◇ ◇

Leadership and Management of Programs for Young Children

SECOND EDITION

CYNTHIA C. JONES SHOEMAKER
George Washington University

MERRILL,
an imprint of Prentice Hall
Upper Saddle River, New Jersey   *Columbus, Ohio*

Library of Congress Cataloging-in-Publication Data

Shoemaker, Cynthia.

    Leadership and management of programs for young children / Cynthia C. Jones
Shoemaker.—2nd ed.

      p.   cm.

    Rev. ed. of: Administration and management of programs for young children. c 1995.

    Includes bibliographical references and index.

    ISBN 0-13-012940-2 (pbk.)

    1. Early childhood education—United States—Administration. 2. Day care centers—United
States—Administration.   I. Shoemaker, Cynthia. Administration and management of
programs for young children. II. Title.

LB2822.6.S567   2000

372.12—dc21   98-51563
                                                                    CIP

Cover art: Artville

Editor: Ann Castel Davis

Production Editor: Sheryl Glicker Langner

Photo Editor: Carol S. Sykes

Design Coordinator: Diane C. Lorenzo

Text Designer: Ceri Fitzgerald

Cover Designer: Dan Eckel

Production Manager: Laura Messerly

Editorial Assistant: Pat Grogg

Electronic Text Management: Marilyn Wilson Phelps, Karen L. Bretz, Melanie King

Director of Marketing: Kevin Flanagan

Marketing Manager: Meghan Shepherd

Marketing Coordinator: Krista Groshong

This book was set in Century Schoolbook by Prentice Hall Publishing and was printed and bound
by R. R. Donnelley & Sons Company. The cover was printed by Phoenix Color Corp.

Earlier edition, entitled *Administration and Management of Programs for Young Children*, © 1995
by Merrill, an imprint of Prentice Hall.

Photo credits: p. 4 by Carisa Traut Jones; p. 11 by Allison Jones Lundeen; pp. 19, 166 by Barbara
Scanlon; pp. 36, 68, 82, 115, by Barbara Schwartz/Merrill; pp. 64, 86, 106, 150, 180 by Jim
Dullea; p. 134 by Janet Heim Jones; pp. 176, 222, 346 by Cynthia Jones Shoemaker; pp. 194, by
Margaret McLennan Jones; p. 203 by Julie Peters/Merrill.

Printed in the United States of America

10 9 8 7 6 5 4 3 2

ISBN: 0-13-012940-2

Prentice-Hall International (UK) Limited, *London*
Prentice-Hall of Australia Pty. Limited, *Sydney*
Prentice-Hall of Canada, Inc., *Toronto*
Prentice-Hall Hispanoamericana, S. A., *Mexico*
Prentice-Hall of India Private Limited, *New Delhi*
Prentice-Hall of Japan, Inc., *Tokyo*
Prentice-Hall (Singapore) Pte. Ltd., *Singapore*
Editora Prentice-Hall do Brasil, Ltda., *Rio de Janeiro*

◇ ◇

This book is dedicated to all early childhood leaders and directors who support families by inviting parents as well as children into their programs. It is also dedicated to my husband, Douglas Shoemaker, to our children, Roger, Michael, Steven, Allison, Peter and Kate, and to their children.

◇ ◇

PREFACE

If one were flying over the landscape of the United States and looking down with special vision, what are the many varieties of child care programs that could be seen? Non-profit and for-profit child care, infant-toddler programs, preschool and nursery programs, after-school programs, in-home provider child care and myriad others, including federally funded programs. What do these programs need? Leadership, planning, implementation, and good operations, including order, computer systems and evaluation procedures for management learning processes as well as for child and adult learning processes. What impacts these programs? Leadership knowledge, skills, and behaviors such as those listed in the matrix in Figure 2.5.

Set in the context of early childhood organizations, *Leadership and Management of Programs for Young Children* addresses the functions common to leadership, management, and administration. It offers discussion and application of leadership and management concepts and practices to those trained in early childhood education and child development. The book has been reorganized to follow more closely the organization of planning, implementation, operations, and a short discussion of general evaluation along with proposal writing. Less is said on the topic of evaluation since that subject is well covered for staff and children in other materials in education that are more readily available than some of the types of materials offered here.

Originally, the planning material was used after students had basic curriculum and early childhood philosophy courses, and sometimes after a basic administration course. If students have no experience with the mechanics of administration, then moving to the implementation and operations sections might be desirable. However, planning carefully and understanding the dynamics involved before acting can save many missteps. The old joke "ready, fire, aim" versus "ready, aim, fire" sums up this concept of the importance of planning. The principles presented here can be applied in many types and sizes of organizations including child care centers and can be adapted for all the variations of children's programs available.

The importance of facilitating a "supportive workplace" (as opposed to a "defensive workplace") is discussed throughout this book. A supportive workplace allows for the openness, caring, and positive morale so needed by the adults who work with young children. Further, in a supportive workplace there is empathy, concern for the needs and development of others, and a positive regard for the self-esteem of all persons involved (children and adults alike).

The four functions common to administration—planning, implementation, operating, and evaluating—are presented in detail in this book. For example:

1. *Planning.* The chapters on leadership (chapter 2), planning (chapter 3), and parent education and involvement (chapter 10), and the proposal and grant writing section of chapter 14 all relate to the planning function.

2. *Implementation.* The chapters on decision-making (chapter 4), creative and analytical problem solving (chapter 5), staff development and training (chapter 6), motivation (chapter 7), and team building (chapter 8) particularly relate to the implementation of programs. Many of these principles are useful in planning, too, of course. A sample time line can be used as a reference for implementing new centers.

3. *Operation.* The chapters on challenges in early childhood education (chapter 1) and operational issues (chapter 13) offer some guidelines and concepts for the necessary knowledge base for the operation of programs for young children. Chapters 11 and 12 on legal and medical issues are new in this second edition, as they can impact the day-to-day operation of a program. The Home Learning Enablers and Parent Papers in the appendices also give some practical activities for parent involvement, which is an important part of administering programs for young children. The Volunteer Program Papers are new in this edition and were taken from a large number and variety of successful volunteer programs.

4. *Evaluating.* Evaluation is an ongoing process in all parts of a program and is addressed in some way in almost every chapter. Chapter 9 on professionalism is particularly useful in constructing a framework for adult employees. When seen as a continuous circle made by planning, implementation, operation, and evaluation, evaluation feeds back into planning to update goals and processes. On the administrative side, evaluation can include actual enrollments, and reveal where the budget and accounts are in relation to where they should be. Since much has already been written on evaluation and staff performance and on child outcomes, these topics are only touched on briefly here.

◇ ◇

WHY THIS BOOK?

This book was written after the author spent many years teaching preschool and child-care leadership, management, and administration at the college level.

During this period, the author's workshop sessions at the National Association for the Education of Young Children conferences on leadership, motivation, and decision-making (taken from lectures in the courses) were so well received, with requests for written copies, that they eventually became three chapters of this book. Every course the author taught on early childhood leadership, management, and administration led to requests for more courses until there were four: basic and advanced administration courses, a course on group settings for young children, and a course on special needs and problems of children. As the book developed, three of these four course concepts and materials were included. The special needs materials were eventually requested as well, and are presented in this second edition of the book in the chapters on legal and medical issues as they relate to young children.

This book addresses only sound, developmentally appropriate care for children in groups of five or more. Similar suggestions exist for family child care and for groups of under five in the home, but that is not the focus of this book. Involvement of parents in their child's care and education is assumed to be an integral part of high-quality early childhood programs, as is well documented in research. In fact, we believe that training and education for all adults involved in programs for children is the cutting-edge issue for success or failure in meeting positive goals for child care. For this reason, additional references are listed in each bibliography at the end of the chapters.

Parent education, coupled with parent involvement, or providing information plus modeling, always increases learning opportunities. These methods also work to ensure that a program is culturally and ethnically appropriate for children, helping child care contribute to and enhance the multifaceted diversity that makes a community (and, indeed, an entire country) unique. We believe that excellent, developmentally appropriate child care is a real service to the community in that it can (and does) have lasting positive effects on each child's life. Furthermore, the least expensive way to reach all the children is to reach all the parents first, as parent education also benefits the children who are too young or too old for child care.

◇ ◇

ACKNOWLEDGMENTS

I would like to acknowledge the valuable assistance received from Doug Shoemaker, and from Barbara Scanlon, whose wonderful pictures grace two of the chapters. I would also like to thank Sandy Turner and Doug Shoemaker for their contributions to chapter 9; Victoria Youcha, Ed.D., for her contribution of chapter 12; and David Cavenaugh for his contribution to chapter 14.

A special word of appreciation goes to the editorial and production staffs at Prentice Hall. Thanks is also extended to the reviewers of this edition for their help and constructive suggestions: Ivy N. Goduka, Central Michigan University; Craig H. Hart, Brigham Young University; Kim A. Madsen, Chadron State College (NE); and Shirley K. Morgenthaler, Concordia University (IL).

DISCOVER COMPANION WEBSITES

A VIRTUAL LEARNING ENVIRONMENT

Technology is a constantly growing and changing aspect of our field that is creating a need for content and resources. To address this emerging need, we have developed an online learning environment for students and professors alike—Companion Websites—to support our textbooks.

In creating a Companion Website, our goal is to build on and enhance what the textbook already offers. For this reason, the content for each user-friendly website is organized by topic and provides the professor and student with a variety of meaningful resources. Common features of a Companion Website include:

For the Professor—

Every Companion Website integrates **Syllabus Manager**™, an online syllabus creation and management utility.

- **Syllabus Manager**™ provides you, the instructor, with an easy, step-by-step process to create and revise syllabi, with direct links into Companion Website and other online content without having to learn HTML.

- Students may logon to your syllabus during any study session. All they need to know is the web address for the Companion Website and the password you've assigned to your syllabus.

- After you have created a syllabus using **Syllabus Manager**™, students may enter the syllabus for their course section from any point in the Companion Website.

- Class dates are highlighted in white and assignment due dates appear in blue. Clicking on a date, the student is shown the list of activities for the assignment. The activities for each assignment are linked directly to actual content, saving time for students.
- Adding assignments consists of clicking on the desired due date, then filling in the details of the assignment—name of the assignment, instructions, and whether or not it is a one-time or repeating assignment.
- In addition, links to other activities can be created easily. If the activity is online, a URL can be entered in the space provided, and it will be linked automatically in the final syllabus.
- Your completed syllabus is hosted on our servers, allowing convenient updates from any computer on the Internet. Changes you make to your syllabus are immediately available to your students at their next logon.

For the Student—

- **Topic Overviews**—outline key concepts in topic areas
- **Electronic Blue Book**—send homework or essays directly to your instructor's email with this paperless form
- **Message Board**—serves as a virtual bulletin board to post–or respond to–questions or comments to/from a national audience
- **Web Destinations**—links to www sites that relate to each topic area
- **Professional Organizations**—links to organizations that relate to topic areas
- **Additional Resources**—access to topic specific content that enhances material found in the text

To take advantage of these resources, please visit the *Leadership and Management of Programs for Young Children* Companion Website at www.prenhall.com/shoemaker.

ABOUT THE AUTHOR

Cynthia C. Jones Shoemaker became interested in the leadership and management of programs for young children when she served as Vice President and then President of Parent Cooperative Preschools International. Previously, as the local county and state president of cooperative Nursery School Councils, she was involved in management, administration, and parent education and training for adults in early childhood programs for several years. Dr. Shoemaker, a graduate of Cornell University, received her master's degree and Ph.D. in Early Childhood Education with a minor in management from the University of Maryland. Discovering that management and administration were not routinely taught in the early childhood education professional curriculum, she designed and directed the Preschool and Child Care Administration Master's Degree program at Trinity College in Washington, D.C., for over 10 years, and later at Catholic University, also in Washington, D.C.

Dr. Shoemaker is also a founder and President of the Early Childhood Education Administration Institute in Marbury, Maryland, which publishes materials for parents and school systems, and consults nationwide. Currently with the Office of Academic Development and Continuing Education at George Washington University, she coordinates five master's degree programs, including one in Organizational Management and one in Management Information Systems, while continuing her work of helping children and adults reach their full potential. She has taught at the graduate level of early childhood education for more than 20 years.

The author of many publications, including *Leadership in Continuing and Distance Education in Higher Education*, published by Allyn and Bacon in 1998, Dr. Shoemaker has also written *Leadership and the Use of Power in ECE Administration; Motivating Staff, Parents and Children;* and is co-author of *A Family Affair: Education; Teaming Families and Schools for Student Achievement;* and

Success for Children Begins at Home. She has spoken nationally on many of the topics covered in the second edition of this book, as well as coordinated many conferences, including "A Cross-cultural Perspective on Promoting Achievement for Students at Risk" and "Promoting Success for All Students," and has served on federal program proposal review panels, including that for Evenstart.

Dr. Shoemaker is currently a board member of the Southern Maryland Consortium for Children and Families and a Director of the Association for Federal Information Resource Management and has memberships in early childhood professional associations including ACEI and NAEYC. She has been Chairman of the Tri-county Staff Development Consortium in southern Maryland and was a recipient of the National Award for Outstanding Service from Parent Cooperative Preschools International.

Dr. Shoemaker is included in *Who's Who in the World, Who's Who in America, Who's Who in the East, Who's Who in American Education, World Who's Who of Women, Who's Who of Professional and Business Women, Who's Who of Women Executives,* and *Who's Who in Staff Development in Public and Private Schools.*

She is married and has four children and eight grandchildren under the age of six. She is shown here at the beach with one of her newest granddaughters, Valerie Gay Lundeen.

CONTENTS

Challenges and Trends in Early Childhood Education

Of all the many challenges facing education at the beginning of a new century, early childhood education, which includes the youngest children in the educational process, is on the leading edge. The following are just a few of these challenges:

1. Children are attending group care programs at an earlier age and in greatly increasing numbers. The number of programs has not increased as fast as the number of children attending them, resulting in overcrowding in those areas with lower standards. Developmental appropriateness in programs is of acute importance for infants and toddlers as well as for preschool age groups.

2. The number of working parents has dramatically increased. The workplace pressures placed on them have increased as well, leading to longer workdays and longer commutes, and these working parents need to find the best care for their children. The demand for good early childhood programs is increasing due to wider recognition of the critical importance of the early years.

3. There are diverse opinions about what is good for children. Constructive debate should focus on the *needs* of *children*.

4. Parent involvement and education are major trends in early childhood education today as parents become increasingly aware of their influence as their child's first and most important teachers. The recent research on early brain development underscores the importance of working well with parents and communicating across socioeconomic, cultural, and educational contexts. It often is difficult to work well with parents and to provide them with parent education information, whether it be in the form of send-home information, handouts or workshops. Chapter 10, "Parent Education and Parent Involvement," deals with this subject more intensively as does all of Section 4 on "Helping Children Overcome Problems" both legally and medically related.

5. Those influencing early childhood education are changing. Federal, state and local governments have become decision-makers in early childhood education and need informing. Private sector involvement is widespread and issues need to be addressed from the standpoint of private companies and corporate child care. High quality child care needs to be articulated and presented to the business world using business and cost/benefit terminology.

6. There are increasing differences in the staffs of early childhood programs both in professional knowledge and skills and in cultural diversity. Turnover is high where salary and working conditions are poor. Continual learning has become a necessity for teachers and directors alike.

The certification of teachers and the accreditation and licensing of programs for young children also reflect the challenges and trends in early childhood education in today's world. Many other countries that have early childhood programs and that have enacted supportive legislation might serve as examples for the United States. Early childhood educators from New Zealand and Australia consistently find regulations in the U.S. less stringent than those in their own countries. In terms of accreditation of preschools and child-care programs, in addition to accreditation by the National Association for the Education of Young Children (NAEYC), most states require that child-care centers be licensed through the state's health or social services departments. A few states, however, provide state accreditation of early childhood educational programs through the Department of Education. In one state, accreditation of nursery schools by the Department of Education was added in the 1940s. When dog and horse training facilities and programs for veterans were being accredited, early childhood personnel at that time had to *request* that their schools be included in the accreditation process. One value of accreditation lies in its ability to regulate the ever-expanding number of children in classrooms.

There are two major changes occurring in society today that affect the early childhood field and its relationship to formal education, and these same circumstances can be seen in the workplace as well. The first change is the ongoing transition into the information age, which has resulted in the use of computers in early childhood program administration and in classroom curriculum. An additional challenge is that some individuals are slow to gain access to new technology and with it the wonderful information resources on the home pages of government agencies, non-profit organizations, and parent organizations. Some of the access barriers can be attributed to cost, but since costs are decreasing, reluctance to change personal communication and research habits may also affect this access. The second change involves the increasingly multicultural population of the nation (U.S. Dept. of Labor, 1989). Cultural diversity in the classroom is not new in early childhood education, but it is still a challenge and a trend. Active parent involvement of many kinds helps to ensure that children's needs will be met in ways that are meaningful and understandable, related to cultural background, and across socioeconomic and educational lines.

Finally, the results of research focusing on the long-term effects of child care for young children are a challenge to all in the early childhood field. These discovered effects are far-reaching, affecting even teachers and principals in the elementary schools into which these children matriculate. The lack of high-quality, developmentally appropriate child care for children now causes school problems and expense later. For example, a child who receives poor-quality child care might find it necessary to repeat grades in school or participate in special education programs. Poor-quality child care also results in low self-esteem, and fosters negative attitudes throughout life. Mental health problems leading to institutionalization, and crime leading to prison crowding problems, cost public budgets far more than would developmentally appropriate child care that encourages parent involvement. With currently more than 70% of children in non-parental care versus 30% in 1970, this good versus poor quality care issue becomes ever more acute (U.S. Department of Health and Human Services, 1996).

It is important that parents retain their perception and their role as their children's most important teachers, and that is why parent involvement and parent education are key factors in any child-care system. Studies done by Jerome Kagan (1970) on the Kibbutz system in Israel, where parents see their children for one half hour per day, have shown that almost no matter what the circumstances, the child's strongest bond remains with the parent.

Whether early childhood programs provide learning opportunities to educate all adults who are involved with children is an important indicator of success or failure in meeting the challenges and problems just discussed. This training must include parents as well as teachers, aides, and administrators.

Supporters of legislation and funding at the federal and state levels for the care of young children cite the damage being done to young children who are left at home alone while single mothers work; children who are taken to the mother's workplace without adequate care arrangements; and children who are cared for in unlicensed centers in states that have low standards, with the danger of resultant child abuse. These concerned citizens see child care as a societal problem, not as an individual problem, and one that will be destructive to society if not regulated and supported. Indeed, the society will suffer if large numbers of young children are damaged. In light of the recent research on early brain development, lack of appropriate regulation and support of early childhood programs has been called a "brain drain" for the United States.

1

Challenges in Developing Programs for Young Children

The need to develop a warm, trusting, sincere environment for children, and to have this goal be top priority for staff and parents, is greater than ever. Children have a desire to learn, to be curious, and to take risks and need to have their parents involved in their learning at least some of the time.

Some appropriate goals for children that will survive challenges and trends include: (1) developing a positive self-image; (2) growing physically, intellectually, and socially; (3) building imagination and thinking skills; and (4) being encouraged to participate, feel important, feel relaxed, and be a part of the program or center. Treating each child as an individual, providing a well-rounded program with many experiences, and maintaining a provision for health concerns are all components of integrating children's needs into a child-care program, regardless of the developmentally appropriate curriculum model used. Children with special needs or who speak English as a second language will need special attention. A child with limited English proficiency who also has special education needs or physical challenges will need assistance in particular.

◇ ◇

PHILOSOPHY

The philosophy of the preschool or child-care center is the foundation on which the total program is built. If this statement of purpose is carefully developed and easily understood by all, many of the problems that occur in child-care leadership, management and administration could be prevented: interstaff problems, staff-to-parent problems, and parent-to-parent problems. A typical statement of educational philosophy might discuss what is meant by individual acceptance. It might use terms such as "freedom within limits" and espouse a "child-sized world." It might advocate a relaxed and friendly atmosphere where a child can explore, investigate, share, play, and communicate with other children his or her own age. Parent participation and teacher-parent-child, or three-way, sharing should be included.

A group decision to help children develop into happy, confident, productive, whole individuals who are able to face and cope with the problems they encounter is a good first step toward a high-quality program philosophy. Parents and staff need to agree on goals such as the following: (1) children can learn to respect themselves; (2) they can establish in themselves a sense of confidence and self-esteem, while learning to respect others and their ideas and rights; (3) they can learn to make choices, to solve problems, and to explore new ways of doing things without being afraid to try; and (4) they can become confident, whole individuals who are able to cope with what lies before them. Once such goals are established, mutual understanding about the curriculum and activities can follow in an atmosphere of discussion and learning.

◇ ◇ ◇ ◇ ◇ ◇ ◇ ◇ ◇ ◇ ◇ ◇ ◇ ◇ ◇ ◇ ◇ ◇ ◇ ◇

ESTABLISHING THE CENTER

The first step in organizing a preschool or child-care center is taken when a number of interested persons meet to discuss plans for organization. Assuming they agree on the need for an early childhood program in their geographical area and on the type of education desired, the next step will be to examine the community and evaluate the facilities already available. The group may then wish to form a committee to conduct research.

The first task for a research committee should be to check the U.S. census tracts (in the public library) for local demographics, numbers of young children, births, socioeconomic levels, and other available information. One research committee such as this developed a census tract map and colored in the areas with the households containing the most young children. Then they looked for a location in the center of a shaded-in area.

The committee's second task might involve the use of the survey shown in Figure 1.1 to compare three or four programs for young children. Many ideas for using indoor and outdoor space emerge from this exercise, in addition to discovering needs and a market niche.

Once a general location and perhaps one or two alternatives are selected, a committee member can approach employers in the area to generate support. Options to present to employers might include housing the center, publicizing and supporting the center by advertising it to their employees and prospective employees through the distribution of flyers, and/or supporting the center by purchasing 5, 10, or 15 "contract" slots to be paid for in advance and then held for their employees, perhaps as part of their benefit package. At this stage, developing a decision tree, as described in Chapter 4, can be very useful for sorting out the benefits of purchasing an existing site, remodeling a site, or building a new center, if all these options exist in the desired location. More information will emerge as the group identifies and critiques the options available.

If these preliminary investigations yield positive results, the group can begin its work. Committees are selected to do the following: (In a corporate setting, numbers 1 through 3 may be done by the central office.)

1. Find out about county and state requirements and, at the appropriate time, make application for licensing.
2. Find suitable housing as previously discussed.

Center name	Price	Number of children	Use of indoor space	Use of outdoor space	Special features or theme	Characteristics missing or poorly handled (lighting, space, teachers, education, etc.)
Center A						
Center B						
Center C						
Center D						
Our Center						

FIGURE 1.1
Competition Survey

3. Develop the philosophy and its statement.

4. Plan the budget.

5. Hire the staff.

6. Publicize the service available for children or visit a social service agency or corporation to determine the number of funded children that might be available in the area.

If the organizing group feels unprepared to decide on an educational program, and hence to select a teacher, they might find it useful to set up a meeting or two with an experienced early childhood teacher in order to discuss child development and preschool education. This would greatly aid the group in setting the goals for their projected center. The all-important philosophy really is the first step.

◇ ◇

ORGANIZING STRUCTURES

The Executive Board

In most organizing groups, an Executive Board is elected by the interested parties to manage the business operations of the center or school. The Board, which carries out the administrative duties in accordance with the purposes and bylaws of the group, leaves the teachers free to concentrate on the educational philosophy and the program. Board members should be members of the community who have a high level of interest in the proposed center; prospective parents are a good resource. Assigning Board members specific roles—that is, involving them in tasks with which they feel comfortable—provides an excellent opportunity for them to learn about good early childhood education. This learning takes place through the "hands-on" process of researching a particular area, which might be the equipment needed, or planning the budget, or the regulations that must be met. Such involvement also provides group cohesiveness and good public relations in the community. This source of energy and interest, leading to support of the goals of the center, should not be underestimated, even by profit-making centers.

During the organizing period, an interim Executive Board may be established. Later, as the center becomes operational, the interim Board can be replaced by a permanent Executive Board, the members of which are elected for one, two, or three years. The usual offices of President, Vice President, Recording Secretary, and Treasurer may be augmented by advisors from the community and by permanent committee chairs for the following areas:

- Housing and Licensing
- Bylaws and Incorporation

- Membership/Enrollment and Public Relations
- Equipment and Supplies (The teacher/director, if hired by this point, is an ex-officio member of this committee.)
- Teacher Hiring and Personnel Committee
- Treasurer and Finance Committee

Additional committees may include:

- Educational Standards Committee
- Handbook Committee
- Communications Committee (responsible for a newsletter, calendar, and bulletin board)
- Hospitality/Social Committee
- Parent Education/Program Committee

Organizing a center or school involves a great deal of work. Each committee has its own job and set of objectives. Those committees found in the first list are the ones that must be organized as soon as possible. In the beginning, there may not be enough people to cover all of the needed committees, so organizers should prioritize which needs are the most urgent until there are enough interested persons to cover all aspects.

These committees are useful even in a corporate setting as parents and staff can learn a lot about early childhood (and get to know each other as well) while working together.

The Child-Care Center or Preschool Board

After the center is organized, a working Board of Advisors or Board of Directors is necessary to avoid having the director work 50 to 60 hours a week (see Part II, "Leadership and the Role of the Director"). A child-care center with a prestigious Board of Advisors or Board of Directors whose members include professionals drawn from a church or business sponsor and from the community may consider setting up a second Executive Board (or choose another appropriate title that will give some honor to the participants). This second group's function should be to work and not merely oversee and advise, and at least 51 percent of its membership should be parents whose children are presently enrolled in the center. In fact, all members of the Executive Board may be drawn from parents currently involved with the center. However, some of the members of this Executive Board also may include (1) alumni parents of other programs (perhaps necessary at start-up); (2) alumni parents from your center as it develops; and (3) interested members of the community or church if the center is housed in a church.

The director and teachers may be voting members of this Executive Board, depending on whether the parent members determine this to be beneficial. Whether or not they are voting members of the Executive Board, the job of the professional staff in the center is to design an educational policy and curriculum that recognizes the philosophy of the parents, staff, and Executive Board. The professional staff should choose and implement the specific education curricula and give advice and guidance on those areas of administration in which the Executive Board is involved. In other words, the director's job is to educate the parent Executive Board in practices that are supportive of children and to interpret the preschool program. In today's world, there are many more experts in administration than experts in early childhood education, as evidenced by the popularity of master's degrees in business administration versus master's degrees in early childhood education. The help of the latter group can be valuable.

Bylaws and Operating Rules

Each preschool program should develop a set of bylaws to organize their group, give it structure, and prepare the center for nonprofit incorporation status, should this be pursued. Bylaws should be kept simple and similar to each other in form. If the parent group as well as the Executive Board is required to vote on major changes in the bylaws, much more participation in and support of the goals of the program are possible. By using a democratic structure such as this, the group develops teamwork right from the start.

Operating rules or policy regulations can be added to the bylaws in a separate section or can be made into a separate document, which makes them easier to change. These rules and regulations are not addressed here since they will be unique to each group. For example, such a document may even include job descriptions for paid and volunteer jobs. The Executive Board usually sets these policy regulations without a vote of the parent group, unlike the bylaws.

A table of contents for a typical set of bylaws follows. As can be seen, the decisions that need to be made to write these bylaws are a useful part of the development of a center or a school.

Sample Table of Contents for Bylaws

A. Statement of purpose or philosophy
B. Name of program
C. Enrollment
    1. Methods of applying for children
    2. General responsibilities of parents

Infants and toddlers are new to many programs.

        3. Health requirements

        4. Meeting attendance requirements and committee participation requirements for parents

  D. Organization

      1. Board of Advisors

         a. Election and duration of term

         b. Duties

         c. Meetings

      2. Executive Board

         a. Election

         b. Duties and powers

         c. Meetings

      3. Staff

         a. Duties

         b. Contract procedure

      4. Standing Committees

         a. Appointment

         b. Duties (job descriptions can be included in the operating rules/policy regulations section)

  E. Treasury
      1. Amount of tuition and fees
      2. Method of payment
      3. Fee arrangements in the event of withdrawal
      4. Insurance and fees
      5. Hours and holidays
      6. Late tuition payment policy
  F. Amendment Procedure
  G. General Rules
  H. Dissolution

Incorporation

Incorporation, whether as a nonprofit educational organization or as a profit-making corporation, is highly recommended for child-care programs that are separate entities. Unless a center is incorporated, Executive Board members can be individually responsible for damages awarded to any person claiming negligence, on the part of the center, resulting in personal injury. Incorporation also protects Executive Board members from responsibility for financial difficulties, and allows the program to enter into legal contracts, such as contracts with teachers or a rental lease. Incorporation may require legal advice.

In many states, a *nonprofit corporation* is specified as an organization that does not sell stock; does not withhold service on the basis of race, creed, or color; and, upon dissolution, distributes its assets to another nonprofit corporation (such as a church or other nonprofit child-care center). To incorporate, a copy of the organization's bylaws must be attached to the Articles of Incorporation, and then must be submitted to the State Department of Assessments and Taxation of the state in which the center is located. Often this department will have a brochure available that contains helpful advice on incorporating. Tax-exempt status for state sales tax, which is different from the nonprofit exemption from federal income tax, may be requested separately once nonprofit status is granted, and can result in substantial savings on the purchases of equipment and supplies. A surplus line in the budget, that carries over into the next year's operating expenses or is kept as a contingency fund, is permissible in a nonprofit corporation, since *nonprofit* does not mean *nonsurplus*.

Individual incorporation of a center protects the housing facility, such as a church or other institution in which the center is located, from damages in case of a negligence suit. The incorporation process is slow, so application should be made while other start-up tasks are being addressed.

Site Selection

Site selection can be a difficult problem, unless a suitable site is obvious. For many years, obtaining housing has been the most difficult problem for those starting a child-care program. A rough outline of the information presented in the bylaws could be combined with the following information to serve as a useful packet for prospective landlords: (1) the hours during which children's classes and parent meetings will occur; (2) the facilities required (indoor and outdoor, including parking); (3) the qualifications of the educational staff; and (4) the names, addresses, and telephone numbers of the program's contact persons. The proposed rent should be high enough to cover the expenses of the housing institution, including janitorial services, but also should be low enough to allow lower-income families access to the program. Housing a center in a rent-free facility often leads to problems with the landlord, who may lose patience with a non-paying group faster than with a rent-paying operation. See chapters 13 and 14 for new initiatives in financing center construction or build out.

Licensing in most areas is handled by local and state agencies who inspect nursery schools and child-care centers. Although licensing takes time, an interim permit often is issued to allow the program to get under way while awaiting health, fire, and safety inspections. It may be necessary to alter a building to meet the necessary regulations and obtain a license. For instance, installing fire doors might be one example of an alteration. The cost of such alterations may be covered or shared with the landlord in many cases.

In choosing a site, it may be necessary to deal with regulations or standards in any or all of the following areas:

Zoning

Business licensing

Fire safety regulations including fire extinguishers, smoke alarms, fire alarms, exits, and escape plans

Educational standards including teacher/pupil ratio, indoor space/child ratio, outdoor space/child ratio, staff qualifications, and health requirements

Equipment

Parking regulations

Building codes, including those for electricity, plumbing, heating capacity, and access

Health regulations including food preparation, food storage, number of bathrooms, lighting, and ventilation

Transportation regulations or licensing

Most high-quality early childhood programs have educational standards that far exceed any regulations that may be required by legislation. Thus, when government standards are raised, these programs do not find themselves having to lobby for the standards to be lowered, thereby finding themselves in a position of fighting against the best interests of the children.

Membership Committee

The task of the membership committee is to recruit families for the program and members must have a good understanding of the philosophy, goals, and curriculum of the program. This committee is the outreach and public relations arm of the program, and, together with a committee for publicity, plans ways to present the child-care program to the community through all types of media: newspapers, radio, television, bulletin boards (electronic ones as well as physical ones), and flyers distributed to corporations and company personnel offices. This committee may plan an open house, take pictures of classes in session after the center opens, distribute recruitment posters, and develop brochures. The duties of the membership committee may be extensive, so occasionally the membership chairman is given a partial scholarship or tuition remission in return for these services.

An enrollment committee may emerge from the membership committee as the center grows. Several excellent computer software programs exist to help with this task. The group or an administrative assistant maintains enrollment forms, a waiting list, and arranges admission interviews. The committee also helps to plan orientation meetings in the fall and perhaps offer an orientation every quarter for a year-round child-care program.

Teacher Hiring or Personnel Committee

A committee to help advertise positions and schedule and conduct interviews of the prospective teaching staff, and even, on occasion, the director, is valuable in any early childhood program. The quality of the program will depend largely on the knowledge and skills of the director and the teachers. If the Executive Board of a community group or an already existing center is establishing the new child-care center, key personnel to be hired may already be identified. However, an interviewing procedure that spreads the decision-making responsibility among several persons is always wise for future hiring and for the additional hiring that needs to be done as the center is being established. More information on this important topic can be found in chapter 6.

Advertisements for teaching staff may be placed at local colleges and universities and in newspapers. These listings should include educational requirements for the job, hours, and a range for salaries. Provide at least two contact phone numbers, or, if it is preferred, have applicants mail in résumés to an address listed in the advertisement.

As inquiries begin to come in, send out an application form in response to each. The application should include a deadline for return. In partnership with the whole personnel committee (three to five persons), screen the completed applications for each applicant's experience, education, and qualifications. Rank the applicants by priority and set up an interview schedule.

Preplanning the interview questions, so that each candidate is asked the same questions, is important for fairness. (Suggestions for questions are given in chapter 6.) The committee may wish to reinterview the top two or three candidates after the first round of interviews. A note of thanks should be sent to all interviewees for their time and to let them know when the position has been filled.

A formal contract should be signed by the teacher/director selected. At this point, the teacher is introduced to the interim Executive Board and is invited to participate immediately in selecting equipment, planning classroom space, developing the educational program, and planning parent orientation meetings.

A final organizational note: The secretary should maintain a personnel file for each employee, which includes their application form, contract, reference letters, health form, and yearly evaluation.

Treasurer and Finance Committee

A sound financial structure is essential to a successful child-care program. Initial tasks of the finance committee include formulating a budget, establishing tuition fees based on budgeted expenses, and setting up the books. If financial policies and structures are well thought out when a program is first developed, these tasks will be easier in succeeding years.

The budget should be planned with the income at 90 percent of enrollment rather than 100 percent, since this provides a leeway that allows for variability and turnover. A reserve fund of one or two months' income, minimum, should also be maintained. The first and last months' tuition may be collected upon enrollment to help start this fund.

Most programs also collect a nonrefundable registration fee at the time a child's application is received; this money enables the program to open its bank account. If the child withdraws before opening day, however, this fee should be refunded. Some schools earmark these registration fees to go toward large equipment purchases.

A well-designed budget is a guide to growth and improvement, and, along with other expenditures, should allow for planned purchases of equipment and annual personnel salary increases.

Written financial policies are important for consistency and fairness. A date by which tuition must be paid and a late fee should be established. Sometimes a provision is made for lower tuition fees if more than one child from the same family is enrolled in the program. The finance committee also should look into possible insurance requirements of the program, which may include: tenant's liability, owner's liability, program liability, employer's liability, bonding (for the Treasurer), fire and theft insurance, unemployment insurance, and medical and accident insurance for children and employees.

Equipment and Supplies Committee

A rich variety of equipment is needed for a preschool program since children learn through interaction and the stimulation of play. A short-term, two- to five-year loan for start-up expenses prevents the burden of initial equipment costs from falling on first-year enrollees. The equipment list should be developed while working with a trained early childhood teacher. Members of the equipment and supplies committee might also visit other early childhood programs and preschools for ideas in addition to subscribing to educational supply catalogs. Conferences and early childhood magazines also are good resources for equipment information. More detail on categories of equipment and supplies is given in chapter 13.

As ideas are gathered, committee members compile lists of equipment and supplies. Once purchases have been made, as the year goes on, committee members are responsible for checking equipment for wear and seeing if repairs are needed. Small toys and puzzles may have pieces missing, and repairing or replacing these is part of the committee's task.

The "job descriptions" for other possible and helpful committees are given in chapter 14, but the ones described here are especially useful in initiating a program for young children.

◇ ◇

LEGISLATION, CERTIFICATION, AND ACCREDITATION

The staff of child-care centers as well as parents need to keep current with local, state, and national legislation and with the variety of teacher certification and center licensing regulations that are mandated by each state. At the time of this writing, many regulations are under review (at all levels), and should be obtained from the appropriate agency in the particular state in which a center is located.

Within each state, licensing is usually granted by one or more agencies which include Health, Welfare or Social Services, and (in a very few states) Education. Accreditation by state departments of education and by the National Association for the Education of Young Children (NAEYC) is also desirable. Possible and desired trends in legislation include the greater involvement of parents and families in their children's education. The Council of Chief State School Officers (CCSSO, 1991) says, "If the potential resources available to the school and the family resulting from the synergy of their partnership is realized, schools and families will have powerful new tools for ensuring education success for children." (p. 1)

The *Families in School* booklet published by the Council of Chief State School Officers (1991) encourages educational agencies at several levels to implement programs that enhance teachers' capacity to work with families as partners in the improvement of their children's education. The booklet also guides families in making decisions that affect the quality and content of the schools and education programs for their children.

At the preschool level, this involvement is especially important since the foundations are being laid for the education system of school-age children. As family involvement becomes an integral component of setting standards for good schools and quality education in the K through 12 age group, it will be following the lead that good early childhood programs have established for several generations of children and parents (Parent Cooperative Preschools International, 1985).

Family involvement can and should become a key component of school and center improvement, while also lending energy, talent, and other scarce resources to these educational programs. As a result, it is hoped that local school districts and state education agencies would continue developing and implementing family involvement in new education programs and initiatives (CCSSO, 1991).

Legislation involving early childhood education in other countries makes "setting up" grants available. For example, in New Zealand, the funding to cover the cost of start-up is granted after the center has passed accreditation standards. International legislation for early childhood programs is indeed a fertile source of new ideas for some of the problems faced in the United States today (New Zealand, Education Department Standards, 1968).

◊ ◊

CURRICULUM MODELS IN EARLY CHILDHOOD EDUCATION

The director and the teaching staff should discuss whether their philosophy, as spelled out in the curriculum, will be developmentally appropriate for the children involved. It is possible to blend curriculum models, and different philosophies can be utilized by different teachers. Within one center, however, there should not be too many divergent classroom curriculum approaches. The director is the "educational leader," so a clear philosophy is especially important and may require extra reading or coursework to stay current.

There are many excellent curriculum models in early childhood education; in fact, an entire university course could and should be devoted to curriculum alone. Some broad curriculum approaches are presented here that should give an overview of some of the possibilities. The multiplicity of curriculum choices is yet another challenge and change in early childhood education. It is best to keep in mind that choosing developmentally appropriate practices, whatever the curriculum approach or slant, is the overall goal in developing a successful program (Bredekamp, 1990; Bredekamp and Copple, 1997).

Developmentally Appropriate Curriculum

Developmentally Appropriate Practice (DAP) curriculum promotes the view that children construct knowledge in an active rather than a passive manner in the context of interactions with their environment: materials, other children, and adults. This is based on the theories of Piaget (1952), Erikson (1963), and Vygotsky (1978), among others. Guidelines, principles and practices were formalized by Bredekamp (1990) and further revised by Bredekamp and Copple (1997). A knowledge of child development from birth to age eight (or the primary grades) is essential for using this approach and all approaches, in order to match curriculum with how young children think and learn. The child becomes the primary source of the curriculum, which therefore accommodates cultural nuances and non-typical developmental sequences regardless of age, gender, disabilities or socio-economic status. Providing options and choices for children and facilitating learning experiences through non-directive mediating and cognitive questioning extensions replaces developmentally inappropriate practices (DIP) of expecting all children to do the same thing at the same time or academic skill-based instruction (which actually could be called "training"). The latter has been shown to lead to negative motivation and intellectual and social stress (Hart, Burts, & Charlesworth, 1997).

Project Approach

The project approach to planning curriculum helps teachers decide with the children on themes and units that are important to the children. New ways of assessing children's interests build an intriguing in-depth curriculum (Katz & Chard, 1989).

Any setting can be a setting that helps build ideas.

The three phases through which projects develop are:

(1) Discussion and getting started: Do the children see and want to know more about worms? Dinosaurs? The possibilities are as varied as the children's imaginations.

(2) Investigation and gaining information: Should there be field trips? What kinds of materials should be in the classroom? Should there be parent visitors? Representation and documentation can be done in many ways such as through the use of sample charts, webs, and illustrations.

(3) Concluding the project and display: Activities such as building the dinosaur or looking at worms in a "worm table" (a sand table with dirt and worms in it). Display of final learning may include photos or even a video.

Activity Approach

The activity approach is the traditional, whole-child development curriculum. Goals and objectives are often listed in relation to holidays, seasons, themes, or units. This approach provides a wide range of experiences that build self-confidence and competence. The materials for this approach allow children to see, hear, feel, smell, and experience. The child is encouraged to learn through his or her senses and the materials provide for this.

Reggio Emilia Approach

The Reggio Emilia approach is the name given to describe the philosophy of a system of 22 municipal full-day (7:30 A.M. to 6:20 P.M.) preschool centers in the Italian city of Reggio Emilia, plus 13 infant-toddler centers, for children newborn to 6 years of age. This approach fosters intellectual development through a systematic focus on symbolic representation. Young children are given opportunities to explore and express themselves in many ways, called the "Hundred Languages of Children," in the title of a book and a well-known exhibit of the Italian children's work (Edwards, Gandini & Forman, 1996). These "languages" might include words, dramatic play, movement, drawing, painting, building, sculpture, shadow play, collage, music and more. Children are encouraged to repeat important experiences, re-observe them, re-consider them and re-represent them. By systematically "documenting" these activities, through the use of slide shows, posters and videotapes, educators provide children with a concrete and visible "memory" which helps them construct a new jumping-off point for their next activity. This documentation provides helpful information to researchers and educators as well.

Reciprocity, exchange and dialogue lie at the heart of this approach and represent a shared culture of exploration between children and adults. In helping children construct this "diary" in their hundred languages (before they can read and write), surprising levels of skill and creativity have been discovered in children of all kinds including those with special needs. Parents and the general public can learn about what happens in these centers and schools through these various "documentations." Close community management and parent relationships are also a hallmark of these programs as they grew out of a parent cooperative movement. Thus, the Reggio Emilia approach is structured more along the lines of an extended family than an industrial "school" model (Edwards, Gandini, & Forman, 1996).

Space is seen as having educational content, so internal spaces are developed to encourage interactions and social development. Mirrors, for example, invite children to interact and play with their own images and are often used in the classroom. External space is seen as an extension of the classroom, so children are given opportunities to explore landmarks and neighborhoods in the city. Planning is understood as preparation and organization of space, materials, occasions for learning, thoughts and situations among children, parents and educators.

This philosophy, developed in Italy in the Reggio Emilia preschools and adapted to the U.S. setting over the last several years, includes new ways of relating to children. Three critical elements include space, conversations and visual representations. Reading the materials and attending workshops has stimulated many early childhood teachers and directors to think about new possibilities and approaches to early education. One school instituted the "open snack" with children helping themselves to melon pieces and raisins as they were hungry, and found that their after-kindergarten and after-school groups improved tremendously. Apparently the children arrived hungry or became hungry earlier than the scheduled snack time. This very adaptable approach will spark discussions for staff development and through its uniqueness promote a "fresh look" at curriculum.

Process Skills Approach

The process skills approach has as its goal enabling the child to adapt to an ever-changing society. Units or goals in this curriculum approach are labeled creative skills, interactive skills, or cognitive skills. These skills or processes include decision-making, cooperating, caring, communicating, creating, perceiving, observing, loving, knowing, and problem-solving. The child takes an active part in experimentation, exploration, construction, and selection. An example of an activity or learning opportunity of the process skills approach might be: Children will use decision-making skills as they choose alternatives and predict implications during free-choice time. The *process* is more important than the product.

◊ ◊

HISTORICAL FOUNDATIONS AND CURRENT TRENDS

In early-era America, child care on a large scale was unnecessary, since children were physically close to their parents as they worked on the family farm, tended the family store, or worked outside but nearby the family home. Even as recently as 50 years ago, the majority of American families were "traditional" in the sense that fathers worked full-time while mothers stayed at home to care for the children. However, child care connected to the workplace does have a place in American history.

The beginning of large-scale child care associated with the workplace is linked to funding by the federal government, which at the time had the needs of the nation in mind rather than the needs of individual children or their families.

In August of 1942, the office of Defense, Health, and Welfare was directed by the War Manpower Commission to set up a program of federally supported child-care centers for children of working mothers in war-related industries. The Lanham Act was passed at this time, which made an additional $150 million available for facilities, including child-care centers, operating in expanded war-industry areas.

One company that took advantage of the Lanham Act was the Kaiser Shipbuilding Corporation in Portland, Oregon, which opened two child-care centers that served 4,014 children from eighteen months to six years of age. The buildings and equipment for these programs were provided by the United States Maritime Commission. In addition to the preschool program, the centers were open to school-age children during holidays, weekends, or whenever necessary. Other nonenrolled children of working parents could attend if their regular child-care arrangements broke down. Some comprehensive services such as health care, home service food, parent information, and other benefits were also made available. The purpose of these centers was to provide services to parents who were required to work long hours.

Federal funding ceased when the war ended, so most child-care centers closed. Many mothers returned to their homes and families. However, if a family still needed child care, it was most often filled by family in-home care providers.

It was not until 1969 that corporations became active in child care. Service areas in which women were expected to work, such as textiles, light manufacturing, assembly-line work, and hospitals, were the first to respond to the need for adequate child care. The programs run by corporations offered very little parent involvement and often were seen as instruments to make working women more vulnerable. Industry-owned and industry-managed child-care facilities controlled employee turnover and the possibility of employees striking for better working conditions by threatening to withdraw child-care programs.

The diversity of child-care programs utilized by working parents and the complexity of emotions concerning who should be responsible for the care of children did not encourage widespread employer involvement in quality child-care issues. Although the economic recessions of the 1970s and the women's movement brought more women into the workforce and created a greater need for child care, the federal and state governments, also affected by the recessions, provided little legislation to support child care. A 1978 survey by Perry, cited by Waxman (1991), found there were only nine industry-sponsored child-care centers in the United States. Also in 1978, just 110 U.S. employers offered their employees some type of child-care assistance (Smith, 1991).

Although the 1980s saw increased demands for quality child care for the growing number of working women, there were conflicting reports on the effects of child care on the healthy development of children. Early studies of child care in the 1960s had shown positive results; however, by the late 1980s, contradictory evidence had been reported. While children were reported to demonstrate positive gains in social, language, and cognitive development, disturbing evidence of negative emotional, aggressive, and uncooperative behaviors was found. The evidence was most distressing in regard to infants placed in child care during their first year (National Research Council, 1990). Much of the detrimental evidence was correlated to the quality of child care and the large size of the groups to which the children were exposed. While the quality of child care was accepted as a major concern, the delivery and regulation of quality child-care service became a major debate.

In the 1990s, many child-care options were developed in response to assessments of employees' needs. In 1990, 5,400 employers offered child-care *assistance* to their employees (Smith, 1991). Waxman (1991) noted that as of 1991, the number of industry-sponsored child-care *centers* had grown to between 500 and 1000 centers in just 13 years. A research group based in New York, called the Families and Work Institute, has created a "family friendly index" to help companies develop a plan of action in addressing work and family issues (Bernstein, Weber, Driscoll, & Cunes, 1991).

Quality on-site or near-site employer-sponsored child care can lead the way for meeting the comprehensive needs of families and children. It can also address the national need for quality early childhood education. The rapid growth of the relationship between employers and quality child care, in addition to provisions for the uniqueness of the development and management of these centers, must be closely monitored.

As seen from the previous discussion, child-care arrangements increasingly are moving outside the home, with children's development often placed in the hands of strangers or near-strangers. As late as 1985 only 14 percent of preschool children were cared for in an organized child-care setting. By 1990, this figure doubled and half the children of working parents were either being cared for in a center or in another home. Today over 70% are in non-parental care. In 1985, 25 percent of working mothers with children under the age of five used a child-care facility as their primary form of care, compared with only 13 percent in 1977 (Hamburg, 1991). Currently more than 13 million children under the age of six, including 6 million babies and toddlers, are in non-parental care some or all of the day (Carnegie Corp., 1996). However, while today there are three times as many children enrolled in child care, there are only two times as many centers, leading to overcrowding and staff turnover. The number of children in child care centers doubled again by 1995, and even if the number of centers continues to increase, the gap will grow even larger since the number of centers is behind enrollment numbers already.

On the whole, this transformation in child-care arrangements was unforeseen, unplanned, and is still poorly understood. Many public opinion surveys report that American parents are deeply troubled about raising their children in today's society (Hamburg, 1991).

A shift toward placing younger children in centers has also occurred, reflecting the increased proportion of mothers of very young children who are in the labor force. Between 1976 and 1990, the proportion of infants under 12 months of age in center care increased from 1 percent to 4 percent, and the number of toddlers aged 1 to 2 nearly doubled from 3 percent to 5 percent (Willer et al., 1990). The proportion of infants in family child care remained stable at 25 percent from 1976 to 1990. The proportion of employed mothers of children under the age of 5 who use center care increased four times between 1965 and 1990, from 6 percent to 28 percent, with an accompanying decrease in the use of in-home providers (Willer et al., 1990).

A major challenge of the next decade will be to increase the number of high-quality child-care centers. The number of children requiring care may continue to increase and more options for increasing the number of developmentally appropriate centers will be necessary. One such option, discussed in chapter 14, is the possibility of existing accredited centers marketing their services to, and perhaps adding satellite centers for, nearby corporations at a corporate group rate. This option would provide a certain number of reserved enrollment slots for company employees and would help centers maintain and expand their operations (Duncan & Thornton, 1993). A 1991 National League of Cities survey of 278 of America's larger cities reported that 96 percent of these cities cited child care as the most pressing need for urban children. This becomes completely understandable when the current number of good care options are reviewed (Child Care Information Exchange, 1991; Carnegie Corp., 1996).

◇ ◇

PROBLEM-SOLVING: CHALLENGES AND TRENDS

Brainstorming for Solutions

In the first and last classes of the semester, conduct a class activity in which students brainstorm ideas in answer to the question, "What would lead to better child care in the United States?" (Brainstorming is a technique in which students generate ideas without sorting them. Chapter 5 provides more details on this activity.) To assist the class in finding solutions, have them build a discussion around each of the following questions:

1. What is the problem? (It often needs redefining.)
2. What more do we need to know?
3. Who needs to be involved?
4. What would a solution look like?
5. What is the first step?

When a number of ideas have been generated, the class can vote to select 10 or fewer solutions, along with their respective first steps, as the ideas that should have priority. These ideas can be developed as small-group projects, term papers, or even as a graduate thesis.

This problem-solving framework can be used for both large and small problems. Initially, one problem should be done with the whole group for practice, then other problems can be worked on by small groups that report back to the whole group. One method of generating problems to discuss might be to have class participants, at the beginning of the class period, hand in problems they would like "think tank" help on.

The following list was generated by one class at the end of a semester in answer to the question, "What would lead to better child care in the U.S.?"

1. Learn from/copy England, Australia and New Zealand for ways to develop more slots/spaces to serve children. (In England, child care centers receive extra grants for creating more spaces, for creating spaces for children with disabilities, for involving the elderly, and for meeting other special requirements. In New Zealand, they have "setting up grants," which are disbursed once the standards for a new center are met.)

2. Require NAEYC accreditation for centers to receive public funding.

3. Require parent education and parent involvement for centers to receive public funding.

4. Have many paths to better child care be accepted: public school prekindergarten; federal and other public programs; accredited non-profit and profit-making programs.

5. Build centers on public school grounds; include Head Start programs in high schools.

6. Encourage corporate-sponsored child care and publicize the benefits (to children, parents, and the corporation).

7. Encourage corporate personnel benefits offices to give corporate vouchers to approved/accredited child-care programs; these vouchers can be redeemed for tuition assistance that is billed to the corporation. "Cafeteria-style" benefits allow for this.

8. Require Parent Board Chairpersons to sign grant and budget documents (as is required in some Federal programs).

9. Attach accredited child-care centers to hospitals.

10. Attach accredited child-care centers to government agencies at all levels of government (county, state, federal).

◊ ◊

SUMMARY

The very words *child care* convey different images to different people. Some see a brightly decorated, modern facility filled with the sounds of children's laughter and tumbling block towers. For too many others, the vision is one of an overcrowded room filled with unruly children and frustrated teachers. In a country as wealthy as the U.S., a country that houses some of the finest universities in the world, a country that considers itself to be the leading world power, it is sad that an issue as crucial as the future of its own children is not receiving the attention it deserves. Why is the U.S. entrusting its future to child-care facilities that have little or no minimum standards for their teachers? Why is one teacher permitted to be responsible for as many as 12 infants at one time, as is the case in Idaho (Wingert & Kantrowitz, 1990)? Some continuing challenges in child care include:

(1) *Lack of federal regulations with regard to the care of young children.* As Wingert and Kantrowitz (1990) so aptly wrote, "The government offers consumers more guidance choosing breakfast cereal than child care" (p. 227).

(2) *Parental fear about the long-term effects of child care on children.* More and more studies, such as those done by Jay Belsky (1984) at Pennsylvania State University, suggest that children who attend day-care/child-care programs are at a greater risk of exhibiting social and emotional problems later in life, as well as at risk of demonstrating higher levels of aggression and disobedience. Recent studies have shown that more than 86% of center-based child care is "mediocre (not growth-enhancing) to poor" (meaning growth-harming). Only one in seven centers provides a level of care that promotes healthy development (Child Care Bureau, 1997; Carnegie Corp., 1996).

(3) *High turnover among child-care workers.* Those who work in child care often fall victim to the stresses of overcrowded classrooms, understaffing, and lack of financial incentives, and they leave the profession. A high turnover in caretakers leaves children with a sense of insecurity. (Some studies show that 50 percent of child-care centers have a 50 percent turnover rate.)

(4) *Lack of alternatives for caring for children when they are sick.* Parents are not always able to stay home with a child who has a cold. Sending him or her to school puts all of the other children and teachers at risk of infection.

(5) *High cost of child care.* Lower cost alternatives in child care, such as hiring immigrants who do not have proper papers to work as nannies or placing children in vastly overcrowded classrooms, are sometimes

illegal. Low-income parents need sliding scales for fees, and parents of all incomes need proof that the facility in which they are placing their children is certified, licensed, and has valid references; this provides peace of mind that their children will not be harmed and will be helped to grow developmentally. Individual licensing of all staff responsible for children both in child care centers and in-home provider child care is being called for in some states (Kagan & Bowman, 1997).

In conclusion, it is known that what happens to a child in the first several years of life lays the foundation for a long, healthy lifespan (Hamburg, 1987). It is important to be resourceful in finding ways of putting this knowledge into practice for healthy child development. Meeting the challenges of developing a program for young children is one step.

Integrating some of the challenges and trends in early childhood education into programs to meet the needs of young children is another step. Caring for children is important work for any human being, and is fundamental to the future of society. Parents can and must help with this work, as we shall see in chapter 10. The role of the director in leading, planning, decision-making and problem solving are nearly as important as the director's knowledge and promotion of developmentally appropriate curriculum practices, as we shall see in the next section.

◇ ◇ ◇ ◇ ◇ ◇ ◇ ◇ ◇ ◇ ◇ ◇ ◇ ◇ ◇ ◇ ◇ ◇ ◇ ◇

SUGGESTED CLASS ACTIVITIES AND DISCUSSIONS

1. *Challenges and Trends—Brainstorming for Solutions.*   Brainstorm challenges and trends in early childhood education today. Record this list on the board and ask small groups to brainstorm on different topics thus recorded. Start with one challenge to do as a whole group for a model.

Brainstorming specific topics relating to the question "What would lead to better child care in the United States?" is a class activity that can be conducted during the first and last classes of a semester. The class brainstorms (that is, generates ideas without sorting them. See chapter 5 for more details) ideas for each of the following questions:

    a. What is the problem? (it often needs redefining)

    b. What more do we need to know?

    c. Who needs to be involved?

    d. What would a solution look like?

    e. What is the first step?

Sometimes it helps to determine the number of small groups of 3 or 4 students, possibly, and give students that number of votes. Vote on the whole list of challenges and give the top 5 or 6 to a specific subsection of students for analysis, using these questions.

When a number of ideas have been generated, the class can vote to select ten or fewer ideas, from questions d or e, above, as the ideas that should have priority. These ideas can be developed for small group projects, term papers or even a graduate thesis.

This question framework can be used for large and small problems. One problem should be done with the whole group for practice, and subsequent problems can be worked on by small groups that report back to the whole group. At an early class, participants can hand in problems they would like "think tank" help on at the beginning of the class period.

2. *Implications for Social Policy Issues Based on Developmental Ages.* Building on child development material, construct a chart in class as follows:

Age	Physical Development	Intellectual Development	Social/ Emotional Development	Implications for Social Policy Issues
0 – 12 mo.				
12 – 24 mo.				
24 – 36 mo.				
36 – 48 mo.				
5 years				
6 years				
7 – 8 years				

Ask students to fill in the blanks on the types of development that occur at each age individually or in small groups. In class, brainstorm the social policy issues these developmental needs at different ages might generate. Are better standards needed for certain ages, or all ages? Are more Head Start programs needed?

3. *Set-up Simulation.*   Role-play jobs of various Board Members—Membership Chairman, for instance. Stage a sample telephone conversation with a prospective parent or role-play the Teacher Hiring Committee Chairman demonstrating a sample telephone conversation screening prospective teachers. An on-going class simulation can show the child care center at various stages of development: (a) early planning, (b) implementation, (c) operation,

and (d) evaluation. A more thorough review of a given stage with handouts, posters and resource materials would make a good small group final project. Incorporation, constitution and bylaws materials can be included in the handouts.

4. *Panel of Directors.*   Invite a panel of directors representing programs with different philosophies and different structures to speak to the class and answer questions. Programs represented might include private non-profit, private for-profit, extended day programs in a public school, Head Start, a city- or county-sponsored child care program and a program that serves special needs or handicapped children. After the directors describe their programs and schedules (for their job and/or for their centers) ask some questions, such as: What qualities do you look for in hiring teachers? What happens when your budget is in trouble? What is your main goal (or top priority) as a director? How often does your staff receive pay increases? Do you think a director should have prior teaching experience? Class discussion will generate more such questions.

5. *Comparison of Legislation and Standards.*   Collect materials on local, state and federal licensing and standards. Discuss the *purpose* of licensing (to protect the children) and, if possible, how it came into being in your state. Posters can be made on such subjects as: (1) the differences in state regulations; (2) comparisons of the states providing child care to the largest numbers of children and types of care children are receiving (in-home, family day care, center care, part-time and full-time, etc.); and (3) federal programs that fund child care initiatives. Role play an interview with a legislator on "How to Influence Your Legislator," which might include focusing on one issue at a time and telling him or her how you would like to be represented on that particular issue. Have a group present an array of ideas on how to influence their legislator(s).

◇ ◇

BIBLIOGRAPHY

Association of Teacher Educators, & National Association for the Education of Young Children. (1991). Early childhood teacher certification. *Young Children, 47*(1), 16–21.

Belsky, J. (1984). Two waves of day care research. In R. C. Ainslie (Ed.), *Quality variations in day care.* New York: Praeger.

Bernstein, A., Weber, J., Driscoll, L., & Cunes, A. (1991). Corporate America is still no place for kids. *Business Week* (3241), 234–238.

Bredekamp, S. (Ed.). (1990). *Developmentally appropriate practice in young childhood programs serving children from birth through age 8.* Washington, DC: National Association for the Education of Young Children.

Bredekamp, S., & Copple, C. (Eds.). (1997). *Developmentally appropriate practice in early childhood programs: Revised.* Washington, DC: NAEYC.

Breitbart, V. (1974). *The day care book: The why, what, and how of community day care.* New York: Alfred A. Knopf.

Burchinal, M. R., Ramey, S. L., Reid, M. K., & Jaccard, J. (1995). Early child care experiences and their association with family and child characteristics during middle childhood. *Early Childhood Research Quarterly, 10,* 33–61.

Cadwell, L. B. (1997). *Bringing Reggio Emilia home.* New York: Teachers College, Columbia University.

Carnegie Corporation of New York. (1996). *Years of Promise: A comprehensive learning strategy for America's children.* New York: Author.

Chase-Lansdale, P. (1994). Families and maternal employment during infancy: New linkages. In R. D. Parke & S. G. Kellam (Eds.), *Exploring family relationships within other social contexts* (pp. 29–47). Hillsdale, NJ: Erlbaum.

Child Care Bureau. (1997). *Child Care Bulletin,* Issue 16. Washington, DC: Department of Health and Human Services.

Child Care Information Exchange. (1991, March/April). Did you know? *Child Care Information Exchange, 78,* 15.

Click, P. M., & Click, D. W. (1990). *Administration of schools for young children.* Albany, NY: Delmar.

Council of Chief State School Officers. (1991). *Families in schools.* Washington, DC: Author.

Duncan, S., & Thornton, D. (1993, January/February). Marketing your center's service to employers. *Child Care Information Exchange, 89,* 53–56.

Edwards, C., Gandini, L., & Forman, G. (Eds.). (1996). *The Hundred Languages of Children: The Reggio Emilia approach to early childhood education.* Norwood, NJ: Ablex.

Eiselen, S. S. (1992). *The human side of child care administration: A how to manual.* Washington, DC: National Association for the Education of Young Children.

Erikson, E. (1963). *Childhood and society.* New York: Winston.

Field, T. M. (1994). Infant day care facilitates later social behavior and school performance. In H. Goelman & E. V. Jacobs (Eds.), *Children's play in child care settings* (pp. 69–84). Albany, NY: State University of New York Press.

Finn, M. (1991). *Fund raising for early childhood programs.* Washington, DC: National Association for the Education of Young Children.

Galinsky, E. (1990). The cost of not providing quality early childhood programs: Reaching the full cost of quality in early childhood programs. *Young Children, 45,* 229–236.

Godwin, A., & Schrag, L. (1988). *Setting up for infant care: Guidelines for centers and family day care homes.* Washington, DC: National Association for the Education of Young Children.

Gonzalez-Mena, J. (1990). *A guide to routines.* Sacramento, CA: California Department of Education.

Governors' 1991 Report on Education. (1990). *Results in education.* Washington, DC: National Governors' Association.

Halpern, R. (1989). Community-based early intervention: The state of the art. In J. Shonkoff & S. Meisels (Eds.), *Handbook of early intervention.* New York: Cambridge University Press.

Hamburg, D. A. (1987). *Fundamental building blocks of early life.* New York: Carnegie Corp.

Hamburg, D. A. (1990). *A decent start: Promoting healthy child development in the first three years of life.* New York: Carnegie Corp.

Hamburg, D. A. (1991). *The family crucible and healthy child development.* New York: Carnegie Corp.

Hart, C. H., Burts, D. C., & Charlesworth, R. (Eds.). (1997). *Integrated curriculum and developmentally appropriate practice: Birth to age 8.* State University of New York Press.

Hayes, C. D., Palmer, J. L., & Zaslow, M. J. (Eds.). (1990). *Who cares for America's children: Child care policy for the 1990's.* Panel on Child Care Policy, Committee on Child Development Research and Public Policy,

Commission on Behavioral and Social Sciences and Education. Washington, DC: National Academy Press.

Hechinger, F. M. (Ed.). (1986). *A better start: New choices for early learning.* New York: Walker.

Hetherington, E. M., & Parke, R. D. (1986). *Child psychology: A contemporary viewpoint* (3rd ed.). New York: McGraw-Hill.

Hewlett, S. A. (1991). *When the bough breaks: The cost of neglecting our children.* New York: Basic Books.

Isenberg, J., & Quisenberry, N. L. (1988). Play: A necessity for all children. *Childhood Education,* 138–145.

Kagan, J. (1970). White House conference on children. Washington, DC: U.S. Government Printing Office.

Kagan, S. L. (1990). *Excellence in early childhood education: Defining characteristics and next-decade strategies.* Office of Education Research and Improvement, U.S. Department of Education. Washington, DC: U.S. Government Printing Office.

Kagan, S. L., & Bowman, B. T. (1997). *Leadership in early care and education.* Washington, DC: National Association for the Education of Young Children.

Katz, L. G., & Chard, S. C. (1989). *Engaging Children's Minds.* Norwood, NJ: Ablex.

Kostelnik, M. J. (1992). Myths associated with developmentally appropriate programs. *Young Children, 47*(4), 17–23.

Lazar, I., & Darlington, R. (1982). Lasting effects of early education: A report for the consortium for longitudinal studies. *Monographs for Research in Child Development, 47*(2–3, Serial No. 195).

Maughan, B., & Rutter, M. (1985). Education: Improving practice through increasing understanding. In R. N. Rapaport (Ed.), *Children, youth, and families* (pp. 26–49). New York: Cambridge University Press.

Minnesota Department of Education. (1990). *Challenge 2000: Success for all learners.* St. Paul, MN: Minnesota Department of Education.

Modigliani, K., Reiff, M., & Jones, S. (1991). *Opening your door to children: How to start a family day care program.* Washington, DC: National Association for the Education of Young Children.

National Association for the Education of Young Children. (1991). *Accreditation criteria and procedures of the National Academy of Early Childhood Programs.* Washington, DC: Author.

National Governors' Association Committee on Human Resources and Center Policy Research. (1987). *Focus on the first sixty months: A handbook of promising prevention programs for children zero to five years of age.* Washington, DC: Author.

National Institute for Early Childhood Professional Development. (1991). A Vision for Early Childhood Professional Development. *Young Children, 47*(1), 35–37.

National Research Council. (1990). *Who cares for America's children?* Washington, DC: National Academy Press.

New Zealand, Education Department Standards. (1968). *Standard for the administration and organization of play centres recognized by the director-general of education.* Appendix XI, circular memorandum B16613, pp. 42–43.

Overman, S. (1989). States offer incentives for corporate child care programs. *Personal Administrator, 5,* 31–41.

Parent Cooperative Preschools International. (1985). *How to start a co-op.* Indianapolis, IN: Author.

Piaget, J. (1952). *The origins of intelligence in children.* New York: International Universities Press.

Recio, I. (1991). Beyond day care: The company school. *Business Week* (3239), 142.

Rutter, M. (1985). Family and school influences on cognitive development. In R. A. Hinde, A. N. Perret-Clermont, & J. Stevenson-Hinde (Eds.), *Social relationships and cognitive development* (pp. 83–108). Oxford, UK: Clarendon Press.

Seitz, V., & Provence, S. (1990). Caregiver-focused models of early intervention. In S. J. Meisels & J. P. Shonkoff (Eds.), *Handbook of early childhood intervention*. New York: Cambridge University Press.

Sher, M., & Brown, G. (1989). What to do with Jenny: A corporate child care decision that greatly affects the bottom line. *Personnel Administrator, 5,* 31–41.

Smith, D. M. (1991). *Kincare and the American corporation solving the work/family dilemma.* Homewood, AL: Business One Irwin.

U.S. Department of Health and Human Services. (1996). Blueprint for action: Healthy child care America campaign. (Pamphlet.)

U.S. Department of Labor, Bureau of Labor Statistics. (1989, November). New Labor Force Projections Spanning 1988–2000, *Monthly Labor Review, 112*(11), 3–11.

Volling, B. L., & Feagans, L. V. (1995). Infant day care and children's social competence. *Infant Behavior and Development, 18,* 177–188.

Vygotsky, L. S. (1978). *Mind in society: The development of higher psychological processes.* (Eds. and Trans. M. Cole, V. John-Steiner, S. Scribner, & E. Souberman.) Cambridge, MA: Harvard University Press.

Waxman, P. L. (1991). Children in the world of adults—On site child care. *Young Children,* 16–21.

Willer, B. (1992). An overview of the demand and supply of child care in 1990. *Young Children,* 19–21.

Willer, B., Hofferth, S. L., Kisker, E. E., Divine-Hawkins, P., Rarquhar, E., & Glantz, F. B. (1990). *The demand and supply of childcare in 1990.* Washington, DC: National Association for the Education of Young Children.

Wingert, P., & Kantrowitz, B. (1990, Winter/Spring). The daycare generation. *Newsweek,* pp. 226–228.

Zaslow, M. J. (1991). Variation in child care quality and its implications for children. *Journal of Social Issues, 47*(2), 125–138.

Zigler, E. F., & Weiss, H. (1985). Family support systems: An ecological approach to child development. In R. N. Rapaport (Ed.), *Children, youth, and families* (pp. 166–205). New York: Cambridge University Press.

Zigler, M. J., & Lang, M. E. (1991). *Child care choices: Balancing the needs of children, families, and society.* New York: The Free Press.

Leadership and the Role of the Director

Leadership, planning, decision-making, and problem-solving are some of the main components that comprise the role of the director. These functions are the foundations of the administrative and management structures of a center and if they do not form a strong foundation, the structure is not as steady or secure as it might be. A center that creates an attitude of excellence in personnel hiring and training, team building, motivation, and professionalism can move forward with the tasks of implementation, operation, and evaluation. Time management and good assistance are important as well. Assistance can be supplied by technology (such as computers), as well as by experienced people (such as a good administrative assistant).

As a center is growing, the director needs to be increasingly aware that one third or more of his or her time should go to parent relations and community outreach. A director should assess the percentage of time spent on:

1. functions, such as talking on the phone, doing paperwork, working with people one-on-one or in groups; and

2. the categories of people with whom this time is spent, such as children, staff, parents, and/or the community.

More categories can be added to these assessments to accommodate unique situations. Pie charts showing these percentages of time spent, such as those seen in the figure below, can reveal rewarding insights.

Director's Time Analysis (Sample)

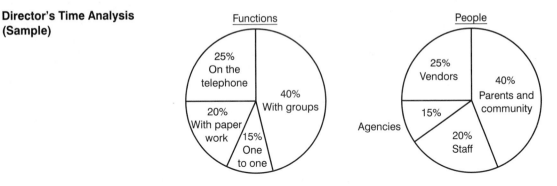

When planning for assistance, adequate human resources will be necessary, in addition to the use of one or more computers and useful child-care software packages. As a center grows to serve 25 to 50 children, a head teacher or education director may need to be added. A full-time administrative assistant may replace a secretary and take over more of the administrative duties. However, the director is still in charge of overall policy-making, budgeting, personnel development, and any activities that might take him or her out of the center.

As a center grows to an enrollment of 25 to 50 children, classes also might grow in number. For example, the center may expand from two classes to four classes, accommodating the younger children in the smaller classes. The director continues to handle parent admissions activities, and the teachers handle routine daily parent contacts. The administrative assistant deals with fee collection. As a center expands to an enrollment of about 50 students, the director usually is freed from in-center activities. More time spent on fund-raising, making agency contacts, and admissions work is required. Meetings and planning become slightly more formal; many of the ideas given in the next four chapters may be even more useful and necessary.

As a center grows to serve 75 children, many of the director's activities remain the same, but, because of the growth, they become more complex and require more time and effort to perform. The director is still the overall administrator, and deals with policy-making, budgets, hiring and dismissals, and staff salaries, as well as plans with the staff and the Board to determine long-range goals. He or she remains the chief link to outside agencies for resources and sponsorship. An assistant director may take on the short-term staff training and many administrative duties, such as purchasing (using the director's guidelines). The advisory capacity of the assistant's position is mostly in the areas of child care and teaching. The secretary/bookkeeper handles the administrative duties that can be delegated, assists with scheduling, and answers the telephone. A center of this size might have six classes of children, so age, maturity, and special needs can be addressed in even more discrete ways.

An analysis of how much time the director spends on functions and categories of people becomes even more important as the center grows. If one feels that "doing paperwork" is the most important part of the job (or is the largest part of the job), some changes may need to be made to involve other members of the staff more. Directors report that they work between 40 and 60 hours a week, but as the number of hours approaches 55 and 60 hours per week, the likelihood of burnout increases and the individual may leave the field. Assessment of management functions needs to be continuous, and many of the ideas in chapter 5 for individual problem-solving can be used to analyze and break down tasks and projects into manageable parts. Facilitating the group of adults who are involved in a center—staff, Board, and parents—to move toward center goals requires an understanding of leadership and the use of power, which are presented in the next chapters.

chapter 2

Understanding Leadership and the Use of Power

An awareness of sound leadership principles can offer new insights to those responsible for providing well-run, quality programs for children. Leadership includes the ability to create a vision, articulate it and develop strategies, along with the management tasks of planning, implementing, operating, and evaluating. Because working with young children is one of the most important occupations to which a person can devote his or her life, excellence should be the goal of all aspects of child care, especially the leadership aspect.

◊ ◊

LEADERSHIP

Leadership in early childhood education administration means planning for change, then implementing, putting into operation, and evaluating those changes. Leadership functions are designed to accomplish change for the improvement of the organization, and not just for change's sake. Administrative functions and responsibilities, as well as leadership functions and responsibilities, may be carried out by the same person; however, administrative roles and leadership roles are different. Administrative duties focus on keeping the center running, through committees, policies, and regulations. Administration alone is not leadership; instead, it is the activity of using old processes to obtain old or ongoing goals. Leadership, on the other hand, uses new processes to achieve ongoing goals, old processes to achieve new goals, or new processes to reach new goals (Figure 2.1).

For example, in a child-care or preschool situation, a leader might be called upon to uphold an ongoing, tried-and-true goal of developing happy, competent children. The leader might decide to use a new process to help reach this goal, such as having the staff brainstorm types of training they want or need, and then, with the staff's help, planning four to eight training sessions from this list.

A new goal for a child-care center might be that of opening another branch of the center in a new location; the leader could use "old" processes, such as the same administrative foundations and sequence of steps that were used to open the first center, to accomplish this new goal. An example of a new goal that could be accomplished through a new process might be that of adding a parent workshop series to the center's offerings, with topics planned by parents during brainstorming sessions and with parent chairpersons responsible for running the workshop series. The possibilities are endless.

How does a director or leader make significant changes that will achieve better quality results? Usually this goal involves long-term changes, which may take one or two years to plan, and then two to three years to implement. This process requires leadership. Under the terms of social exchange, which bases leadership on successful interactions and the ability to persuade others

FIGURE 2.1
Leadership and Vision vs.
Administration and
Management

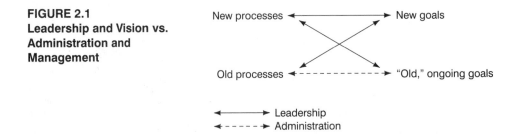

toward group goals (rather than on force), leadership is an interaction between persons in which the first person presents information in such a way that the second person is convinced that the benefits to himself/herself will be greater than the benefits to the first person (cost-benefits improved). In this way, the interaction avoids direct confrontation and moves the persons or groups toward goals without making status or power differentials obvious (Jacobs, 1971, p. 237).

A good example of this can be found in the story of a director of a large Midwestern child-care center. The center was located in a small town in the middle of flat, hot, dusty farmland. Even so, the director always managed to hire extremely able assistant directors, who were competent, productive people. How did she do this? She told them that if they would do their best work for her for four years, she would then write a persuasive letter of recommendation to any of the biggest child-care systems in the country that they chose. (They could see their cost-benefits improving.) The director made it clear that she didn't expect these assistants to stay with her forever, just for four years. Without this leadership gesture, which provided young professionals the chance to see the direct benefits of giving their boss their best efforts, this director might have had assistants quitting in one year. She also might have had a hard time enticing able people to her locality at all.

Obviously, this type of leadership requires interpersonal interaction skills in persuading other people. Some employees prefer an *authoritarian* (autocratic) type of leadership and some followers or employees prefer a *humanitarian* (friendly or kindly) type of leader. The choice will depend on the situation, the leader, and/or the followers.

Leadership in organizations has been well documented. Knowledge of the components of leadership is an invaluable asset to an individual charged with new kinds of tasks in early childhood care and education. Natural skill and ability in leading has always been an asset but knowledge of the various behaviors that increase the effectiveness of a group, in addition to planning new goals and/or new processes makes any effort needed more focused for leaders.

Perhaps a review of the basics would be valuable. The original human relations management perspective emerged from experiments done at Western Electric's Chicago Hawthorne Plant in the 1920s. The results of this experiment came to be known as the Hawthorne Effect in which a seemingly non-intrusive experiment produced striking results in human behavior. The basis of the study was to determine the relationship between working conditions and the level of employee productivity. It was found that lighting in the plant, whether bright or dim, had no impact on worker production (Gay, 1992). What made employees feel important and subsequently increased their productivity was the attention from management they received and not the illumination of their workplace. The conclusion at the basis of this perspective is that leaders and managers CAN affect the behavior of their subordinates. In many cases improved morale and working conditions influenced employees' productivity and attitudes more than financial incentives. It has always been assumed that educators at any level received stimulation and encouragement from each other and from their professional associations. This may or may not be true, but as staff and administrative employees fill many different kinds of jobs in early childhood education, without necessarily having extensive backgrounds in early childhood education, peer attention and encouragement may not be sufficient to gain the results that a leader sees as goals. In considering leadership knowledge, leadership skills and abilities, and leadership behaviors it is interesting to note the source of the material on leadership behaviors.

The behavioral approach to predicting leadership ability draws its data from descriptive observations of: (1) how managers/leaders spent their time at work; and (2) comparisons of the behavior of effective and ineffective leaders. The behaviors were documented through: (1) job descriptions; (2) direct observations; (3) reviews of managers' diaries; (4) anecdotes; and (5) questionnaires. Researchers identified specific leadership behaviors that could serve as guides for effective leadership. A synthesis of these behaviors later became the basis of an instrument used to describe leadership entitled the *Leadership Behavior Descriptive Questionnaire*. This questionnaire was developed at Ohio State University and is still in use today (Likert, 1961).

Likert's early studies on managers identified other behaviors that made individuals successful. He identified five specific actions that successful managers and leaders took that distinguished them from their less successful counterparts in the same company. These behaviors, with their specific associated tasks, created a climate of: (1) understanding; (2) mutual trust; (3) respect; (4) success among their subordinates; and (5) high task orientation. The five behaviors and their accompanying interpretations will be discussed later in this chapter in the section on effective and ineffective leaders.

Likert (1961) determined that another important behavior for managers to possess involves informing skills. Informing is defined as a process by which a leader communicates task-relevant information needed by subordinates, peers, or superiors. Likert believed that informing serves as a linchpin between the work unit, the rest of the organization, and the outside environment.

The situational approach to leadership which was developed by Blake and Mouton (1982) looks at: (1) work performed by the leader's organizational group; (2) the organization's external work environment; and (3) the characteristics of the followers. Their *Managerial Grid* has been used in organizations to assess the way that work is performed, and the relationship of these three variables to that work. Yukl (1998) emphasizes that the assumption underlying situational leadership is that different leader behavior patterns will be effective in different situations, and that the same behavior pattern is not optimal in all situations.

In his book *Leadership in Organizations*, Yukl (1998) identifies specific leadership behaviors that facilitate the "management of the work" and the "management of relationships." Each of these functions resulted from studies done on managers and leaders who had been successful since the early 1950s. Yukl compiled and analyzed the research and pinpointed the following behaviors as important. Leadership behaviors to manage human relationships include:

1. Supporting
2. Developing
3. Recognizing
4. Rewarding
5. Team building and conflict management
6. Networking

Specific behaviors to manage the work include:

1. Planning
2. Clarifying
3. Monitoring
4. Problem Solving
5. Informing

In summation, Yukl states that research on these specific categories of managerial behavior is limited. Nevertheless, the findings suggest that each of these categories of leadership and managerial behavior has the potential to improve leadership and managerial effectiveness if they are skillfully used in appropriate situations (1998, p. 113).

◇ ◇

THE DIFFERENCE BETWEEN MANAGEMENT AND LEADERSHIP

Briefly stated, management provides consistency, control, and efficiency—with or without new ideas or processes. Leadership is needed to foster purpose, creativity, imagination, and drive. The specific roles of manager and leader have undergone a great deal of analysis in the field of business. This research points out that there are differences between these responsibilities and that the individuals who manage have specific roles that are determined by the organization. Organizational leadership, on the other hand, can come from a variety of people in a number of roles. In a time of constant change, which has also been called "permanent white water" (Vaill, 1989) managing well requires elements of leadership.

Gardner (1990) defines leadership as "the process of persuasion by example by which an individual induces a group to pursue objectives held by the leader or shared by the leader and his or her followers" (p. 1). Gardner also describes managers as individuals who hold a "directive" post in an organization. They preside over the resources by which an organization functions, allocate resources prudently, and make the best possible use of people. According to Gardner, leadership and management are not separate entities, and a delicate balance must be struck between the two roles. He calls individuals with the ability to play both these roles, leader/managers. Gardner does, however, differentiate between leadership and management with respect to the role the manager accepts in the workplace. He suggests that the word manager indicates that the individual so labeled presides over processes, resources and making the best use of people.

Yukl (1998) suggests that most definitions of a leader or manager, including Jacobs' (1971), reflect the assumption that leadership involves a process of social influence, whereby intentional influence is exerted by one person over other people in order to structure the activities and relationships in a group or organization. Yukl (1998) and others view effective leadership in a variety of ways, but there is general agreement that it is a group or organizational process that contributes to the overall effectiveness of a group or organization. Administration and leadership/management are similar in the description and in Figure 2.1 shown earlier. However, leadership is distinct from administration in that leaders must deal with the issue of implementing long-term change, and must use new processes to achieve on-going goals (e.g., technology might be one), old processes to reach new goals, or new processes to reach new goals.

◇ ◇

SOURCES OF POWER

There are different *sources of power* described in management theory; by combining two or three of these sources, an administrator can "widen" his or her power base. Remember, *power is the ability to influence others,* and, according to this definition, is always granted from below. It is *authority* that is granted from above and is the right to *attempt to influence others*. The following sources of power, therefore, are ways leaders can seek to influence others' behavior.

Reward Power

Reward power is derived from one person's capacity to reward another person in exchange for his compliance with desired behavior. This compliance is expected to happen without supervision, and works best when the person's acceptance of direction and evidence of providing effort (results) *can be seen*. If a director notices good teaching practices or positive relationships between a teacher and children, it is important that praise or a rewarding smile be given at the moment it is observed. So much of what is important in early childhood is not tangible and cannot be viewed easily at just any time. If a positive action or situation is reinforced when it occurs, then it can be referred to later when the director considers the person for a raise, or selects a candidate for "Teacher of the Month."

Coercive Power

Coercive power is not the result of merely withholding rewards; it is the capacity to actually inflict something negative on a person, such as through reduction of hours or dismissal. Using this kind of power produces negative outcomes and can cause employees to "cover up," lie, turn in false reports, and perhaps sabotage the goals of the organization. In early childhood education, coercive power is particularly undesirable since physical punishment of children is prohibited; if it is used, it may produce undesirable behavior in children as well.

Legitimate Power

Legitimate power is just that: Because the director is the director (holds that job), people *expect* him or her to lead and delegate responsibility by asking others to do things. However, the leader's efforts to make changes must appear to be "reasonable and correct" to the group. If they do not appear to be reasonable, the leader will need to make his or her position clear by informing the group of his or her point of view or by helping them understand more about the responsibility the position entails. Elected officials utilize this type of "legitimate power."

Referent Power

Referent power results when people find the leader so attractive, competent, and understanding that they want to *identify* with him or her, often wishing to please by seeking to do as the director asks. This kind of leader "inspires" people, and often those being led have no idea of the power this leader has over them. Referent power is one of the most effective sources of power and is a valuable one for all early childhood administrators, since it is important for staff and administrators to model behavior that inspires parents and children alike.

Modeling behavior after a leader affords the leader great influence. In such a situation, people act in certain ways because they admire, wish to please, and want to emulate the leader. People have different areas in their lives, or groups of reference, that might involve different referent people; for example, work life, social life, family life, and religious life are all groups of reference.

Expert Power

Expert power lies in the employees' view that the administrator has more knowledge and ability in a given area. This is an easy power source for a leader to maintain and increase by updating knowledge with workshops and courses, keeping up with professional reading, *and talking about it*, either informally or through staff training meetings. Employees often will support and follow directions without supervision in relation to how expert they think the leader is.

Those who are experts should remember that when dealing with other peoples' ideas, work, or property, one should always maximize the person's self-esteem, and give credit at the end of a project when it is successful. If a project is unsuccessful, the "idea person" will be grateful to be saved from the embarrassment of criticism.

◇ ◇

SOCIAL EXCHANGE: HOW TO MAKE INTERACTIONS WORK FOR YOU

The concept of applying social exchange to leadership can be compared to a checking account. A leader can have a plus or minus balance of "credit," and he or she can add to this or subtract from it.

In social exchange theory, the central question is *why* a group member subordinates himself to someone of higher status. The answer lies in the type of "balance" a leader builds, whether it be positive or negative. A leader starting out in a newly created position usually has a neutral balance. From that point on, everything the leader says builds plus or minus credit. The leader's follow-up on what he or she says then builds plus or minus credit (for example, if the leader delivers resources as promised, a plus credit is built). Plus or minus credit is built by the reward or punishment the leader gives to those who do well or poorly in relation to organizational goals.

A new leader may start off with a slight plus credit, because of the position of "leader," unless the leader or director who came before did an unusually poor job. In the latter case, the leader may start off with a slight minus credit, and must allow a longer time to "build trust." Barring a particularly positive or particularly negative predecessor, the new leader will have a "neutral" balance as mentioned before.

When a leader begins a job, the organization can publish an item in the newsletter to help give him or her a "plus credit" start. Even if the previous leader left with a minus credit, however, there is only a limited carry-over effect, since credit is mostly based on the new individual, and what he or she does. A new leader also earns a small plus credit because people assume he or she has access to resources.

Making a positive change can be a slow and deliberate process, and a new director must have the group's support, or at least their indifference, rather than their opposition. If the group doubts the leader, the cohesiveness of the group may be split. Some individuals in a group work slowly and cautiously to split the staff, thereby ruining the organization. In order to prevent this, the leader has to make the proposed rewards great enough to satisfy employees and encourage them to work, while also not promising anything that cannot be delivered.

A leader can always earn more credit if he or she has a plus credit to begin with, but as credit grows, so also does the blame when plans do not succeed. Directors should decide if they want this accountability and if they have the competency for it. Perhaps a given individual's competencies lie in areas other than leadership.

Idiosyncrasy Credit

The term *idiosyncrasy credit* refers to the number of peculiarities, or idiosyncrasies, the director or new leader is "allowed" to have. Idiosyncrasy credit, sometimes called personality credit, develops slowly, over time. In the beginning, then, it is best for a leader to present only one or two idiosyncrasies until credit is well established.

A new director or principal often enters a program with a view toward things that he or she would like to change. Writing these ideas in a notebook will be useful later, since after a while the fresh perspective wears off and the needs of the program may not be identified as clearly. After making a list, the director should choose only two ideas and decide how to implement them in the next six months. Two more ideas can be focused on in the following six months. One director reveals this plan in a letter to the staff, which she includes as the first page in her staff notebook. (The staff notebook is a resource given to each staff member, and includes schedules, policies, rules, a calendar, etc.) In this letter, the director states her philosophy, either generally or for the specific upcoming year:

> Our philosophy this year will emphasize *respect*—respect for children, respect for adults, respect for materials, and respect for new ideas.

or

> Our philosophy this year will emphasize physical fitness, which will include the addition of a new piece of playground equipment and serving more nutritious snacks.

Following the paragraph on philosophical topics, the director includes a paragraph describing her two idiosyncrasies.

> I would like to remind you that I am upset and very uncomfortable when I see someone discipline a child for wetting or dirtying his pants. I'd like to ask you all to refrain from this type of discipline out of respect for me. Also this year, I'd particularly like to have a special emphasis on having the children sing more during the day.
>
> Thanks for being such a great staff. This center wouldn't be the best center in town if it weren't for each person's special efforts. I want you to know how much I appreciate them.
>
> Sincerely,
>
> Sue Smith, Director

The idea here is that the director is allowed to have two idiosyncrasies—even if they are a little unusual—just because she *is* the director. This acceptance of her idiosyncrasies, or her idiosyncrasy credit, builds with time and with her abilities in social exchange and interactions. Generally, leaders have a greater positive balance of idiosyncrasy credit than do followers.

Studies show over and over again that employees desire a fair exchange in their work situations, and that they prefer more than pay in return for their efforts. If they feel they gain self-esteem and status from working in a good center where their extra efforts are especially valued, they will feel that they are getting a fair exchange. This in turn earns the leader more credit.

The amount of credit a leader receives is based on the *perceptions* of the group members relative to the accomplishment of group goals. A leader, therefore, should let the group know when the center is praised or group goals are met.

In summary, to gather credit, a leader must:

1. facilitate group attainments and assist the group in knowing when they are attained. (The leader can't tell them, however; they must get their perceptions through interactions.);

2. resolve conflicts;

3. increase resources.

Since a leader's credit is partially built as a result of his or her ability in social exchange, it is important to realize that social exchange is popularity-based. Employees *like* to be with a leader who makes them feel good about themselves. The followers feel that they provide a service to this kind of leader, and like being helpful to him or her (referent power).

Popular leaders can tolerate, accept, and appreciate a wide range of values—they are not dogmatic. Of course, a leader can never know exactly how employees will interpret his or her behavior, or what they will do in response. Most groups within an establishment develop fairly strong informal organizations. The leader's goal should be to have the purpose of this network be the same as the purpose of the center, for instance having the best center in town.

Minimum Effort vs. Maximum Effort

When an employee begins work, there is usually a written or unwritten "employment contract" stating that the employee will accept direction and will provide effort without question. This requirement is called a *minimum effort*, and dictates what an employee must do unless he or she wants to risk getting fired.

One goal of leadership is to obtain, at least part of the time, individual effort from employees that far surpasses this minimum effort. To obtain this greater effort, there must be some sort of process that leads individuals to be concerned about the achievement of organizational objectives for reasons other than just their pay and fringe benefits. The employees must be genuinely concerned about the welfare of the center itself, either by identifying with it, or by feeling that the goals themselves are right and proper. Either attitude will lead to superior efforts. Such employees take pride in saying, "I work for the best center in town."

Perhaps the most important aspect of the interaction between adults involved in a child-care center and the center is that the center convey to the adult his or her importance, thus providing a feeling of personal worth. Each person has a strong need to feel accepted and appreciated by others. To the extent that a center communicates a feeling of worth and support to an individual, whether staff or parent, that individual will feel rewarded; *in exchange*, that person will feel motivated to repay the center through greater cooperation and the encouragement they give to other adults and the children. This exchange occurs when adults know they will receive even more respect if their behavior continues and improves.

One large system of child-care centers in Philadelphia has a wonderful program of gradually improving rewards. Hourly records are kept of how much time each parent "gives" the center; this time might be spent attending parent-officers meetings, going along on field trips, providing classroom assistance, checking out library books for the center's use, painting or repairing equipment, or helping in any of the other myriad ways parents can help. These volunteer parents record their hours on a chart posted in the hall near their child's room. At the end of the year, the director provides rewards such as corsages for parents who provide 10 to 15 hours of help, a large gift selected by the Board and presented to the parent who provides the most number of hours of help, and smaller gifts to the runner(s) up for the most hours given. Each year the parents' committee votes for new "prizes," and then earns the money to pay for them through fund-raising events.

When looking for ways to maximize the effort given by the adults involved in a particular center, the leader should remember that commitment is very slow to build, but very easy to destroy! It is precious, and something to be nurtured.

Organizational Variables

In his books *New Patterns of Management* (1961) and *The Human Organization* (1967), Rensis Likert found that organizations have three sets of variables, as illustrated in Figure 2.2. If long-term change is the goal, the leader must provide input into the first set, which then affects the second set, and then the third set. These variables are as follows:

1. *Causal variables.* The organization has some control over these, which include policies, rules and regulations, salary, fringe benefits, interpersonal relations, and hours.

2. *Intervening variables.* These include perceptions, attitudes, and loyalty, which are built on the causal variables.

3. *End variables.* These result from the attitudes and loyalty of a center, and include as an end goal happy, competent children (our definition of productivity for the early childhood world) and cooperative staff and parents. On the negative side, end variables may include waste, pilfering, turnover of staff, lateness, and absenteeism.

Most of Likert's research is based on *perceptions*. Although perceptions may not reflect what is really going on, *perceptions are what count*, because they affect the end variables. If undesirable behaviors are noted in the end variables column of the chart in Figure 2.2 when it is applied to a specific center, plans can be made to make changes in causal variables. Perhaps it is time to ask the staff as a group to review and update staff policy. Although salary is often a problem in the early childhood work world, almost all of the other causal variables can be changed easily to better benefit or accommodate the staff, which in turn creates more positive feelings and more loyalty. Salary, of course, can be changed also, but external as well as internal factors are involved in making such a change. Appendix C provides some Leadership Enablers that give a few

VARIABLES		
Causal	**Intervening**	**End**
Policy	Perceptions	Happy, competent children (productivity)
Rules	Attitudes	Cooperative staff/parents
Salary	Loyalty	
Fringe benefits		Waste, pilfering, lateness, staff
Interpersonal relations		turnover, absenteeism
Hours		
6 months–2 years*	6 months–2 years*	

Note: Remember to consider the *time factor* in the above process. For the variables in each column to effect a change in the next column, the time or "institutional lag" needed between sets of variables is six months to two years.

FIGURE 2.2
Likert Model

ideas for possible changes in causal variables as these are the only variables that can be changed directly.

The following story of Mary, an aide, illustrates how a simple change in causal variables can affect other variables.

> Mary was always 20 to 30 minutes late for work each morning, which upset the staff-child ratio during those 20 to 30 minutes. The director had spoken to Mary several times, but no change in Mary's lateness had occurred. Finally, in a one-on-one conference, the director learned that Mary had a six-year-old child who left for school at 8:15 A.M. Mary's bus to the center left at 8:00 A.M., and she usually missed it. This director quickly saw that a tender-hearted person like Mary wasn't about to leave a crying six-year-old for the sake of any job. So she adjusted Mary's work schedule to start and end half an hour later. Mary was very grateful (intervening variable) for this understanding attitude on the director's part, and was loyal to the center and kind to the children for the rest of the time she was employed there (several years).

The time lag in Mary's change of perception—from feeling that this was just a job with inconvenient hours to a feeling of gratitude—occurred considerably faster than the six months shown on the chart, but then this was a small change.

Unfortunately, this chart works in reverse, too. Where there is waste, absenteeism, staff turnover, and unhappy children, a director or an observer might find disloyal staff who perceive the policies and regulations as harsh and unfair or who have other complaints (whether justified or not). This is a larger problem, and the full two years might be needed after some of the causal variables have been changed for attitudes to change as well. Output changes, and the development of really happy, competent children may occur two *more* years after the attitudes change.

Because of this time lag, it is important never to judge a program, and perhaps drop it, after only one year. As mentioned earlier, when a new director comes into a program, he or she often sees many things that could be changed. Since this initial time is a time of building trust, the changes should come gradually. After a year, the director may look at the four areas chosen to work on (two every six months), and find it difficult to see noticeable improvement. The Likert model suggests the benefits of waiting another year before dropping these efforts, since attitudes and perceptions change slowly, but are often well worth waiting for.

◊ ◊

CHARACTERISTICS OF SUCCESSFUL LEADERS

While studying large companies with many branches, Likert (1953) compared the 30 most successful managers with the 30 least successful managers in the same company. He found that the major differences between the two groups fell into five categories:

1. *Providing social support for employees and groups.* This factor was found to be the most important characteristic; it is a causal variable that a leader can control to develop good attitudes.

2. *Providing high task orientation.* Successful leaders always clarify the overall goals of the organization and remind employees of their importance.

3. *Providing a high degree of technical expertise.* Successful leaders know their fields. They take courses and workshops to keep up professionally, and thus are able to be problem-solvers and help train their employees.

4. *Maintaining a high degree of role differentiation.* While successful leaders are friendly with their staffs, they do not "go out drinking with the boys" or share details about their recent divorce. By being sure to do the things that only a leader can do (set goals, resolve conflicts, increase resources), and avoiding the temptation of "pitching in" with everyone, leaders serve their organizations better. This is not to say that leaders should not pitch in sometimes (such as when the fish tank breaks!), but they must reserve time for planning and keeping up with professional reading.

5. *Providing general supervision.* In contrast to providing "nosy" and specific supervision, successful leaders meet with groups of people in a *gen-*

eral way. General training and direction can be offered at staff meetings, for example. The concept here is that employees are hired because they are competent, and are trusted to do a good job. It was found that specific, close supervision makes people feel mistrusted. Even praise that is too intrusive can lead to uncomfortable feelings of being hemmed in. People who feel mistrusted immediately develop attitudes of disloyalty to and nonsupport of the organizational goals.

In a child-care situation, adhering to these five conditions creates a climate that leads to happy, competent children as well as to other positive results.

People want a leader who can be a focal point. It is much easier to follow a leader who supplies resources, provides goal orientation and facilitates group attainments, and resolves conflicts between people.

Leaders also characterize the organization that they lead. For example, Likert (1961) divides organizations into four types, as illustrated in Figure 2.3, based on the management style of the leader(s):

System 1:   exploitative authoritative

System 2:   benevolent authoritative

System 3:   consultative

System 4:   participative group

System 1: Exploitative authoritative	System 2: Benevolent authoritative	System 3: Consultative	System 4: Participative group
Workers afraid to talk to management	Workers less afraid to talk	Workers fairly free to talk	• Extensive, friendly interaction: People really are working with you • Productive, problem-solving atmosphere; not win-lose • Management knows what workers' problems are

FIGURE 2.3
Likert's Four Systems of Management

In extensive and numerous (300 to 400) studies, Likert found that when organizations change from System One to System Four management, their income shifts from 15 to 20 percent *below* their projected budget to 15 to 20 percent *above* their projected budget. This benefit of a System Four management style—which is characterized by extensive, friendly interaction with people—reflects the fact that the most valuable asset of any organization is its people. When a director becomes overly task-oriented, she is selling short her most valuable asset—people. In fact, when leaders operate under the philosophies of "let's run a tight ship," "clean it up," and "let's have less noise," the most productive employees leave first, since they get better offers elsewhere.

A System One organization in which employees are afraid to talk to management usually enforces norms very harshly; job threats, for example, are a frequent occurrence. Quite often there is something being "covered up" at higher levels of management, which restricts the professional employee's desire for free-flowing information. In one such instance, a director took a nap in the broom closet every afternoon, and this was the "forbidden secret." This particular director's center was clearly a System One center, and employees were disciplined for questioning the leadership. This is a true example, and is only recorded here to show how peculiar these indiscretions might be. Other more usual "secrets" may include excessive drinking or misuse of funds. Suffice it to say, System One is often a "deficit model," with the leader feeling easily threatened.

A System Two management style, in which employees are less afraid to talk, often comes into being when a new director replaces a System One director, and the employees cannot quite believe the improvement. The six months needed to build trust, as described earlier in this chapter, will be the minimum time in this case, since 18 to 24 months may be necessary to allow for "institutional lag."

System Three represents the reality in many well-run child-care programs that have directors who were "socialized" under System One and Two organizations themselves, but who are attempting a more open and participative style that harmonizes better with the early childhood field. However, people tend to manage in the way *they* were managed as employees; first managers can be strong models, whether positive or negative ones.

System Four directors usually have experienced, and have been greatly helped by, this particular style in other situations. They are believers in the extra power, creativity, and motivation that a System Four style can unleash. Role-playing each of these management styles can demonstrate to observers the strengths of System Four and the weaknesses of other styles, since real-life observations are not usually possible.

Treasurers and Executive Boards often do not have the vision to build toward a System Four management style, and often suggest some short-term, budget-oriented solutions to problems instead. The specifics of how to apply System Four management goals will vary with the individual organization, but it must be remembered that people first have to be treated well before they become willing to put any extra effort into changes. This indicates that leaders need to respect each individual's human dignity within that person's *own* framework.

A director or supervisor who is curious about what type of management system his program utilizes, can ask any employee the questions provided in the staff questionnaire found in Figure 7.3 of chapter 7, along with, or instead of, the question, "How much confidence and trust do you feel your superior has in you?" When reviewing the results of such a questionnaire, keep in mind that the formula for a successful organization involves supportive relationships (including opportunities to advance), high performance goals, and technical competence.

> Supportive Relationships + High Performance Goals + Technical Competence = Successful Organization

When a leader begins to work at building positive attitudes, loyalty, and perceptions, "productivity" may decline in the first six months. This is because, before undertaking this new goal, *all* resources were put into productivity, whereas now some resources are divided.

Some people in the organization may have been waiting for an opportunity to reveal their problems to the leader, only now bringing their many needs to his or her attention. To survive this phase of "building attitudes," the leader can find other ways to maintain productivity, such as:

1. using up inventory
2. borrowing
3. cutting back in other ways.

In the long run, a worker who feels respected will be much more willing to give his or her maximum effort. Such effort leads to the realization of the goal—the center really *does* become the best in town, and everyone associated with it takes pride in providing really excellent care for young children. This is true productivity.

◇ ◇

THE USE OF POWER

Sometimes power is erroneously defined as negative and coercive. The positive aspects of power, however, already have been discussed in the context of leadership. For the purposes of this discussion, the following definitions of power and authority will be used:

- *Power* is the ability to influence another's behaviors. This influence is always granted from below, that is, by the people over whom it is exercised. Therefore, power is not guaranteed; some people would rather die than change their behavior for someone else. (For example, those who fought in the Revolutionary War.)

- *Authority* is the vested right to try to influence others. This right is always granted from above.

In the context of these definitions, power has to be earned, whereas authority is given.

Power actually increases when it is given away, since more employees, and thus more ideas, become involved. The graph in Figure 2.4 illustrates this relationship. Some people think the more power they give away, the less they have. (A few elementary-school principals demonstrate this belief.)

For example, suppose Director Smith approached the Executive Board and said, "We need to have a fundraiser this spring, and I think Mrs. Williams and Mrs. Adams could co-chair it." What could happen? Mrs. Williams and Mrs. Adams might feel imposed upon and decide that they are much too busy to help out this spring. However, if Director Smith turns the power of deciding how to solve their fund-raising problems over to the Board, the outcome might be *three* fundraisers: a "no-bake" sale, a fair, and a center-wide picnic. Since each person is confident about the success of her project and likes the idea so well, she is more willing to work on it, and the center benefits. The total amount of "power" is multiplied.

However, there *are* times when a director needs to take the lead and be "in charge." For example, when there is an emergency, clear leadership is needed. Another example in which a leader should take charge would be in implementing the ideas resulting from planning-group discussions such as those described in Chapter 4, perhaps facilitating the discussion of a scenario and then putting into action a plan to build more of a physical fitness theme (or other theme) into the center day. Clear leadership and modeling may be necessary to get started.

FIGURE 2.4
Perceptions of Power

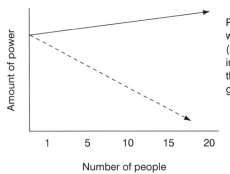

Power actually increases when you give it away. (More ideas and workers are involved.) But some people think the more power they give away, the less they have.

Two things determine whether or not attempts to make changes will work: The potential costs and consequences of the change the leader is initiating, and the employees' view of the director's responsibility. When contemplating a change, the director needs to consider the employees' views and, if necessary, modify them by providing more information about his or her own responsibilities. This is a good time to develop joint goals to solve the problems that created the need for changes.

Working as a group to develop joint goals implies positive potential consequences of the change being initiated; the staff sees that the leader values their input and ideas. Additionally, this helps to offset any potential costs of the change being initiated, large or small, such as having to rearrange schedules, classrooms, or coffee breaks.

If the staff forms a coalition in the leader's favor, they will accept many more of the leader's ideas. To facilitate this, a director should talk one-to-one with staff members. It is hoped that such a coalition would include the entire staff, but if the majority, or even a few employees, understand the change and have had time to make suggestions during informal chats, the coalition will help the leader reduce his or her costs. Although a coalition risks costs to the leader, more often it will help the leader to avoid costs (that is, the costs involved with presenting an idea and having it turned down).

In an interesting doctoral study done on leadership in early childhood education (Pipa, 1997), ten top center directors, as measured by the Program Quality Review and the Coordinated Compliance Review in California's San Francisco Bay area, were interviewed for their leadership knowledge, skills, and behavior. These reviews are done on all child care centers that receive funding from the California Department of Education. Next, the teaching staffs of these directors were sent questionnaires about the leadership knowledge, skills, and behaviors of their directors. Interestingly enough, some of the best knowledge, skills, and behaviors these leaders demonstrated were ones that they were unaware of, or at least did not mention. These included setting the direction for the center; using his or her power and abilities to help the center in the external environment; and using power in the internal environment, reported to some extent by directors, but by all teachers. This may be because the directors' knowledge of external and internal politics is learned informally, perhaps on the job with their own governance structures. Whether mentioned in this particular study or not, all five categories in Figure 2.5 (I to V) are important for successful leadership in early childhood programs and in many other educational organizations as well. Figure 2.5 adds to, adapts and combines these questionnaires into a matrix and also shows the results with a symbol (o) for the knowledge, skills and behaviors the leaders mentioned, and a different symbol (+) for the knowledge, skills, and behaviors the staffs observed and reported. (Note: The references to Herzberg in Item IV are discussed in Chapter 7, "Motivating Staff, Parents, and Children.")

	Knowledge	Skills and Abilities	Behaviors
I. Is skilled in setting the direction for the center • Directors didn't see or report + Teachers saw and reported	___ knows the vision he or she has and tells staff, informally	___ articulated vision when started in the role; set goals and implemented them ___ is skilled at setting and implementing goals and moving the group towards them	___ tells them this vision at meetings but doesn't invite their participation in developing this vision ___ does invite their participation
A. Conveys and translates this vision to staff	___ tells them formally once or twice a year	___ re-articulates the vision often and translates it ___ tells only some staff of this vision ___ makes sure the group moves towards the goals	___ articulates a commonly shared purpose for the center ___ has a retreat once a year
B. Understands and believes in high expectations for teachers and children	Yes ___? No ___?	___ sets and clarifies expectations for the entire center	___ has a strong vision of what the center should look like ___ translates the vision for the staff, parents, and visitors
C. Takes the time to be highly visible in center and with staff in classrooms	___ manages by walking around ___ stays in the office only/mostly	___ they never see him or her—uses e-mail, or notes ___ chats with people at all levels while walking around—has frequent short conversations	___ they see him or her dropping in for planned and unplanned visits
D. Understands and is committed to staff achievement	___ knows that their good work will reflect well on him or her—therefore is encouraging to all	___ guides planning for problem solving as needed ___ influences behaviors and attitudes of staff ___ provides opportunities to promote improved teaching, and classroom atmosphere and management	___ maximizes the effort made by staff through recognition

FIGURE 2.5
Leadership Matrix and Questionnaire

II. Staff Development

A. Maintains and increases own knowledge through participation in courses, reading, conferences
- + Both Directors and teachers saw and reported

____ takes courses and workshops

____ sends e-mail, posts notices giving date and time of new courses and workshops

____ discusses course work and readings at staff meetings

____ attends conferences

____ takes staff to conferences

____ helps with problems and center evaluations

____ influences the behavior and attitudes of teachers

____ holds meetings for staff development

____ brings in useful literature and shares

____ keeps curriculum and child development textbooks on a "library" shelf

____ has staff rotate conducting seminars on useful articles and books

____ provides positive, constructive feedback to staff

____ spots problems and takes action early

B. Discusses course work and readings at staff meetings

____ shares useful literature and articles

____ encourages staff attendance at conferences, workshops, and courses

____ understands how to empower staff through their involvement in the decision-making process

III. Instructional Leadership

A. Understands and is aware of children's needs

B. Sets and clarifies performance expectations for the entire staff
- + Both Directors and teachers saw and reported

____ knows and demonstrates various educational and instructional approaches

____ is aware of children's needs in various classrooms

____ understands and is aware of teacher's needs

____ uses some of this knowledge in meetings with staff

____ provides resources for activities and instruction

____ guides instructional planning through evaluating children's competence and abilities, and through developing plans for helping to solve learning problems

____ uses a seminar approach for staff development meetings

____ maximizes the efforts made by staff

____ encourages professional growth

____ encourages staff to go to conferences and courses

____ provides constructive feedback to teachers to improve teaching

Leadership Matrix and Questionnaire, *continued*

	Knowledge	Skills and Abilities	Behaviors
IV. Internal Environment A. Has know-how about the politics that take place in the organization B. Uses his/her power within the organization to achieve goals for center and for parent programs. • + Both Directors and teachers saw and reported	___ knows that empowerment comes through participatory management and brings strength and creativity to the center	___ builds friendly interactions at meetings to aid problem-solving and risk-taking ___ uses his or her power to achieve program goals for the organization internally	___ gets along well with staff and provides Herzberg's hygiene factors ___ provides (or sees that Herzberg's motivator factors are provided): autonomy, recognition, esteem, worth of the work, sense of achievement and growth ___ gets teacher input formally or informally in decision making ___ takes time to be highly visible and visits each classroom on a regular basis
V. External Environment Uses his/her power outside the organization to achieve goals for the center and programs • Directors didn't see or didn't report + Teachers saw and reported	___ knows how to reach out to build liaisons, and to build up the budget and other resources ___ builds connections with the community	___ develops external liaisons to achieve goals for the centers and programs ___ uses his or her power to achieve program goals for the organization externally ___ tells the staff about these efforts and how well they're working	___ takes various staff members to meetings on occasion ___ creates supportive coalitions and alliances within the community to make things happen for the centers and programs ___ encourages professional staff to create alliances also, to develop the program and build public relations

Leadership Matrix and Questionnaire, *continued*

◊ ◊ ◊ ◊ ◊ ◊ ◊ ◊ ◊ ◊ ◊ ◊ ◊ ◊ ◊ ◊ ◊ ◊ ◊ ◊

SUMMARY

Social exchange behaviors for *leadership* are partly learned in early childhood. When children learn these behaviors, high self-esteem and a strong self-concept are developed at an early age. They learn that they are desired, loved, and popular. This knowledge helps them to take risks and to make decisions, and because these children are popular, they are asked to make decisions or to take risks.

Adult leaders as well as children can learn to value the benefits that result from risk-taking (such as asking the staff to implement a change). Both adults and children also can learn to accept failures that may result from risk-taking. By learning from their mistakes, leaders can say, "I won't make the same mistake twice" or "I can usually do *something* to help correct a wrong decision." It is important to remember, however, that it is difficult to change behavior and to maintain this change over a long period of time. In stress situations, a person's behavior will not change considerably; instead, it will remain fairly consistent with that person's most comfortable style, whether this style is "human-oriented" or "task-oriented."

Some leaders realize how others perceive them, and some leaders do not. The leader who does not learn to read others' perceptions keeps going out on a limb and then finds that she has no support. To read others' perceptions, leaders must first become aware of behavior and "body language." They need to be sensitive to the emotions and actions of others. If a leader doesn't feel she has support, it is better *not* to take a stand; instead, she should discuss the issue more ahead of time, informally, in one-on-one conversations, thereby building trust. Since stress can block some of this discussion, arranging a more relaxed situation, such as having a meeting over coffee or food of some kind, might be helpful.

The more valuable the leader is perceived as being, the greater the credits, rewards, and salary he or she receives. Just as directing one child-care center can help families and improve the quality of life for their children, directing three child-care centers, or even adding 20 more openings in one center, can help an increased number of families or children.

◊ ◊ ◊ ◊ ◊ ◊ ◊ ◊ ◊ ◊ ◊ ◊ ◊ ◊ ◊ ◊ ◊ ◊ ◊

SUGGESTED CLASS ACTIVITIES AND DISCUSSIONS

Note: The Leadership Enablers in Appendix C provide many additional activities and can be used in a double role play for the "right" and "wrong" ways to demonstrate leadership and use power. Students can develop their own "leadership enablers" in small groups and then report back for class discussion. It might be helpful to develop one leadership enabler with the whole class first.

1. *Role Play and Discuss Feelings About Cost-benefits*.   Demonstrate that interaction and social change tend to be reciprocal in a role play in which each participant receives a cue card, listing their current situation at a center. Number off the class in groups and give out the following cards:

> Number ones and fives: Feel left out, feel indifferent, feel peeved at the leader for leaving them out, feel they "get nothing."
>
> Number twos and fours: Are getting a raise in salary.
>
> Number threes: Are having their lunch hour reduced to half an hour, and their working hours increased.

Conduct a model staff meeting with the instructor or a class member as the director. Then elicit and discuss the feelings the "staff" members had in relation to their cost-benefits as just acted out.

2. *Brainstorm Advantages and Disadvantages of Different Types of (Less Than Perfect) Leaders*.   Describe three directors with different characteristics and ask the class to brainstorm benefits and disadvantages possible for each. This can be done as a large group or in three or more small groups. Leader styles can include:

> (a) *The Lone Ranger*—Thinks his or her part is more important than the whole, works alone, but is afraid to act. *Possible advantages*: bulletin boards are good; redoes the files; seems sure of self and projects well to the community. *Possible disadvantages*: communications breakdown, is a poor group leader, turns off some parents.
>
> (b) *The Power Tripper*—Over supervises. *Possible advantages*: gets things organized, gets equipment, supplies and funds, gets things done. *Possible disadvantages*: poor or no interpersonal communication, low or no autonomy allowed, has a hard time accepting people as they are.
>
> (c) *The Frightened Fawn*—Is apologetic when giving assignments. *Possible advantages*: is more considerate of people's feelings, is a good listener, allows autonomy. *Possible disadvantages*: is afraid of higher authority, tries to please everyone and no one is happy or knows where he or she stands.

3. *Skits Demonstrating the Use of Power*.   Ask two groups to prepare skits/role plays to share with the class showing a first meeting with a new director taking over a center that is on the verge of collapse. One group can show the new director in a hurry listing priorities and rushing off. The second group demonstrates more of a Likert System 4 approach with a slower, friendly

manner and discussion of workshops, planning time, and plans for committees to work on other problems and solutions.

4. *Examining Five Power Bases.*   Discuss the five power bases described in the text (some authors list even more). Fill in the chart that follows and then discuss the insights that this provides.

Requirements for Employees	Referent	Coercive	Reward	Expert	Legitimate
Amount of Conformity Behaviors Likely					
Attitudes Likely					

5. *Evaluating the Underlying Basis from Exchange.*   Using Figure 8.1 "Behaviors Demonstrating Social Change" in chapter 8, have students evaluate different problems in small groups and decide which of the 10 exchange categories each problem demonstrates. Problems can be handed in by students from actual situations. One problem might be analyzed first by the class as a whole to demonstrate applications of the levels. For example, using the late tuition problem from chapter 4, paying tuition late is number 5 level, maximizing benefit to the parent and the center will be at number 6 level, awareness of the high cost of coercion. (On the other hand, the center will close down if everyone is casual about paying tuition.) How might this be handled?

◊ ◊ ◊ ◊ ◊ ◊ ◊ ◊ ◊ ◊ ◊ ◊ ◊ ◊ ◊ ◊ ◊ ◊ ◊ ◊

BIBLIOGRAPHY

Ackoff, R. L. (1970). *A concept of corporate planning*. Philadelphia, PA: Wiley.

Allen, R. W., Madison, D. L., Porter, L. W., Renwick, P. A., & Mayes, B. T. (1979, Fall). Organizational politics: Tactics and characteristics of its actors. *California Management Review, 22*(4), 77–83.

Banfield, E. C. (1961). *Political influence*. New York: The Free Press.

Bass, B. M. (1985). *Leadership and performance beyond expectations*. New York: The Free Press.

Beach, D. S. (1975). *Managing people at work: Readings in personnel*. New York: Wiley.

Bennis, W. G., & Nanus, B. (1985). *Leaders: Strategies for taking charge*. New York: Harper and Row.

Blake, R. R., & Mouton, J. S. (1985). *Managerial grid III*. Houston, TX: Gulf.

Blau, P. M. (1964). *Exchange and power in social life*. New York: Wiley.

Bloom, P. J., & Sheerer, M. (1992). The effect of leadership training on child care program quality. *Early Childhood Research Quarterly* 7: 579–594.

Bolman, L. G., & Deal, T. E. (1991). *Reframing organizations: Artistry, choice and leadership.* San Francisco: Jossey-Bass.

Boyatzis, R. (1982). *The competent manager.* New York: Wiley.

Brearley, A. (1976). The changing role of the chief executive. *Journal of General Management, 3*(4), 62–71.

California Council of Parent Participation Nursery Schools, Inc. (1968). *Pointers for participating parents.* San Francisco: Author.

Child Care Information Exchange. (1990). *On being a leader: Reprint collection No. 5.* Redmond, WA: Author.

Conger, J. A. (1992). *Learning to lead: The art of transforming managers into leaders.* San Francisco: Jossey-Bass.

Covey, S. (1991). *Principle-centered leadership.* New York: Fireside.

Deal, T. E., & Peterson, K. D. (1994). *The leadership paradox: Balancing logic and artistry in schools.* San Francisco: Jossey-Bass.

Decker, C. A., & Decker, J. (1990). *Planning and administering early childhood programs.* Upper Saddle River, NJ: Merrill/Prentice Hall.

Drucker, P. (1967). *The effective executive.* New York: Harper & Row.

Drucker, P. (1974). *Management tasks, responsibilities, practices.* New York: Harper & Row.

Drucker, P. (1990). *Managing the nonprofit organization: Principles and practices.* New York: HarperCollins.

Fiedler, F. E. (1967). *A theory of leadership effectiveness.* New York: McGraw-Hill.

Fiedler, F. E. (1971). *Leadership.* New York: General Learning Press.

Gardner, J. W. (1990). *On leadership.* New York: The Free Press.

Gardner, H. (1995). *Leading minds: The anatomy of leadership.* New York: Basic Books.

Gay, L. R. (1992). *Educational research: Competencies for analysis and application.* New York: MacMillan.

Herzberg, F., Mausner, B., & Snyderman, B. (1959). *The motivation to work.* New York: Wiley.

Hesselbein, F., Goldsmith, M., & Beckhard, R. (Eds.). (1997). *The leaders of the future.* Drucker Foundation Future Series, San Francisco: Jossey-Bass.

Jacobs, T. O. (1971). *Leadership and exchange in formal organizations.* Alexandria, VA: Human Resources Research Organizations.

Kagan, S. L. (1994). Leadership: Rethinking it— Making it happen. *Young Children, 49*(5), 50–54.

Kagan, S. L., & Bowman, B. T. (1997). *Leadership in early care and education.* Washington, DC: National Association for the Education of Young Children.

Kotter, J. P. (1973). The psychological contract: Managing the joining up process. *California Management Review, 15*(3), 91–99.

Kotter, J. P. (1977, July/August). Power, dependence, and effective management. *Harvard Business Review,* pp. 125–136.

Kotter, J. P. (1978). *Organizational dynamics: Diagnosis and intervention.* Reading, MA: Addison-Wesley.

Kotter, J. P. (1979a). Managing external dependence. *Academy of Management Review 1979, 4*(1), 87–92.

Kotter, J. P. (1979b). *Power in management.* New York: AMACOM.

Kotter, J. P. (1982). *The general managers.* New York: The Free Press.

Kotter, J. P., Faux, V. A., & McArthur, C. C. (1979). *Self-assessment and career development.* Upper Saddle River, NJ: Prentice Hall.

Kotter, J. P. (1996). *Leading change.* Boston, MA: Harvard Business School Press.

Likert, R. (1953). Findings of research on management and leadership. *Proceedings: Pacific Coast Gas Association, 43.*

Likert, R. (1961). *New patterns of management.* New York: McGraw-Hill.

Likert, R. (1967). *The human organization.* New York: McGraw-Hill.

Lorsch, J., & Allen, S. A. (1973). *Managing diversity and interdependence.* Cambridge, MA: Harvard University Press.

McClelland, D. C. (1970). Two faces of power. *Journal of International Affairs, 24*(1), 29–47.

McClelland, D. C. (1975). *Power: The inner experience.* New York: Irvington.

McGregor, D. (1960). *The human side of enterprise.* New York: McGraw-Hill.

Miles, R. H. (1980). *Macro organizational behavior.* Santa Monica, CA: Goodyear.

Morrison, A. M. (1992). *The new leaders: Guidelines on leadership diversity in America.* San Francisco: Jossey-Bass.

Nichel, W. G. (1982). *Marketing principles* (2nd ed.). Upper Saddle River, NJ: Prentice Hall.

Pascale, R. T., & Athos, A. G. (1981). *The art of Japanese management.* New York: Simon and Schuster.

Peters, T., & Waterman, R. H. (1982). *In search of excellence.* New York: Harper and Row.

Pettigrew, A. (1973). *The politics of organizational decision making.* London: Tavistock.

Pfeffer, J. (1981). *Power in organizations.* Marshfield, MA: Pitman.

Pipa, R. L. (1997). *The leadership, knowledge, skills, and behaviors of directors of quality, state-funded child care programs in the San Francisco Bay area.* Unpublished doctoral dissertation, University of LaVerne, (School of Org. Mgt.) LaVerne, CA.

Presthus, R. (1962). *The organizational society.* New York: Vintage.

Rickarts, T. (1975). *Problem solving through creative analysis.* Epping, England: Gower Press.

Rodd, J. (1994). *Leadership in early childhood: The pathway to professionalism.* New York: Teachers College Press.

Rumelt, R. P. (1974). *Strategy, structure, and economic performance.* Cambridge, MA: Harvard University Press.

Salancik, G., & Pfeffer, J. (1977, Winter). Who gets power and how they hold on to it: A strategic contingency model of power. *Organizational Dynamics,* pp. 3–21.

Sayles, L. R. (1989). *Leadership: Managing in real organizations.* New York: McGraw-Hill.

Sciarra, D. J., & Dorsey, A. G. (1990). *Developing and administering a child care center* (2nd ed.). Albany, NY: Delmar.

Senge, P. M. (1990). *The fifth discipline: The art and practice of the learning organization.* New York: Doubleday.

Sonnenfeld, J., & Kotter, J. P. (1982). The maturation of career theory. *Human Relations, 35*(1), 19–46.

Tannenbaum, R., & Schmidt, W. H. (1973, May/June). How to choose a leadership pattern. *Harvard Business Review.*

Vaill, P. (1989). *Leadership as a performing art: New ideas a world of chaotic change.* San Francisco: Jossey-Bass.

Vaill, P. (1996). *Learning as a way of being.* San Francisco: Jossey-Bass.

Vroom, V., & Yetton, P. W. (1973). *Leadership and interpersonal behavior.* New York: Holt, Rinehart and Winston.

Yukl, G. A. (1998). *Leadership in organizations* (4th ed.). Upper Saddle River, NJ: Prentice Hall.

Planning

Good planning is the key to a smoothly running program for young children. Planning can help educators anticipate decisions that must be made; it can help leaders manage interdependent decisions; and it can provide a process by which staff and parents can have input into and develop support for the goals and strategies of the organization. Planning must occur before everything else and requires special attention and skill development to ensure that all components are covered before a program begins, or once yearly for on-going programs. The key to success is to plan effectively *before* a director and staff begin program management procedures.

Some people claim that the main value of planning does not lie in the actual plans produced, but in the process of producing them. In this context, the main benefit of planning comes from the interaction of people and ideas as they think about mid-range and long-range goals for a program or center. Therefore, planning cannot be done *for* a group, but must be done *by* the group. But planning *before* things happen is more desirable than just reacting *after* things happen.

Many of the best ideas of employees may surface in planning sessions, and can be suitably adapted onto a time line along with other "best ideas." Implementing every step of the plan is less important than developing the habit of sharing good ideas and planning for the future, especially when this interaction occurs within a framework that is structured enough to allow good ideas to be captured and thought out. As with children and the curriculum, the process of learning is more important than the product of learning.

During the planning process, both the program being planned for and its environment can change, so it is nearly impossible to consider all the variables at the outset. Therefore, as a plan is being carried out, it is necessary to continuously update it, both individually and as a group. To prevent being "sandbagged" by change, it is important to try to understand the environment systematically on at least five levels: global, national, community, workplace, and individual. (See Figure 3.7 for specific examples of each of these levels.) When changes in each of these levels are considered in relation to the impact(s) they might have on a program for young children, new insights emerge and actions and contingency plans can be developed. In addition, planners can also:

1. try to alter the course of the change,
2. decide how to capitalize on the advantages of the change, or
3. plan to resist the change.

Anticipating change and predicting it helps an organization and its people feel a sense of control and therefore maintains morale. Long-range planning that affects many functions of the organization and that is hard to reverse should be considered carefully. For example, opening another center across town is a long-range decision that could require a great deal of the center's resources in terms of money, person-hours, and equipment or materials. On the other hand, planning next week's lunch menu is a short-range decision; it is hoped that this type of decision-making can be delegated to another person or group, along with most other considerations of short-range planning. (For a discussion of techniques for decision-making, see Chapter 4, "Decision-Making.")

◇ ◇ ◇ ◇ ◇ ◇ ◇ ◇ ◇ ◇ ◇ ◇ ◇ ◇ ◇ ◇ ◇ ◇ ◇ ◇

THREE PHILOSOPHIES OF PLANNING

There are many philosophies of planning, of course, but three that can be seen working in early childhood education programs will be discussed here and include satisficing, optimizing, and adaptivizing (Ackoff, 1970).

Satisficing is arriving at one solution that meets objectives and goals that are feasible and desirable. It implies "being satisfied." The satisficing planner sets a few simple goals and is happy to satisfy them. This outlook harbors the danger of not being long-range enough, or of not considering the outside environment enough, but for some problems it is an appropriate approach. An additional danger of satisficing is that sometimes at the end of a long meeting, when time is a factor, a single solution can look more and more attractive even when it is not the best or the most appropriate solution.

Optimizing is similar to the rational approach taught in business schools. The goal in optimizing is to do as well as possible, and, in this context, many, many alternatives can be generated. Unfortunately, generating all these options takes more time than is always available. In the rational approach, criteria are developed after the problem is defined, then three to five alternatives are considered against these criteria. When weighing the alternatives, some variables can surface that then may be combined in yet a new way. Some variables cannot be controlled, such as weather, economic conditions, the competition, technological developments, and preferences of parents. Unfortunately, the optimizer sometimes ignores these variables, and often ignores goals that cannot be quantified. For example, an optimizer might consider the financial bottom line to be more important than the "happiness" of the children.

Adaptivizing is the name given to planning that adapts, or "gets outside the box," and considers solutions from a very different perspective than does satisficing or optimizing. This type of planning often occurs when the problem is redefined and looked at in new ways. Chapter 5, which discusses problem-solving, suggests a number of ways to do this.

Adaptivizing provides for five different sets of plans:

1. commitment planning,
2. contingency planning for somewhat better conditions,
3. contingency planning for somewhat worse conditions,
4. responsiveness planning for much better conditions, and
5. responsiveness planning for much worse conditions.

These different plans are based on knowledge of the future, which can be certain, uncertain, or completely unknown. Planning for a future that is fairly certain is called *commitment planning*; the center's budget might be an example of this.

Planning for an uncertain future that could be a little better or a little worse than the present situation is called *contingency planning*. Such planning requires two approaches (contingencies): one for somewhat better conditions, and one for less good or somewhat worse conditions.

Planning for a future that cannot be anticipated, or that is unknown, also requires two sets of plans: one for much better conditions and one for much worse conditions. This type of planning is called *responsiveness planning*, and is frequently overlooked. Labeled *responsive* because it builds responsiveness and flexibility into an organization, this planning is *responsive* to outside conditions as well. The plan shown in Figure 5.1 of chapter 5, which includes a suggestion for conducting a computer camp on Saturdays if computers are bought, rented, or given to the center, shows how responsiveness planning might be done for a favorable situation. A responsiveness plan for unfavorable conditions (such as the closing of a major industrial plant or military base near the center) might list financial emergency measures, such as plans to rent out one or two classrooms for other uses such as for small business incubators. Another emergency measure might be to eliminate the most expensive and least used part of the program, such as a breakfast-before-school program.

The adaptive planner attempts to change the system or the structure so that efficiency is the result. Organizations that plan this way tend to use their employees' best potential and therefore are very effective.

◇ ◇

MANAGING CHANGE: OBJECTIVES AND SCENARIOS

Commitment planning, or planning for a fairly certain future, can also be called *reference projection,* because it essentially involves predictions that can be made if nothing new is done. What one would *like* to do can be referred to as a *wishful projection;* the difference between the two (reference projection and wishful projection) defines the gap that can be filled by planning and setting objectives onto a time line. Directors usually have many aspirations for their organizations, and most of these fall under the category of wishful projections. The steps involved in taking a center from its reference projection to a

The block corner is a good place to practice planning and predicting what will happen.

wishful projection are called *planned projections*. To make these steps more efficient, a time schedule can be attached to each step or objective in the planned projection.

Sometimes it is difficult to discover the aspirations, or wishful projections, of those involved in an organization, and to learn the answer to the question: "What kind of center do you want this to be?" An effective way to uncover these aspirations is through the use of scenarios that focus on different topics. In the motion picture industry, a scenario describes what people will do when acting out a story. Scenarios in management planning describe different models of what people will do or what must or might happen in order to reach different goals. In this context, scenarios allow for various areas of wishful thinking to be quantified so that decisions regarding possible goals can be made. Scenarios also help determine any possible goal conflicts. By identifying and resolving goal conflicts early on, and thus reducing conflicts and encouraging useful discussions, any project can be further enhanced.

Scenarios can be developed around policies, programs, procedures, practices, and courses of action. In each case, the person developing the scenario makes a pictorial model of the existing policy, course of action, or other item that needs to be examined. (See Figure 3.2 for an example of a scenario model.) The developer puts a box around each existing step listed in the model. Then, alternatives for each step in the model can be discussed by either a group or an individual. As the four or five (or more) boxes are reviewed and brainstorming occurs, a scenario begins to emerge. Although some of the ideas that emerge may be inappropriate for the particular situation under discussion, they can lead to other, more plausible, suggestions.

Developing a Philosophy

When identifying problems and solutions for a child-care center, it is essential to be clear on the style or values of the center. Discussing the philosophy of the center with both the staff and the parent group will help to define the philosophy more clearly. This discussion, which can take the form of a brainstorming session, should first occur during a staff meeting, followed by having the staff vote on the 5 or 10 most important elements in the philosophy. This list of important elements can then be taken to a parents' meeting (perhaps displayed on a flip chart or large poster) and parents can use these ideas to brainstorm *their* ideas about the philosophy. After parents have taken a vote on the most important items in their list, the staff list and the parent list can be combined; usually an impressive philosophy statement results. This statement can be added to the bylaws, the publicity brochures, the bulletin boards, and wherever else information on good child care is needed. A sample philosophy is given in Figure 3.1.

The philosophy of the Children's Education Child–Care Center is based on the belief that children are individuals who are learning and growing. Within a child-size world, the focus of the center will be:

1. to provide programs which, in balance, enhance a child's development socially, emotionally, physically, and intellectually.
2. to provide individualized attention within the context of a group setting.
3. to foster an acceptance of self and of the differences in others.
4. to develop a sense of respect and a caring attitude that comes from freedom within limits.
5. to learn actively through play.
6. to work with parents as active partners in their child's learning.

FIGURE 3.1
Philosophy

Voting on which elements of the philosophy are most important gives parents a true feeling of involvement and can be repeated every fall during an orientation period. One center added the idea of "physical fitness" to its philosophy one year, then emphasized "respect for children, adults, and equipment" another year. During parent planning meetings, parents have the opportunity to hear the many expectations other parents have for child-care centers; after voting, parents can find out which elements are favored by the majority, perhaps discovering that not all desires can be met. For example, if a parent feels strongly that her child should be taught French, but that same ideal is not held by the majority, the parent may wish to look for another center. On the other hand, after seeing that French cannot be worked into the program, the parent might decide to provide for outside lessons while allowing her child to remain at the center. Whichever option the parent chooses, the director and teacher can be spared a year of complaints and unhappiness on the part of the parent.

Developing Scenarios

After the philosophy is in place, the "style" of your center will be clear; then possible ideas for improvement of one aspect or another can be generated. The director can begin translating into goals these ideas and the values given in the philosophy. At this point, it is important to develop a schedule for attaining these goals. While a director's list of goals may look quite different from the philosophy, they still remain relevant. These goals might include:

- To remain financially afloat by increasing the center's income
- To build quality into the program by focusing on specifics in the philosophy
- To improve safety throughout the center
- To build staff morale

An effective way of working toward achieving these goals is to develop a scenario for one or more of them. Again, a scenario is a description of what an organization might look like at some specified time in the future. It is a description rather than a financial plan. The use of scenarios is based on the idea that what a center becomes depends more on what it does than on what is done to it. It builds on the idea of making the future happen rather than on letting events occur and then asking, "What happened?" A center can design almost any kind of future it wants for itself, given careful planning and involvement of staff and parents. A scenario allows room for wishful thinking for the future. Several scenarios have been developed here as examples.

The first step in developing a scenario, as we discussed previously, is to draw a model of the activities done throughout the day in a center. See Figure 3.2.

The second step in developing a scenario for a particular goal is to brainstorm alone or perhaps with a group about ways that particular goal could be implemented; for each box in the model, two or three ways of implementing the goal can be listed. For instance, for the goal of increasing a center's income, the scenario might look like the one shown in Figure 3.3.

After this step is completed, the director has a number of ideas from which to choose several logical projects that might increase the center's income. Sometimes ideas that are not volunteered during the development of the scenario may remain in the back of people's minds, and the director may hear more about these possibilities next year, as well as hearing some modifications of ideas already used this year.

Another scenario, this one focusing on building quality into the program according to the philosophy given in Figure 3.1, and that also works toward building staff morale, might look like the one shown in Figure 3.4.

Space in the day's activities model does not permit listing all the ideas that can be generated from item 1 in the philosophy (Figure 3.1). When physical fit-

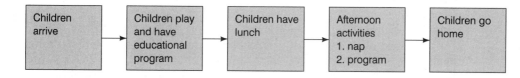

FIGURE 3.2
A Model of Child-Care Activities

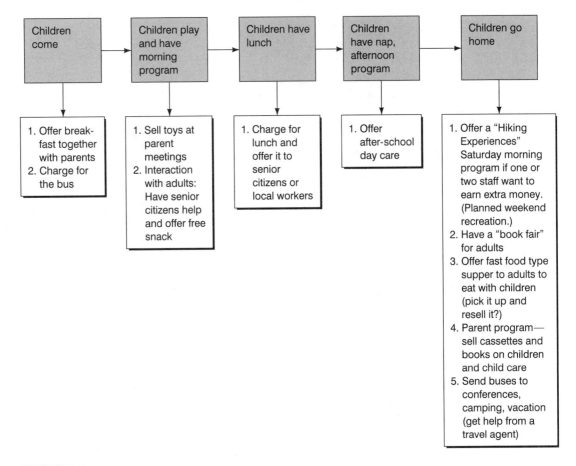

FIGURE 3.3
Increasing a Center's Income

ness is the focus of the year, for example, purchasing more outdoor equipment, finding more imaginative ways to use what is there, and inviting a speaker to come to a staff-parent workshop on Movement Education are a few ideas that could be explored. The possibilities are limitless, and generating them produces a good exercise for beginning-of-the-school-year staff training meetings. If the staff can help choose two or three goals for staff training for the year, then the improvement of quality and morale is off to a good start.

Using the decision-making tree described in chapter 4 can be helpful in deciding which projects the director might invite the group to become involved in planning. Since some ideas would benefit from outside funding, or might require permission from another group, a section on writing proposals has been included in chapter 14.

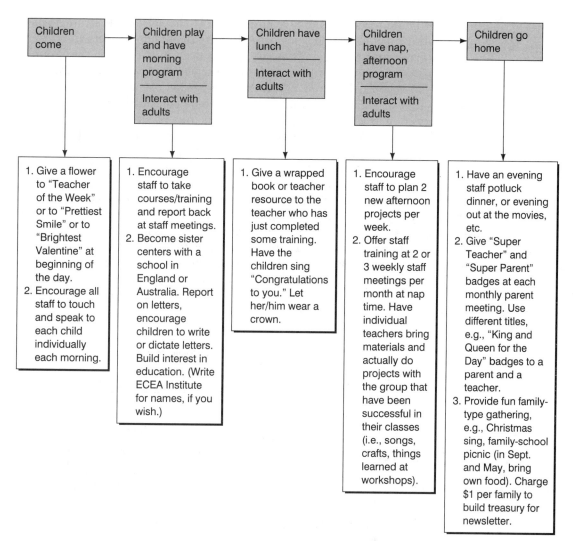

FIGURE 3.4
Building Quality and Staff Morale

◊ ◊ ◊ ◊ ◊ ◊ ◊ ◊ ◊ ◊ ◊ ◊ ◊ ◊ ◊ ◊ ◊ ◊ ◊ ◊

STRATEGIC PLANNING

Strategic planning is the name given to the process of looking first, in an organized way, at outside environmental opportunities and risks, and then focusing on the center's strengths and weaknesses (i.e., its available resources). It is preferable for a center to develop plans and opportunities, instead of responding only when outside events have an impact. At the very least, strategic planning has the effect of adding some predictability to outside impacts.

When arranging a planning session, a first step might be for the group to think of two or three significant events in society that will impact child-care centers and schools. It is not necessary to agree on these events, but as the leader/facilitator collects each person's list, some consensus usually emerges. This first step is called *external analysis,* and is shown in Figure 3.5. Responses might include such things as the changing multicultural demographics and society's move into the information age.

After discussing some of the events that might affect child-care, a "visioning" exercise of some type might be useful. To begin such an exercise, simply ask the group of people involved what they envision telling people about the center in five years, or use the scenarios approach just described. Once this information is recorded, review the mission or philosophy statement for the center. At this point, the statement might need to be rewritten or have some policies added to it. When this is done, the group can review the external analysis done earlier, and then review the internal strengths and weaknesses of the center to develop the *internal analysis,* shown in Figure 3.5. An example

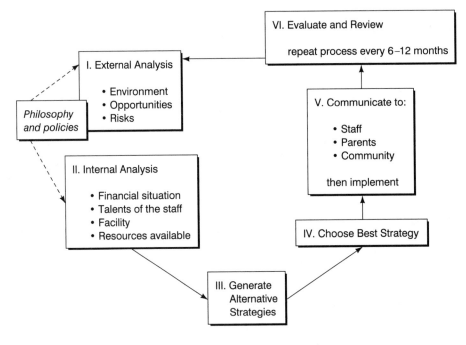

FIGURE 3.5
Strategic Planning Steps

of an internal weakness might include debt, which would not allow the center to expand. On the other hand, a strong line of credit could be considered a strength, since this would allow for expansion. The depth of professional and managerial talent also must be considered when developing an internal analysis.

As with the external analysis, it isn't necessary to reach a consensus on the internal analysis. However, with the combined lists of strengths and weaknesses, it is easier to set priorities and then write objectives for the next three to five years, which should be done when the internal analysis is complete. Then the group is ready to write strategies for new programs and processes.

Generating alternative strategies (Step III in Figure 3.5) can be done alone or in a group brainstorming session. However, to be most effective, choosing and implementing a strategy requires group involvement and outward communication. Steps IV, V, and VI in Figure 3.5 model this process. This planning time can be the most valuable time that a director spends because it prevents management by default. Failure to plan can result in ineffective, undirected action. (This situation has also been described as planning to fail from failing to plan.)

Once several strategies are generated for accomplishing priorities, the best strategy can be agreed upon. (It is important to keep a record of all the strategies generated, even those not chosen, since they may become useful when outside events change.) The strategy chosen as the best should then be communicated to head teachers, to staff, to parents, and to the public, as appropriate (see Step V in Figure 3.5). It is hoped that all but the general public will have been involved in one way or another before this juncture. The last step taken after these plans become operational, and which may begin next year's or next quarter's planning session, is to evaluate and review the chosen strategy and the accompanying choices against the knowledge of what actually happened, thus building improved strategies and choices for the future (see Step VI in Figure 3.5). The whole process, then, is a continuous circle, as shown in Figure 3.6.

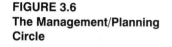

**FIGURE 3.6
The Management/Planning
Circle**

Strategic Planning and Sources and Impacts of Change

Since programs for young children are affected by outside trends, including demographic and economic changes, planning for the future becomes essential. Figure 3.7 shows the results of a brainstorming session on the topic "Sources and Impacts of Change in Programs for Young Children." The results demonstrate how even national and global concerns can affect the workplace, and how individuals must manage the impact of such changes.

Sources	Political Impacts	Economic Impacts	Social Impacts	Physical Impacts	Technological Impacts
Global	World changes have caused cutbacks in the U.S. military and in defense industry spending.	Economic globalization: Pacific Rim countries will be doing more business with the U.S.	Families will be moving and relocating.	Families and children travel, fly more easily to distant places.	Computers and the information age are transcending national barriers.
National	There is a national upsurge in East/West fashion, food, curricula, etc.	Families caught in sudden transition will be short of money while at least one spouse looks for new work.	Even more women with children will enter the work force.	Feature national trips and international trips in classroom learning opportunities.	Public schools are getting more and more computers for children's use.
Community	Some communities have high numbers of "new" minorities, e.g., Asians.	Offices of economic development may look to child care centers to provide jobs.	More and better child care will be needed on all economic levels: deluxe to basic.	Families may move across town to follow new businesses.	Have a community fundraiser to buy the center one or more computers.
Child Care Program (workplace).	Can encourage local legislators to support child care legislation.	Offer learning units about Asia and other countries.	Consider adding some deluxe services to help offset a sliding fee scale.	Share information about trips and where children have moved from.	Make plans for children and staff to use (play with) computers, learning through play.
Individual	Invite legislators to a center picnic or other function. Take their picture and write an article for the paper.	Encourage Asian and other ethnic families to bring in food or share "show and tell" with their children.	Encourage parents to build up their child's self-esteem and competence by doing things with them at home.	Have staff/parent bulletin board with news of trips or places people have moved from, so all can learn.	Encourage staff to take individual computer classes.

FIGURE 3.7
Sources and Impacts of Change in Programs for Young Children

Formulating such data makes an interesting exercise for staff or Board meetings, since the information or ideas in the boxes may change every few months. Scheduling such a brainstorming session also could be a first step in a strategic planning exercise during which all levels of the environment are to be considered for their potential impact. A second meeting, in which Figure 3.7 might be used as a handout, could include more of the strategic planning steps, such as considering the opportunities and risks of each change, perhaps beginning with impacts at the national and community level. The staff might choose one category—such as social, physical, or technological—to develop more fully in terms of the workplace or of the individuals who work there.

After considering possible alternatives, such as the ones listed in the last two rows of Figure 3.7, as well as other alternatives suggested by those assembled, the group can vote on one or two of the best alternatives to pursue. Once the alternatives have been chosen, they should first be communicated to the staff, then to the public and parents. For example, using bulletin boards and the newsletter as a medium, inform parents that the center is teaching a unit on other countries, or will be inviting legislators to a picnic. Different committees might work on each alternative. More ambitious plans that will use more resources, such as opening a center across town, could be tested using the scenario process, which helps a group (or individual) to simulate possibilities and probabilities for the new idea.

◇ ◇

SUMMARY

The excitement and friendly interaction that occurs as ideas are generated in a brainstorming session helps teachers (and/or Board members) "learn through play" (Jones, 1990). It also creates in the participants a feeling of being stronger, more helpful, and more "empowered" (Berlew, 1990). Designing situations in which people can succeed, such as these brainstorming sessions for considering hypothetical scenarios and strategies, unlocks creativity and puts some of the joy and energy back into the sometimes taxing work of being an adult involved with a child-care center. As people come up with ideas, they will be more likely to offer help. Innovation is attractive and new ideas are interesting and draw support. As seen in Chapter 2, "Leadership and the Role of the Director," if the atmosphere at the center has been discouraging for a while, two or three idea sessions may be needed to get useful planning under way.

If a center insists on high quality innovations, it will be ahead of the game when standards rise (Foster, 1986). The center will also earn great word-of-mouth publicity and will probably have happier children attending the center. It might be necessary to have Saturday programs for children to help pay for some innovations, but feeling more in control of the center's future will be worth it.

◇ ◇

SUGGESTED CLASS ACTIVITIES AND DISCUSSIONS

1. *Problem Solving "Outside the Box."*   Draw a model on the board of Ackoff's three problem solving approaches, shown as boxes.

Satisficing	**Optimizing**	**Adaptivizing**

Share a problem or problems for which planning is needed. Select one problem and brainstorm and record solutions according to each approach. For example, with "the sandbox is uncovered" as the problem, a Satisficing approach (one answer) would be to install a cover. Optimizing (as many answers as possible) would list all the parent, staff, and community education that can be done concerning the benefits of sand play as well as covering the box. An adaptivizing approach might be to bring more rolling water tables outside and use them for water, sand, rice, foam chips, beans, and many other pouring mediums. This solution is literally (and figuratively) "outside the box."

2. *Brainstorm a scenario that would add multi-cultural diversity elements to all parts of the center day.*   Draw a model of the center day like the one found in Figure 3.2. Students can then brainstorm activities for each block or module for the day that would enhance the understanding of multicultural diversity. What could be done in the morning program? At lunch? In the afternoon program? For the classroom environment? Discuss the ideas.

3. *Develop a three-year plan for internal and external needs.*   Students can develop a six-part plan for a center, first listing what will be needed for next year *internally* and *externally* (such as more art supplies and advertising to new businesses' personnel offices). Then two similar lists are done for Years Two and Three in the future. Discuss how much more freedom their thinking shows for plans further into the future. In a real center, these plans would move up each year and be revised as Year II became Year I and Year III became Year II, and so forth. Discuss how this might change a future plan.

4. *Brainstorm a scenario that would add "moving into the information age"*
elements to all parts of the center day.   Draw a model for the center day as found in Figure 3.2 (as in #2 above) and brainstorm ways computers and CD-ROM technology might enhance each block. What could be done in the morning program? How could a computer enhance lunch (menu planning, inventory control, etc.)? How could technology enhance the afternoon program? Discuss the ideas.

5. *Brainstorm a scenario that would predict and provide for adaptations needed for children with disabilities throughout the center day.*   Draw a model for the center as found in Figure 3.2 again, only this time brainstorm adaptations or special activities that would be appropriate for children with various disabilities for each block. How could the morning program be adapted? Lunch? Afternoon nap? Discuss the ideas generated and check Chapter 12 for more ideas.

6. *Develop a chart for sources and impacts of change.*   Draw a grid or matrix, as in Figure 3.7 in this chapter and list global, national, regional, community and work place levels down the side. Then, across the top, list impact categories similar to those listed in Figure 3.7: political, social, technological, physical and economic. The class can brainstorm the categories of sources of change, and their impacts at each level on a child care center as illustrated. Discuss the ideas put forth.

◇ ◇

BIBLIOGRAPHY

Ackoff, R. L. (1970). *A concept of corporate planning.* New York: Wiley.

Ackoff, R. L. (1974). *Redesigning the future: A systems approach to societal problems.* New York: Wiley.

Argyris, C., & Schon, D. (1974). *Theory in practice: Increasing professional effectiveness.* San Francisco: Jossey-Bass.

Bennis, W., & Nanus, B. (1985). *Leaders: The strategies for taking charge.* New York: Harper and Row.

Berlew, D. E. (1974, Winter). Leadership and organizational excitement. *California Management Review.*

Berlew, D. E. (1990). Effective leaders make others feel stronger. In *On being a leader* (reprint no. 5), pp. 13–16. Redmond, WA: Child Care Information Exchange Press.

Bradford, D. L., & Cohen, A. R. (1984). *Managing for excellence: The guide to developing high performance in contemporary organizations.* New York: Wiley.

Foster, R. (1986). *Innovation: The attackers advantage.* New York: Summit Books.

Jones, E. (1990). On creating environments where teachers, like children, learn through play. In *Developing Staff Skills* (reprint no. 7), pp. 3–6. Redmond, WA: Child Care Information Exchange Press.

Kanter, R. (1983). *The change masters: The innovation for productivity in the American corporation.* New York: Simon and Schuster.

Kelly, C. M. (1987). The interrelation of ethics and power in today's organizations. *Organizational Dynamics, 16*(1), 4–18.

Kelly, C. M. (1988). *The destructive achiever.* Reading, MA: Addison-Wesley.

Koontz, H., & O'Donnell, C. (1972). *Principles of management* (3rd ed.). New York: McGraw-Hill.

Lindbloom, C. E. (1980). The science of muddling through. In H. J. Leavitt & L. Pondy (Eds.), *Readings in managerial psychology.* Chicago: University of Chicago Press.

McGregor, D. (1960). *The human side of enterprise.* New York: McGraw-Hill.

Naisbitt, J., & Aburdene, P. (1990). *Megatrends 2000.* New York: William Morrow.

Peters, T. J. (1987). *Thriving on chaos: Handbook for managing revolution.* New York: Knopf.

Peters, T. J., & Austin, N. (1985). *A passion for excellence: The leadership difference.* New York: Random House.

Peters, T. J., & Waterman, R. H. (1982). *In search of excellence: Lessons from America's best-run companies.* New York: Harper and Row.

Rogers, C. (1977). *On personal power.* New York: Dell.

Vaill, P. B. (1989). *Managing as a performing art: New ideas for a world of chaotic change.* San Francisco: Jossey-Bass.

Wack, P. (1985, September/October). Scenarios: Uncharted waters ahead. *Harvard Business Review,* p. 72.

Weisbord, M. R. (1978). *Organizational diagnosis: A workbook of theory and practice.* Reading, MA: Addison-Wesley.

Weisbord, M. R. (1987). *Productive workplaces: Organizing and managing for dignity, meaning and community.* San Francisco: Jossey-Bass.

Decision-Making

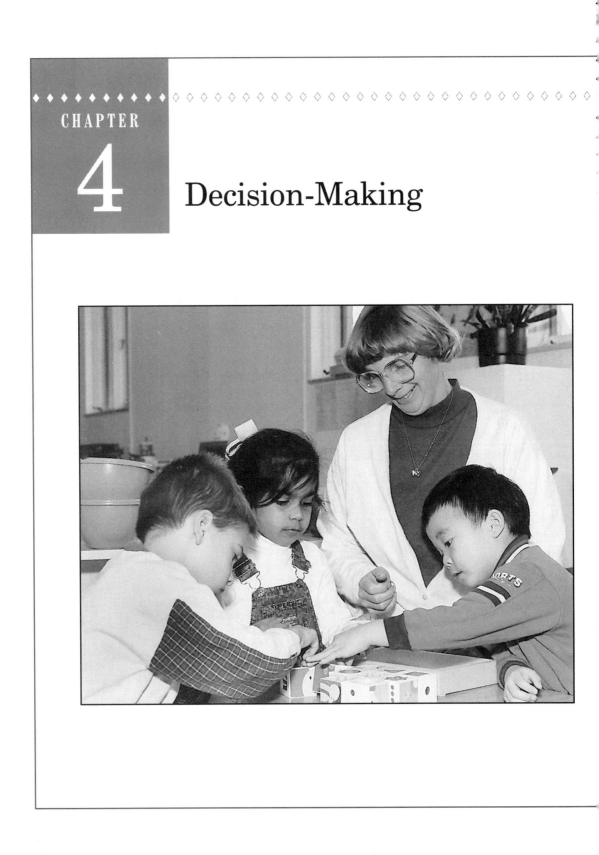

Leadership involves decision-making. To lead effectively, one needs to plan changes that will improve the organization. Enacting these changes may involve using old processes to achieve new goals, using new processes to continue working towards ongoing goals, or using new processes to aim for new goals. Planning should be a continuous process as new resources, goals, policies, or needs arise. If a plan is looked upon as an interim report, as it should be, it is essential that the planners meet at regular intervals to adapt and improve plans that have been made and to generate new plans. Research has shown that leaders build commitment any time they involve staff, parents, or the Board in planning and decision-making. But how and when can leaders do this?

The Greek word for administration is *kuberneseis*, which refers to the work of ships' pilots as they steer the ships through rocks and shoals to the harbor. All administrators have days when they say, "The fog is too thick!" "Where is the harbor?" "Why are there so many rocks?" In the midst of these questions, though, administrators of all kinds need to have wisdom, because if the administration of an organization is not well run, the organization itself will not be able to meet its goals. When an outstanding center is one of those goals, then administrators also need to promote encouragement, confidence, and commitment on the part of staff, parents, and the Board of Directors. Throughout the daily struggle of navigating through the fog and avoiding the rocks, it is rewarding to be part of an organization about which staff and parents can be proud and enthusiastic.

Again, having an outstanding center requires leadership and decision-making skills. Throughout this book, and especially in the chapters on leadership and motivation, the end-of-chapter bibliographies list many early childhood education administration materials that discuss the ideas behind effective leadership. One of the basic premises behind leadership is that the more power a leader gives away—by involving others in decision-making, coordination, or supervision—the more total shared power a leader has. Not all decisions are appropriate for group involvement, however, so further analysis of the decisions to be made and of the decision-making process is necessary.

An important skill in decision-making is knowing when to "re-frame" an issue. This is similar to re-structuring the problem, as will be discussed in chapter 5, but gives more insight into one's own perception and the perceptions of others. If one simplifies decisions in ways that blind one to other options, or to what is significant about this problem, or even to new ways of looking at a problem, the organization can find itself in great difficulty. A director can better understand when change is needed by knowing how important frames are. Some valuable keys to decision-making include: (1) becoming aware of your own frames (and filters); (2) selecting a decision frame carefully; (3) reframing a decision with intelligence when one can see the inadequacy of the present frame; and (4) matching one's frame to the frames of people one wants to influence (How would the Board or parents view this?). Gaining consensus on what the problem actually involves and how it could be re-stated may be as important as the decision-making process(es) selected. The decision tree introduced later in this chapter helps guard against "frame blindness." Chapter 5, "Creative and Analytical Problem-Solving," also gives more techniques for dealing with these issues. Suppose, for example, that the current budget is under constraint; one might ask: "How do other kinds of services and businesses cut costs without reducing quality?" Restaurants limit the menu. Some centers provide lunch only and do not provide breakfast. Other organizations recycle ideas or materials. Car dealers lower prices during the "off" season. Is summer an "off" season or a "high" season? Figure costs and offerings commensurately. If "Parent education" is re-framed as "providing information to parents," there are many other sources of information that can be helpful to parents in addition to what is being provided by their own child's center:

doctor's offices

toy manufacturer's labels (note: be sure to check for developmental appropriateness)

Internet web sites or print outs (try www.homelearning.org, homelearning.net or home-learning.org, www.ed.gov, or www.loc.gov. See Appendix H for a longer list.)

birthday party planning ideas

math, science, and language activity ideas (again, check for developmental appropriateness), and more.

In challenging the traditional frame one puts on decisions, consider:

What boundaries do I put on the question?

What yardsticks or measures do I use?

What reference points or bench marks do I use to measure success? (Better cash flow? Happier children? Fewer complaints?)

What metaphors do I use? (Like a family? Like a baseball team? Like a factory? Like growing a garden? [long-range goals?])

Why do we think about this problem the way we do? (We've always done it this way? Money is always a problem?)

What does this frame emphasize? (The children? The budget? The staff's needs? My needs?)

Do other people in early childhood care and education think about this differently than we do?

Can I summarize *my* thinking about this in a "slogan?" Can I summarize *their* thinking? For example: "We can't keep going without a stronger bottom line" or "To help children grow and learn."

Welcome a diversity of viewpoints in considering these questions and ask people with different thinking styles and backgrounds to be involved in this issue. You can even "role play" your competitors at a staff meeting as a "warm-up" for considering an issue (Russo and Schoemaker, 1990). Consider other metaphors: Should you act more like a general? A religious leader? An orchestra director? A mountain climber? A marathon runner? And *always* ask these three questions:

1. How much do we *really* know?

2. Is our knowledge base truly *representative*?

3. Are our estimates and judgements sound or have we relied too much on intuition and our "gut feeling?"

When gathering information, be wary of only gathering information that is available. Also, be wary of overconfidence and of relying too much on past experience or intuition. These both can produce inconsistent results with a fast-changing outside world. Scenarios described in the last chapter can be used to demonstrate possible optimistic and pessimistic outcomes. The following decision techniques can help create new avenues for approaching decisions.

◇ ◇ ◇ ◇ ◇ ◇ ◇ ◇ ◇ ◇ ◇ ◇ ◇ ◇ ◇ ◇ ◇ ◇ ◇ ◇

EASY DECISIONS

Making a decision that has only two possible outcomes, and in which the leader has no preference, can be as simple as flipping a coin. For slightly more complicated decisions, however, a decision-making strategy is useful, perhaps by listing the pros and cons of a decision in separate columns on a piece of paper. The benefit of this and other decision-making strategies is that they help the decision-maker look at a problem in a more systematic way, thereby revealing relevant questions that may not have been apparent at first.

In a well-run organization, most "easy" decisions can be delegated to an appropriate staff member, after parameters have been set by the leader. For example, deciding where to hold the end-of-the-year picnic might be done by vote, or by a committee, or by asking Mrs. Smith to choose this year. Much has been written about the benefits of delegating such decisions to the lowest feasible level. For example, a leader might announce: "This year the aides will decide on the park where we will have the picnic." Such an approach builds commitment throughout a staff's organizational system.

◊ ◊ ◊ ◊ ◊ ◊ ◊ ◊ ◊ ◊ ◊ ◊ ◊ ◊ ◊ ◊ ◊ ◊ ◊ ◊

HARDER DECISIONS

A *decision tree* is a useful tool for making decisions that are somewhat complex. A decision tree can be generated during meetings with staff, parents, or the Board, and can be a helpful method of providing information and encouraging discussion before a vote is taken. A simple tree also can be used by indi-

Decision making gets harder as one gets older.

viduals to solve personal problems, such as whether to buy a new car, repair the old one, or buy a used car.

To continue with our picnic example, a simple decision tree could be developed to decide whether lunch will be barbecued or whether parents will supply potluck items. The tree might start out looking like this:

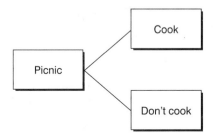

The next step is discussion (or information-gathering), which might focus on whether or not the parks under consideration have facilities for cooking, what hours the parks are available, how much advance notice is necessary, and so forth. The tree begins to look like this:

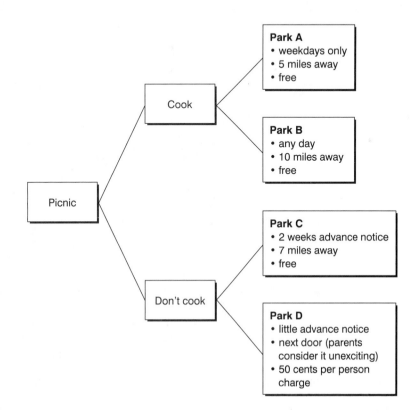

This tree could have additional branches placed to the right as more details are considered, such as the possibility of swimming at the parks, available amusements, or car pool arrangements. Once the tree is completed, it is ready to be used. The group or the decision-maker first considers the items the farthest to the right. The way to start this decision-making process is to rank all the considerations on the far right on a preference scale of 1 to 10 or -1 to -10, as shown in the following example:

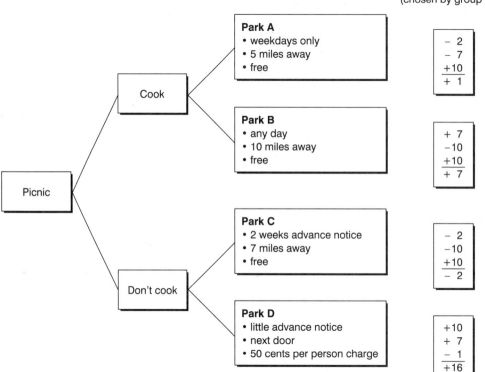

When this ranking system is used, Park D becomes the favorite if parents do not mind providing unheated food. If the group would rather cook, Park B seems more desirable. The question could now be presented at the parents' meeting with a choice between Park B and the cooking option or Park D with no cooking. When parents are given the opportunity to discuss the options, the factor of whether parents consider Park D exciting or not, or whether that is even important to the parents, would surface.

Using a simple tree of this sort is helpful in making other group decisions, either with staff or parents. This method also engages people's interest and often encourages them to research other options for next year's activity. This type of decision-making, then, benefits the organization in the long run because it builds commitment and interest. The remaining question for a leader to ask, then, is, "How many people should be involved in a given decision and how does the leader involve them?"

◊ ◊

VROOM'S DECISION-MAKING TREE

Victor Vroom and Philip Yetton, in their book *Leadership and Decision-Making* (1973), suggest that a series of questions be asked before deciding how many people to involve in the decision-making process. These questions appear at the top of Figure 4.1, but will be discussed first for clarification.

Is there a quality requirement such that one solution is likely to be more logical than another?

This first question assigns a very special meaning to the word *quality*. A decision is categorized as a "quality decision" if a large percent of an organization's money, materials, people, and/or time are to be used. Since "people time" is a very scarce resource in early childhood programs, the amount of time a director or teacher would have to devote to a project is always a consideration. Other factors that must be considered in making a quality decision—in addition to the percent of money, man/woman power, or materials needed—are whether or not the decision uses scarce resources, and whether or not the decision is easily reversible. Examples of quality decisions might include opening a new center across town (this would require a great deal of money and time), changing a major part of the curriculum, or changing in a major way the processes the center uses to relate to its parents.

Do I have sufficient information to make a high-quality decision?

If a leader does not have sufficient information to decide on an issue, and realizes it, then the information-gathering process can begin. For example, if a leader knows she wants to start another center across town, but also realizes she does not know what steps are necessary to carry out this dream, she can start reading books and asking people for more information. If she has gone through the Vroom decision-making tree and has decided to involve her staff at this point, she might invite to staff meetings guest speakers who have successfully started second centers. She might also ask the staff to start researching this issue as a possibility, without necessarily stating that the center plans to open a second branch.

Is the problem structured?

The meaning behind this question is: Does the leader know exactly what information is needed, who possesses it, and how to collect it? In terms of starting a new center, the answer would probably be "no." If the question under consideration were, "What is the jungle gym with the lowest price?," the answer would probably be "yes," because the leader would at least know *how to get* that information.

Is acceptance of the decision by employees critical to effective implementation?

This question is a very important one to ask in connection with many decisions. If employees will be the ones carrying out a decision (such as implementing a new curriculum or a new parent-relations program), then giving the employees enough information and a range of choices to gain their acceptance will be the key to success or failure. With regard to opening a center across town requiring employee support, the question to ask would be whether to hire a totally new staff, or whether to transfer several top teachers for one or two years.

If I were to make the decision myself, is it reasonably certain that it would be accepted by my employees?

This question relates to the previous question, obviously, but serves as a reminder to a leader who might be tempted to go out on a limb. It is always better to allow more time for understanding and discussion if it is apparent that the limb could be sawed off. It also helps the leader to assess the emotional climate surrounding a given issue.

Do employees share the organizational goals to be attained in solving this problem?

It is hoped that in an early childhood organization, the answer to this question would be "yes"; the whole staff should be working toward the goal of happy, competent children participating in their program. However, sometimes people take jobs just to earn money, and if that describes the majority of a staff, then staff training and motivation helps, and perhaps some selective hiring and firing are necessary. On the other hand, if the majority of the staff does identify with the goal of having the best center in town (or any goal that benefits children and parents and is agreed upon by all or most), then involving the staff in decision-making will enhance staff commitment and the organization. When employees share the organization's goals, the group can look together for solutions that are in the best interests of the organization.

Is conflict among employees likely in preferred solutions?

This question can be skipped on the decision tree if employees share the center's goals, but if employees do not share organizational goals, it is important to preplan how to handle possible conflict or to decide if the preferred solution is worth the risk of conflict.

Do employees have sufficient information to make a high-quality decision?

Often employees do not have enough information, and this leads to a natural opportunity for staff training on a given topic. Board members can be invited to attend the staff training too, if that is appropriate. In discussion, or ahead of time, the leader can identify the problem more clearly and, by using the Vroom tree in Figure 4.1, decide which solution and degree of staff involvement is appropriate.

After working through the tree, the leader can use Figure 4.2 to examine possible decision methods for group or individual problems. The codes at the bottom of Figure 4.1, such as AI, AII, CI, CII, and GII, correspond to the possibilities given in Figure 4.2. Where several codes or "feasible sets" are listed in Figure 4.1, the code listed farthest to the left is the fastest method for solving the particular problem being worked through. In these figures, *A* refers to autonomous methods, *C* refers to cooperative methods, and *G* refers to group methods.

Deciding the Degree of Group Involvement

As the solutions progress from AI to GII in Figure 4.2, the more ways it becomes possible to involve the group. In AI the leader makes the decision himself by using the information available at the time. When considering an issue such as whether or not to open another center across town, a leader often chooses this method of decision-making.

If the leader needs more information to make a decision, solution AII suggests that the necessary information be obtained from co-workers and parents, but that the decision be made on his or her own. For example, the leader could gather information by asking staff and parents, "Do you think this town could use another child-care center?" "Where would be a good location?" "What special programs might be an asset?" Depending on the situation, the leader may or may not tell others about his or her plans. Either way, other people serve only as information-providers; they do not participate in the decision-making.

In the next solution, CI, the leader talks one-to-one with staff and parents, but does not meet with them as a group. These discussions can be done informally, such as at a social gathering, and can occur over time or in a number of ways. After the necessary information is gathered, the leader makes the decision on his or her own, perhaps taking others' views into account or perhaps not.

The next solution, CII, is similar to CI in that the leader finally decides alone, perhaps not even using the employees' advice, but this time the employees are gathered together in a group to give their suggestions. This arrangement allows everyone to be familiar with the question and also provides a situation in which people can build upon one another's ideas. If the leader should decide later that she does need help, at least her employees will know what it

A. Is there a quality requirement such that one solution is likely to be more rational than another?
B. Do I have sufficient info to make a high quality decision?
C. Is the problem structured?
D. Is acceptance of decision by employees critical to effective implementation?
E. If I were to make the decision by myself, is it reasonably certain that it would be accepted by my employees?
F. Do employees share the organizational goals to be attained in solving this problem?
G. Is conflict among employees likely in preferred solutions? (This question is irrelevant to individual problems.)
H. Do employees have sufficient info to make a high quality decision?

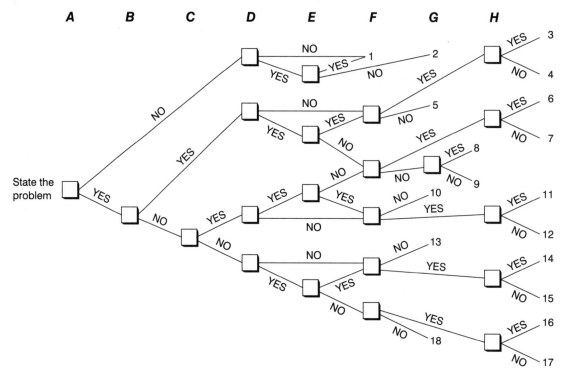

The feasible set is shown for each problem type for Group (G) and Individual (I) problems.

1 { G: AI, AII, CI, CII, GII / I: AI, DI, AII, CI, GI }
2 { G: GII / I: DI, GI }
3 { G: AI, AII, CI, CII, GII / I: AI, DI, AII, CI, GI }
4 { G: AI, AII, CI, CII, GII / I: AI, AII, CI, GI }

5 { G: AI, AII, CI, CII / I: AI, AII, CI }
6 { G: GII / I: DI, GI }
7 { G: GII / I: GI }
8 { G: CII / I: CI }

9 { G: CI, CII / I: CI }
10 { G: AII, CI, CII / I: AII, CI }
11 { G: AII, CI, CII, GII / I: DI, AII, CI, GI }
12 { G: AII, CI, CII, GII / I: AII, CI, GI }

13 { G: CII / I: CI }
14 { G: CII, GII / I: DI, CI, GI }
15 { G: CII, GII / I: CI, GI }
16 { G: GII / I: DI, GI }

17 { G: GII / I: GI }
18 { G: CII / I: CI }

FIGURE 4.1
Decision-Process Flow Chart for Both Individual and Group Problems

Source: From *Leadership and Decision-Making* (p. 13) by V. H. Vroom and P. W. Yetton, 1973, Pittsburgh: University of Pittsburgh Press. Copyright 1973 by the University of Pittsburgh Press. Reprinted by permission.

Group Problems	Individual Problems
AI You solve the problem or make the decision yourself, using information available to you at the time.	**AI** You solve the problem or make the decision yourself using information available to you at the time.
AII You obtain the necessary information from your employees, then decide the solution to the problem yourself. You may or may not tell your employees what the problem is in getting the information from them. The role played by your employees in making the decision is clearly one of providing the necessary information to you, rather than generating or evaluating alternative solutions.	**AII** You obtain the necessary information from your employee, then decide on the solution to the problem yourself. You may or may not tell the employee what the problem is in getting the information from him. His or her role in making the decision is clearly one of providing the necessary information to you, rather than generating or evaluating alternative solutions.
CI You share the problem with the relevant employees individually, getting their ideas and suggestions without bringing them together as a group. Then **you** make the decision, which may or may not reflect your employees' influence.	**CI** You share the problem with your employee, getting his ideas and suggestions. Then you make the decision, which may or may not reflect his or her influence.
CII You share the problem with your employees as a group, obtaining their collective ideas and suggestions. Then you make the decision, which may or may not reflect your employees' influence.	**GI** You share the problem with your employees, and together you analyze the problem and arrive at a mutually agreeable solution.
GII You share the problem with your employees as a group. Together you generate and evaluate alternatives and attempt to reach agreement (consensus) on a solution. Your role is much like that of chairman. You do not try to influence the group to adopt "your" solution, and you are willing to accept and implement any solution which has the support of the entire group.	**DI** You delegate the problem to your employee, providing him or her with any relevant information that you possess, but giving him or her responsibility for solving the problem alone. You may or may not request him or her to tell you what solution is reached.

FIGURE 4.2
Decision Methods for group and Individual Problems

Source: From *Leadership and Decision-Making* (p. 195) by V. H. Vroom and P. W. Yetton, 1973, Pittsburgh: University of Pittsburgh Press. Copyright 1973 by University of Pittsburgh Press. Reprinted by permission.

is she needs help with. Of course, if the leader does follow a particular line of advice, either deliberately or by straw vote, she should let the appropriate person or group know and show appreciation for the help. If the leader does not use the advice, and if an explanation is appropriate or needed, she can explain that circumstances were such that another solution seemed better at the time.

In solution GII, the decision-maker shares the problem with the group and then acts as a discussion leader while everyone generates as many solutions as possible. Then the group votes to decide which solution is best. Whichever solution is chosen by the majority is the one the leader is willing to adopt and implement, and, of course, this solution has the support of the entire group. This method might be very helpful if the leader knows he or she wants to start a new center across town, but is not sure where to locate it. The leader would probably want to have the center in a fairly convenient location for new enrollees. It also may be that one, two, or three teachers will *volunteer* to work at the new center when they learn that they will have some say in choosing the new location and the new equipment.

This GII solution is especially useful in cases where the leader knows that he or she wants to address a big problem, but doesn't know how or where to begin to solve it. Introducing the problem to the group provides more resources and allows for more ideas to flow. The group may decide they want to know more about the problem; guest speakers can be invited and literature provided as everyone learns more and has time to ask friends and acquaintances. Interesting problems *attract* able people, and the leader will find all sorts of resources becoming available. Also, allowing some time to find a solution gives "the grapevine" time to work; for example, an aide might ask a competitor's brother, or some other informal network person, some key "how-to-do-it" questions that would be inappropriate to ask at higher levels.

The list of solutions for individual problems follows the same pattern as for group problems, but is appropriate for one-on-one problems. An additional code, DI, is involved in this list, and indicates delegating the problem and its responsibility to an employee. It goes without saying that politeness in seeking information or asking advice is essential.

◇ ◇

USING THE DECISION TREE

The following section contains several case studies of actual decision-making situations. Practice using the decision-making tree as you consider the situations and the decisions that were made. Figure 4.3 provides a decision-making worksheet that contains abbreviated questions and boxes for decision points. As you use a pencil to trace through the tree, if a question is unclear, go back to Figure 4.1 to study the longer version of the tree and read the accompanying explanation in the text. Figure 4.4 shows the decision tree simplified even more.

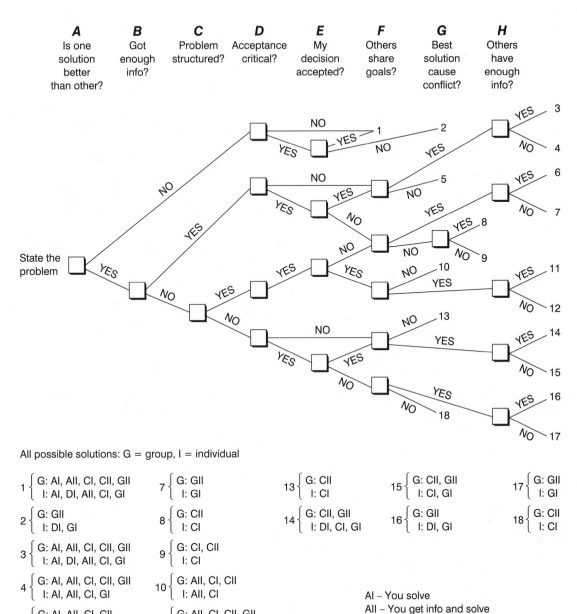

All possible solutions: G = group, I = individual

1 {
G: AI, AII, CI, CII, GII
I: AI, DI, AII, CI, GI
}

2 {
G: GII
I: DI, GI
}

3 {
G: AI, AII, CI, CII, GII
I: AI, DI, AII, CI, GI
}

4 {
G: AI, AII, CI, CII, GII
I: AI, AII, CI, GI
}

5 {
G: AI, AII, CI, CII
I: AI, AII, CI
}

6 {
G: GII
I: DI, GI
}

7 {
G: GII
I: GI
}

8 {
G: CII
I: CI
}

9 {
G: CI, CII
I: CI
}

10 {
G: AII, CI, CII
I: AII, CI
}

11 {
G: AII, CI, CII, GII
I: DI, AII, CI, GI
}

12 {
G: AII, CI, CII, GII
I: AII, CI, GI
}

13 {
G: CII
I: CI
}

14 {
G: CII, GII
I: DI, CI, GI
}

15 {
G: CII, GII
I: CI, GI
}

16 {
G: GII
I: DI, GI
}

17 {
G: GII
I: GI
}

18 {
G: CII
I: CI
}

AI – You solve
AII – You get info and solve
CI – You get advice and solve
CII – Get group's advice and solve
GII – Get group's advice and group solves
GI – Get group's advice and solve together

FIGURE 4.3
Vroom's Decision Tree—Simplified

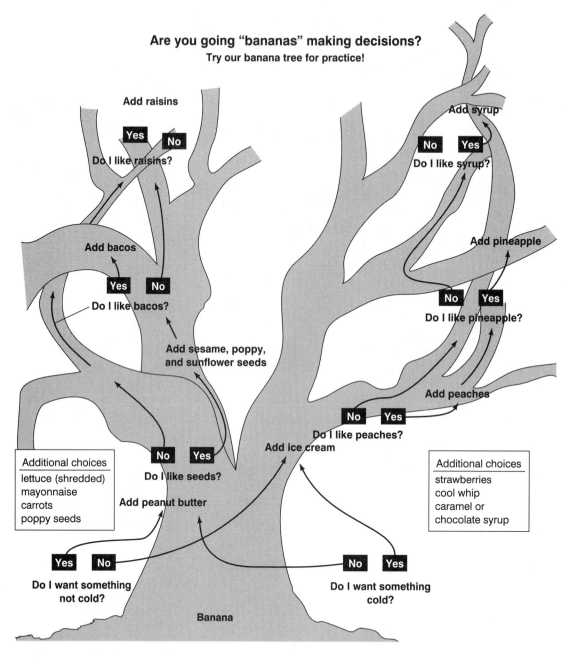

FIGURE 4.4
"Banana" Decision Tree

Case Study A: Unpaid Tuition

The director had trouble collecting tuition from one family and abruptly told them that their child's enrollment was terminated at the center. Other parents were horrified because they knew that this family was a particularly needy one. The father was out of work, the mother was recovering from an auto accident, and they had a new baby in addition to the child enrolled at the center. The director's decision caused a lot of negative talk and complaint. Staff morale dropped to a new low because they viewed the action taken with this family as harsh and unkind.

Using the Decision Tree
Follow these points on the tree in Figure 4.1.

1. *Is this a quality decision?*   Perhaps the answer to this question appeared to be "no" to the director, but actually it should have been "yes," because ultimately the problem took up a very high percentage of director, staff, and parent time.

2. *Did the director have sufficient information to make a quality decision?*   Apparently not, since the only information she took into account was that the center needed to stay afloat financially.

3. *Is the problem structured?*   Yes, because the director knew where to get more information.

4. *Is the acceptance of the decision by staff and parents critical to effective implementation?*   Since the director can decide anything she wants if she owns the center or is sole manager of it, the key word here may well be *effective*. Creating gossip among the staff and community is time-consuming and worrisome. The answer to this question should have been "yes."

5. *If I decided myself, would staff and parents accept it?*   As we know from hindsight, the answer is "no."

6. *Do staff and parents share the organizational goals to be attained in solving this problem?*   Apparently the answer here was "yes," because the adults involved wanted to be helpful to this family. The family had been upstanding members of the community before their string of misfortunes.

7. *Is conflict among employees likely?*   This question is skipped on the branch of the tree we have traveled so far.

8. *Do employees have sufficient information to make a high-quality decision?*   The answer here could be mixed, since the employees knew of the family's needs, but perhaps didn't know about the center's budget problems.

9. *Result.*   Interestingly enough, GII is recommended as the *fastest* solution, whether the answer is "yes" or "no." Taking the decision to the

parent/staff Board turns out to be the solution to try first. This action would allow the director to present her budget problems as well as her hard-and-fast rule that tuition must always be paid on time. The Board could vote on whether this particular situation was a "special exception" for which they could use scholarship funds. If no scholarship funds exist, the Board might resolve to develop a future revolving fund by organizing some fundraisers, although they would not be able to help this particular needy family at this time. If the director had shared the problem *before* taking action, however, the Board could have become aware of the factors involved and could have taken positive steps to help now, or if not now, at least in the future. Months or even years of gossip and complaint could have been averted.

10. *What actually did happen?*   The problem was handled as originally described. A staff member brought it up in a class a year later because she was still upset about it, and the class took it through the decision tree as a learning exercise.

Case Study B: Should a Values/Morals Statement Appear in the Center Philosophy?

The director of a new center couldn't decide whether to include in the center's statement of philosophy any mention of teaching enrollees values and morals.

Using the Decision Tree

1. *Is this a quality decision?*   While implementing this decision might not use a large percent of money, people, or materials, the decision itself might be hard to reverse. If the answer here is "no," the director might decide to include the statement but have parameters put around it (such as, "Don't name a particular church"), and then hand the wording over to a Board or parent group to iron out. If the answer is "yes," we can proceed through the tree.

2. *Does the director have sufficient information to make a quality decision?* In this case, the director did not know what the majority of the parents preferred, or whether there was a strong feeling either way.

3. *Is the problem structured?*   Yes, because the director did know from which group she could get more information.

4. *Is the acceptance of the decision by staff and parents critical to effective implementation?*   Yes, because a philosophy that causes conflict is not representative of the program.

5. *If I decided by myself, would staff and parents accept the decision?* Since the director really didn't know how others would respond, she decided to say "no."

6. *Do the staff and parents share the organizational goal of having a top-quality center?*   The director answered "yes" to this question.

7. *Is conflict among employees and/or parents likely?*   Again, this question is skipped.

8. *Do staff and parents have sufficient information to make a high-quality decision?*   Yes, because they know how they feel about this issue.

9. *Result.*   The solution that was recommended by the tree as the fastest way to solve this problem was GII.

10. *What actually happened?*   The director took the problem to the parent group since the staff was indecisive. The parents voted to include a phrase in their philosophy about teaching children values and morals, so there was no problem after all. The parents were pleased to be asked about something they cared about.

Case Study C: Late Pick-up of Children

The center was plagued by a few parents who were habitually arriving from 6:10 P.M. to 6:25 P.M. to pick up their children, when the center was scheduled to close at 6:00 P.M.

Using the Decision Tree

1. *Is this a quality decision?*   The director decided that this was a quality decision because the parents would be very unhappy if the center imposed a stiff penalty for lateness or did not allow for genuine emergencies. On the other hand, the staff was always complaining about having to stay late for the sake of a few parents.

2. *Did the director have sufficient information to make a quality decision?*   The director felt that she needed more information.

3. *Is the problem structured?*   Yes. The director decided to ask the Executive Board of the parent group to make a recommendation.

4. *Is acceptance of the decision by employees critical to effective implementation?*   Yes. If the problem continued, staff members would probably quit.

5. *If I decided myself, would staff and parents accept the decision?*   The director was unsure of the support she would receive if she made a decision that employees did not agree with.

6. *Do staff and parents share the organizational goals to be attained in solving this problem?*   The director answered "no" to this question, based on her perceptions of employees' attitudes. (The answer to this question is always based on the "gut feeling" of the client or person with the problem.)

7. *Is conflict among employees likely in preferred solutions?* Yes.

8. *Result.* On the tree, the solution at which the director arrived was CII, which suggests sharing the problem with the group, getting their suggestions, and then making the decision alone.

9. *What actually happened?* The director did ask the Executive Board of the parent group for ideas and suggestions on this problem. The group felt it was a very severe problem, because if one parent took advantage, others would also be tempted to do so. The suggestions ranged from charging $1 per minute for lateness, to $5 per 15 minutes, to sending the child by taxi to an emergency neighbor's house, to requiring the offending parent to paint equipment on a Saturday. The director settled on charging $1 per minute and announced the decision at the parent group meeting with the support of the Executive Board. Lateness has dropped off dramatically at this center. The lateness policy is also clearly communicated so that everyone knows about the rule.

◇ ◇

SUMMARY

Decision-making is indeed key in leadership processes. However, the ability to structure decisions and then break them down into manageable parts as necessary in decision-making are skills that can be learned. For a leader, sometimes making a decision oneself can be the *slowest* way to a resolution when group support is needed and group involvement would be preferable (and faster). Taking three to six months to involve the Board, the staff, and the parents is often the fastest decision approach possible when a large decision is involved and when an individual decision might result in years of controversy.

It is well to keep in mind that decision research over the last 20 years has shown that people in a wide variety of fields tend to make the same kinds of mistakes in decision-making (Russo and Schoemaker, 1990, p. xvi). Ten of the most common errors include:

1. *Plunging in.* Gathering information and reaching conclusions before taking time to think through the crux of the issue—and to think through *how* you believe this type of decision should be made.

2. *Frame Blindness.* Trying to solve the wrong problem because the mental framework that you hold has allowed you to overlook some of the best options or some important objectives. This is a hazard seen in Case Study B above. Framing decisions is important.

3. *Lack of Frame Control.*   Failing to consciously define the problem in several ways (always more than one), or being influenced by the mental framework created and held by others. *Your* framing of decisions is important.

4. *Overconfidence in One's Own Judgement.*   Not collecting key facts and looking at the evidence, because one is too sure of one's own opinions and assumptions. (Experienced directors need to be wary of this one.)

5. *Taking Short Cuts for the Short Run.*   Relying on "yardsticks" or "rules of thumb" and/or placing too much trust in information that is easily and readily available and convenient. (A hazard shown in Case Studies A and C). Coming to conclusions requires looking at mid-term and long-term goals as well.

6. *Winging It and Shooting from the Hip.*   Thinking one can keep all the information in one's head and rushing ahead rather than using a systematic procedure for making a final decision. (See Case Study A—months of controversy resulted.) Information gathering is important.

7. *Failing to Manage the Group Decision-Making Process.*   Assuming that good people will make good choices without using a method to arrive at this desired result can be costly.

8. *Inaccurate Interpretation of Feedback.*   Not interpreting feedback realistically—whether one is protecting one's own ego or the egos of others, or because of being "tricked" by hindsight (e.g. "It seemed to work last time"). Learning from feedback is important.

9. *Not Keeping Track.*   Failing to keep track of results of past decisions and to analyze these results in ways that reveal their key lessons.

10. *Failing to "Audit" the Decision Process.*   Failing to develop an organized approach to understanding one's own decision-making leaves one exposed to mistakes 1 to 9 above. To begin to do this, list the frames and "yardsticks" or "rules of thumb" you generally use and your preferred strategies for arriving at conclusions. Ask which phase of the decision process is the hardest for you, which of these areas can you improve on by becoming more aware of them, and which require formal steps. These might include changing how you make estimates; formalizing processes; analyzing learning after making major decisions (perhaps in a group); or keeping better records. List the steps you should take. Rank yourself from A to F on these 10 areas or "decision traps."

Think about what your present frames emphasize and minimize. How do you measure success? Frequency of problems? Sense of partnership? Usefulness of other people's input? This chapter outlined some of the parameters to consider when approaching a decision, and the following chapter on problem-solving provides additional tools that may be useful.

◇ ◇ ◇ ◇ ◇ ◇ ◇ ◇ ◇ ◇ ◇ ◇ ◇ ◇ ◇ ◇ ◇ ◇ ◇ ◇

SUGGESTED CLASS ACTIVITIES AND DISCUSSIONS

1. *Use of Decision Tree with Class Members' Problems.*   Students can turn in problems that they would like to see processed on the decision tree. Select one that represents a "high quality" decision that is irreversible or that uses a large amount of resources, whether time, money, or materials. Take the problem through the decision tree with the owner of the problem as the "client" who therefore has the final say. If other problems turned in are "high quality," ask small groups to take them through the decision tree separately and report back to the class.

2. *Role Play with Decision Tree Chart Taped on the Floor.*   A small group of students can make a full-sized decision tree on the floor with masking tape, that "decision-makers" could walk through. The role play can even be presented as a dream sequence with "Mrs. Jones, the director" dreaming about her staff walking through a problem and coming up with each teacher volunteering an idea and agreeing by consensus. One group developed the idea of volunteers and parent volunteers coming in with a physical education program at noon. A week later, the director follows up with praise (in the role play). Since this is a dream, hypothetical situations can be tried out. Other problems and group solutions from the class can be "walked through" on this chart on the floor.

3. *"Decision Tree," Television's Latest Decision-Making Game.*   A small group of students can present the decision tree, or a modification of it, as a television game show. Again, the game context allows hypothetical problems to be simulated. One example to use might be "Miss Rotten's poor room arrangement," characterized by poorly defined areas in the room. Solutions can include putting the art area near the sink and placing the cars and trucks near the blocks. Students can contribute other questions or problems for this "game show."

4. *Unexpected New Funds Exercise.*   Address the following problem in small groups, using the decision method of choice. A benefactor has given your center the sum of $10,000. The benefactor is a member of the church that sponsors and houses the center. The money must be used now and with the following restrictions:

   a. The money cannot be used for salaries.

   b. The present equipment cannot be replaced or repaired.

   c. No building may be added.

   d. The center must remain a part of the church. A report must be turned in this month to the governing board of the church for the use of the money. Have small groups do outlines of their possible reports and report back to the class.

5. *Class Discussion on Risk Taking.*   Discuss some of the following statements on risk taking:

- Groups are more willing than individuals to take risks.
- A risk is taken when one accepts change, which may represent a gain or a loss.
- The best guard against loss is primarily a matter of the quality of the solution.
- In reaching a consensus in a group, someone must change.
- The person who changes in a group can be an asset or a liability depending on where the high quality solution may be coming from.

◇ ◇ ◇ ◇ ◇ ◇ ◇ ◇ ◇ ◇ ◇ ◇ ◇ ◇ ◇ ◇ ◇ ◇ ◇ ◇

BIBLIOGRAPHY

Argyris, C. (1985). *Strategy, change and defensive routines.* Boston, MA: Pittman.

Beach, D. S. (1975). *Managing people at work.* New York: Wiley.

Blake, R. R., & Mouton, J. S. (1964). *The managerial grid.* Houston, TX: Gulf Publishing.

Chambers, G. S. (1971). *Day care—resources for decisions.* Washington, DC: U.S. Government Printing Office.

Cosier, R. A., & Schwenk, C. R. (1990, February). Agreement and thinking alike: Ingredients for poor decisions. *Academy of Management Executive,* pp. 69–74.

Decker, C. A., & Decker, J. (1992). *Planning and administering early childhood education.* Upper Saddle River, NJ: Merrill/Prentice Hall.

Drucker, P. F. (1967). *The effective executive.* New York: Harper and Row.

Fiedler, F. E. (1958). *Leader attitude and group effectiveness.* Urbana, IL: University of Illinois Press.

Ford, R. C., & Fattler, M. D. (1995, August). Empowerment: A matter of degree. *Academy of Management Executive,* pp. 21–31.

Garvin, D. A. (1993, July/August). Building a learning organization. *Harvard Business Review,* pp. 78–91.

Goldman, T. A. (1967). *Cost effectiveness and analysis: New approaches in decision making.* New York: Praeger.

Lakein, A. (1973). *How to get control of your time and your life.* New York: Signet.

March, J. G. (1994). *A primer on decision making: How decisions happen.* New York: Free Press.

Messeck, D. M., & Bazerman, M. H. (1996, Winter). Ethical leadership and the psychology of decision making. *Sloan Management Review,* pp. 9–22.

Millett, J. D. (1968). *Decision making and administration in higher education.* Kent, OH: Kent State University Press.

Robinson, S. L. (1996). Trust and breach of the psychological contract. *Administrative Science Quarterly,* 41, 574–599.

Russo, J. E., & Schoemaker, P. J. H. (1990). *Decision traps*. New York: Simon & Schuster.

Schoemaker, P. J. H., & Russo, J. E. (1993, Fall). A pyramid of decision approaches. *California Management Review*, pp. 9–31.

Senge, P. (1990). *The fifth discipline: The art and practice of the learning organization*. New York: Doubleday.

Stata, R. (1989, Spring). Organizational learning—The key to management innovation. *Sloan Management Review*, pp. 63–64.

Vroom, V. H. (1967). *Methods of organizational research*. Pittsburgh, PA: University of Pittsburgh Press.

Vroom, V. H. (1973). *Leadership and decision-making*. Pittsburgh, PA: University of Pittsburgh Press.

CHAPTER

5

Creative and Analytical Problem-Solving

A director's problems often comprise a group of subproblems or activities. Breaking down these larger problems into parts can be helpful, but a director also needs a perspective of the total situation. Vision is an important component of any formula for success. It holds the keys to the future and, for this reason, vision is listed early in the leadership knowledge, skills and abilities questionnaire in chapter 2. Therefore, when beginning to solve a problem, it is helpful to state the problem in as open-ended a way as possible; then a selection can be made from any or all of the problem-solving techniques that might be appropriate.

◇ ◇ ◇ ◇ ◇ ◇ ◇ ◇ ◇ ◇ ◇ ◇ ◇ ◇ ◇ ◇ ◇ ◇ ◇ ◇

STEPS IN PROBLEM-SOLVING

The first step in problem-solving is to ask the initial question: *Is the problem within the problem-solver's (director's) sphere of influence?* If it is, then using individual problem-solving techniques to solve the problem may be enough. If the problem is not within the director's/administrator's sphere of influence, then group techniques are necessary. It is helpful at this point to identify key persons and involve them in whichever group techniques are chosen. Several aids to decision-making exist, such as the decision tree discussed in chapter 4, and brainstorming and synectics, which are group techniques that will be discussed later in this chapter.

The next step in problem-solving is to ask: *Are time and change important?* Problems can be further divided into those for which time and/or change are important, and those for which time and/or change are less important. For example, planning a new curriculum for next year would fall into the second, or static, category (not changing rapidly, under less time pressure); on the other hand, meeting a proposal deadline this month would fall into the first, or more dynamic, category (with high time pressure and the possibility of change). Obviously, there will be situations that fit both categories, since time and change are both important.

◇ ◇ ◇ ◇ ◇ ◇ ◇ ◇ ◇ ◇ ◇ ◇ ◇ ◇ ◇ ◇ ◇ ◇ ◇

INDIVIDUAL TECHNIQUES

The individual analytical techniques described in the following section should be quite familiar, since they are often used in everyday situations. The section that follows analytical techniques, which describes individual creative techniques, lists many procedures that also can be used for group problem-solving. An administrator can first "walk through" the technique alone, or he or she might want to gather group ideas first.

Individual Analytical Techniques

Many of the techniques used when making individual decisions are analytical in nature. For example, checklists are a familiar analytical problem-solving aid, as are lists of "pros" and "cons" that relate to a specific decision or problem. Using a scale of 1 to 10 to weigh ideas on a checklist or list of pros and cons (that is, rating ideas from 1 to 10 or -1 to -10 according to the problem-solver's feelings or some particular criteria for measuring) also helps clarify priorities and is an individual analytical technique. An attribute list, which is described in the section on creative techniques below, can also be used as an analytical technique. The decision tree used in chapter 4 is analytical in nature, and can be used both by individuals or a group.

Another analytical technique could be called the "Six-Question Approach." To demonstrate this, let us use the example of deciding to purchase a new piece of playground equipment. First, gather catalogs (or other reference materials appropriate to a given problem). These resource materials help prepare an individual or group and serve as a springboard for discussion. As possibilities are chosen, ask these six questions:

What is it?

What must it do?

What *does* it do?

What will it cost?

What else might do the job?

What will that cost?

Thinking through these questions one by one sharpens one's thinking and clarifies the issues involved.

Computer-Aided Problem-Solving

Computer software systems designed specifically for child-care center management are other aids to individual decision-making and analytical problem-solving. There are three types of software that are useful for centers: (1) planning software (that is, software that aids in making projections, establishing long-range plans, and setting up cash-flow patterns and budgets); (2) communications and printing software; and (3) record-keeping software.

The planning software also can be used to develop scenarios (possible plans for the future) as a director considers the five outlooks discussed in chapter 3:

- Things will go as expected.
- The situation will get a little better.
- The situation will get a little worse.
- The situation will get much better.
- The situation will get much worse.

Simulating the numbers, budgets, and other factors of a one-year, five-year, and ten-year plan can help a director explore a possible scenario. These "pilot program views" are subject to error, of course, since the future *is* uncertain and computers are famous for only projecting the known or linear possibilities that have been entered into them. However, uncovering hidden possibilities or predicting problems is worth the effort involved (Senge, 1990).

Individual Creative Techniques

Morphological Analysis

Morphological analysis is a comprehensive method of listing and examining all of the possible solutions to a problem, as well as combinations of these solutions. The steps of this method, which can be done individually or with a group, include:

1. Define the problem broadly.
2. List the interdependent variables.
3. Enter the variables on the horizontal axis of a chart.
4. Select the most promising alternatives and list them on the vertical axis of the chart.

The object of morphological analysis is to review all possible solution combinations. Figure 5.1 illustrates this technique. In this example, the problem is how to expand a center's services and increase its income.

Figure 5.1 shows a gradual progression of goals and objectives that can be applied to future years. While a lack of floor space and expertise might pose problems, planning for using the extra space available during the summer or

Variables	Old Population	Some New Population	New Population
Old product	Child-care center	Advertise for school-age/after-school program	Advertise summer day camp to the geographic area
Some new product	Offer Saturday games and hiking program	Have older children also come to the games and hiking program (with their parents for some events)	Have separate Saturday program of games, hiking, and other enrichments for school-age children
New product	Offer summer or Saturday computer camp	Offer computer camp to older children	Advertise summer computer day camp—Offer it to teenagers 12–15 also

FIGURE 5.1
Morphological Analysis: How to Expand Services and Increase Income

hiring teachers who are trained in both computers and child development might solve these dilemmas. When first contemplating changes, an organization should consider building upon old strengths of either the product (present services) or the population served at present to avoid significant risk. *Starting changes by instigating a new service for a new population is the riskiest alternative.* By providing a familiar service to a new population or providing a new service to a familiar population, the organization is more likely to succeed.

Morphological analysis can also be used with a group in a brainstorming session to gain more ideas and add details to concepts already suggested. The exercises used in this analysis process are designed to generate ideas, and may greatly benefit a staff training session. The combining and recombining of functions and possible alternatives provides numerous opportunities to look at a problem and develop fresh, novel solutions.

Attribute Lists

A specialized form of morphological analysis is the *attribute list*. This type of analysis is done by listing attributes of the functions desired (or not desired) on one side of a matrix, and then listing possible forms across the other side of the matrix. In this manner, form and function are separated and new insights emerge. The advantage of using the matrix is that each function can be considered as it would appear in each form. Also, elements within each function can be considered.

Figure 5.2 is an example of an attribute list of this type. In this particular case, the list was used to better understand a difficult personnel problem involving a grievance that was filed by an administrative assistant. This problem was resolved when the individual took a three-month medical leave without pay and, while on leave, acquired a new job. In looking back at the circumstances of her hiring, it was found that her references had not been checked closely; if they had, it would have been discovered that she had exhibited this behavior in the past. Her grievances against a large number of people in this organization (17 out of 23) were found to be unsubstantiated.

Attribute lists are also intended to help generate ideas about a service, situation, or product under consideration. In these types of situations, the list is generated and then analyzed to find items that would improve the situation, service, or product (happy, competent children in the case of early childhood programs). For example, an individual or a group (staff or Board) might want to improve the outdoor area around the center while minimizing any hazards. A list of attributes or features could be developed similar to that found in Figure 5.3.

Checklists can be developed for each item and then forced relationships can be developed next or later. (A forced relationship develops when participants are given a new word, concept, phrase, or object and asked to relate it to the problem being studied. The idea is to find new stimuli to "force" creativity.) When this activity is done in a group setting, the leader or facilitator can intro-

Dimensions of the problem	Elements within the dimension
Rudeness	Of administrative assistant to professionals, parents, visitors
Incompetence	Late work, lost work, surliness about complaints
Programs threatened	Income and prestige loss, relationship with community agencies threatened
Wants all requests to be made in writing	Delays work, creates rigidity, violates norms of informality
Filed grievance citing sexism and racism as reasons for the behavior described above	Involves legal language and delays, learning about parameters involved; can work to the benefit of management or the employee

FIGURE 5.2
Attribute List

duce a new word, concept, phrase, or subject relating to the main task, and then, before returning to the main task, the group can brainstorm ideas that stem from the new subject. For example, to help a group brainstorm ideas relating to the main task of improving the outdoor area, the facilitator might introduce the phrase "playing in a garden." This phrase generates thoughts of integrating *beauty* into the children's play area. Ideas might include allowing children to plant seeds in the beds (zinnias, carrots, and radishes, for example). For centers with almost no outside area, container gardens could be used and then brought indoors during the winter.

For the subject "picnic/snack area," subtopics such as "benches," "tables," and "trash cans" can be generated and discussed. The same procedure can be used with any other topic; finding comparisons among other lists can help enhance this problem-solving method, because it is an interim step in the main problem-solving task.

In the outdoor play area example, using a word like "beauty" creates forced relationships and generates new ideas in one direction. Introducing the phrase "physical fitness" initiates a whole new group of relationships and steers ideas in another direction. Adding another column (entitled "Expense") to the attribute list also could help clarify certain situations. For example, when expense is considered, the cost of building a stone wall might be too high, but if a stone wall already exists, the cost of making it safe and usable might be feasible.

Item	Beauty Attributes	Physical Fitness Attributes
Lawn	Adds to beauty	Used as a running area and for large muscle exercise
Beds—flowers	Add to beauty	Do not add to fitness since they cannot be walked in or touched
Beds—nonflowering (e.g., ivy)	Add to beauty (Is sturdy and harder to damage)	Do not add to fitness
Fences	Can be attractive	Required to make safe areas for outdoor fitness
Flowering trees	Add to beauty (Cannot easily be damaged at the tree trunk level, once mature)	Do not add to fitness
Other shade trees	Add to beauty (Lend shade and comfort for outdoor activities)	Do not add to fitness
Shrubs	Add to beauty	Do not add to fitness
Hedges	Add to beauty	Do not add to fitness
Walks, tricycle paths	Can be attractive	Used for many large muscle activities
Stone walls	Can be attractive	Can be a safety hazard near outdoor play
Picnic/snack areas	Can be attractive	Add to ambiance and variety of outdoor play
Signs	Can be attractive	Add to safety of outdoor play
Outdoor play equipment (as listed in Chapter 13)	Can be attractive	Required for children's fitness

FIGURE 5.3
Attribute List with Forced Relationships

Using the Senses and Working in Color

Since effective early childhood programs use "learning by the senses" as often as possible, using all the senses in problem solving may be easy for leaders and other adults working with young children. To build creativity into solutions, think of a subject from the perspective of sight, sound, touch, taste, and smell. Consider each sense separately at first. How does it *look*? How does the playground *sound*? (Shall we sing outside?) *Smell*? (Are the flowers planted?) *Taste*? (Outdoor snacks?) *Feel*? (Is it a hard or soft surface if a child falls? Are nuts and bolts carefully taped over?) Then consider the senses in combinations with one another. (Sing songs before snack time outside? Bring an air mattress or two outside to jump on?) Brainstorm more combinations for a creative exercise before a staff meeting. Inventing the new, as well as rearranging the old in a new way, are part of creativity and the analytical approach of forced attribute relationships and allows more creative ideas to flow, in this case using the senses.

Another suggestion is to use four colors of markers, or a four-color pen to record ideas. Use green for the outdoor ideas, red for the urgent ideas (e.g., remove or cover the asphalt under the play equipment), blue for things with a due date (plant bulbs in the fall), and black for the main body of notes. Also, more colors can be used for underlining major points and for elaborating with details. Imaginative people are inspired by working with colors and this simple technique can add life to problem solving sessions (Vance and Deacon, 1997).

Problem Redefinition

Whether creative problem-solving is done by an individual or a group, *redefinition of the problem* may be needed. While there are many redefinitional techniques, only a few will be reviewed in this chapter. Since those who work in programs for young children are usually quite creative, applying these skills to administration problems in this setting can be very useful. The book *Applied Imagination* by Alex Osborn (1960) is filled with additional ideas as are the books by Michael Michalko (1991, 1998).

- Questioning is always a favorite redefinition technique. Some sample questions might include: What would happen if I made it (the center, the program, etc.) larger? What if I made it smaller? What would happen if we turned it upside down (e.g., ran it all night instead of all day)? What if we put it on the top floor instead of the bottom floor? (Or the bottom floor instead of the top floor?) What if we rearrange it differently?
- Restating the problem by using key beginning phrases is another helpful redefinition technique:

    What would I do if I had three wishes?

    You could also define the problem as . . .

The main point of the problem is . . .

The problem, put in another way, is like . . .

Another, even stranger, way of looking at it is . . .

The worst thing that could happen is . . .

- Another creative redefinition approach is the "List Ten Ways This Can Be Done" method (or "List Ten Ways This Might Look," or some other similar phrasing that helps generate ten aspects of a problem).

- Another redefinition technique is to ask the question "How does a similar event occur in nature?" This tactic is sometimes called the Bionic Approach. An example of this method might be: If a mighty oak grows from a little acorn, maybe a system of child-care centers can be grown from an acorn of an idea.

Boundary Examinations

Another type of problem-solving technique, the boundary examination, involves first writing down the problem. Then, underline the nouns, verbs, and adjectives. Using a dictionary or thesaurus, find two or three substitutes for each underlined word. This technique produces new ways to define a problem and thus can yield new solutions. For example:

Solutions that arise from this particular boundary examination include setting aside time for talking with parents during the lunch hour, or scheduling parent education meetings in the evenings to help parents deal with stress in their lives. The education meetings might include help with child-raising, career strategies, and methods for understanding and resolving conflicts with children or the center.

PROBLEM:

Angry   mothers take up too much of the teacher's

(upset)   (caretakers)   (counselor's)

(frustrated)   (relatives)   (administrator's)

time at the beginning of the morning.

(hours)   (mid-morning)

(minutes)   (lunch time)

(attention)   (evening)

FIGURE 5.4
Boundary Examinations

Wishful Thinking

Wishful thinking, another creative problem-solving technique, can make a valuable contribution to formal problem-solving situations. To begin, have participants complete the sentence: "If I could break all the constraints, I would. . . ." For example, experts who conduct budgeting seminars always advise organizations to design an "ideal budget," or one that is based on what is really needed and wanted, and then work backwards to tailor the budget to what can be afforded. Beginning this way rather than starting out with an "actual budget," or one that is based on the present dollar amount, allows a record to be made of the organization's priorities and goals, so that when money does become available, it can be better used. In child-care situations, sometimes one of a center's dreams becomes the latest trend in programs that receive government grants. One center posted a long sheet of paper inside the director's office. As people thought of ideas, they jotted them down on this "wish list." When requests for proposals came from the state or federal government, the center checked the list to find any topics that matched. One year, for example, programs involving helping the elderly and other programs focusing on reading were the ones that were most successful in acquiring grants. The center developed a proposal and subsequently received funding for an "Adop-

Predicting what will happen next is part of learning for children and adults.

tive Grandparents" program that featured older adult volunteers who read to the children, cuddled them, and helped them with learning activities in the classroom.

Many kinds of restraints can be ignored in wishful thinking. The size of the building, the salary of workers, or the training budget are only a few examples. This wishful thinking device sets up new thinking patterns. The next phase is to return to the practical realm with statements such as: "I can't really do that, but I *can do*. . . ."

Analogies and Metaphors

Devices often found in early childhood storybooks—analogies and metaphors— can also be used in administration. An *analogy* is a direct comparison between two objects or ideas that have similar characteristics. In contrast, a *metaphor* is a figure of speech in which one word or phrase is used in place of another object or idea to show the similarity between the two. For example, "the ship of state" and referring to old age as "the evening of life" are both metaphors. It is said that Aristotle thought that metaphors were the highest form of thought (Michalko, 1998).

Both analogies and metaphors are useful in problem-solving because they generate data and help to produce ideas about or solutions to a problem. Metaphors are more powerful because they demand a greater change of perspective, but both devices help participants see new principles. For example, when considering the metaphor "evening of life," the images called to mind might include softening light, singing birds, and quietness. Other common metaphors include "quiet leadership," "bear hug," "paper shuffler," or even "brainstorming." Many women who own small businesses use the analogy of "bearing a child and watching it grow" to describe their feelings about their enterprise. To them, this analogy captures the great joy of creating something where before there had been nothing.

A discussion that involves analogies can be a useful introduction to a group creative problem-solving session in which participants will be using brainstorming or synectics techniques. A current discussion topic in education is the role of child-care personnel. One analogy is that child-care personnel serve as "architects," helping the parent develop the child according to the parent's goals. An opposing view is that of the child-care staff serving as "physicians," diagnosing ills and prescribing cures. When deciding which role your center supports, both analogies generate a whole cluster of concepts and thus create good springboards for discussion at either staff or parent meetings. Another possible analogy is that of the director as a "nurturing parent," since both directors and parents are concerned with the growth of those for whom they have responsibility.

Direct analogy, which can be denoted by the words "as if," might be used in certain situations to benefit everyone involved. For example, suggest to the child-care staff that they consider rude parents "as if" these parents had experienced a terrible tragedy in the past. This builds compassion and patience in the listener before the parent even begins talking and may even be true but unknown.

Creating Ideas

In thinking of ways to add value to your center, innovation is always attractive and creating something original or adding to or improving services that have already been provided adds freshness. But how does one think about this? You can begin by making a large chart or matrix with place, people and product (in this case good child care) written along the side. (Vance and Deacon, 1997). For a variety of perspectives, look at two or more of the following:

A new *invention* might be to offer appealing and good child care not only during the daytime, but also on evenings and weekends. This might mean hiring a Weekend and Evening Coordinator (or Associate/Assistant Director) to supervise the additional hours with staff. It also would mean developing a fee structure, although this service would maximize an expensive asset of most centers: the actual location and a place that the children know and trust.

An *extension* might be to choose an especially good part of your program and offer extra versions of it on Saturday mornings or afternoons. A large muscle/gym class; a story program, perhaps with puppets; or a singing or

I. Place (ECE Center)	**Inventions** *(What's new?)*	**Things** *(Selling toys and materials for parents—e.g. photocopies of Appendix A HLE's?)*
II. People (Our staff is great—add consultants for gym and computers?)	**Extensions** *(What could be extended?)*	**Thoughts** *(Thinking activities for children? See Appendices)*
III. Good Child Care (Add appealing and good child care on evenings and weekends for center enrollees?)	**Uninventions** *(What can be replaced— how to use the Internet—for communication with parents, staff and the public?)* Functional Substitutions *Flexibility?*	**Social Relationships** *(Work more with parents? Community? Politicians?)*

FIGURE 5.5
Creating New Inventions

music and dance program would spotlight your center and perhaps generate extra income. Even a "parent-child computer class" with bring-your-own-laptops would be a fresh new innovation that promotes the appeal of your center. This class could feature many children's CD-ROMs and software and show parents how to distinguish the good from the developmentally inappropriate. (Is the print too small, when it appears? Does the child just watch or listen while the voice reads aloud?)

An *"uninvention"* is a term for an invention or idea that reduces the effect of another invention or of competition in your geographic area. For instance, showcasing good child care "uninvents" using the television as a babysitter, by showing how much children are involved, actively participating and learning in developmentally appropriate programs.

Functional substitutions show how one invention substituted for another can also create fresh and original new approaches. Substituting "open snack" for snack time is one example. Computers that replace typesetting for books are another functional substitution. Creating an Internet website for your center and allowing parents of prospective enrollees to sign up for tours or even having your own "on-line" tour to substitute for "live" tours, substitutes easier-to-manage electronic means for live visits and phone calls and shows parents what a wonderful center it is. An interactive registration form or tour sign-up form would give the center access to information about interested parents and new geographic areas the center might expand into. These potential enrollees could also be added to your mailing list for receiving center notices and newsletters to again showcase what an excellent program your center offers.

Drawing a Model

Several problem-solving approaches suggest drawing a situation model of the problem to show the relationships involved. The model could contain boxes or circles, much like the models for scenarios shown in chapter 3 on planning. As shown in Figure 5.6, the situation model's developer can expand this basic outline of the problem or situation by drawing boxes that show elements that are outside of the problem but that are closely related to it. Broken lines are used to connect these "outside" elements to the main problem. This method of expansion can uncover the possible causes of or factors in a problem and can encourage decision-making or planning.

◇ ◇

GROUP TECHNIQUES

Individual analytical techniques, such as creating a checklist or listing pros and cons, can also be done effectively in a group. Decision aids can be

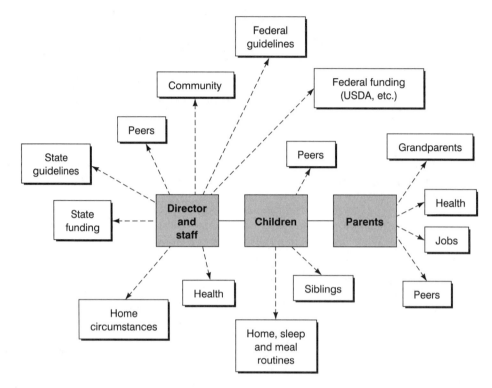

FIGURE 5.6
Factors Outside of the Situation Model

processed individually or in a group as well. (More suggestions about using decision aids can be found in chapter 4 on decision-making.) One of the best methods for group problem-solving might be to address the following five questions:

What is the problem?

Who needs to be involved?

What more do we need to know?

What would an ideal solution be?

What would be the first step(s) in realizing a solution?

For more details on organization and communication add eight more questions:

What needs to be done?

Who needs to do it?

When should it be completed?

What will be required in training and education for this to happen?

Who needs to know?

What do they need to know?

When do they need to know it?

What ways would communicate this best?

Using these questions to begin a group discussion can uncover a problem and result in some solutions, which can be written on a chalkboard or flip chart for later consideration.

The creative group techniques that will be discussed in this section include brainstorming and synectics. Brainstorming during a problem-solving session produces a great number of ideas but does not necessarily provide more insight into the overall problem. Adding the technique of "cardstorming," described below, helps to capture and organize these ideas. Synectics, unlike brainstorming, requires someone to play the part of the client with the problem. This method produces fewer, but more in-depth, solutions.

Brainstorming

When using the brainstorming technique at a parent or staff meeting, it works best when the group becomes familiarized with the topic about to be discussed. This warm-up may be as simple as a detailed description of the issues to be considered. The questions listed in the previous section provide a good practice drill for solving various problems. After using this particular warm-up exercise, the group can brainstorm about possible first steps. Before the group discussion begins, an individual warm-up activity might be to ask each person to write down three or more ideas about the topic or to suggest three possible solutions.

The brainstorming procedure is divided into two parts. The first part involves idea generation, and includes set rules for this stage:

1. All ideas are given equal respect.
2. There is no criticism of any suggestion, no matter how impractical.
3. All ideas are written down on a chalkboard or flip chart that can be seen by the group. This allows everyone to view the ideas and build on other members' suggestions or link ideas.
4. Add "cardstorming" next for large initiatives.

Writing down the ideas sets the stage for the second part of brainstorming in which the ideas are ranked or given priority. One approach to ranking is to give every group member 3 to 7 votes (depending on the total number of ideas that will be ranked). By allowing 3 to 7 votes per person rather than just one, greater nuances within a solution are revealed. As voting occurs, a natural ranking appears. If the client or person with the problem is present, it should always be made clear that he or she may choose among *all* the solutions generated by the group, and need not follow the solutions ranked high by the group. The client, after all, knows the problem most intimately; he or she may have received new insights during the idea-generation session and might prefer to use one of these discoveries instead of the ideas voted on by the group.

Cardstorming

A variation on brainstorming that captures ideas in a more flexible way, rather than just listing them, is called "cardstorming." Using 5 X 8 or 4 X 6 cards, ask each person in the group to write on three cards, three responses or ideas involving major elements of a problem that have been identified in brainstorming. If the group hasn't yet identified major elements, category headings for notes on cards can include: major points, resources, recommendations, definitions, applications, background, and perhaps miscellaneous headings for the loose ends. These headings or the element headings then can be taped across the top of a board. As the card responses come in, they can be read aloud and placed into the correct column. This exercise helps uncover details about unknown aspects of a problem or about making processes work. Activities from these cards can then be placed on a Time Line or a Calendar. If there are tasks that need to be assigned, an Assignment Chart or a Communication Chart can be added, as well as a schedule for making sure the proper communications are made (to the Board? the parents? the general public? your suppliers? the children?). As a project or program progresses, various people can be assigned the duty of keeping the Time Line and other charts current. These people can keep track of what's been done, what's under way, what's left to do, new inputs and any hindrances or obstructions. When leadership begins thinking and functioning using these tools, the organization will grow and develop in new ways as never before (Vance and Deacon, 1997).

Reverse Brainstorming

Reverse brainstorming is also a useful technique. To approach the problem using this method, ask: "What are all the possible ways things could go wrong?" In other words, reverse brainstorming is a way of looking at the problem from the reverse side of the discussion question.

Synectics

Synectics is a Greek word that means "joining together different and apparently irrelevant elements." In this context, synectics is a group problem-solving technique that joins together different people and their different ideas. It requires a leader to serve as a facilitator and also requires a "client." The client has the ultimate say as to whether a solution will work or not, as he or she "owns" the problem. The client also can decide how to correct a factor that blocks the use of a particular solution. The group's role is to act as a "think tank" for the client. While the client is the evaluator in this technique, other group members can hear the ideas generated and see them written on a flip chart or chalkboard and are thus free to use them in their own way.

After providing a suitable warm-up for the group, staff, or Board during which time the situation is described, the facilitator writes out the problem, defined in an open-ended way, for all to see. Solutions then are generated by the group and are written in columns below the problem, as shown in Figure 5.7. After this step is completed, the client is asked to respond to the solutions and give them a plus or minus rating. If a solution is given a minus sign, a comment about why the solution would not work is written on the visual aid. The minus responses are then addressed by asking "How to avoid" questions, and new solutions are generated. Figure 5.8 shows this approach to solving the broad current problem of how to have a U.S. policy on child care, the subject that was addressed by a graduate public administration class in policy analysis. This topic is a good discussion springboard for a professional association meeting or other similar group.

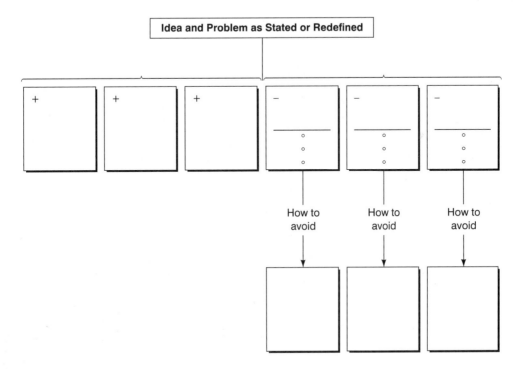

FIGURE 5.7
Synectics Model

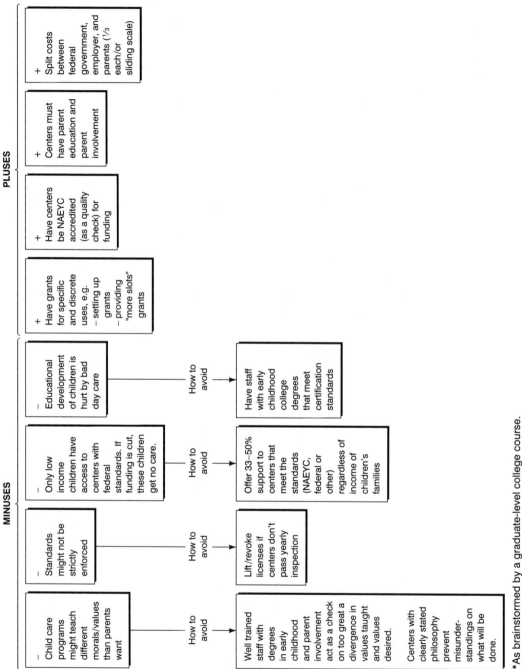

MINUSES

PLUSES

- Child care programs might teach different morals/values than parents want

- Standards might not be strictly enforced

- Only low income children have access to centers with federal standards. If funding is cut, these children get no care.

- Educational development of children is hurt by bad day care

+ Have grants for specific and discrete uses, e.g.
  – setting up grants
  – providing "more slots" grants

+ Have centers be NAEYC accredited (as a quality check) for funding

+ Centers must have parent education and parent involvement

+ Split costs between federal government, employer, and parents (⅓ each/or sliding scale)

How to avoid

How to avoid

How to avoid

How to avoid

Well trained staff with degrees in early childhood and parent involvement act as a check on too great a divergence in values taught and values desired.

Centers with clearly stated philosophy prevent misunder-standings on what will be done.

Lift/revoke licenses if centers don't pass yearly inspection

Offer 33–50% support to centers that meet the standards (NAEYC, federal or other) regardless of income of children's families

Have staff with early childhood college degrees that meet certification standards

*As brainstormed by a graduate-level college course.

FIGURE 5.8
How to Have a U.S. Policy on Child Care (Synectics Problem-Solving Example)

124

◊ ◊

SUMMARY

Since problem-solving is a continuing component of administering and managing programs for young children, applying creativity to problem-solving can encourage educators as well as uncover new ideas. Unleashing the tremendous creativity and innovative potential of those who work in early childhood education and who are already on the payroll can yield unexpected dividends. Early childhood educators know that creativity builds children's self-esteem; it also builds adults' self-esteem and feelings of competence. By reading through this chapter and trying some of the ideas, perhaps beginning with a small sphere of influence before branching out to a larger one, educators may find the inspiration needed in working with young children. Figure 5.9 gives a useful overview of the techniques discussed in this chapter and categorizes them as individual or group techniques and as creative or analytic approaches. Many of the cre-

INDIVIDUAL	**EITHER**	**GROUP**
Creative	*Analytic*	*Creative*
1. Morphological analysis and attribute lists	1. Checklists and attribute lists	1. Brainstorming
2. Redefining the problem	2. Decision trees and other aids	2. Synectics
3. Reversals	3. Six-question approach	
4. How is it done in nature?	4. Computer-aided projections and scenarios	
5. Boundary examinations		
6. Drawing a model		
7. Wishful thinking, big dream, inspired approach		
8. Analogy and metaphor		
9. Questioning		
10. Ten ways this can be done		

FIGURE 5.9
Creative and Analytical, Individual and Group Problem-Solving Techniques

ative approaches listed under individual techniques also make interesting and useful exercises for groups or classes.

Decision-making, as opposed to problem-solving, is usually future-oriented because it is concerned with future consequences and the probability of success. According to Peter Drucker (1977), problem-solving often looks back at a particular situation. That is, when a problem is solved, a decision is no longer needed because things are restored to "normal," or to a "steady state." On the other hand, decisions lead to change and to changed circumstances, so that problem-solving often is needed again.

If directors see change as opportunity, when small problems occur, they are more inclined to practice problem-solving techniques ahead of time, whether alone or in groups. Directors with this perspective are better equipped to make decisions that focus on the future and that create a new optimal stage for their centers. Effective follow-up to problem-solving sessions—both to assess growth after using various techniques and to identify the adequacy of these techniques—can occur in the form of three-month, six-month, and twelve-month check-ups with staff members. Taking the time to look back on a particular problem and to reflect on the chosen solution, or to build upon the solution at the present time, is a useful exercise and an essential part of evaluation and reflection in practice. Large corporations use this method to follow up with managers in order to assess adaptation, growth, and change after six and twelve months. Child-care programs could also benefit from the use of this reflection process.

Several analytical approaches can be used to predict success. These can include:

1. Asking "What will guarantee success? What will guarantee failure?"
2. Listing "Our Expectations" and "Our Concerns," in separate columns, to facilitate analysis.
3. Listing "Anticipated Risks" and "Ways of Overcoming Risks," in separate columns, in a device similar to synectics.

To disregard some of the negative questions that are likely to be asked when a new plan is being considered would be ignoring reality. Using these analytical approaches to sharpen the issues, and facilitating the analysis by thinking through both positive and negative aspects, helps prepare the director and/or staff for their new optimal stage or plan.

One final list of some common "do's and don'ts" in problem-solving might include the following:

- Try to identify the real problem, not just symptoms of the problem.
- Identify the "owner" of the problem if possible. Asking the wrong group to solve the problem can lead to resentment, noncooperation, and even charges of meddling.

- Try to identify all the possible alternatives, since high-quality problem-solving and decision-making require a good look at all the choices.
- Develop a written plan for implementation. No solution is better than the plan to activate it. This means getting consensus on who does what, how, and when.
- Monitor the implementation. Appoint a monitor, coordinator, or trouble-shooter who can use time and staffing charts developed jointly. Using flip charts, rough drafts of these can be developed at consensus meetings and then later refined. This avoids bottlenecks, frustrations, finger-pointing, and slippages. One center even organized a "problem-solving committee" with representatives from each classroom that met once a month to share ideas on how to improve working conditions in various ways. They acknowledged the problem, came up with practical solutions, and monitored the implementation.

The best problem-solving situation supports and facilitates decision-making and helps programs advance to a more optimal stage or condition. Using problem-solving techniques helps the director and the group progress through each of the following stages: generating ideas, making a decision, planning a course of action, considering alternatives, planning, implementing, operating, and evaluating. A trained facilitator even can be brought in to help solve serious problems or decisions that will affect a large percentage of the program's resources.

Problem-solving often uncovers the need for more resources or better operational systems, and the next two sections deal with ongoing implementation and operational issues such as working with parents, legally and medically related issues, and facilities, equipment, room arrangement, scheduling, finances, and proposal development.

◇ ◇ ◇ ◇ ◇ ◇ ◇ ◇ ◇ ◇ ◇ ◇ ◇ ◇ ◇ ◇ ◇ ◇ ◇ ◇

SUGGESTED CLASS ACTIVITIES AND DISCUSSIONS

1. *Blocks to Problem Solving: Discussion and Brainstorming.*   Discuss six types of blocks to problem solving and write them as column heads across a board. Types of blocks and possible examples under each one include: (These are real examples from a class.)

Perceptual blocks—such as not being observant every day as to what is really happening; bringing perceptions from a former job or boss to this job.

Cultural blocks—such as "playfulness is for children only"; "fantasy is a waste of time and is lazy"; "problem solving should be serious and not humorous"; "tradition is better than change."

Environmental blocks—such as lack of trust and support in the organization; or having an autocratic boss.

Physical blocks—such as telephone calls and interruptions.

Emotional blocks (since creativity occurs in the subconscious)—such as the ego saying "I can't do it"; the super ego saying "don't think that way"; fear of failure; not being able to tolerate ambiguity; fear of success; inability to relax and "sleep on it"; delays.

Intellectual blocks—such as inability to communicate.

The class can brainstorm and add to each list as students think of more examples for each type of block.

2. *Assets and Liabilities of Group and Individual Problem Solving.*   List column headings on the board for "Assets" and "Liabilities." This enables a group discussion on the processes of problem solving. At the left of this matrix, list "Group" and below it "Individual" headings. Examples of *group* problem solving *assets* include: a greater sum of knowledge available; a less informed person may volunteer unique contributions; a greater number of approaches are possible; participation increases acceptance, gains mutual goals, and better comprehension of the decision and gives strengthened social support and exchange; and the group reduces the individuals' fear of total responsibility unless so designated. These group assets become the *Individual Liabilities* as an individual problem solving loses these assets.

Assets for individual problem solving include: one pursues one's own philosophy; and one can feel good about one's self and about the decision. Additional group liabilities become individual assets and include: groups may provide a low-quality decision with a high rate of acceptance (although this can be more effective than a high-quality decision with low acceptance). The class can further brainstorm assets and liabilities for group and individual problem solving.

3. Problem Redefinition and Restructuring Exercise.   The class can identify several problems that are important to them in a center setting. Try some of the redefinition techniques described in the text on appropriate problems, such as questioning and restating the problem, boundary examinations, wishful thinking, and analogies or metaphors. Restructuring may be needed after redefinition and questions to ask the client (the person with the problem) include: Is time a factor? Is the problem within your control? Does the group need an outside consultant to come in and provide more information? If time is not a problem (such as a proposal deadline due), more creative techniques can be used. If the problem is not within the client's control, then group techniques must be used. Many kinds of outside expertise or consulting might be helpful for particular problems such as landscape advice. This expertise might be available at little or no cost from the parent group or the community.

4. *Round Robin "Trigger Session Brainstorming."*   Class members jot down ideas for two minutes on a relatively easy problem such as: "Develop a menu guide for the center Parent's Dinner which is nutritious, easy to make, cheap, easy to buy, balanced and uses our special resources." Then share these ideas in groups of 5 or 6. Individuals can pass their ideas to the person on their left. Follow with a large group sharing of two ideas from each group. Comment on the process and how many *more* ideas were developed. Move on to more difficult problems.

5. *Synectics Practice Session.*   After introducing synectics as a process, role play a staff meeting in a child care center. The question under discussion might be: "How to have a parent education meeting on the discipline of three- and four-year olds." On one side of the board, list the benefits or pluses of such a meeting. On the other side of the board, list the minuses or problems of such a meeting. Below each problem identified, list a "How to Avoid" solution as shown in the chapter. In this discussion, one can interrupt the problem solving with an "excursion" or a "spur" with a question that invites speculation or a "far-out" answer or that invites an analogy. One analogy is "disciplining a four-year-old is like driving a fine race car—it can be all speed and no control; it can be wrecked with sudden turns; one must understand its mechanisms to drive it properly." Then return to the problem solving exercise and see if any new insights have been gained for the parent meeting.

◇ ◇ ◇ ◇ ◇ ◇ ◇ ◇ ◇ ◇ ◇ ◇ ◇ ◇ ◇ ◇ ◇ ◇ ◇

BIBLIOGRAPHY

Ackoff, R. L. (1987). *The art of problem solving.* New York: Wiley.

Ailes, R. (1994, January/February). Break the rules and win. *Success*, p. 37.

Blake, R. R., & Mouton, J. S. (1969). *Building a dynamic corporation through grid organization development.* Reading, MA: Addison-Wesley.

Cartwright, D., & Zander, A. (1960). *Group dynamics.* New York: Harper and Row.

Chase, S., & Chase, M. T. (1951). *Roads to agreement.* New York: Harper and Row.

Cummings, P. W. (1988). *Open management.* New York: American Management Associations.

Drucker, P. F. (1954). *The practice of management.* New York: Harper and Row.

Drucker, P. F. (1977, March/April). Peter Drucker on the manager and the organization. *Bulletin on Training*, p. 4.

Dyer, W. G. (1978). When is a problem a problem? *The Personnel Administrator*, pp. 66–71.

Eitington, J. E. (1984). *The winning trainer.* Houston, TX: Gulf Publishing.

Fisher, B. A. (1974). *Small group decision making: Communication and the group process.* New York: McGraw-Hill.

Harris, P. R. (1985). *Management in transition.* New York: Jossey-Bass.

Harrison, E. F. (1975). *The managerial decision-making process.* Boston: Houghton Mifflin.

Hawkens, P. (1987). *Growing a business.* New York: Simon & Schuster.

Hyman, R. T. (1975). *School administrator's handbook of teacher supervision and evaluation methods.* Upper Saddle River, NJ: Prentice Hall.

Kilmann, R. H. (1985). *Beyond the quick fix.* New York: Jossey-Bass.

Lakein, A. (1973). *How to get control of your time and your life.* New York: Signet/New American Library.

Lee, I. J. (1952). *How to talk with people.* New York: Harper & Row.

Likert, R. (1961). *New patterns of management.* New York: McGraw-Hill.

Likert, R. (1967). *The human organization: Its management and value.* New York: McGraw-Hill.

Marrow, A. J. (1972). *The failure of success.* New York: American Management Association.

McGregor, D. (1960). *The human side of enterprise.* New York: McGraw-Hill.

Miller, D., & Starr, M. (1967). *The structure of human decisions.* Upper Saddle River, NJ: Prentice Hall.

Murnighan, J. K. (1981, February). Group decision making: What strategies should you use? *Management Review*, pp. 55–62.

Osborn, A. (1960). *Applied imagination.* New York: Scribner's.

Parent Cooperative Preschools International. (1984). *Leadership development: A facilitator's handbook.* Indianapolis: Author.

Parnes, S. J., Noller, R. B., & Biondi, A. M. (1976). *Creative actionbook.* New York: Scribner's.

Parnes, S. J., Noller, R. B., & Biondi, A. M. (1977). *Guide to creative action.* New York: Scribner's.

Philips, M., & Rasberry, S. (1981). *Honest Business.* New York: Random House.

Pinchot, G. (1985). *Intrapreneuring.* New York: Harper & Row.

Rawlinson, J. G. (1981). *Creative thinking and brainstorming.* New York: Wiley.

Rich, D., & Jones-Shoemaker, C. (1978). *The three R's plus: Teaming families and schools for student achievement.* Washington, DC: The Home and School Institute.

Senge, P. (1990). *The fifth discipline: The art and practice of a learning organization.* New York: Doubleday.

Sinetar, M. (1991). *Developing a 21st century mind.* New York: Villard Books.

Sinetar, M. (1993). *Reel power.* New York: Liguori/Triumph Books.

Toffler, A. (1985). *The adaptive corporation.* New York: McGraw-Hill Books.

Torrance, E. P. (1962). *Guiding creative talent.* Upper Saddle River, NJ: Prentice Hall.

Ulschak, F. L., Nathanson, L., & Gillan, P. G. (1981). *Smallgroup problem solving: An aid to organizational effectiveness.* Reading, MA: Addison-Wesley.

Vance, M. & Deacon, D., (1997). *Think out of the box.* Franklin Lakes, NJ: Career Press.

Wiles, K., & Lovell, J. (1975). *Supervision for better schools.* Upper Saddle River, NJ: Prentice Hall.

Leadership and Implementation/Human Resources Issues

The first task in establishing an early childhood center, as discussed in Chapter 3, Planning, is to determine the center's philosophy. Once a philosophy has been decided, the tasks of team building, motivating and perhaps assembling or re-assembling a team to carry out this philosophy can begin. Staffing, training, motivating, team building, and displaying professionalism are all part of the reality of today's well-run programs for young children. These concerns are based on and go hand-in-hand with leadership, planning, decision-making, and problem-solving. Directors who are already experienced in running a child-care facility, but who are setting up a new center, might want to reread the previous chapters as they discuss the topics just listed. It might be a helpful review of the leadership foundations that successful human resources management rest upon. Although this book addresses center child care primarily, some suggestions could be adapted to family child-care settings as well.

Since human resources are the most valuable resources of an organization (Peters & Waterman, 1982), they are of prime importance in implementing programs. Readers who are would-be practitioners can think about how *they* would handle various situations if they were the administrators. Current administrators can adapt and apply suggestions. This book is based on the premise that every organization should be a learning organization. As Peter Senge (1990) laments, some organizations are not learning organizations but have "learning disabilities."

When the professional "team" within a program or center becomes aligned in a common direction, these individuals' energies harmonize. Less energy is wasted, and a shared vision and understanding of how to complement one another's efforts emerges. The shared vision becomes an extension of individuals' goals, such as "working for the best center in town," or "helping children reach their potential." When individual goals and directions are aligned, and many of the exercises in the following chapters promote this, then empowering the individual leads to empowering the whole team (Senge, 1990).

To maintain common goals and vision, however, there needs to be an ongoing "visioning process" in which personal and local ideas and visions continually interact with organizational ideas and visions. An organization's combination of shared purpose, vision, and values creates a common identity that can demonstrate great strength. Senge (1990) sees the chief task of directors, along with other leaders, as working to develop this common identity. However, it is important that the director be a curriculum leader and expert also. If the school has a project philosophy or wants to adopt one, or embraces the Reggio Emilia philosophy, then having staff attend workshops together, such as an "Emergent Curriculum Workshop," can initiate new ideas and a fresh approach to what may have become routine.

The idea of planning as a learning tool is a common theme in most of the chapters. Since children are always learning from others and from their environment, it is appropriate that adults be in a continuous learning environment also. Now that leadership, planning, and decision-making have been discussed, careful attention will have to be paid to staff selection. In addition, the development of staff is greatly enhanced by some of the group processes described in the previous chapters, and self-evaluation is also further enhanced by some of these processes. Teachers and family child care providers have valuable insights to offer, including insights on the implications of policy changes for children and families. Group processes encourage everyone to share their perspective and ensure the opportunity to do so. In considering issues about staff and human resources, keep in mind that what we know about how humans learn is not restricted to children; it is important that we pay attention to adult learning and growth as well (Jones, 1986). Today's learning organizations demand a new view of leadership, and the activities in all of the chapters will help in building a learning organization that espouses such leadership. Once an organization clearly develops its vision and exhibits it in many ways for all to see, the educational team can work together with energy and enthusiasm to make that vision a reality.

CHAPTER 6

Staff Selection, Development, and Evaluation

The careful choice of teaching and support staff is essential to the administration and management of a child-care center. The staff, and the staff training made available, are two key elements of a successful program. This chapter discusses the hiring committee, staff training and meetings, evaluation, and Advisory or Executive Board training. Sample staff evaluation forms are provided for use with programs, policies, and meetings.

◇ ◇

SELECTION

Careful staff selection, with a high priority given to "the most crucial staff characteristic" of combined training in early childhood education and child development, has an effect on whether child care "helps or harms children" (Kuykendall, 1990, p. 48). The National Day Care Study (Abt Associates, 1987) found that "only one teacher characteristic predicts program quality and effectiveness: the amount of job-related training in early childhood education that a teacher has received" (Schweinhart, Koshel, & Bridgeman, 1987, p. 527). In this study, caregivers with such training delivered better care resulting in somewhat better developmental effects for children (Snow, 1983; Abt Associates, 1987). By establishing specific requirements that caregivers must meet in order to be hired, such as having a background in early childhood education and child development, a director can ask the Executive Board for help with the hiring process. Spreading the decision-making over a larger group, instead of relegating the responsibility to the director alone, provides a learning opportunity for the parents and/or community Board members involved. Unfortunately, recent studies have shown that among center-based teachers nationally, only approximately one third have earned a bachelor's degree or higher degree (Whitebook, Howes, & Phillips, 1990; Cost, Quality, and Child Outcomes Study Team, 1995; Whitebook, 1997).

The Hiring Committee

An Executive Board with a hiring committee composed of three to five members can be extremely helpful to a director, both by assisting with telephoning and screening tasks, and, as mentioned previously, by allowing the decision-making to be spread over a larger group. The director should make clear to the chairperson of the hiring committee the amount of education and experience that are minimum requirements for the job. Application forms should be sent only to those applicants who qualify. Interviews can then be scheduled and handled by the hiring committee, the director, and perhaps a teacher. The interview sessions should be conducted as a group interaction, with one person, perhaps the committee chairperson, acting as the lead speaker. During the process of hiring aides, the director may want just one teacher present rather than the entire hiring committee, or he or she may prefer to have the committee's help.

The Interview

Since the interview is an important component of the hiring process, the following sample format is provided to help readers construct a pattern that benefits their own specific situations. At the beginning of the interview, after introductions, the chairperson might begin by asking the applicant to describe his or her education and training. Following this, questions relating to experience in the field and how the applicant would handle various situations that can arise with individual children yield much useful information. Some sample questions might be:

- How would you handle two children who are fighting?
- How would you handle a child who stands outside the group, continuously sucking his thumb?
- How would you handle a child who disrupts quiet activities by running about and hitting other children?
- How might you further enhance learning during art experiences or during story time?

Always remember to ask "How is your health?" and to check references carefully. In some jurisdictions, fingerprinting and a negative TB test are also required. Be aware that the person may have strengths in interacting with adults but not with children, or with children and not adults. The reference check will help uncover these possibilities. Qualities of loving and caring for and about children are, of course, paramount.

Applicants should be made aware of expectations that go along with becoming a part of the center's team. For example, regular training and staff meetings featuring new ideas for the curriculum should be offered at least once a month; such programs are important components of having employees become assets to the center, and of offering a quality program that is developmentally appropriate for children.

◊ ◊

DEVELOPMENT

The importance of providing training and development updates to all of the adults involved with a child-care center (staff, Executive Board members, and parents) cannot be emphasized too greatly. The more these involved adults understand the goals of developmental children's programs and know what excellent programs look like and aspire to, the more helpful a center will be to children and families. As a center focuses on children's needs, excellence and quality will emerge in the program. This quality is characterized by establishing goals that exceed minimum state regulation or certification requirements in terms of meeting the needs of children and families, and in terms of building a professionally accepted knowledge base. To make such goals a reality, the budget needs to provide for the development of staff, Executive Board members, and parents.

Staff Training

Position statements from professional organizations consistently mandate knowledge of child development and early childhood education as a requisite for teaching (Bredekamp, 1987; Gotts, 1988; National Association of State Boards of Education, 1988). As part of the staff, directors also need this knowledge base; a director's lack of education in the area of child development and/or curriculum can "frustrate and impede the work of skilled teachers" (Kuykendall, 1990, p. 49). Directors who lack child development knowledge, and who consequently hire staff without making child development expertise a priority, can perpetuate this frustration on the part of the staff. A director without this background can take courses to gain it.

While another source of this training is through professional organizations and associations, research by Whitebook, Howes, and Phillips (1990) showed that only 14% of center staff teachers belong to any professional or occupational group. Nearly 25% of Head Start employees belong to a union but virtually no for-profit center staff did (Morin, 1991). While licensed or regulated family child care providers or those involved in the Child Care Food Program may be associated with family child care associations (Galinsky et al., 1991), the majority of child care employees do not participate in organizations or classes that might enable them to build validated and sanctioned leadership skills, as well as other skills. Family child care providers have an even more difficult time participating in training activities of any kind—or leadership and advocacy activities—because they work exceedingly long hours with no provision for paid leave and substitute coverage (Whitebook, 1997).

Meeting Format and Structure

Regular weekly meetings for all staff, during which announcements are made and one learning area is explored each week, build a firm foundation of excellence for a child-care center. If all the aides and teachers cannot be free at the same time (such as during the children's nap time), a rotating schedule could be established, or half the group could meet on each of two days. Such an arrangement allows all the staff to participate without dividing it along lines of educational background (which may create conflict and lead to a divisive atmosphere).

Meeting Content

In deciding what topics to cover in staff training meetings, one successful format is to have two weekly meetings per month on curriculum content areas, a third weekly meeting on administrative matters and problem-solving, and a fourth weekly meeting on special topics such as (1) working with parents; (2) special problems children encounter including divorce, death, adoption, and foster care (see chapters 11 and 12); (3) caring for children with disabilities; and (4) other topics drawn from the multitude of child-care issues.

As training sessions are set up, keep in mind that the best learning, for adults as well as for children, occurs as a result of doing. A center might select 10 to 12 curriculum topics to cover in a 6- to 12-month period, such as block building, art, science, nature, or physical fitness, plus supervisory topics. Then, as the director observes good examples of these topics in classroom activities, he or she can ask different teachers to make half-hour presentations of their activities and then allow a second half hour for the staff members to actually *do* the activity. These training sessions might be preceded by distributing handouts or articles from journals on the "Topic of the Week." The opening or closing half hour of a 90-minute meeting could be used for the usual announcements and routine business.

Teacher aide curriculum meetings might include developing classroom activities similar to the Program Enrichment Papers in Appendix C. Small groups could be made responsible for designing an activity focused on the theme under discussion in that particular week's meeting. A curriculum library or resource center stocked with books and materials relating to discussion topics and activities can be a valuable resource for a center.

The once-a-month special topics training session can be facilitated and enhanced by (1) distributing and then discussing articles on given topics; (2) scheduling guest speakers; (3) watching videos or other resources; (4) reading and discussing a particular book; or (5) listening to a report from a staff member reporting on a college or university course he or she is taking. Some centers use these types of training sessions to discuss particular children who exhibit a problem related to the topic of discussion, but others consider this an invasion of privacy. Often, scheduling a "toy patching" session quarterly or twice a year provides a valuable learning time by allowing a chance for staff members to openly share feelings while their hands are kept busy. The Program Enrichment Papers in Appendix C also give more ideas for teachers' and aides' curriculum planning.

The monthly meeting on administrative topics provides a scheduled time for discussing organizational matters. Directors of large centers might want to divide extra responsibilities among the staff, one for each, according to their preferences, such as:

1. planning and scheduling field trips,
2. checking supplies inventory,
3. checking playroom maintenance,
4. organizing parent education programs,
5. serving as liaison for continuing education, and
6. serving as representative to community groups.

These assignments can change each year, and, in addition to spreading the responsibilities over a wider group, this system enables other professionals in the center to have input and learn about the over-all needs of the program. Chapter 1 lists more "job descriptions" that can be shared among parents, volunteers, or paid staff.

Beginning staff can find more references and resources in such materials as the Child Care Information Exchange's "Beginnings" series and through NAEYC materials. Perhaps a big sister/mentor program can be established within a center or across a small group of centers with senior staff and "junior" (or new) staff.

Board Member Training

If the center has an Advisory Board and/or a Parent Executive Board, the director will need to plan to train these Board members, or to assist with training if this is the responsibility of others. As the principal proponent of and educational resource for excellent early childhood education in the program, the director's input into Board training is invaluable and should not be omitted, even though Board members serve on a volunteer basis. Understanding the goals and needs of a good child-care program and its facility is essential if Board members are to perform well on the ongoing Board committees. A Board manual containing job descriptions, written in the early stages of the center's operation, is very helpful and eases the director's job.

When training Board members, the director should have in mind the kinds of committees the Board will comprise. Some useful Board committees include an equipment and supplies committee, a purchasing committee, a marketing and public relations committee, a hiring committee, a newsletter committee, and a parent education committee. As an example of ways to involve the Board, one center, for one of its fall orientation meetings that included both the Board and the staff, had the group watch a film showing good developmental child care. Before the film, one-third of the group was assigned to observe the teacher's interactions with the children; one-third was to observe the equipment and supplies in use; and one-third was to look for ideas that could be used in public relations and advertising. A discussion of quality child care followed the film, and then each group reported back with their observations. Other films could be analyzed in a similar way. Chapter 1 lists additional ways to involve Board members and utilize their expertise.

Attending Professional Meetings

Attending professional association meetings and conferences is another valuable form of staff and Board member training. The overall effectiveness of the center can be greatly enhanced if the attendees are asked to report on interesting new ideas they have learned from a meeting or conference. Communication research reports that if an individual member of a group sorts through material and reports back to the group, the group makes an assumption that useless aspects of the material have been discarded; as a result, group members attend to the presentation of a colleague with more interest (Rogers & Shoemaker, 1971).

◇ ◇

EVALUATION

Yearly evaluations along with self-evaluation exercises encourage an employee to improve his or her own performance and goals. For example, the teacher checklist in Figure 6.1 shows a sample self-evaluation form that helps teachers determine whether decision-making in the classroom is based on structure or child preferences.

The group evaluation sheets shown in Figures 6.2, 6.3, and 6.4 will help facilitate yearly center evaluations. All of these evaluations (Figures 6.1 to 6.4) can be distributed and collected once or twice a year, kept in a folder, and then reviewed in a one-to-one meeting with a staff member to see how (or if) things have changed for the center in general, or the individual in particular.

As stated previously, updating both new and experienced employees on recent developments in early childhood education and building a climate of respect, help employees reach their peak performance. Encouraging new employees to ask questions also eases their transition onto the center staff.

◇ ◇

SUMMARY

Hiring the best staff possible and providing regular, well-organized staff training is very important to a well-run center. By providing opportunities for interaction in a number of ways while keeping all eyes on the goal of a developmentally appropriate curriculum and center, a happy and productive adult team can be established. Part 2 addressed the leadership role of the director and included discussions on power, planning, decision-making, and creative and analytical problem-solving, all issues that are also of central importance in human resource management. The following chapters on team building, motivation, and professionalism give more insights into the dynamics of human resource issues.

Yes	No		Child-Care Center Characteristics
___	___	1.	Children move freely about the playroom and playground.
___	___	2.	Children select and use materials without adult interference.
___	___	3.	All children usually engage in the same activity at the same time.
___	___	4.	Children are expected to join in and remain with a group activity that is directed.
___	___	5.	Children's activities are interrupted when the clock says it is time for the next scheduled activity.
___	___	6.	Children may spend as much time as they choose to complete their work or their play.
___	___	7.	Group activities are encouraged more than are individual activities.
___	___	8.	Loud and boisterous play is prohibited at all times.
___	___	9.	The teacher requires materials and equipment to be shared, regardless of the child, situation, or activity.
___	___	10.	Materials and equipment are always put away by the children following their use of them.
___	___	11.	The teacher often sits near an activity without entering into it, indirectly encouraging and facilitating play.
___	___	12.	Adults talk and listen to a child on a face-to-face level.
___	___	13.	When children speak, offer ideas, contribute suggestions, share an experience, etc., adults listen to them.
___	___	14.	The teacher and other adults tell children what to do.
___	___	15.	The physical environment, with its clearly defined centers of interest, tells children what they may do.
___	___	16.	Children are required to walk in line when moving from place to place.
___	___	17.	Children speak only when given permission.
___	___	18.	The teacher positively acknowledges children's contributions whether they are ideas, suggestions, experiences, or actions.
___	___	19.	Children wait for teacher instructions and patterns before constructing their own products.
___	___	20.	The teacher and other adults speak to children in positive language.
___	___	21.	Children's requests, desires, or wishes often are ignored.
___	___	22.	The teacher and other adults freely give praise to children for each child's efforts.
___	___	23.	Children initiate ideas and plans for work and play, and adults are available to help the children carry them out.
___	___	24.	The schedule of the day's events or plans is rigidly adhered to.
___	___	25.	Materials and equipment for the children's use are placed where children can help themselves to them.

FIGURE 6.1
Teacher Checklist

Program Evaluation for 20____ to 20____ (year)

Please fill in the blanks as honestly as you possibly can, so we can strive for better programming in the coming year. You do not have to sign this.

1. The working conditions are _____

2. The staff I work with is _____

3. The equipment is _____

4. The food is _____

5. The supplies are _____

6. The coordinators are _____

7. My working surroundings are _____

8. My training was/is _____

9. Communication is _____ _____

10. The growth of the children has been _____

11. My supervision/supervisor has been _____

FIGURE 6.2
Program Evaluation

12. Cleanliness of site/office/classroom, etc., has been _____
    _____
    _____

13. Administration is _____
    _____
    _____

14. The director has _____
    _____
    _____
    _____

15. The agency (if appropriate) has _____
    _____
    _____

16. The parents have _____
    _____
    _____
    _____

17. The volunteers have _____
    _____
    _____
    _____

18. Other: _____
    _____
    _____
    _____

Additional Comments:

Program Evaluation, *continued*

**Policies and Procedures
Worksheet for 20____ to 20____**

Please list items that you would like to see specific policy on to avoid confusion and disagreement. This will aid in better communication come September of the coming year.

Policy: _____
_____

Procedure: _____
_____
_____

Policy: _____
_____

Procedure: _____
_____
_____

Policy: _____
_____

Procedure: _____
_____
_____

**FIGURE 6.3
Policies and Procedures Worksheet**

1. The staff meeting was:
   Boring ____   Too Long ____   All Right ____
   Exciting ____   Well-organized ____   Unplanned ____

2. I am   glad ____   sorry ____   I came.

3. I think staff meetings should be _____
   _____
   _____

4. The luncheon was   tasty ____,   enough ____,   not enough ____,
   unnecessary _____,   nice _____.

5. I suggest _____ at _____ for staff
             day   time
   meetings in September.

**FIGURE 6.4
Staff Meeting Evaluation**

Case Study: An April Visit to a Sunshine Program

Context: One state's child development regulations for state funded programs included a Program Quality Review—much like a "self-study" in accreditation processes for higher education. Then a Coordinated Compliance Review occurred a year later to see if any gaps identified in the self-study were closed and specific, listed requirements were met.

A large and varied child care program of 112 children included a preschool program for three- to five-year-olds and a toddler (two-year-old) all day program in one building, and an after-school program for kindergartners in another building from 11:30 A.M. on. First, second, and third graders arrived later. Some of the space in the second school-age building was used by the preschool groups in the morning. The groups were arranged according to the teachers names and the children were roughly divided by age, ability and special needs, such as having limited English-speaking skills. Where possible, a child was placed in a group with a teacher who spoke his or her language. One teacher was taking Spanish courses at the local community college and the children were enjoying helping her learn by correcting her words. The parents who spoke little English were emboldened to try out their skills with this teacher as they heard her mistakes in trying to speak their language.

The Center had just held an "emergent curriculum" day sponsored by the local Director's Association and were adapting some of the Reggio Emilia approaches. Children in all groups were having "open snacks" (e.g. available over a longer period), with melon pieces and crackers set out for the younger group and carrot sticks, celery, strawberries and crackers set out for the older group. The director commented that the school-age group "had a much better afternoon" when this practice was instituted. Previously, some children had been "super cranky" by the school day's end. But now, those children who were hungry were allowed to go into the kitchen and help themselves to a plate of grapes and crackers. A regular "timed" snack was also given between 3:30 and 4:00 P.M. The children were happy and busy at this center.

The director also commented that the Director's Association had a Mentor program for new directors. Each intern or protégé was paired with an experienced director for help and advice during their first year or two as a director. The Association had applied for a state grant to provide funding for this and the curriculum training programs.

What staff development elements do you see in this case study description?

What director development elements do you see?

What could be developed further?

What more could be done?

What could your center try or add?

◇ ◇

SUGGESTED CLASS ACTIVITIES AND DISCUSSIONS

1. *Teacher Hiring Interview Role Play.*   Role play a teacher hiring interview using suggestions given in the text. Possible roles needed in addition to the Director and the Teacher Applicant might include an Advisory Board member, another teacher of the same age or close-in-age children and a parent. It is important to keep the group number an uneven number to prevent ties in decision-making. Follow the role play with a discussion of additional responses to expect from the role players.

2. *Staff Training Centers.*   Students can (perhaps as a Final Project) set up curriculum-content centers to demonstrate new ideas for a sample staff training meeting. Centers can feature art, music, literature, self-expression, science, math, or any number of topics "teachers" select, or the whole activity can center around "The Importance of Experiences" or "Creativity" or a similar theme the group(s) select. Students set up the centers as they would for children and the class as "teachers" participate in each center to practice new ideas or new applications of ideas.

3. *Brainstorming Program Enrichment Papers.*   The class as a whole group at first, and then in small groups, can brainstorm topics for Program Enrichment Papers (PEPs). Students can choose a particular age or topic area such as "Infant-Toddler Appropriate PEPs" or a subject-matter area, perhaps Geography or History for School Age Day Care. Do an outline of the whole-group PEP on a board to demonstrate the large number of ideas needed to formulate one PEP. Have the groups write up the activities they develop and distribute copies to the class.

4. *Board Training Role Play.*   Role play a Fall Orientation meeting for Board members, teachers and staff. Have the group watch a movie or video showing good developmental child care. Assign one third of the class to watch the teacher interaction with children, one third to watch for equipment and supplies used, and one third to watch for advertising or public relations ideas. After the video is shown, let groups meet to consolidate their ideas and present them to the class. Other topics can be used with part of the class role playing parents, and the topic of the video shown (or a panel presented) on discipline. Divide the class in thirds to observe and brainstorm about different aspects of the topic.

5. *Home Visit and Special Needs Role Plays.*   Ask two or more members of the class to role play a home visit as part of a staff training meeting. This allows practice on points given in the text on home visits and also allows special needs or unusual situations to be spotlighted, such as a parent-teacher conference with a single father. The context for the single father might be a

young widower, and resource materials on parenthood and child development might be a feature. Other special instances such as foster care, adoption and divorce can be treated in other role plays, whether as home visits or parent-teacher conferences at the center. Practice in these areas helps the staff with training and provides a vehicle for articles and resource materials to be shared.

◇ ◇

BIBLIOGRAPHY

Abt Associates. (1987). *Preliminary findings and their implications: National day care study.* Cambridge, MA: Author.

Bredekamp, S. (Ed.). (1987). *Developmentally appropriate practice in early childhood programs serving children from birth through age 8.* Washington, DC: NAEYC.

Bredekamp, S., & Willer, B. (1992, March). Of ladders and lattices, cores and cones: Conceptualizing an early childhood professional development system. *Young Children, 47*(3), 47–50.

Child Care Employee Project. (1992, July). On the horizon: New policy initiatives to enhance child care staff compensation. *Young Children, 47*(5), 39–42.

Cost, Quality and Child Outcomes Study Team (1995). *Cost, Quality and Child Outcomes in Child Care Centers. Public Report.* Denver Colo.: Univ. of Colo.

Daniel, J. (1990, May). Child care: An endangered industry. *Young Children, 44*(5), 23–26.

Galinsky, E. (1989). The staffing crisis. *Young Children, 44*(2), 1–4.

Galinsky, E., & Friedman, D. (1986). *Investing in quality child care: A report to AT&T.* Basking Ridge, NJ: AT&T.

Galinsky, E., Howes, C., Kontos, S., & Shinn, M. (1994). *The study of children in family child care and relative care: Highlights of findings.* New York: Families and Work Institute.

Gotts, E. E. (1988). The right to quality child-care. *Childhood Education, 64,* 268–275.

Jones, E. (1986). Teaching adults: *An active learning approach.* Washington, DC: NAEYC.

Jorde-Bloom, P. (1988). Closing the gap: An analysis of teacher and administrator perceptions of organizational climate in the early childhood setting. *Teaching & Teacher Education: An International Journal of Research and Studies, 4*(2), 111–120.

Jorde-Bloom, P. (1989, Winter). Professional orientation: Individual and organizational perspectives. *Child and Youth Care Quarterly, 18*(4), 227–240.

Jorde-Bloom, P. (1993). But I'm worth more than that: Addressing employee concerns about compensation. *Young Children, 48*(3), 65–68.

Kisker, E., Hofferth, S. L., Phillips, D., & Farquhar, E. (1991). *A profile of child care settings: Early education and care in 1990.* Washington, DC: U.S. Department of Education, Office of the Under Secretary.

Kuykendall, J. M. (1990, July). Child development: Directors shouldn't leave home without it!! *Young Children, 45*(5), 47–50.

Leavitt, R. L., & Krause-Eheart, B. (1985). Maintaining quality and cost effectiveness through staffing patterns. *Child Care Information Exchange, 45,* 31–35.

Morgan, G. (1987). *The national state of child care regulations, 1986.* Watertown, MA: Work Family Directions, Inc.

Morin, J. (1991). *Taking matters into our own hands: A guide to unionization in the child care field.* Berkeley, CA: Child Care Employee Project.

National Association for the Education of Young Children. (1990). NAEYC position statement on guidelines for compensation of early childhood professionals. *Young Children, 46*(1), 30–32.

National Association for the Education of Young Children. (1992, November). *NAEYC model of early childhood professional development.* Washington, DC: Author.

National Association of State Boards of Education. (1988). *Right from the start: The report of the NASBE task force on early childhood education.* Alexandria, VA: Author.

Neugebauer, R., & Neugebauer, B. (1998). *The Art of Leadership: Managing Early Childhood Organizations.* Redmond, Washington: Redleaf Press.

Peters, T. J., & Waterman, R. H. (1982). *In search of excellence.* New York: Harper & Row.

Phillips, C. (1994). The challenge of training and credentialing early childhood educators. *Phi Delta Kappan,* 76(3), 214–217.

Rogers, E. M., & Shoemaker, F. F. (1971). *Communication of innovations: A cross-cultural approach.* New York: MacMillan.

Rowan, B. (1994). Comparing teachers work with work in other occupations: Notes on the professional status teaching. *Educational Researcher,* 23(6),17–21.

Schweinhart, L. J., Koshel, J. J., & Bridgeman, A. (1987). Policy options for preschool programs. *Phi Delta Kappan, 68,* 524–530.

Senge, P. (1990). *The fifth discipline: The art and practice of a learning organization.* New York: Doubleday.

Snow, C. (1983, November). *As the twig is bent: A review of research of the consequences of day care with implications for caregiving.* Paper presented at the Annual Conference of the National Association for the Education of Young Children, Atlanta, Georgia.

Spencer, L. M., Jr., McClelland, D. C., Spencer, S. M. (Eds.). (1994). *Competency Assessment methods: History and state of the art.* Boston: Hay/McBer Research Press.

The staff shortage: 41 ideas on how to respond. (1986). *Child Care Information Exchange, 47,* 33–41.

Stephen, K. (1990, June). Is child care a good business? *Child Care Information Exchange, 13.*

Whitebook, M. (1986). The teacher shortage. *Young Children, 41*(3), 10–11.

Whitebook, M. (1994). Advocacy to challenge the status quo. In *The early childhood career lattice: Perspectives on professional development,* eds., J. Johnson and J. McCracken, Washington, DC: NAEYC.

Whitebook, M. (1997). Who's missing at the table? Leadership opportunities and barriers for teachers and providers. In S. L. Kagan, & B. T. Bowman (Eds.), *Leadership in Early Care and Education,* pp. 77–84. Washington, DC: NAEYC.

Whitebook, M., & Ginsburg, G. (1985). *Comparable worth: Questions and answers for childhood staff.* Oakland, CA: Child Care Employee Project.

Whitebook, M., Hinatiuk, P., & Bellman, D. (1994). *Mentoring in early care and education: Refining an emerging career path.* Washington, DC: National Center for the Early Childhood Work Force.

Whitebook, M., Howes, C., & Phillips, D. (1989). *Who cares? Child care and the quality of care in America. Final report of the National Child Care Staffing Study.* Oakland, CA: Child Care Employee Project.

Whitebook, M., Howes, C., & Phillips, D. (1990). *The National Child Care Staffing Study: Who Cares? Child Care Teachers and the Quality of Care in America.* Oakland, CA: Child Care Employee Project.

Whitebook, M., Pemberton, C., Lombardi, J., & Galinsky, E. (1990). *From the floor: Raising child care salaries.* Oakland, CA: Child Care Employee Project.

Whitebook, M., Phillips, D., & Howes, C. (1993). *The National Child Care Staffing Study Revisited: Four years in the life of center-based child care.* Oakland, CA: Child Care Employee Project.

Willer, B., & Johnson, L. C. (1989). *The crisis is real: Demographics on the problems of recruiting and retaining early childhood staff.* Washington, DC: NAEYC.

Motivating Staff, Parents, and Children

The best leaders, directors, administrators and managers of all kinds agree on one thing: People support what they help to create (Senge, 1990). This idea also applies to the process of understanding and building vision, goals, and strategies within an organization. When employees are involved in developing the philosophical components of an organization, a task structure is more likely to evolve that will capitalize on the natural motivation inherent in all people. Everyone is motivated by something, so the director's task is to create a supportive climate with high performance goals to try to access this natural motivation (Senge, 1990). This will promote a self-fulfilling prophecy—that of an excellent center where excellent people work. By encouraging people to take responsibility and by constantly checking one's own assumptions about people, being wary of multicultural or gender filters, a director is well on the way to having a center where people motivate themselves.

Two theories of motivation give new insight into how actions on behalf of employees produce certain effects. The first is a two-factor motivation theory, developed by Herzberg, Mausner, and Snyderman (1959). The second theory discussed here is that developed by Maslow (1970), which can be viewed as a one-factor motivation theory. Maslow's theory of motivation looks at individuals, and is based on the assumption that things that are absent will satisfy when they are present. Herzberg's theory, on the other hand, looks at motivation within organizations. Of the many theories of motivation, these two are particularly useful in the administration of early childhood programs.

◇ ◇

TWO-FACTOR MOTIVATION THEORY

"What would motivate my teachers to really work towards the goal of enabling children to be happy and competent?" a director asked. "I wish I had more money to pay them. Maybe I'll give Sue a small raise—that's only a few dollars a week more. Then I think I'll ask Mary if she'd like to attend that all-day conference next month. It costs $45, but it's only a one-time expense." What would be the results of these two experiments? In this case, the teacher who received the raise asked for another raise in three months; the teacher who received the training, however, was able to use those new skills for several years.

In two-factor motivation theory, as outlined by Herzberg, Mausner, and Snyderman (1959) and diagramed in Figure 7.1, two types of factors are needed to motivate employees. The first type of factors are termed the dissatisfaction or "hygiene" factors, and are shown in the left-hand column of Figure 7.1. The second type of factors, shown in the right-hand column, are called motivator factors. The vignette in the previous paragraph about Mary and Sue illustrates this theory, in part.

Dissatisfaction or Hygiene Factors

The words *hygiene factors* used along with the term *dissatisfaction factors* really denote the extrinsic or outer factors of a facility—the things in a child-care center that a director can do something about. Dissatisfaction factors are group-oriented factors that surround a person at work, and they set the tone of

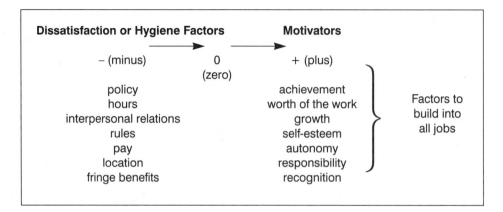

FIGURE 7.1
Herzberg's Two-Factor Motivation Theory

the working atmosphere. Dissatisfaction factors include salary, working conditions, interpersonal relations, policy, hours, status, security, and quality of supervision (which can be measured by observing whether the director monitors the staff too closely, or whether the director trusts the staff). These are the factors that a leader usually chooses to improve upon when he or she feels there is a need to strengthen motivation in an organization. For example, if morale is low, many leaders think the solution is to increase employees' salaries, improve work hours, organize more staff parties (to enhance interpersonal relations), or improve on some other hygiene factors. However, Herzberg found that even if all of these factors are excellent, this excellence will merely prevent employees from being dissatisfied. In Figure 7.1, this situation is illustrated by the arrows, which show employees moving from a minus position up to a zero position. In other words, while employees may not complain as much, they are still not motivated to do their best work.

Although studies have shown that improving hygiene factors does not necessarily lead to increased motivation, they are still very important. If a person is greatly dissatisfied in a work situation, the motivating factors will hold no interest. It is important to realize that even in the best organizations, one or two of the hygiene factors may be beyond the leader's control. In child-care situations, for example, the hours and the wages are somewhat controlled by outside factors. The two-factor theory of motivation is still particularly applicable in these situations, however, because all of the motivator factors can be implemented within a given program while costing the child-care center very little or nothing.

Motivator Factors

According to Herzberg, motivator factors are the second type of factors needed to inspire employees to do their best. These factors, shown in the right-hand column of Figure 7.1, are successful in motivating people because they are internal. It has been found that when motivation comes from within rather than from outside circumstances, people are happier and more able to successfully fulfill their responsibilities. Leader/directors, then, need to incorporate motivators into the structure that can become internalized. For example, feelings of job satisfaction are internal motivators that are likely to come from the work itself. These feelings include a sense of achievement, a sense of responsibility, and a sense that the work itself is worthwhile.

In early childhood education, a tremendous benefit can be gained from internal motivators, because working with children is inherently worthwhile. Working with children, whether as teachers or parents, can be emotionally and psychologically draining, however; the hours are long, and the repeated crises that arise are stressful. On the other hand, working with children can be emotionally fulfilling and is an important life's work, because the consequences are far-reaching (Hamburg 1987). Those who take an active part in early child-hood education participate in shaping the future of this country as well as the world. It is essential that parents and teachers are reminded of this often, and thanked for their efforts in this important work.

In contrast to the importance and reward of careers involving work with young children are jobs that employees feel are unimportant and unrewarding. For example, those who work in factories, turning three bolts or inserting three computer chips all day, everyday, will have to find motivators other than job satisfaction, since the work itself will never be as inherently interesting and as far-reaching as working with young children. Factory owners are aware of this problem; assembly line workers are often paid high wages and morale problems are assumed to be an inherent part of the business.

Even though job satisfaction may be more difficult to find in some jobs than in others, motivator factors that allow employees to feel a real sense of satis-faction in their work instead of an absence of dissatisfaction *can* be developed by any administrator. Aside from job satisfaction, other motivators include: (1) building employees' self-esteem; (2) encouraging them to grow and learn; (3) giving them opportunities for professional growth and advancement; and (4) providing them with some autonomy, by allowing them to work on their own. In the child-care field, this last motivator means giving aides, parents, chil-dren, and teachers opportunities for independence.

Studies have found that people will stay in a job longer if they are satisfied or motivated by the work, even though it may not pay well. Some people say, "If I only earned more, I wouldn't care what I did." This generally is not true, however. Earning more in an unrewarding job may please a person for a year or two, but burnout soon occurs. Finding really satisfying work can be one of the most gratifying aspects of life.

Recognition is another important motivator for adults as well as children. Everyone likes to be recognized for something, whether it be a bright smile, a job well done, a special hobby, or other unique qualities, job-related or not.

Such motivating factors are the variables that allow people to be motivated and happy in their work. Hygiene factors are important; in fact, they build job commitment. But when motivating factors are also present, *organizational commitment* is built along with job commitment. *Organizational commitment* is a commitment to the goals of a particular organization. In early childhood education, these goals may be providing the best quality child care in town, or developing happy, competent children. Every child-care center has some over-riding goals beyond just running the center. One such overall goal might be for the parents to have a sense of pride in having their children enrolled in such a fine program. Whatever goals are chosen, however, it is essential that the entire staff be committed to them. Developing motivator factors within the working conditions of an educational program helps to secure this vital com-mitment of staff and parents.

Knowing the two-factor motivation theory can help in finding the right job. In fact, one interviewee uses this motivation theory as a criterion for selecting a job. When she goes for an interview, she asks the other people working there, "What do you like about working here?" If the replies are mostly, "The pay is regular" or "The hours are good" (hygiene factors), she doesn't take the job. On the other hand, if the employees reply, "They let you try out your own ideas" or "They'll support you when you get going in a project" (motivator factors), she will usually take the job, even if it pays a little less than another job with plenty of positive hygiene factors.

More time should be spent incorporating more motivators into child-care job settings. As stated before, these motivators are not only important, but they are also free of cost, or at least easily affordable. When determining how best to include motivators in a center, however, remember that the goal is job enrichment, not job enlargement. Motivators should not add so much extra work and challenge that the job becomes overwhelming. When motivators are used effectively, the payoff in commitment and motivation on the part of the staff benefits the center and encourages maximum effort much of the time. (Minimum effort, in contrast, is the minimum amount of work an employee must do to avoid getting fired. See chapter 2 for more on this subject.)

The goal in integrating motivators into the program is to help people realize their potential. For example, if there is an aide working at the center who is very creative, give him or her more opportunity to design bulletin boards, to produce newsletter illustrations, or to use that talent in any other way that benefits the center and helps him or her to grow. When an organization realizes its obligation to recognize the potential in people, both individuals and the organization profit. If the center believes in people, these same people will reward the center by being motivated to expend more effort on the center than on something else. Many organizations waste valuable talent because of their failure to motivate people. The loss that results is not only economic, but also a loss of human happiness. While hygiene factors can inspire a person's work performance, motivator factors allow a person to become his or her own generator.

◇ ◇

CLOSING THE EXPECTATIONS GAP

The two-factor theory of motivation parallels what early childhood educators believe in: the importance of building a child's self-esteem and of helping a child reach his or her potential. Adults as well as children respond to those who believe in them and who recognize their potential. Just like children, adults have a need to create and achieve, to be responsible and to grow. Within each person, however, there is often a gap between what a person does and what he or she is capable of doing (Figure 7.2). Someone who is encouraged to create and achieve will be using more of his or her potential, whether that potential is perceived or not. For example, in early childhood programs,

FIGURE 7.2
Expectations Gap

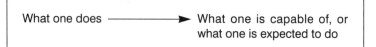

encouraging aides to reach their potential can be done in many ways. Changing the job title of aide to perhaps program assistant or associate teacher, which reflects more expectations and abilities, might be one step. The next step might be to enlist these people in any task that needs creativity: Have them help create a section of a morning curriculum activity; ask them to think up a song with children's names in it; encourage them to create new endings for stories; or invite them to develop new activities for rhythm and movement. The more an organization can help to close the gap between a person's actions and a person's abilities, the more of a sense of commitment its employees will feel towards the organization's goals.

Helping people realize their potential involves training them to handle more *responsibility* and find the satisfaction that goes along with it. Along with taking on more commitments, people need to build a sense of competence and confidence, as well as a sense of growth. It is unrealistic to assign tremendous responsibility and expect employees to derive satisfaction and happiness from it.

When training people to manage more responsibility, it might be useful to set aside a small section of each day during which one member of the staff who is familiar with a particular task can train another person in that same task. For example, the staff member usually in charge of story hour may want to teach an aide to take over this task. In the same way, parents and/or volunteers can be trained to take responsibility for specific tasks, such as reading stories, supervising the finger painting corner, or working in the puzzle corner with children. Such a method of delegation instills a sense of achievement and responsibility into the job.

Emphasizing the *value of the work* is another way to help employees reach their potential. While the value of child-care work is one of the easiest things to reinforce, it is often not stressed. Frequently remind people of the center's philosophy—in the newsletter, in the center's bylaws, and on bulletin boards. Condense your goals into a simple sentence, such as, "We believe in having a good program for children—respecting children, respecting materials, and respecting adults." Repeat this sentence often to the staff. Consider varying the goals every year, to keep interest in them high.

Recognition is also easy to give, and reinforces the attempts people make to reach their potential. For staff, have a "Teacher of the Month" (or Week) bulletin board. For this display, show a picture of the teacher and list his or her birthday, hobbies, favorite jokes, pets, and the names of his or her children.

Place it where parents can see it as they come in, so they can feel more at ease when they greet the teacher. Remember that encouraging the staff produces a better attitude toward the children.

Directors need encouragement too, and it is important for them to attend workshops, conferences, or courses to gain new ideas and to receive some recognition for what can be a lonely and isolated job. Since there are many problems a director cannot share with his or her staff, it is important to become involved in a program that includes people with similar problems.

Encouraging professional *growth* is an important means of helping people close the expectations gap. Assisting this growth by offering to pay for parents or teachers to attend local or regional conferences, or by offering regular staff and parent training at the center, can reap great rewards. Even if only two or three people benefit from training programs provided at the center, offering such education on a regular basis is still an opportunity for growth. College courses fall under this category also. Inform the staff that the center is interested in their personal growth and their future employment prospects. If employees feel that they are growing and getting something rewarding out of working for an organization, they will benefit and will appreciate one of the best things a program can offer.

In a field in which people are asked to give constant nurturing, centers are obligated to give staff something in return—a sense of fulfillment, perhaps—so that they in turn can be warm and loving to the children. Studies on stress show that people can only give so much before they burn out. As a general rule, the more a leader can support staff, help them feel good about themselves and their personal worth, and help them feel that what they are doing is really worthwhile, then the more confidence and self-esteem they will develop.

The director can personally encourage staff to realize their importance to the center, to the children, and to the parents. Feeling good about ourselves is an undeniable human need. Even though there are times a leader feels discouraged, helping people feel good about themselves is not a difficult task. If the staff can derive a sense of recognition or an increase in self-esteem from the efforts it gives to the center, then it is likely that the fruits of this appreciation will eventually benefit the center and the director as well. This is true empowerment.

The questionnaire shown in Figure 7.3 and its accompanying key (Figure 7.4) can help centers find out just how their staff feels and in what areas motivating factors might be increased. As mentioned before, hygiene factors are easy to complain about and when rated at 100% still only keep people from being dissatisfied. The motivator factors in other question areas are much more important for lasting success and an optimistic outlook for the future. A total score of 44 to 57 is good. Below 44, look into the motivator factors. Below 22, a director may begin to see absenteeism and high turnover and should look into the hygiene factors, also.

Question	Fantastic	Pretty Good	Just Okay	Not So Good
1. How do you like the work you do?	Highly exciting; it's the work you always wanted	Promising; better than average; somewhat gratifying	Average; so-so; worthwhile	Routine; dull and confining; meaningless
	SCORE: 3	SCORE: 2	SCORE: 1	SCORE: 0
2. How much control do you have over the way you do your job?	You're the captain of your ship, and do it your own way	You decide what to do and have your plan approved by supervisor	You and director decide what you are to do (together)	You do as you're told
	SCORE: 3	SCORE: 2	SCORE: 1	SCORE: 0
3. What kind of relationship do you have with your supervisor?	Effective; he/she really does understand you	More often effective than not	Effective sometimes and ineffective others	Ineffective relationship
	SCORE: 3	SCORE: 2	SCORE: 1	SCORE: 0
4. What kind of relationship do you have with your coworkers?	Great group; they're your kind of people	Some likeable	Pleasant, but "dull"	"Wet cement"
	SCORE: 3	SCORE: 2	SCORE: 1	SCORE: 0
5. How do you feel about the progress you've made over the past year?	Involved in new and more difficult tasks	Have some new job tasks not previously handled	New tasks, but they are small, routine duties	Not going anywhere; same old thing
	SCORE: 3	SCORE: 2	SCORE: 1	SCORE: 0
6. To what extent do you participate in decision-making?	In most cases, opinions are asked for and used constructively	Ideas are asked for	Not involved in decision-making, but informed of matters necessary to know about	Not informed of job-related matters
	SCORE: 3	SCORE: 2	SCORE: 1	SCORE: 0

FIGURE 7.3
"Analysis of Staff Motivation" Questionnaire

Question	Fantastic	Pretty Good	Just Okay	Not So Good
7. Are you given opportunities to attend conferences, in-service classes, or workshops in your area of specialization or interest?	Regularly SCORE: **3**	Occasionally SCORE: **2**	Rarely SCORE: **1**	Never heard of those SCORE: **0**
8. Have you been given a raise in salary, promotion, or a better work location recently?	Every 6 months SCORE: **3**	Once a year SCORE: **2**	Over 18 months SCORE: **1**	Never SCORE: **0**
9. All in all, how do you feel about your pay?	Earning top dollar; likely to be rich in 10 years SCORE: **3**	Generous; can make a good living SCORE: **2**	Average; ordinary SCORE: **1**	Miserly pay, little hope for the future SCORE: **0**
10. In the past year, have you received any awards or acknowledgments for a job well done?	Every time you turn around SCORE: **3**	Occasional pat on the back SCORE: **2**	Almost never SCORE: **1**	Don't even know you're alive SCORE: **0**
11. Do you feel sure of steady employment?	Very sure SCORE: **3**	More sure than unsure SCORE: **2**	More unsure than sure SCORE: **1**	Don't know what tomorrow holds SCORE: **0**
12. Do you like where your job is located?	Ideal SCORE: **3**	Sub-ideal SCORE: **2**	Could be closer SCORE: **1**	It's an overnight trip on the freeway home SCORE: **0**

Question	Fantastic	Pretty Good	Just Okay	Not So Good
13. What is your work setting like?	Luxurious facility; tons of resources and equipment	Comfortable; nice place; sufficient resources and equipment	Run down	Dismal; cockroach carnival
	SCORE: **3**	SCORE: **2**	SCORE: **1**	SCORE: **0**
14. What kinds of fringe benefits do you receive?	Long vacation, tuition aid, pension plan, life and medical insurance	Most of these	Some of these	Few of these
	SCORE: **3**	SCORE: **2**	SCORE: **1**	SCORE: **0**
15. How does your supervisor address you?	By your first name, or name you prefer			Avoids calling you by your name
	SCORE: **3**			SCORE: **0**
16. Who evaluates your progress?	You evaluate your own	Cooperate in evaluation with supervisor	You are given a chance to review and discuss the evaluation given you	Given an evaluation
	SCORE: **3**	SCORE: **2**	SCORE: **1**	SCORE: **0**
17. Does your job role or status give you authority over others?	To a high degree	Somewhat	Very little	Not at all
	SCORE: **3**	SCORE: **2**	SCORE: **1**	SCORE: **0**
18. How much time and freedom does your job allow?	Your time is your own; freedom to come and go	Some free time (1 hour or more per day)	Little or no relief (10 minutes or less)	Slave driven
	SCORE: **3**	SCORE: **2**	SCORE: **1**	SCORE: **0**
19. What kind of guidance do you receive on the job?	Well-planned with individual attention	Periods of no guidance	Once in a while; vague	Poor; little or no attention
	SCORE: **3**	SCORE: **2**	SCORE: **1**	SCORE: **0**

Figure 7.3, *continued*

Total: 13 factors
(7 hygiene) + (6 motivators)

Score: hygiene = 21 points (50%)
motivator = 36 points (50%)

Questions:

Hygiene Factors

Salary—#9
Supervisor—#3
Coworkers—#4
Location— # 12
Fringe benefits—# 14
Working conditions—# 13
Security—# 11

Motivators

Autonomy—#18, 16, 2
Worth of work—#1
Recognition + Achievement—#10, 15
Growth needs—# 19, 7
Advancement—# 5, 8
Responsibility—# 6, 17

FIGURE 7.4
Key to Motivation Questionnaire

Incorporating Motivator Factors into a Child-Care Program

An interesting exercise would be to take the list of motivator factors and then brainstorm ways in which more of these motivators can be written into the job description of an aide, a parent and/or volunteer, a teacher, a director, or into the plans for children. The following groups of motivators were developed to help parents become more involved since that is a key part of a good child care program. They were gathered from two sources: a "staff meeting" role-play group organized during a motivation segment of a college credit child-care management course, and a 1993 teacher-directors conference. The Motivator Activities provided in Appendix C also show some ways of facilitating motivators for staff, parents, and children.

Motivator Activities for Parents

Responsibility

1. Train parents to hold offices on the center's Advisory Board.
2. Train parents to be classroom volunteers, then provide opportunities one or two hours a week or every two weeks. For example, some opportunities might include breakfast helpers, late afternoon helpers, or Sat-

urday yard clean-up helpers. Such a program gives parents a sense of "ownership" in the center and in their children's education.

3. Invite creative parents to make instructional materials for teachers to use in their classrooms. One center organized an "International Week" in which a different country was presented as the topic each day, and parents provided input on snacks, stories, activities, and crafts.

The Value of the Work

1. Send home "happygrams"—flyers that have a smile face on them—describing something the child did well that day. (Run off a group of blank forms on a copier.) Send "happygrams" to the staff and parents for their efforts, also.

2. Send home ideas of ways that parents can help the center, or send home lists of items the center can use and that parents can contribute. Thank parents in the newsletter for anything they *do* contribute.

3. Send home ideas for learning activities that parents can do with their children. Frequently remind parents that they are their child's most important teacher. (See the Home Learning Enablers in Appendix A.)

4. Invite a parent to participate in a children's class or a staff meeting as a guest speaker. Ask the person to tell about his or her own job, career, or hobbies; for example, children might be interested in hearing a dentist talk about his or her work. Staff might enjoy hearing from a person with a career or background in music, art, or dance.

5. Share good ideas on parenting issues or tips on single parenting in brainstorming sessions, and then publish the best ideas in a newsletter.

6. Praise parents in the newsletter or in person when they build a support network for each other, such as by picking up the children of a parent who is sick.

Recognition

1. At a parent gathering, give a certificate with a gold seal on it to a parent for her or his *first* contribution to a center. Have a "warm fuzzy" note pad and send home one or two notes a day to parents for their contributions.

2. In each month's newsletter, mention names of those who have helped the center in some way.

3. Award "thank-you" corsages at the end of the year to parents who have volunteered 10 hours (or some other attainable goal) of time over the course of the year. On a chart in the hall (where all can see), keep track of the hours volunteered. Give a more elaborate "thank-you" gift at the end of the year to parents who help 25 hours, and a still more elaborate

gift to those who help 40 or 50 hours. Have the Parent Advisory Board decide what the gifts should be, and perhaps hold a fundraiser to earn money to pay for the gifts. One center calls these gifts the "Above and Beyond Awards."

4. Create a "Parent of the Week" display on a bulletin board or in a newsletter. Describe the featured parent's hobbies, interests, job, family news, and so forth. List compliments given that person, or have the person's child write "I love my mommy (or daddy) because . . ." sentences. Do the same for other family members, such as grandparents. Post pictures of children new to the center and of their parents so all can get to know them.

5. Acknowledge and implement parents' ideas whenever possible. At meetings, validate their input for solutions that are useful.

6. Praise parents in front of their children. Reinforce and complement parents' positive interactions with children.

7. Display a toy a parent has made or a craft done by a parent. At a potluck supper, distribute recipes that parents have developed, with the cook's name written on the cards.

8. In the newsletter, have a section that focuses on one or two parents a month.

9. Involve children in drawing pictures for parent recognition and thank-you notes.

Growth

1. Invite parents to attend workshops and conferences.

2. Train parents to advance to responsible volunteer positions and then allow them to attend selected teacher's meetings. Develop a "theme for the year," such as fitness or music, to add focus to these meetings.

3. Help parents with their own jobs/careers. Put out a listing of local jobs available; have a meeting on résumé writing. Share information about adult stages of human development and about the types of support that adults need at different stages in their lives.

4. Send home some Home Learning Enablers, which are one-page activities that describe a 5- or 10-minute activity parents can do with their child. (Some example activities include counting steps, stacking soda or soup cans, and making instant pudding. For more examples, see Appendix A.)

5. Tell/share information about resources in the community.

6. Encourage parents to read library books on different topics, both child-related and adult-related, and then have a meeting in which parents and staff vote on books to give their "seal of approval." Develop a parent library to allow parents access to these resources.

7. Invite parents to attend early childhood conferences.

8. Share child development information frequently.

◊ ◊

ONE-FACTOR MOTIVATION

Abraham Maslow (1970) is quite well-known in the field of psychology, and his work on the hierarchy of human needs is also used in management. This theory states that the bottom level of needs in the triangle or hierarchy (shown in Figure 7.5) must be met before an individual can or will want to move on to the next level. A person therefore is motivated by one factor: whether or not personal needs are met on a particular level of the hierarchy. This theory, when applied as a motivation theory, assumes that by meeting a person's needs on a particular level, the person will be *motivated* to go on to the next level. When a specific need is filled, the person is satisfied and ready to move on.

As was stated before when comparing the two-factor and one-factor theories of motivation, Maslow's theory looks at individuals, whereas Herzberg's theory looks at motivation within organizations. Maslow's hierarchy of needs is based on the assumption that those things absent will satisfy when they are present. In this context, in order to motivate people, you need to meet them at the level they are on and then help them move forward to the next level. Of course, it is difficult to correctly estimate another person's level of need. Some suggestions to increase the accuracy of estimating someone's level of need include finding out more about the person's background, discovering the person's place in the family when growing up (birth order), and learning about the person's general situation at present. Fulfilling this list can be very difficult, since many times

FIGURE 7.5
Maslow's Hierarchy of Needs

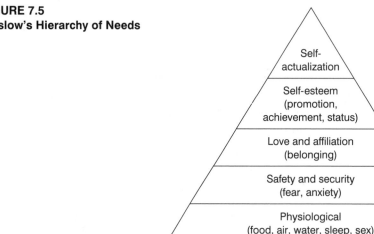

important pieces of information are not known even by the individual. Knowledge about birth order is helpful, however, and is in the realm of polite conversation. A number of books on this topic help educators understand children *and* adults better.

Physiological Needs

Humans tend to focus on meeting physiological needs before higher level needs. In the child care field, there is concern that wages may be so low that many employees may be at this "survival" level. As child care is sought by parents of all income levels (low to high), a higher standard of pay, education, and training becomes more possible, as it is imperative to increase quality and prevent a national children's "brain drain." However, when the needs at this level are partially satisfied, other needs emerge. The classic example of this is the early missionaries' attempts to preach to people who were starving. Hungry people need to be fed before they can hear any message that is being brought to them.

Anxiety, Safety, and Security Needs

One can see the effect that anxiety, safety, and security needs have on an individual's personality by observing elderly people who live in urban areas. Their concerns about break-ins and being mugged are so great that many of them have five locks on their doors. This fear and worry is so great (need for safety and security), that the higher level needs do not concern them. An individual at a higher level may also experience these anxiety, safety, and security level needs after a traumatic experience, such as an auto accident, occurs. For several months following the accident, the person might be quite fearful and worried about safety while driving or riding in a car. According to Maslow's theory, then, it is important to "meet people where they are." However, once a person has been at a higher level, that person will return to that level as the "interrupt" anxiety or other need is eased.

Love, Affection, and Belonging Needs

Maslow believes that most of America is at this level. The strong need for love, affection, and a sense of belonging can be seen often in children. Staff development and parent activities can help meet this need with staff and parents at the adult level.

Self-Esteem Needs

If a person feels loved, is not really feeling threatened or unsafe, and is not really hungry or in need of rest, then, according to Maslow, that person would

Food is a basic motivator—for all ages.

not mind increasing self-esteem in some way, perhaps by taking on additional responsibilities or becoming chairperson of a committee. A person with pressing needs in another area, however, does not need or want status responsibilities on top of their other worries.

Self-Actualization Needs

The highest level needs, self-actualization needs, are satisfied only after needs at the four lower levels have been met. At this fifth level, the individual is concerned with the development of his or her potential. This person has peak experiences of insight or understanding. The person at this stage, which many people never reach, has a better perception of reality, accepts self and others, is more creative, and is better able to become completely human in the realization and development of his or her full potential. Truth, goodness, beauty, and meaningfulness are recognized and enjoyed by this person.

Some theorists say that only older people can reach the self-actualization level; however, this author has met many people in the field of early childhood education at this level who periodically have had peak experiences—times of feeling really good about their work with young children of all ages. For example, a director who has planned a good staff training program and can see that it has really helped the staff may experience the self-actualization level. It is important to take time to value this feeling, since it is a "pay-off" of a kind for the effort expended. A director might take a moment to think, "I worked hard on that, and it really seems to be benefiting the center." Similarly, people must learn to value the insights that come to them about what to do next. Perhaps such insights can be written down and reviewed until the time is right to put them onto a long-range or short-range goals list.

◇ ◇

APPLYING ONE-FACTOR MOTIVATION

The previous section discussed some practical ways of motivating adults by using the one-factor theory. This section will apply the theory to children and their needs. Some time will also be devoted to identifying the need levels of adults as well, since the same ideas for motivating children also can be used with adults.

The first step in motivating children is to think of different behaviors or problems a child might show based on each level of Maslow's hierarchy of needs. For instance, a child who is a discipline problem could be exhibiting any of the five levels of needs on the hierarchy.

- What physiological needs might cause a child to be a discipline problem?

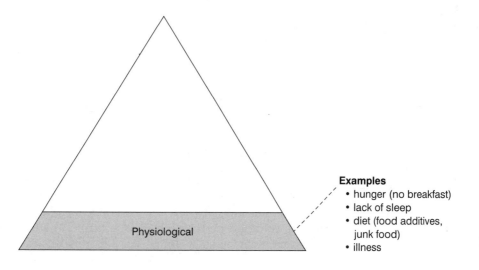

Examples
- hunger (no breakfast)
- lack of sleep
- diet (food additives, junk food)
- illness

Physiological

- What safety concerns, fears, or anxieties might result in a discipline problem?

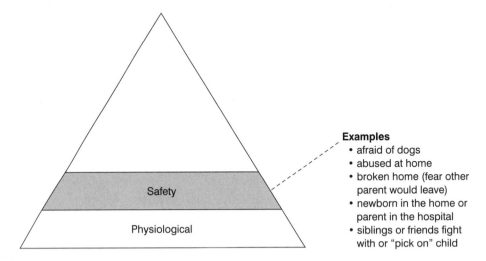

Examples
- afraid of dogs
- abused at home
- broken home (fear other parent would leave)
- newborn in the home or parent in the hospital
- siblings or friends fight with or "pick on" child

- What love, affection, and belonging needs could cause a child to be a discipline problem?

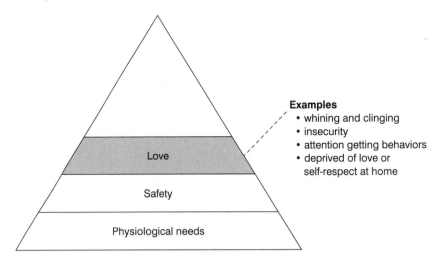

Examples
- whining and clinging
- insecurity
- attention getting behaviors
- deprived of love or self-respect at home

One idea for motivating children who exhibit love, affection, and belonging needs is to implement a "Child of the Week" activity. One center took a picture (or a picture could be drawn) of a different child each week, mounted the picture in the middle of a large piece of construction paper, and had all the children say one nice thing about the child. For example, the comments children made about Tommy included such things as: "I like his shoes," "He shared the green truck with me," and "He tells good jokes." After these comments were written around the picture, this "Child of the Week" poster was sent home. Tommy's family loved the poster and sent it to his grandparents after posting it on their own refrigerator for a month. This is self-worth and self-esteem building in action.

This "Child of the Week" activity is good not only for the child receiving the attention that particular week, but also for all the children, because they learn what it sounds like to hear and to say nice things about another child. Television shows that emphasize put-downs as comedy have become so popular, and this behavior has become so accepted as children get older, that learning to say positive things about one another becomes doubly valuable and needed when children are young. Children need to receive more credit and positive reinforcement for saying good things about people. Similar activities, such as choosing a "King" or "Queen" for the day, also build self-esteem. (Have two or three crowns on hand for emergencies.) Even adults respond to such esteem-building activities.

• What self-esteem needs would cause a child to be a discipline problem?

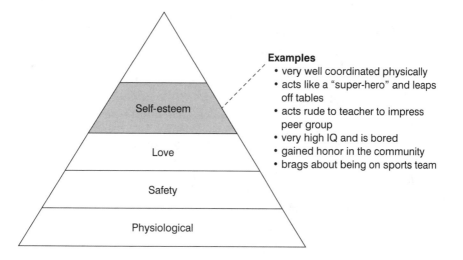

Examples
• very well coordinated physically
• acts like a "super-hero" and leaps off tables
• acts rude to teacher to impress peer group
• very high IQ and is bored
• gained honor in the community
• brags about being on sports team

Self-esteem

Love

Safety

Physiological

From this discussion, one can see that children (or adults) might act the same way for many different reasons. For example, in one child-care situation, a boy came to school each morning and pinched every child. The teacher realized that this action was the boy's way of saying "hello." She then was able to teach him better ways of greeting the other children. This child's discipline problem was an outward sign of his love, affection, and belonging need. However, another child could act the same way (pinching her classmates) because she feels threatened by the other children (anxiety, safety, and security need) or because she wants to impress her peer group (self-esteem need). Clearly then, the director's or teacher's analysis of what level a child is on must be accurate. Seeking more training on this topic can be very helpful in sharpening one's analytical skills, since determining a particular child's level can be difficult. As a teacher, for example, it might be tempting to tell a child who is talking loudly, fidgeting, and punching his neighbor that he will get some attention in a few moments if he behaves properly. If the child's real problem is that he is hungry, however, more attention will not help much.

Similar problems arise when applying the one-factor theory of motivation to adults. If someone has specific needs at one level, solutions based on another level of need will not be effective motivators. For example, a teacher who grew up in a large family and never had a room of her own was having trouble sharing cupboard space with other teachers. By assigning her some cupboard space of her own in which to keep her materials, the director met the teacher's deep-seated need to protect her "stuff" and to have her own space. This solution was more effective in meeting this teacher's need than perhaps a workshop on efficient use of storage space might have been.

An administrator must try to think about each employee, decide if he or she has a pressing need, identify it, and then try to work with the employee on that level. The level of physiological needs should not be ignored; adults can be operating on this level when they come to work without having eaten breakfast or after having too little sleep. One center actually decided to have employees come in early each day for their morning coffee break and use this time for a social exchange. Staff members took turns preparing coffee and providing food, and everyone's day got off to a better start.

In addition to the *physiological level* discussed previously, other levels of need and some other problems that adults have that could be better understood by applying Maslow's theory are:

Anxiety, Safety, and Security Level

- worries about a health problem
- worries about financial problems
- spouse lost job
- sudden divorce
- spouse abuse

Love, Affection, and Belonging Level

- single parent
- conflict with spouse

Self-Esteem Level

- loss of job or spouse

Self-Actualization Level

* not enough opportunities to use talents, skills, and abilities

Obviously a center's director or Executive Board is not usually equipped to deal with many of these problems, but acknowledging their existence and referring employees to appropriate community resources might be a first step. Encouraging all adults involved with the center to treat others with support and kindness also builds a positive climate in the workplace.

Occasionally an administrator may have an employee with such a strong need that he or she really should not work in a child-care situation. One example is that of a teacher, a very good teacher up to this point, who was having tremendous problems at home with an alcoholic husband and an ensuing divorce. Although the administrator did not know all the circumstances, the entire staff had noticed that the teacher had begun yelling at the children and even hit them on occasion. The administrator realized that the center could not meet this teacher's pressing needs, and encouraged her to find another kind of work, for a year or two, and then return. Another alternative would have been to have her help in the office with administrative work for a year or so. Not all jobs require perfect patience all day long; other jobs are available for people who cannot reasonably be expected to change their behavior during difficult circumstances.

Maslow's theory encourages one to look carefully at an individual, try to identify his or her level (or one's own) correctly, and then work towards solutions based on this level. It can be helpful to draw the hierarchy triangle chart and brainstorm (alone or with a trusted colleague or friend) some of the possible causes for a person's behavior at each level. This exercise will help prevent identifying the wrong level in a particular situation.

Two other process theories about motivation, not often seen in early childhood care and education but still observable, are an "expectancy" theory and an "equity" process theory. The expectancy theory states that persons fill positions because they *expect* better positions to evolve from them. The equity theory states that persons are in jobs because they see them as "fair" and "equitable" (Hellriegel, Slocum, & Woodman, 1998). This is often heard in political campaigns (what is "fair" and "equitable"). Education and training are becoming the keys to a long and productive work life in almost any field, in view of the prediction that the average worker will probably have eight jobs and up to five careers in the future.

Encouraging staff, parents, and children to do their best, to reach for their full potential, and to feel good about themselves is a valuable life's work. This encouragement will reap tremendous returns for the organization and for the individuals who provide this motivation.

◇ ◇

SUMMARY

Certain themes that are known to facilitate any organization and are particularly appropriate in early childhood programs are found throughout this chapter and this book. One of these themes includes providing a supportive workplace rather than a defensive one. A supportive atmosphere establishes the openness, caring, and good morale so necessary for all adults who work with young children. In a supportive workplace there is empathy and a realistic concern for the needs and development of others, as well as a positive regard for the self-esteem of all persons involved (children and adults). Spontaneity, creativity, and a willingness to try new things (risk-taking) are valued in both children and adults. Providing the opportunity for all concerned to take part in problem-solving, regardless of rank or status, is another hallmark of the workplace climate needed in an open, caring early childhood program. The focus of such programs should be on finding solutions to problems and the use of technical expertise and training to solve issues rather than on interpersonal fault-finding. This leads to concern about mutual learning and the development of strategies to improve the way things are done. In short, a supportive climate includes the following characteristics:

1. descriptive (of behavior),
2. solution-oriented,
3. vision driven,
4. empathetic,
5. collegial (friendship among equals), and
6. experimental.

With this theme in mind, many of the chapters in this book, in addition to this one, stress ways to involve everyone in the planning and implementation of programs for young children. This approach is the most professional one, and is further developed in the following chapters.

◇ ◇

SUGGESTED CLASS ACTIVITIES AND DISCUSSIONS

1. *Role Play of Different Levels of Parents or Children in Maslow's Hierarchy.*   Ask one or more small groups to develop a skit around one of Maslow's levels in the hierarchy and present it to the class. One example: (physiological level). The child is upset. Further inquiry reveals that the father has left the home and the mother is worried about having money for groceries. Stop and

ask what level this is for the parent. Then continue the role play for solution possibilities and referrals needed. Another example: Role play children wearing masks and pick out the child with activities showing security.

2. *Evaluate Center Newsletters for Herzberg Motivators.*   Ask the class to bring in examples of Center newsletters. Evaluate them for: growth (for example, child development articles), recognition, self-esteem, the worth of the work, achievement and autonomy. Mark these for parents and/or staff motivators and label the articles or columns by motivator.

3. *Analyze the Maslow-Type Needs of Parents of Handicapped Children.* Hand out problems for small groups to analyze and report back to the class showing special needs children's parents' problems. Problem examples: A father, who, when told to get counseling, refuses just as he refuses to admit the child has a problem (level: low self-esteem plus other factors); a mother who does not meet the needs of the four-year-old, because her two-year-old became deaf after spinal meningitis and requires extra attention. Ask the class to contribute or brainstorm other problems. Another category of need is the young widow who hangs back from attending parent meetings. She may need to meet other widows, and have a sponsor invite her to parent meetings (Love and Belongingness level).

4. *Role Play Demonstrating Hygiene Factors.*   Ask a small group to role play a center situation with poor hygiene factors: There are 45 children, the room is dirty and too small, two of the staff are retiring, a co-worker keeps interfering with the teacher and the director puts the teacher down. Analyze the hygiene factors, including: company policy, working conditions, and quality of supervision. Then role play a corrected situation, possibly after brainstorming for solutions.

5. *Self-Motivation on the Job.*   Ask the class to write essays on "What Motivates Me on the Job?" after reviewing Herzberg. Where do job content, skills, and the motivators fit in? Discuss the essays in class.

◇ ◇ ◇ ◇ ◇ ◇ ◇ ◇ ◇ ◇ ◇ ◇ ◇ ◇ ◇ ◇ ◇ ◇ ◇ ◇

BIBLIOGRAPHY

Adler, N. J. (1991). *International dimensions of organizational behavior*. Boston, MA: PWS-Kent Publishing.

Barley, J. E. (1986, September). Personnel scheduling with flex-shift: A win-win scenario. *Personnel*, p. 63.

Bass, B. M. (1985). *Leadership and performance beyond expectations*. New York: The Free Press.

Bass, B. M., & Stogdill, R. M. (1989). *The handbook of leadership* (3rd ed.). New York: The Free Press.

Beach, D. S. (1975). *Readings in personnel*. New York: Wiley.

Bennis, W. (1989). *Why leaders can't lead: The unconscious conspiracy*. San Francisco: Jossey-Bass.

Bennis, W., & Nanus, B. (1985). *Leaders*. New York: Harper and Row.

Birch, D., & Veroff, J. (1968). *Motivation: A study of action*. California: Brooks/Cole.

Blake, R., & Mouton, J. S. (1964). *The managerial grid*. Houston, TX: Gulf Publishing.

Boettger, R. D., & Greer, C. R. (1994). On the wisdom for rewarding A while hoping for B. *Organization Science, 5,* 569–582.

Click, P. M., & Click, D. W. (1990). *Administration of schools for young children*. New York: Delmar.

Cone, W. F. (1974). *Supervising employees effectively*. Don Mills, Ontario: Addison-Wesley.

Conger, J. A. (1989). *The charismatic leader: Behind the mystique of exceptional leadership*. San Francisco: Jossey-Bass.

Cook, C. W. (1980, April). Guidelines on managing motivation. *Business Horizons*, p. 23.

Decker, C. A., & Decker, J. R. (1988). *Planning and administering early childhood programs*. Upper Saddle River, NJ: Merrill/Prentice Hall.

Driver, M. J. (1979). Individual decision making and creativity. In S. Kerr (Ed.), *Organizational behavior*. Columbus, OH: Grid Publishing.

Drucker, P. F. (1977). *People and performance: The best of Peter Drucker on management*. New York: Harper's College Press.

Eiselen, S. S. (1992). *The human side of child care administration: A how to manual*. Washington, DC: National Association for the Education of Young Children.

Eysenck, H. J. (1964). *Experiments in motivation*. New York: Macmillan.

Fuller, J. L. (1962). *Motivation: A biological perspective*. New York: Random House.

Gellerman, S. W. (1963). *Motivation and productivity*. New York: American Management Association.

Greenberg, J. (1990). Employee theft as a reaction to underpayment inequity: the hidden costs of pay cuts. *Journal of Applied Psychology, 75,* 561–568.

Greenberg, J. (1990). Looking fair vs. being fair: Managing impressions of organizational justice. In L. L. Cummings and B. M. Staw (Eds.), *Research in Organizational Behavior, 12,* 111–158. Greenwich, CT: JAI Press.

Hamachek, D. E. (1968). *Motivation in teaching and learning*. Washington, DC: National Education Association.

Hamburg, D. A. (1987). *Fundamental building blocks of early life*. New York: Carnegie Corporation.

Hammer, W. C. (1979). Motivation theories and work applications. In S. Kerr (Ed.), *Organizational behavior*. Columbus, OH: Grid Publishing.

Hannaford, E. (1967). *Supervisor's guide to human relations*. Chicago, IL: National Safety Council.

Harvis, P. R., & Moran, R. T. (1990). *Managing cultural differences*. Houston, TX: Gulf Publishing.

Hellriegel, D. J., Slocum, J. W., Jr., & Woodman, R. W. (1998). *Organizational Behavior* (8th ed.) Cincinnati, OH: South Western College Publishing.

Hersey, P., & Blanchard, K. H. (1988). *Management of organizational behavior: Utilizing human resources*. Upper Saddle River, NJ: Prentice Hall.

Herzberg, F. (1982). *The managerial choice: To be efficient and to be human* (2nd ed.). Salt Lake City, UT: Olympus Publishing.

Herzberg, F. P., Mausner, B., & Snyderman, B. (1959). *The motivation to work*. New York: Wiley.

Jones, C. C. (1981). *Motivation*. Rockville, MD: ECEA Institute.

Jongeward, D. (1973). *Everybody wins: Transactional analysis applied to organizations*. Reading, MA: Addison-Wesley.

Jorde-Bloom, P. (1988). *A great place to work: Improving conditions for staff in young children's programs*. Washington, DC: National Association for the Education of Young Children.

Klein, S. M., & Ritti, R. R. (1984). *Understanding organizational behavior*. Boston: Kent Publishing.

Klimoski, R. J., & Hayes, N. J. (1980, Autumn). Leader behavior and subordinate motivation. *Personnel Psychology*, p. 33.

Kotter, J. (1988). *The leadership factor*. New York: Free Press.

Lawler, E. E. (1973). *Motivation in work organizations*. Monterey, CA: Brooks/Cole Publishing.

Locke, E. A., & Latham, G. P. (1990). *A model of goal setting and task performance*. Upper Saddle River, NJ: Prentice Hall.

Maslow, A. H. (1970). *Motivation and personality* (2nd ed.). New York: Harper and Row.

Mason, R. H., & Spick, R. S. (1987). *Management: An international perspective*. Homewood, IL: Richard Irwin.

McClelland, D. C., & Burnham, D. H. (1976, March). Power is the great motivator. *Harvard Business Review*, p. 54.

McGregor, D. (1960). *The human side of enterprise*. New York: McGraw-Hill.

Murray, E. J. (1964). *Motivation and emotion*. Upper Saddle River, NJ: Prentice Hall.

Quick, J. C. (1979, July). Dyadic goal setting within organizations: Role-making and motivational considerations. *Academy of Management Review*, p. 4.

Senge, P. M. (1990). *The fifth discipline: The art and practice of the learning organization*. New York: Doubleday.

Stahl, M. J. (1983, Winter). Achievement, power and managerial motivation: Selecting managerial talent with the job choice exercise. *Personnel Psychology*.

Taylor, B. J. (1989). *Early childhood program management*. Columbus, OH: Merrill.

Terry, G. R. (1974). *Supervisory management*. Homewood, IL: Richard Irwin.

Vroom, V. H. (1964). *Work and Motivation*. New York: Wiley.

Wagel, W. H. (1986, April). Opening the door to employee participation. *Personnel*, p. 63.

Weiss, J. W. (1996). *Organizational Behavior and Change: Managing Diversity, Cross-Cultural Dynamics, and Ethics*. St. Paul, MN: West.

Winter, D. G. (1988). The Power Motive in Women and Men. *Journal of Personality and Social Psychology, 54,* 510–519.

Team Building and Small Group Interaction

Small groups, whether they exist in the workplace or in voluntary organizations, provide an important source of satisfaction to the group members. What is accomplished in these small groups is vital to any leader. A small group is usually considered to be more than two, less than 20, and is often less than 12. To gain the most benefit from a group this size, it is necessary to understand some of the processes that go on within small groups (or teams); such an understanding helps develop group stability, group health, and group effectiveness. The internal dynamics and factors within a group can make it more or less productive. Since the staff of many small centers may comprise just one "small group," it is important that it be productive.

◇ ◇

THE IMPORTANCE OF SMALL GROUPS

The basic reason why group membership proves so beneficial is that groups provide their members with social support and a feeling of personal worth. The foundations for mature social exchange are established early in life through child-to-child and child-to-adult interactions; favorable interactions are quickly perceived by children as indications of acceptance and approval. Thus, acceptance and approval continue to be important motivators in adult life.

It has long been established that small groups or teams in the workplace will be more effective if they contain "friendship groups," that is, if they take into account the small groups that already exist in the "informal organization." Individuals like to interact with people who like them. Sometimes the thoughts of others are the only basis on which a person can evaluate his or her own perceptions. People like to have a feeling of certainty about their beliefs, opinions, and attitudes, and often gain affirmation through the shared values in a small group.

A negative aspect that affects the dynamics of small groups is that members with low self-esteem tend to find frustrating conditions *more* frustrating than do members with a higher self-esteem. Consequently, in difficult circumstances, those with a very low self-esteem may give up while those with a high self-esteem might persist and stay on the job. Another negative factor can be the "free-rider." Most team and group members dislike free riders as they violate an equity or fairness standard, a social responsibility standard, and a standard of reciprocity or fair exchange. Carefully selecting people for a group can modify this problem or variable.

◇ ◇

STAGES OF SMALL GROUPS

According to Tuckman & Jensen (1977), there are five observable stages that occur in establishing a new small group: (1) forming, (2) storming, (3) norming, (4) performing, and (5) adjourning (if the team has a short-term objective). These stages can be observed in any small-group situation, whether it be during an evening parent meeting or during a three-month-long staff assignment, or in an on-going functional team such as two team teachers with two or three aides.

The *forming stage* occurs as the group begins and a status hierarchy develops within the group. Status can be based on a person's performance skills, interpersonal skills, or the job he or she holds. Different roles begin to emerge in the group during this stage: the "tough leader," the "friendly helper," and the "clear thinker," for example. Providing the group with clear expectations helps speed this forming process along; for example, by appointing a discussion leader, a group will get into a discussion more quickly. Sometimes a group leader might be chosen merely on the basis of resources, such as the person who has the pencil and paper designated as the leader.

The *storming stage* can cause tension, and occurs when one or more group members think the leader of the group is going in a direction with which they disagree. An example of this occurred during a teacher training activity for which the assigned task was to write out a philosophy of discipline for a center. Several small groups were working on the same task as a first step towards developing a unified written statement. One person started her group off with a strong statement about her views, which favored a fairly harsh philosophy of discipline. Another teacher, in obvious disagreement, said, "Now, *wait* a minute." The possible impasse was avoided when a "clear thinker" member of the group suggested checking other written philosophies, thus channeling energies along another line. This person who broke the deadlock, incidentally, became the leader. It should be noted that this rough start was partially created by assigning an "unclear task," the characteristics of which are discussed later in the chapter.

The *norming stage* follows quickly in a short-term small-group situation, or can last several weeks or years for a work group assigned to a large task. *Norming* is defined as creating a social standard for the group. In the workplace, this norm can be a performance standard imposed from the outside, or a standard of behavior (perhaps unspoken) expected of informal group members who share the same or some of the same values. In at least some areas of reference (social, work, church, political), norming is based on shared beliefs and opinions. Group members need to feel that their objectives are worthy of attainment. They develop expectations about how people should feel about certain issues. There is usually some agreement about what is relevant and what is not. Interestingly enough, if group members perceive a difference in one of these areas, they will talk *more* about it rather than less, perhaps trying to persuade the others to their point of view.

Group norming leads to group members exerting pressure on others to conform. In the workplace, for example, an informal group might together define what constitutes "a fair day's work." Then the group members, as well as other workers, might work towards achieving this specific goal. Such group norming can increase overall effectiveness when the goals of the group are lined up with the goals of the organization. On the other hand, a negative group norm can be detrimental to the organization. If the informal group, for example, defines a fair day's work as very limited, other workers might feel pressured not to go beyond that "norm."

Rules or norms also benefit the group or team by making the group more effective and fairer for all. Norms or standards reduce the need for making decisions on routine matters and also reduce the need for using personal power.

This is a "clear task," with "leader position power" as described in the next section. "Leader-member relations" may or may not exist, but they still have a successful puddle.

Performing then follows and shows how effectively and efficiently the team can achieve results. Some teams continue to grow and learn from their experiences and each other. Current management literature calls this part of "knowledge management." They know how and when to work together and when to work independently. A team with low norms may only work at the level needed for survival, however. How successful a team is will vary partly due to the competencies related to the task and to group processes that team members bring in. See Figure 8.1.

Adjourning refers to the closure that occurs for pre-set tasks, such as during a single meeting or for a specific problem-solving task. Ongoing functional teams may continue indefinitely or until one member resigns or is re-assigned. Then, with a new member, this sequence will appear again—although moving faster—as other team members already know each other and are used to working together.

In the context of discovering how groups begin to develop norming behaviors, Figure 8.1 provides an interesting exercise for a class, for a staff meeting, or for a group just wanting a review of the ways in which people interact. To use the chart, the observer checks off behaviors that occur in the twosome or group under observation. This exercise is good practice in that it helps sharpen one's observation skills in the context of a small group. The behaviors described on the chart are arranged from least beneficial (number 1) to most beneficial (number 10). For example, the comment "What date shall we set for our next meeting?" is beneficial; it demonstrates a means of facilitating the attainment of group goals (number 10). The behavior given in number 6, "to become aware of the high cost of coercion," is beneficial because becoming

Tally
Behaviors
Used

	1. To obtain approval of others: Agreement, compliments, conformity—generally spontaneous	
	2. To reward others: Asking advice, compliments, positive responses—generally calculated	
	3. To reciprocate: Interacting or responding on the same level	
	4. To obtain marginal return: Supplying rewards that benefit, yet obligate the other person	
	5. To maximize benefit/cost ratio: Consulting indirectly, i.e., talking about a problem to get advice rather than asking for it directly; seeking advice from a group member percieved to be more like self	
	6. To become aware of the high cost of coercive attempts: Showing shrewd manipulation of the group toward the leader's point of view, perhaps using debts from past exchanges	
	7. To indicate superior bargaining position: For example, having the only copy of a book in the library checked out to you; demonstrating a skill in a technique or knowledge needed by the group	
	8. To make unique and valuable contributions in return for status: Presenting knowledge which is superior to that given by other members of the group; taking more responsibility than other members	
	9. To develop or clarify group goals: Action to ascertain that group member is certain of group goals	
	10. To facilitate attainment of group goals: Structuring the group; keeping the group to goal-directed behavior	

FIGURE 8.1
Behaviors Demonstrating Social Change

aware that coercion sets back the whole group's ability to interact helps group members avoid this approach and shows competency in group processes.

Figure 8.1 can be used either as a formal exercise or as an informal one. The observer might want to tally one person's behaviors in the left-hand column and a second person's behaviors in the right-hand column. This chart is particularly useful during staff meetings; for example, the group can do this exercise while two staff members role play a teacher-parent conference. The person role playing the part of the parent might be asked to exhibit a specific personality style that the staff selects. For instance, when the personality style chosen is that of an abusive or neglectful parent, a number of behaviors often surface. Such parents, if they talk much, usually will exhibit an overwhelming array of problems. Often, however, they do not say much at all. The leader of this exercise can interrupt the role play and ask each of the participants how they feel. The person in the teacher role usually feels frustrated and unsuccessful. The person in the parent role, however, sometimes feels more trusting and supported, and may plan to work more with the next younger child. This activity can therefore be very encouraging to teachers who are dealing with difficult situations. They become motivated to see the situation from a more long-term viewpoint and to realize that even when they see no obvious success, it does not mean that success is not occurring.

◇ ◇

SPECIALIZED ROLES

As a small group develops, two or three types of leaders can emerge. One person, for example, might focus on the task and then compete for, or take over, the position of power and influence in the group. Some researchers call these types of behaviors *goal behaviors*. Another person might work to reduce tensions in the group by telling jokes and might have an ability to develop a high interaction rate with individual group members. These people-oriented behaviors can also be called *maintenance behaviors*. The first type of leader could be said to fill the role of "tough leader," and the second, to take on the role of "friendly helper." Another label for "tough leaders" is task specialists, and for "friendly helpers," social specialists. A third role that often can be seen in small groups is the "clear thinker," which occasionally is combined with the personality characteristics of the "tough leader."

These roles are so important for group or team success that certain individuals might find themselves filling different roles in different groups, because they understand intuitively that the group will not be effective without someone stepping into a particular role. Some people might also fill different roles and provide different services at different stages in their lives. For example, a person just beginning a career might act as the "friendly helper." A person new in the community might offer to serve on the telephone committee. These different role structures in a group permit the organization to rapidly fulfill assigned tasks.

◇ ◇

PREDICTING GROUP PERFORMANCE

Fiedler (1967) developed a model, which has been reaffirmed many times (Fiedler & Garcia, 1987; and Hellriegel, Slocum, & Woodman, 1998), that would predict group or team effectiveness based on leadership style, group variables, and task variables. He found that three main factors within a situation affect group performance:

- Leader position power, or the actual power to hire and fire
- Leader-member relations, or group atmosphere (how well individuals get along)
- Task structure, or clearness of task (e.g., Can it be written down?)

On the subject of the task structure variable, Fiedler further described four ways a task might be judged clear or unclear:

1. Using an impartial measure, determine whether or not a decision can be "proved" correct. For example, do statistics or other quantitative or measurable behaviors support the decision? This is called decision verifiability.
2. Determine if the group members understand the requirements of the task. A routine task with a small number of steps is likely to be a clear task.
3. Determine if more than one procedure can be used to accomplish the task. For example, in baking a cake, there is usually only one procedure that will produce an attractive cake.
4. Determine if the problem has more than one correct solution. For example, the task of educating young children (or of all children, for that matter) is not a clear task—there are several effective ways to do it and several correct solutions to most problems.

If a task is unclear, as in steps 3 and 4 of the list, then further steps should be taken to agree on one procedure or one solution, such as agreeing on the philosophy in an early childhood program. Any tools that can add clearness to the task are helpful, such as the materials provided in Appendices A, B, and C.

Fiedler (1967) found that any group that exhibited two out of three of the major factors listed earlier (positive leader-member relations, clear task structure, and a powerful leader position) would probably be effective. Taking this discovery into account, when working in the field of education where the task is unclear, one can see that positive leader-member relations and leader position power become essential. Conversely, anything that can be done to make the task more clear (such as producing written goal statements, developing curriculum, using checklists, providing handbooks for the Executive Board or staff members) will help a small group become more effective in the field of education and in many fields. Leaders can really help group effectiveness by taking a disorganized, ill-defined problem and structuring it somewhat before presenting it to the group or team. At the other extreme, when a task is completely non-routine, a leader may have no more idea of how to perform a task than the employees do. Such a task is likely to have unclear or changing goals and multiple paths to accomplishment. At this point the other two variables will be needed for success, so a friendly, interactive problem-solving atmosphere is needed, along with some of the tools for problem solving from chapter 5, perhaps some outside resources, and a clear leader position. Fiedler believes that leaders can be taught how to become better leaders (Hellriegel, Slocum, & Woodman, 1998).

Examples of Different Group Factors

Leader Position Power

A parent committee (or any volunteer group) provides an appropriate illustration of a situation in which there is no leader position power. For example, let us say that the members and the chairperson of a parent committee are asked to design a flyer for a parent education meeting. Since there is no leader with hiring or firing power (i.e., leader position power) in any volunteer group, including this one, the other two factors become very important. Let us assume this particular group has good interpersonal relationships, or leader-member relations, and we already know that they have a clear task. When something like a written draft for a flyer is requested (a clear task), it enables an appropriate committee (presumably a Parent Education committee) to confirm all of the details involved—such as time, place, topic, theme, refreshment plans, costs, and schedule for the meeting—before writing it down in the form of a flyer. When the two factors of a clear task and positive leader-member relations are present, a group is able to successfully complete its task, in this case, producing an effective flyer. A second level of this task might be to ask the committee to write a recommended list of 20 parent education topics from which the whole parent group can select 10. This type of group interaction is diagramed in Figure 8.2.

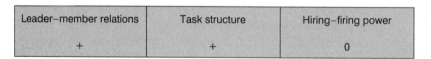

Leader–member relations	Task structure	Hiring–firing power
+	+	0

FIGURE 8.2
No Leader Position Power

Unclear Task

A different combination of factors can be seen in a staff meeting in which a director is meeting with teachers to update the curriculum to incorporate more Project and/or Reggio Emilia concepts. Updating curriculum is an unclear task, but the director does have leader position power. If the group members get along well (leader-member relations), invariably they will succeed at this task. The first step an observer will see in such a situation, however, will be numerous efforts to clarify the task. For example, they perhaps will divide into two subgroups, one for Reggio Emilia and one for project curriculum, according to their interests. Hopefully they will want to read books, articles and check the Internet for more ideas. Attempts to list major headings or categories will come next. A leader also might bring in sample curricula dealing with these approaches. Anything that can be done to clarify the task from the beginning will help the group work more effectively. Figure 8.3 provides a diagram of this type of group.

Leader-Member Relations

A third type of interaction might be seen when a director meets with staff to compose a letter to the parents on the topic "How the staff and director feel about discipline," with the intention of placing this letter in the front of both the parent handbook and the staff handbook. This is a specific task. When it has been completed, a written document will be the result. Even though the task is specific, that does not mean it will be easy; it touches on the purposes and means of discipline, a very unclear topic at best. If the members of this group get along well with each other, and with the director, so much the better. If they do not (poor leader-member or interpersonal relations), the director may want to ask each person to write an individual draft. The director can then compile these into one or two versions before presenting them to the group as a whole. Figure 8.4 provides a diagram of this type of group interaction.

Leader–member relations	Task structure	Hiring–firing power
+	0	+

FIGURE 8.3
Unclear Task

Leader–member relations	Task structure	Hiring–firing power
0	+	+

FIGURE 8.4
Poor Interpersonal Relations

Another example of Fiedler's theory can be seen when it is applied to the example of a family as a small group, which, of course, it is. Using the Morphological Analysis approach from chapter 5, one can see the progressions over the last century of the changes in the dynamics in many families as society moved from the industrial age into the information age. A set of variables, based on the small group factors for success according to Fiedler, can be listed across the top of the chart. Alternatives in family management styles can then be listed on the vertical axis.

Fiedler's Theory Shown in Morphological Analysis

Variables—Alternatives	Leader Member Relations	Clear Task	Strong Leader Position Power
1. (Industrial Age) Autocratic, Victorian Father (1850–1950)	zero (Therapy may be needed later)	"Father Knows Best" "Do as I say"	Announcements (e.g. "The family will move across the country")
2. Parents share leadership with or without a plan (1940–1980–2000)	Yes	No	No
3. (Information Age) Spouses claify tasks for a combined leadership (1995–2050[?])	Yes	Yes	Less, but shared and workable

Level Three of clarifying the task for combined family leadership is "in sync" with modern management in the information age of sharing information and decision-making to the lowest possible level. This requires more discussion and more information on the stages of child development so that expectations for different ages of children will be appropriate (See Appendix B, "Parent Papers"). It also requires use of information technology such as leaving messages on a home answering machine for one's self or spouse, or the children. One family even set up their e-mail so that with one or two clicks of a mouse the children could call Daddy's pager and tell him Mom was going into labor. (This writer was shown the message on his pager). He left his meeting with alacrity when the message came.

Sharing leadership through clear tasks allows the family to accomplish more, as can be seen even with geese. Wild Canadian geese flying south or north and even in pairs rather than flocks, alternate leadership so that they can go further by transferring to each other the burden of cutting the wind as they fly. "Even a goose knows enough to share the load" has become an expression.

Level One, the Victorian father, carried vestiges into the late 19th and 20th centuries dating from when "Father really did know best" as men had more access to education and career opportunities and were usually the only source of income. Beginning with World War II and into today, women have more education, have active careers and a longer life, and have a lot of input in their families as sources of knowledge, income and as resources for decision making. Many are or have been, single parent heads of households (which again reinserts the variable of "Strong Leader Position Power"—because there is only one). In the times of Victorian autocratic fathers, two of the three variables were in place. So successful families resulted and it mattered less that father had poor "leader-member relations" or wasn't liked much in regards to successful outcomes for children. A lot of emotional damage was done in these times, however.

There followed a period in which leadership between parents became shared, often without clarity, and fathers and mothers *did* get along well with the children, but only one factor (leader-member relations) was present and many of these children had few goals, no clearness in their lives (for tasks or anything else quite often) and often were still living at home in their twenties and thirties, sapping their own (and others') self-esteem.

One easier solution to this dilemma lies in the clarifying of the tasks in raising a family in many ways that are possible, including frequent discussions of goals, tasks, and activities. Sharing information is good for children's vocabularies and is the "Information Age" secret to good parenting and successful families and organizations. Love will always be the main ingredient in successful families, however.

◇ ◇

TEAM LEARNING AND SHARED VISION

Now that some of the dynamics of small groups have been analyzed and understood, a better understanding of "team learning" is possible. As was mentioned previously, as a team becomes more aligned, a shared vision and philosophy emerges, and individual energies harmonize (Senge, 1990). A musical ensemble is an example of this same cohesiveness, or synergy, in which the whole becomes greater than the sum of its parts.

Educational organizations that emphasize continued learning on the part of staff (team learning) can work together with shared energy and enthusiasm. According to Senge (1990), such organizations need people who continually expand their capabilities; this leads to greater understanding of the complexities of the task, to clearer vision, and to an improved sharing of mental models, whether these are mental models for curriculum or scenarios for the center and the parents (see chapter 3 on planning). For those aspiring to build such a team, being responsible for the learning opportunities of children, adults, and one's self is a first step. Senge (1990) sees leaders as designers, stewards, and teachers, and notes that while learning disabilities are tragic in children, they are fatal in organizations.

◇ ◇

THOUGHTS ON TEAM BUILDING

Coming together is a beginning; helping together is progress; working together is success.

Henry Ford (1863–1947)
American Industrialist

People acting together as a group can accomplish things which no individual acting alone could ever hope to bring about.

Franklin Delano Roosevelt (1882–1945)
Thirty-second U.S. President

Let each of you look out not only for your own interests, but also for the interests of others.

Philippians 2:4

Success becomes possible the minute you realize you can't do it alone.

Robert Shuler
"Possibility Thinking" speaker and author

A team is the most advanced form of group.

Jerry Spiegel and Cresencio Torres,
Managers Official Guide to Team Working (1994)

In assessing a child-care center's team and "teamness," consider constructing appropriate rating scales (Eitington, 1984, pp. 361–364). Figure 8.5 shows an assessment scale that provides a list of characteristics describing "teamness"; the person using this tool is asked to use a scale from 1 to 5 to rate how well each characteristic applies to the group. The completed assessment provides not only a measure of the group's present effectiveness, but also establishes a goal to strive for. Such a rating scale can be given out as an exercise at a staff meeting. Small groups could then divide up the five top selections (and perhaps the five bottom selections also) and discuss implementation strategies. Then the whole group can reconvene to discuss the ideas.

Another rating scale can be constructed that assesses team communication. The scale, similar to Figure 8.6, can be constructed with 8 or 10 statements describing communication when it is at its best.

A rating scale that assesses team problem-solving and creativity might show statements about group problem-solving, similar to the scale shown in Figure 8.7.

Once these scales are developed and adapted for the center, they can be distributed to staff for self-assessment. These measures can be used as a springboard for discussion at a staff meeting, and they can be especially useful as an occasion for praise and recognition of a staff that is really working well together.

Please rank from 1 (doesn't apply) to 5 (strongly applies)

_____	Sense of ability	_____	Empowerment
_____	Cohesion	_____	Cooperation
_____	Pride, sense of competence	_____	Communication
_____	Decision-making	_____	Goal setting
_____	Openness	_____	Creativity
_____	Trust	_____	Conflict
_____	Team self-assessment	_____	Support
_____	Team membership identification	_____	Mutual respect
_____	Leadership	_____	Commitment
_____	Feedback to leader	_____	Atmosphere

FIGURE 8.5
"Teamness" Assessment Rating

FIGURE 8.6
A Rating Scale to Assess Team Communication

Please rank from 1 (strongly disagree) to 5 (strongly agree)

_____ 1. Members listen to each other.

_____ 2. The leader listens to all team members.

_____ 3. There is freedom to be candid with each other.

_____ 4. Constructive feedback is freely interchanged to improve the group.

_____ 5. Members all participate at meetings.

_____ 6. Members double-check with each other before taking action.

_____ 7. "Air-time" is shared fairly at meetings.

_____ 8. Resources are available for information needed by the team.

_____ 9. Information is shared willingly and not withheld, including information on new policies, projects, and pay.

_____ 10. Members are not afraid to tell the leader "bad news."

_____ 11. The leader is candid about performance so that there are no surprises at personnel evaluation time.

_____ 12. The team communicates well with other groups in the organization.

FIGURE 8.7
Assessing Team Problem-Solving and Creativity

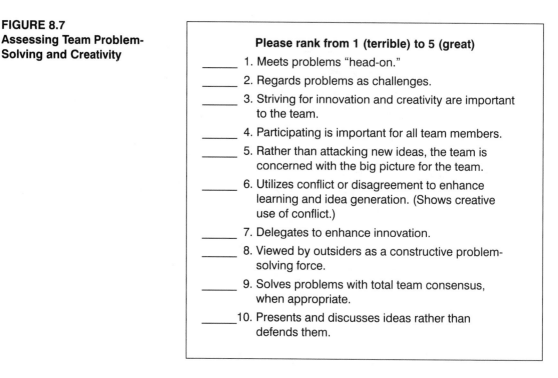

Please rank from 1 (terrible) to 5 (great)

_____ 1. Meets problems "head-on."

_____ 2. Regards problems as challenges.

_____ 3. Striving for innovation and creativity are important to the team.

_____ 4. Participating is important for all team members.

_____ 5. Rather than attacking new ideas, the team is concerned with the big picture for the team.

_____ 6. Utilizes conflict or disagreement to enhance learning and idea generation. (Shows creative use of conflict.)

_____ 7. Delegates to enhance innovation.

_____ 8. Viewed by outsiders as a constructive problem-solving force.

_____ 9. Solves problems with total team consensus, when appropriate.

_____10. Presents and discusses ideas rather than defends them.

Why focus on getting work done by teams? Early childhood programs have naturally and informally relied on teams for generations, but knowing the hallmarks of high performing teams helps:

1. Clear, realistic expectations of the team
2. Common understanding of the team leader role
3. Adequate resources (people, facilities, equipment, information, time and money needed to accomplish their mission)
4. Empowerment (have some authority to take action and make decisions)
5. Feedback (internal and external)
6. Importance (team members have greater motivation when they realize the importance of their work)
7. Compatibility (must be willing to work with each other).

Evaluate your teams on these essentials. When the team has high scores on each of these areas, both productivity (happy, competent children) and job satisfaction will be high.

◇ ◇

SUMMARY

A small group exists when two or more people have a unifying relationship, such as common goals or physical proximity. Utilizing the characteristics of groups is an important skill of leadership, and understanding their dynamics as described by Fiedler or other theorists can be useful. Team dynamics and outcomes are affected by the interplay of context, goals, roles, size, member roles, norms, cohesiveness and leadership. Characteristics of groups include norms, which are standards of behavior expected by group members, and individual roles, which can consist of a person's total pattern of expected behavior or of behavior during certain situations.

An informal group is defined as two or more people associated with one another in ways different from the formal organizational structure. Informal group leaders can be powerful and may be chosen by consensus, or to fill a leadership vacuum, but they are usually trusted. As such, an informal group leader is a good person for a formal leader to have on his or her side, and often is able to explain things to the community. Informal leaders are sometimes called "opinion leaders" in sociology. The synergism and energy that teams and small groups can provide are a beneficial force for accomplishing an organization's objectives.

◇ ◇ ◇ ◇ ◇ ◇ ◇ ◇ ◇ ◇ ◇ ◇ ◇ ◇ ◇ ◇ ◇ ◇ ◇ ◇

SUGGESTED CLASS ACTIVITIES AND DISCUSSIONS

1. *Small Groups Demonstrating Fiedler Variables.*   The class can form into three small groups. Then give a discussion assignment to each group demonstrating different combinations of variables as described in the text. One group could be a volunteer (no hiring-firing power) group from the Board and/or parents' group designing a flyer (clear task) for an upcoming event. Another group might be teachers and the director writing a Discipline Position Statement for the center (unclear task). A third group could be teachers without the director present asked to clarify the language arts used in the curriculum. (An unclear task, no hiring-firing power: One would expect this group to get "stuck"). As the groups are forming, have an observer in each group (assigned privately) to record the "forming," "storming," and "norming" of the group. When the groups report back, have the observer report back also.

2. *Role Play Using the Behavioral Change Checklist (Fig. 8.1).*   The class can be observers for a role play and distribute copies of Figure 8.1 from the text. Ask two class members to be players with one trying to persuade the others to do something. The class can use the columns on the left and right of the

chart, one per role player, to check the number of times that behavior is demonstrated. A situation for the role play might be the director trying to tell a teacher to take a course or her job will be jeopardized. If these coercive words are actually used, the "teacher player" immediately tries to obtain some benefit in return such as released time or more pay. Without any instruction this role play uncovers some natural problem-solving talents on the part of students.

3. *Teamness Assessment Rating Use.*   Using Fig. 8.5 or an adapted version designed by the class, role play a staff meeting in a small group in front of the class (sometimes called a "fish bowl" role play). Have the class circle five good behaviors they see and five poor behaviors they see. After the role play, have the class discuss how this staff meeting could have been improved. A difficult problem should be discussed (such as moving the center to another building).

4. *Team Communication Rating Scale.*   Following the Staff Meeting role play described above, or a second staff meeting role play, have the whole class, including the role players, fill out the chart in Figure 8.6. Discuss how the staff "team" could have had better communication.

5. *Board Meeting Role Play: Team Problem Solving and Creativity Rating Scale.*   Ask the class to observe another role play in a "fish bowl" setting with the Board discussing a difficult problem, such as the need to raise tuition. Distribute copies of Figure 8.7 to the whole class, (to Board Member role players after the role play), fill out the chart and discuss the role play.

6. *Analyze the Seven Types of Differences Between Teachers and Parents Trying to Work Together.*   Discuss in turn the *power, goals roles, personal* and *professional images, pay* and *objectives* perceived by the teachers and by the parents. Do this both for the teacher half of the group and for the parent half of the group in a role play with half of the class in each group. Generate solutions and strategies to rise above these differences. For example, parents think teachers have power, especially power over their child's life for that year. Teachers often feel relatively powerless. Understanding these "structural role conflicts" better helps to build the team of teacher and parent to help the child learn.

◇ ◇ ◇ ◇ ◇ ◇ ◇ ◇ ◇ ◇ ◇ ◇ ◇ ◇ ◇ ◇ ◇ ◇ ◇ ◇

BIBLIOGRAPHY

Argyris, C. (1962). *Interpersonal competence and organizational effectiveness.* Homewood, IL: Dorsey Press.

Argyris, C. (1985). *Strategy, change and defensive routines.* Boston: Pittman.

Beach, D. S. (1980). *Managing people at work: Readings in personnel.* New York: Wiley.

Bonner, H. (1968). *Group dynamics: Principles and applications.* New York: Harper and Row.

Cartwright, D. (Ed.). (1968). *Group dynamics, research and theory*. New York: Harper and Row.

Eitington, J. E. (1984). *The winning trainer*. Houston: Gulf Publishing House.

Feldman, D. C. (1984). The development and enforcement of group norms. *Academy of Management Review*, 9, 47–53.

Fiedler, F. E. (1967). *A theory of leadership effectiveness*. New York: McGraw-Hill.

Fiedler, F. E., & Garcia, J. E. (1987). *New approaches to effective leadership*. New York: Wiley.

Gersick, C. J. (1988). Time and transition in work teams: Toward a new model of group development. *Academy of Management Journal*, 31, 9-41.

Hellriegel, D., Slocum, J. W., & Woodman, R. W. (1998). *Organizational behavior*. Cincinnati, OH: South-Western College Publishing.

Hitchcock, D., & Willard, M. (1995). *Why teams fail and what to do about it*. Homewood, IL: Irwin.

Jacobs, T. O. (1970). *Leadership and exchange in formal organizations*. Alexandria, VA: Human Resources Research Organization.

Jaffee, C. L., & Lucas, R. L. (1969). Effect of rates of talking and correctness of decisions on leader choice in small groups. *Journal of Social Psychology, 79,* 247–254.

Kiefer, C., & Stroh, P. (1984). A new paradigm for developing organizations. In J. Adams (Ed.), *Transforming work*. Alexandria, VA: Miles Riler Press.

Larson, C., & LaFasto, F. (1989). *Teamwork: What must go right/What can go wrong*. Troy, NY: Sage Publications.

Mankin, D., Cohen, S. G., & Bikson, T. K. (1996). *Teams and technology*. Boston: Harvard Business School Press.

Obert, S. L. (1983). Developmental patterns of organizational task groups: A preliminary study. *Human Relations*, 36, 37-52.

Parker, G. M. (1994). *Cross-functional teams*. San Francisco: Jossey-Bass.

Pritchett, P. (1992). *The team member handbook for teamwork*. Dallas, TX: Pritchett Publishing Co.

Schon, D. (1983). *The reflective practitioner: How professionals think in action*. New York: Basic Books.

Senge, P. M. (1990). *The fifth discipline: The art and practice of the learning organization*. New York: Doubleday.

Stoneman, K. G., & Dickinson, A. M. (1989). Individual performances as a function of group contingencies and group size. *Journal of Organizational Behavior Management*, 10, 131-150.

Strata, R. (1989, Spring). Organizational learning—the key to management innovation. *Sloan Management Review*, pp. 63–64.

Tuckman, B. W.(1965). Development sequence in small groups. *Psychological Bulletin*, 62, 384-399.

Tuckman, B. W., & Jensen, M. A. C. (1977). Stages of small group development. *Group & Organization Studies, 2,* 419-427.

Wageman, R. (1995). Interdependence and group effectiveness. *Administrative Science Quarterly, 40,* 145-180.

Zander, A. (1994). *Making groups effective* (2nd ed.). San Francisco: Jossey-Bass.

Zenger, J. H., Muselwhite, E., Hurson, K., & Perrin, C. (1994). *Leading teams*. Homewood, IL: Irwin.

Professionalism:
More Than Meets the Eye

After World War II, the word *professional* was used in the U.S. workforce almost interchangeably with the words *experienced* or *trained,* as in reference to a doctor or a lawyer. The Industrial Age, which Toffler (1980) calls "the Second Wave," put experts on a towering pedestal. One of the basic rules of this period, according to Toffler, was "specialize to succeed" (p. 262). In the late 1970s, the word *professional* referred to a specialist in a general field; for example, a special education teacher or a dental hygienist fit the definition of *professional.* The 1980s brought the term *professional* into the affective domain by characterizing the word as a mental focus or an attitude. A professional was a total package, a complete entity. This affective attitude came at a good time for those working in the child-care industry in the 1990s, because of the U.S. President's interest in child care. With today's new child care and training issues, child care has become a national political issue as well as a state and local one. Thus, the field of early childhood has now evolved into a true profession, which currently encompasses early childhood education, child development, preschool, and child care. Each of these aspects also has its own subfields related to the umbrella profession.

The educational reform movements of the 1980s and 1990s also influenced the professionalization of the early childhood field. As the nation focused on issues such as quality education, developmentally appropriate curriculum and practice, and better teacher training, those who were part of the early childhood field had legitimate data to present. Currently, education is facing even more reforms, and the early childhood field has an even stronger role in building a solid educational foundation. David Elkind (1990) said,

> I am not an economist. But I can do simple arithmetic. When I subtract the cost of psychological and educational remediation at later age levels (from the cost of developmental child care), I come up with a huge surplus. From that simple-minded calculation, I argue that money spent on insuring quality child care is a wise investment that in the long run will save the nation both money and anguish. (p. 28)

In a discussion of why teacher professionalism is important at all levels, nursery through grade 12 (or N–12), Michael Fullan (1993b) states that teaching and teacher development are fundamental to the future of society. He calls for action that links initial teacher development with continuous teacher development, even if this means restructuring universities and schools and their relationship to each other. Since child-care personnel are frequently called "teachers," and in fact are teachers, child-care centers should be included in this restructuring as well. These centers deal with children in the formative first four or five years of life.

Systems such as the N–12 education system do not change by themselves; it is the actions of individuals and small groups working on new concepts and approaches that produce the breakthroughs. One of these breakthroughs is the new paradigm for teacher professionalism, which covers all elements of children's programs for all ages of children (Fullan, 1993b, p. 17).

◇ ◇

PROFESSIONALISM: A NEW PERSPECTIVE

It is helpful to look at the attributes of all professions when discussing the early childhood profession and the adult professionals who work in programs for young children. The attributes of a profession include:

1. Specialized knowledge;
2. Agreed-upon principles and ethics;
3. Knowledge that is based on the practical rather than the academic (e.g., the precedents in law versus those in philosophy);
4. Theoretical knowledge that is not known to lay persons;
5. Membership in professional associations or in societies that publish journals, give conferences, and promote continuing education;
6. Prolonged specialized training required by all professions;
7. "Standards of Practice" are adopted by a profession;

8. A code of ethics is adopted and shared by a profession as the client is in a "lower power" position;

9. Work is performed with autonomous practice. Members of a profession work with some autonomy with respect to the client (e.g., they do not dictate to the client) and with respect to the employer (the employer does not dictate the practice and values of the profession); and

10. An altruistic mission or vision. A profession sees itself as altruistic, that is, doing work that is essential to society. Professionals identify their goals with the good of humanity. This altruism can mean working longer hours on occasion and inhibits professionals from slipping into customer/sales language. (Katz, 1987)

Child-care professionals provide education, care, nurturing, safety, and security to young children, but the service of providing child care is given to the parents or guardians of those children, rather than to the children themselves. These parents and guardians perceive child-care providers as being service-givers, whether in the public sector or the private sector. Therefore, a look at the history of public servants is warranted.

In his discussion of the evolution of American public service, Frederick Mosher (1968, 1982) outlined the chronology of public servants, an adaptation of which is shown in Table 9.1.

Government by the Gentleman

When the United States Constitution was ratified, a great many of those in influential positions in the new government were landed gentry (wealthy landowners) who were loyal to the new government and showed great fitness of character. These men were veterans or supporters of the War for Independence, and, as such, were thought to have proven their loyalty, and their service was viewed as a personal investment in the new government. These positioned gentlemen held high ideals about the new democracy, and contributed much to this new form of government " . . . of the people, by the people, for the

TABLE 9.1
Chronology of Public Servants

1789–1830	Government by the Gentleman
1830–1883	Government by the Common Man
1883–1906	Government by the Good
1906–1937	Government by the Efficient
1937–1960	Government by the Administrator
1960–2000	Government by the Professionals

Adapted from *Democracy and the Public Service* by F. Mosher, 1968, 1982, New York: Oxford Press.

people. . . ." This period was also called the "guardian" period as those in public service were "guarding" this precious new government. The standard of "fitness of character" and high moral standards was applied and the criteria included family background, educational experience, and having a high status occupational background.

Government by the Common Man

The election of Andrew Jackson in 1828 ushered in the "Era of the Common Man." Jackson was the first candidate to appeal to and depend on voters to elect him to office rather than on the backing of a particular political machine. Beginning with this election, the ordinary citizen began to participate in the workings of the government. Entry into the process was through the "spoils system," that is, government appointments in return for political support. Although Thomas Jefferson, president from 1801 to 1809, was probably the first to make use of the spoils system by refusing to appoint Federalists to political office after his Democratic-Republican party was established, it was during Jackson's presidency that the phrase "to the victor belong the spoils" was introduced and openly practiced.

While the spoils system did much to increase loyalty to particular candidates and political parties, this arrangement also proved to be a breeding ground for corruption, incompetence, and nepotism. A classic example of this system gone awry was the Tammany Hall establishment in New York City. The Society of Tammany, which was originally begun to further the ideals of independence, liberty, and federal union of the country, soon turned to political activities. Many scandals are associated with the Society of Tammany as its power as a Democratic political machine overstepped its bounds. Another example of the spoils system under Andrew Jackson that brought this process closer to home was the political appointment of local postmasters.

This spoils and patronage period brought with it more of an equal opportunity for public service, based on party loyalty of course, but it also brought about the decline of public service in popular esteem. Additionally it introduced the concept of simplicity of government/public service work, that is, work that is so simple that even the "common man" can do it. Later, the legal profession began to receive many of the executive non-career appointments (Mosher, 1982).

Government by the Good

The Pendleton Act, or the Civil Service Act of 1883, ushered into public service the concepts of merit pay and promotion, and gave rise to moral crusades like child labor laws. President Woodrow Wilson called for the separation of administration and workers, and public servants were asked to remain politically neutral. To this day, *neutral competence* is the watchword of public servants as administrations change, in an attempt to separate policy and politics from administration. The merit pay system brought with it competitive exams with "open" service and entry possible at all levels. Civil service reform was considered a "moral imperative." The Civil Service Commission was formed at this time, but later when it became the Office of Personnel Management also became somewhat politicized.

Government by the Efficient

In the late 1940s, Frederick Taylor's scientific management theories became popular. Using scientific methods, Taylor studied and measured the problems of the workplace. Time and energy management and specialization of tools, machines, and people were some of the concepts he introduced. He emphasized rationality, quantitative measurements, specialization, standardization, and efficiency; in other words, "maximum output, minimum upkeep" (Taylor, 1947). Currently, some bureaucracies who look backward to the Industrial Age rather than forward to the Information Age still aspire to this goal. Some even confuse machines with people when it comes to the expectations made of personnel.

The science of work and management included personnel management and brought in position classification with the concept of rank and pay being attached to the job and not to the person. Specialization proliferated, with each specialization attempting to develop a career ladder. Quantitative measurement and the concept of "one best way" (rigorously followed) came in with standardization, which may have been applicable to machines in industry, but certainly is NOT applicable to young children. Some of the specialization still hinders the field of early childhood care and education as it attempts to bridge the social work and education disciplines and expectations (or lack of expectations) of experts and specialists in each field diverge.

Government by the Administrator and Manager

Because of the great economic and social problems that occurred during the Great Depression era, the federal government assumed a much larger role in the everyday lives of U.S. citizens. Franklin Roosevelt, whose administrative effectiveness ranks him as one of the United States' most innovative Presidents, created many new government agencies to deal with the problems the country faced. In fact, so many new organizations were created that Roosevelt felt the need to establish a committee to recommend solutions for the new administrative tangles all these agencies brought about. One recommendation made by this new committee, called the Brownlow Committee, was that the Civil Service Commission become a federal agency headed by a single administrator who would report directly to the president. The committee also recommended that personnel management be integrated with general management. In doing so, personnel functions were decentralized, allowing middle and lower management greater input into the decision-making processes.

In 1949, the Classification Act was passed, which formally outlined the responsibility of government agencies to provide job descriptions, performance evaluations, and promotions. Principles of Management, sometimes known as POSDCORB (Plan, Organize, Staff, Develop, Coordinate, Operate, Review, Budget), became a teachable discipline. Other similar strategies and theories became popular as well. More flexible management, better motivated management, rewards and penalties for good and bad management, development and selection of better managers and more innovative management all were instituted during this period.

Government by the Professionals

Currently, one out of every three public servants is a professional; that is, they have formal training, a license or certification, and belong to a professional organization. Expertise is power, and knowledge is the most flexible, versatile, and basic kind of power (Toffler, 1990, p. 474).

The Civil Service Reform Act of 1978 eliminated the bipartisan Civil Service Commission, and in its place established the Office of Personnel Management (OPM), the Merit System Protection Board, and the Federal Labor Relations Board. Each of these organizations has leadership with professional credentials, even if they are politically appointed.

Unionization of public employees has accelerated during the last two decades. Although unions have existed in the American workplace for many years, it was President Kennedy, through an executive order, who allowed government employees to organize into unions or to engage in collective bargaining (Moore, 1985), thus allowing professionals more input into decision-making.

Viewed broadly, the professions are social mechanisms wherein knowledge, especially new knowledge, is transmitted into action and service. Professions have become a larger proportion of the labor force, and professional attitude and status is sought after in many fields, as well as in early childhood care and education. In fact, for the information or knowledge age, effective professional service is considered a top goal (as compared with efficient mechanical output as a goal for the industrial age) (Peters, 1992). In the public service field, a professional conveys knowledge and theory into areas of public service. Professionals provide leadership in a number of public agencies and through education, examinations, accreditation, and licensing they largely determine what the profession is, in terms of knowledge, skills and work.

Professionals influence public policy and the definition of public purpose, in the fields in which they operate; they provide or control the recruitment, selection and many personnel actions for the professional members; and they (can) shape the structure and the social organization of many public agencies, large and small, including a child care center. Some conflicts arise between government's bureaucratic controls and the treasured ideal of individual autonomy in professionalism, service to (and fees from) individual clients, and vocational self-government which can be seen in the NAEYC accreditation system. However, professional managers and professional employees are mutually supportive and see themselves as both representative of the interests of the profession (in this case children and parents). Furthermore, the objectives and standards of an agency or organization are usually not in conflict with the aspirations and goals of the professional workers. (In this case they both want "what's best for the child.") Conflict can arise, as mentioned earlier, when the goals and aspirations of social service agencies and professionals collide with different goals and aspirations of educational agencies and professionals in early care and education, which bridges both worlds. This conflict may be due to different educational backgrounds, cultures, standards, or perceived prestige. Both of these fields need the mutual support of the other as they have common objectives for early care and education, if not common funding sources.

◇ ◇ ◇ ◇ ◇ ◇ ◇ ◇ ◇ ◇ ◇ ◇ ◇ ◇ ◇ ◇ ◇ ◇ ◇ ◇

PROFESSIONAL WORK: SOME CHARACTERISTICS

In his book *What Every Supervisor Should Know* (1985), Lester Bittel outlines four unique characteristics that separate professional work from other types of work. These characteristics are complementary to, but different from, those qualities described by Lillian Katz at the beginning of this chapter.

1. *Professional work is investigative in nature.* Assignments that are approached from a professional point of view are done so with observation skills, record keeping, analysis, and follow-through. Conclusions and problem-solving done any other way are more or less haphazard.

2. *Professional work requires individual contributions.* In an organization where all team members have a common goal of excellence, each professionally minded person will make a personal commitment and contribution to the goal.

3. *Professional work is not routine or repetitive.* This may seem an odd characteristic when thinking about the child-care field, but looking at each child creatively is far from routine and repetitive. Professional people look for creative, enriching ways to go about everyday tasks and view children as unique and individual.

4. *Professional work increases in importance and difficulty, but the increase does not occur in discrete stages.* Just as children do not all develop in the same way and at the same time, neither does a job well-done. There are wide ranges between the simple and the complex in the field of child care and in the administration of programs, but as administrators and staff capitalize on their strengths and work on their weaknesses, the program as a whole becomes more productive.

Bittel also answers the question, "How can I, the supervisor, learn to modify my approach when dealing with each individual employee's perception of professional work?"

1. *Realize that professional employees want to be recognized as members of a profession.* Truly professional employees are more often career-oriented than company- or center-oriented. They are usually individualists who are constantly evaluating themselves. They dislike regimentation and compulsion.

2. *Ensure credit and recognition from top management and parents is given to employees for outstanding work and unusual accomplishments.* Generally speaking, professional employees guard their own ideas and do not appreciate it when someone else, especially a supervisor, takes credit for their ideas.

3. *Give proper dignity to the title of each position held by each employee.* Job titles are as important as the job itself.

4. *Adopt liberal policies with respect to time off for personal reasons.* Professional employees enjoy a work environment where rigid control of the time clock and the policy manual are the exception rather than the rule. People respond positively to "being treated like a professional."

5. *Encourage knowledgeable workers to take part in the activities of their professional societies.* Networking with other child-care professionals can validate an employee's work.

◇ ◇

TEACHER/DIRECTOR BURNOUT AND FATIGUE

Katz (1975), in listing the principles of teaching teachers, suggests that teachers will interact with children in the way that they themselves have been taught. If respect is shown to teachers and their self-image is valued, they are more likely to pass this respect on to other adults and to the children they teach. Human development research reports that employees in the service fields need to experience basic fulfillment in order to do their best jobs helping

Continued, loving attention to children is a goal in excellent early care and education, but this can be hampered by low morale and burnout.

others, whether children or adults. In fact, the degree to which these workers feel fulfilled will be reflected in the degree to which they give of themselves.

Consider the very real problem of teachers in role conflict. According to Katz (1975) and Fuller and Brown (1975), this conflict is especially felt in the first year of teaching. Teachers and child-care administrators often see themselves divided into two contradictory roles: the executive, who is directive, supervisory, and critical; and the counselor, who is supportive and oriented toward the pursuit of knowledge. The constant tension between these two roles, plus the stress caused by insufficient time for extraneous (or required) duties, takes a toll on the personality. Sometimes, no matter what reforms are made, teachers leave their building each day discouraged, angry, and depleted. These consequences are detrimental to teacher morale and effectiveness, and many teachers resign or become ultra critical.

The concern in teacher education and administration for the feelings and self-concept of teachers is perhaps the result of this perception of the "psychological drain" that occurs in helping professions such as teaching children. Teacher and director burnout and fatigue can develop if these concerns are not addressed. It is generally being recognized that teachers learn by doing, just as children do (Jones, 1973), and that active involvement in the learning process is the most likely method of developing and changing feelings, beliefs, attitudes, and understandings in teachers. In other words, by providing teachers with opportunities to learn, burnout and fatigue can be avoided or lessened.

College courses and staff development programs can be a great asset to administrators of early childhood programs. Those who have participated in such sessions have listed problem-solving activities and "the feeling of support gained from finding out that others share the same dilemmas" as the most valued experiences in these programs. Other comments found in program evaluations by early childhood directors include: "It's nice to know of others with the same problems"; "This is the kind of 're-charging' I need after a year and a half of solo work"; "I feel better about everything now"; "I'm changing my priorities to support teachers more now"; "This was an inspiration to tackle many of the things I've put off—I've been bogged down in day-to-day busy work." Topics felt to be of particular value were staff relationships, home learning activity enablers, newsletter writing, brainstorming techniques, incorporation procedures, and budgeting time. Experiencing the feeling that "we are all working together" and that there are many different solutions to similar problems is a valuable benefit to administrators in the thick of day-to-day childcare operations.

Administrators can help bolster teachers by realizing that effective administration of programs for children requires that warmth and sincere support be given to the teachers, who are directly involved with the children. Helping teachers find rewards and job satisfaction in daily encounters with children and adults, and seeking and providing training in all aspects of a program from budget to curriculum to the building of satisfactory interpersonal relationships, seem reasonable goals. The teacher must be respected, cared for, and fulfilled.

To handle the many stresses of the early childhood field, it is essential to learn coping mechanisms, one of which is developing self-management skills. Other strategies might include: (1) seeking knowledge of group dynamics and motivation theory; (2) seeking skills relevant to, and awareness of, one's own personal style; (3) seeking knowledge of alternative ways of presenting curriculum content; and (4) sharing problems and solutions with peers. Suggestions for mechanisms include: (1) selecting a goal, (2) recording the quantity and circumstances of behavior, (3) changing the settings for events, (4) establishing effective consequences, and (5) focusing on environmental contingencies.

Teachers and administrators need to develop the ability to self-encourage, so that they can sustain their efforts when others are not around to provide support. Taking part in self-management training programs can help teachers maintain their enthusiasm rather than becoming discouraged when personal difficulties and frustrations are encountered. Winklestein (1976) suggests that the usability, availability, and continuity of such training are basic considerations in helping teachers maintain professionalism and avoid burnout and fatigue. Katz (1975) recommends that the time of training be shifted so that more training is available to the teacher *on* the job rather than *before* it. Many teachers say that their preservice education has had only a minor influence on their day-to-day activities in the classroom, which suggests that strategies and techniques learned before employment often will not be used in actual job situations.

According to Katz (1975), and as implied by Winklestein's (1976) requirements for the availability and continuity of training, timing or pacing of teacher training is important for early childhood education teachers as well as for teachers of children of all ages. Research points to "developmental stages" that occur during teaching, with special needs marking each stage. Katz (1972) lists these stages as survival, consolidation, renewal, and maturity, each of which lasts about one year. In writing about how teachers' feelings affect the way they deal with children, Katz believes (and other writers agree) that the way administrators treat teachers is the same way that teachers will then treat children. By thinking of teachers as being in developmental stages, it is easier to determine the right, and therefore most useful, timing of possible training offerings.

Wade (1977) found, in a review of teacher education research, that teachers valued mutual support and encouragement; pooling ideas and resources; and the chance to reflect and develop judgments by comparing individual responses to the same experiences. Child-care directors and early childhood teachers particularly benefit from these components when they are incorporated into teacher training. These items could be set as goals for methodology in the early childhood teacher training curriculum.

Incorporating a methodology concerned with the basic needs of teachers into the curriculum, and timing the presentation of staff development and workshop offerings so that on-the-job adults can participate, are ideas supported in the research as well as in some successful programs currently offered.

◊ ◊

PROFESSIONALISM: REALISTIC GOALS FOR CHILD-CARE ADMINISTRATORS

When considered realistically, professionalism is not a trait inherent at birth. It is an attitude that takes time, experience, and a solid knowledge base to acquire. Some goals for which a professional child-care administrator should strive are:

- A solid knowledge base of the varied fields of early childhood education and of basic, good leadership and management principles
- Appropriate practice based on that knowledge base

- Strategic planning, in which short-term and long-term goals are set and achieved (see chapters 2 and 3)
- Networking within professional organizations such as the National Education Association (NEA), National Association for the Education of Young Children (NAEYC), state and local Associations for Young Children (AYCs), Child Care Information Exchange, and local professional, early childhood, and business organizations
- Providing meaningful in-service training and participatory decision-making for center employees, which conveys a message of professionalism and empowerment to the staff (See chapter 4 for a discussion of decision-making.)

◇ ◇

PROFESSIONALS IN A GROWING PROFESSION

As child-care professionals identify new needs in their field, more models of effective child-care centers are required. One method of envisioning ways to develop new or additional centers (or organizations) is described by Toffler (1990). In the context of what he calls a "flex-firm," smaller units are able to draw information, people, and money from one another or from other outside organizations. This concept might be particularly useful for professional child-care administrators who wish to develop more child-care slots and additional centers under one umbrella. Within the flex-firm, the units may be next door to one another—as in California where centers purchase one, two, or more residential homes and convert them to child-care centers—or across town, across the state, even across continents. With a computer, a telephone, and a facsimile machine, these units can enjoy a free, fast flow of information. Unit functions may overlap or be divided logically (such as preschool and school-age children in separate units), geographically, or financially. Individual units can choose to either use or adapt central services provided by headquarters. People can thus trade ideas, data, hints, insights, facts, strategies, kindly gestures, and smiles that are essential to an efficient organization (Toffler, 1990, p. 187).

Connecting the right people with the right information is the key to effecting change at every level. With the need for child care tripling and quadrupling while the number of child-care centers is only doubling (Hamburg, 1990), the need for excellent, professional child-care programs to expand in one way or another is evident. Research reports that centers of 60 children or fewer are ideal for children (Spodek and Saracho, 1990), but more centers are needed. The flex-firm umbrella concept, along with modern technology and child-care software programs, enables this effort.

Future Needs for Early Childhood Professionals

Since there are a variety of settings for early childhood professionals as well as a variety of programs, many competencies and a broad knowledge base are needed. Spodek and Saracho (1990) list 12 predictions regarding the profession of early childhood education.

1. The field of early childhood education will continue to expand and there will be an increasing need for early childhood practitioners.

2. The children enrolled in early childhood programs will continue to be more diverse (and younger and younger), making teaching a more complex task.

3. The role of the early childhood teacher will expand to become increasingly responsible for out-of-class activities. (These activities will include parent education components as well as health, nutrition, and social services elements.)

4. A distinction between the care and the education of young children will continue to be made, as will a distinction between the practitioners who provide those services.

5. There will continue to be distinct levels of professionalism among early childhood practitioners, as well as varied ways of entering the field.

6. Practitioners will continue to enter the field with a wide range of levels of preparation.

7. The move toward better educated and better prepared certified teachers of young children will continue, which will include more teacher preparation programs that go beyond a four-year degree.

8. Early childhood personnel training programs will continue to expand at the vocational and community college level.

9. Use of electronic media will be expanded in the preparation of teachers. (Note: This is true for many disciplines.)

10. While the older ideas of competency-based and field-based teacher education programs will continue to decline, new approaches to field-based programs will be elaborated with the creation of university-related professional development centers.

11. Professional associations will continue to press for higher standards of practice and higher standards for entrance into the field of early childhood education.

12. The knowledge base of early childhood education will continue to expand both through research and through contributions from such fields as medicine, sociology and anthropology.

As Saracho and Spodek point out, these are predictions, not inevitabilities; however, in a field as diverse and fast growing as early childhood education, they are helpful. In the future "one stop shopping" may be needed for parents and families to bridge the fields of early childhood education and social services. At higher levels, these two sets of professionals differ in terms of education, organizational culture and bureaucracy, and goals and expectations.

"Bridging" of these two fields (and others) can be done with information technology as an aid. The federal government is working towards "one stop shopping" and self-service by the public and by partnering agencies. Other country's governments have improved efficiency, provided new services, gained benefits from new technology, and increased service to the citizens (in early care and education this means children and families), by integrating eight or more agencies to be accessed through a single computer window. Ireland is preparing to set up a system like this, Australia calls its system "Centrelink," and in Portugal the INFOCID system is available in kiosks in public locations. Vertical integration can be seen at the local, state, and federal levels for children (and also for the aging) in the state of New York.

The next step for self-service governments is to integrate commonly requested services into a single computer accessed window. Innovative funding is needed to do this with taxes and bonds, grants, and the sale of public assets. In the early childhood field, children in education programs could receive the social services supports that they need, and in other organizational local or state structures, children in social services programs could gain enhanced educational benefits both through parents and in the child care setting. In the United States the Women, Infants and Children program (WIC) is considered "Tier II" for electronic benefits as it requires more difficult technology than Tier I programs for adaptation, and will be integrated at the federal level next (McDonough, 1998). Professionals in the early childhood care and education fields would do well to gain new knowledge and skills in information technology, as these supports and new infrastructures, already in place in smaller and English-speaking countries, may be around the corner for U.S. early childhood programs.

◇ ◇ ◇ ◇ ◇ ◇ ◇ ◇ ◇ ◇ ◇ ◇ ◇ ◇ ◇ ◇ ◇ ◇ ◇ ◇

ORGANIZATIONAL CULTURE AND CHANGING PARADIGMS

Organizational culture represents a complex pattern of beliefs, expectations, ideas, values, attitudes and behaviors shared by members of an organization (Hue, 1993). Organizational culture exists on several levels, which can differ in their visibility and in their resistance to change. The most superficial level is that of cultural symbols or slang, jargon, gestures, and pictures of objects. In early childhood care and education there are a number of these. Shared behaviors and norms are the next level and are somewhat more visible and also easier to change than the remaining two levels which are cultural values and shared assumptions. These are less visible and more difficult to change. Cultural values include collective beliefs and feelings about what is good, normal, rational and valuable—in short, what employees feel deeply about. The least visible component of organizational culture at the deepest level is shared assumptions. These represent beliefs about reality and human nature that are taken for granted. If a center or an agency assumes that employees are naturally lazy and must be tightly controlled in order to enhance their performance, the reward system developed will reflect this (Hellriegel, Slocum, & Woodman, 1998).

Writers on organizational culture have developed four labels for common types of organizational culture: the baseball team, the club culture, the academy culture, and the fortress culture. The distinctive characteristics of the club culture are that it values age and experience and rewards seniority. The "club culture" provides stable, secure employment and rewards loyalty, commitment and "fitting in." Quick upward mobility is unusual. Government agencies, the U.S. military, utilities, and most commercial banks are thought to fit into this category (Hellriegel, et al., 1998). The academy culture hires recruits early—often right out of college—and emphasizes training and expertise in a particular area. The academy culture stresses continuity of service, functional expertise, and institutional wisdom. This culture appeals to "steady climbers" versus "fast trackers" and is the most similar to early childhood organizations. However, with franchised child care chains and on-site corporate child care, some of the other cultures described may be predominant. The fortress culture is preoccupied with survival. These organizations promise little in the way of job security and have difficulty rewarding employees for good performance. Such organizations do not appeal to those who desire a sense of belonging, opportunities for growth or a secure income. Many organizations are a blend of one or more of these "generic" types. Some early childhood centers are a combination of academy culture, club culture (as they also hire younger people early in the career cycle), and the fortress culture, as many centers appear to be in a "survival" mode, which may or may not be the actual case. Effective and professional service organizations, which many organizations are seeking to become in the 21st century, including child care organizations, emphasize professional growth in their culture.

How does organizational culture develop? Schein (1985) suggests that organizational culture forms in response to two major challenges:

1. External adaptation and survival, and
2. Internal integration.

Internal integration involves the internal relationships of an organization including the language and shared meaning of concepts; group and teaching team boundaries; power and status issues and the means for acquiring, maintaining and losing power and status; and rewards and punishments. The organizational culture emerges when group members discover means of sharing knowledge and assumptions and uncover ways of coping with internal integration (or with external adaptation or survival).

External adaptation includes how well the organization finds its niche (in the community or within a larger organization) and copes with a constantly changing environment. Mission and strategy; goals; means to pursue the goals and selection of the organizational structure and rewards to pursue those goals; and measurement criteria for how well individuals and teams are accomplishing their goals are all part of external adaptation (Hellriegel, et al., 1998).

Maintaining Organizational Culture

The ways an organization functions and is managed maintains or changes organizational culture. Some organizations hire individuals that "fit in" with the existing culture and discourage those who do not. A powerful method of maintaining organizational culture can be seen in what directors and teaching teams pay attention to, measure and control. Further methods include how they handle organizational crises and critical incidents; the director's role modeling, teaching and coaching that goes on (to try innovations or extend cognitive abilities, or to reject innovations); criteria for rewards and status; criteria for recruitment, promotion and displacement; and organizational ceremonies and story-telling. In particular, the manner in which a crisis is dealt with can validate and reinforce the old culture or bring out new values and norms that change the culture in some way.

Changing Organizational Culture

Conversely, each of these areas can be used to change an organizational or agency culture by:

- Changing what directors pay attention to,
- Changing how crises are handled,
- Changing criteria for recruiting new employees,
- Changing criteria for promotion internally,
- Changing criteria for reward distribution, and
- Changing center or agency ceremonies, rites of passage, and staff development.

Rewarding employees for attempting more challenging tasks or goals might be a start. For example, offering an award for innovative ways to document children's progress (with snapshots? audio tape? written observations? camcorder?) or using information technology (e-mail? multimedia?) in a vision-related way to share with parents are some ideas that might be implemented.

Changing organizational culture can be difficult and as Peter Drucker (1991) cautions in his article "Don't Change Corporate Culture—Use It," deeply held, core values of an organization might not be amenable to change. Drucker thinks it better to focus on changing ineffective procedures and behaviors. Changing behaviors works best if it can be based on existing culture.

A second difficulty is assessing organizational culture correctly. Many large organizations have more than one culture. These "subcultures" can be multiple but Schein (1985) argues that *all* organizations have at least three cultures: (1) an operating culture (the "line employees" or teachers); (2) a technical or "special skills" culture (cooks and bus drivers); and (3) an executive or director management culture. Effecting change within groups with such different "world views" can be difficult and may require different approaches for each group. Where would a first, early success be possible?

Steps to changing organizational or agency culture include:

1. Understanding the old culture.
2. Providing support for employees and teaching teams who have ideas for the new culture and are willing to act.
3. Finding the most effective subculture or classroom and using it as an example from which other employees can learn.
4. Not attacking culture directly but finding ways to help individuals and teams do their jobs most effectively.
5. Using the vision of a new culture as a guiding principle (only) for change.
6. Recognizing that significant organizational change takes 5 to 10 years.
7. "Living" the new culture because actions speak louder than words (Dumaine, 1990).

◇ ◇

ORGANIZING PRINCIPLES FOR THE INFORMATION AGE

Ten of the new theories of organizing in early childhood care and education that may be seen in the 21st century (and in the next 20 years) may include:

1. Developing a feel for the whole task will be essential. Children from infant-toddler care into and through elementary school are still the same children, with the same parents.

2. Trust is essential. An atmosphere of trust is essential, particularly when trying a new curriculum (Project? Reggio?) (Staley, 1998), or getting the information technology or other system right.

3. Who reports to whom will change over time, and accountability for a goal will be a higher priority than "pleasing the director."

4. New evaluation schemes are critical. They might include assessing team interaction, relationships with outsiders, unique expertise, a commitment to learning and improving, and the passing on of lessons to team members and the broader network.

5. Organizational learning will be highly rewarded. Contributing to the knowledge development process of the center organization as a whole will be one of the primary dimensions upon which performance and compensation are judged, especially over the long haul.

6. Information technology is essential to success, but applying new technologies to outmoded organizational structures is disastrous.

7. Real-time (current) access to all information is a must for everyone in the organization. Large amounts of time and money must be spent on communication. More clearinghouses with information resources for children with problems in their lives will be needed. Federal agencies, especially Health and Human Services and the Department of Education, have begun to provide these resources through web pages on the Internet. (See www.ed.gov, www.hhs.gov, and www.homelearning.org and www.homelearning.net.)

8. Everyone will fill "project management" roles directly or indirectly (e.g., planning field trips, helping with Saturday programs or parent programs, etc.) Attention to those skills and education and training in them will be important. Small, ad hoc groups can be very effective and leadership of these "project teams" can rotate. Listing these activities on a resume can be a career builder.

9. Service to the citizen (in this case, parents and children) will be a function of the organization or agency. This service will be a function of the power of the networks and referral systems available to it at any time, and not only of the amount of resources owned outright.

10. Partnerships and subcontractors will add value and innovativeness (music and movement teacher? computer teacher?) but using them is NOT a way to contract out problems. Using them allows the organization to respond with a new set of partners to unforeseen opportunities, challenges and problems (Peters, 1992, pp. 153–6).

◇ ◇ ◇ ◇ ◇ ◇ ◇ ◇ ◇ ◇ ◇ ◇ ◇ ◇ ◇ ◇ ◇ ◇ ◇ ◇

SUMMARY

As a society moves into the information or knowledge age, relationships between classes, races, genders, professions, nations, and other social groupings change, according to Toffler in his book *Powershift* (1990). These groupings are altered by shifts in population, ecology, technology, culture, and other factors. The profession of early childhood education is at just such a juncture. It could well rise to the status and visibility it deserves, as the importance of a far more heterogeneous workforce and population is realized. A solid education is required to help citizens develop a strong self-esteem and the competencies necessary to cope with the changes that will occur as the information age moves forward.

As the country works to protect and invest more in its future, as evidenced by its concern with the information age and its involvement with environmental issues, investment in young children, who are the country's future citizens, is also wise. In discussing early childhood education and other national issues, Charles Bowsher, Comptroller General of the United States from 1981–1996, stated that consumer attitudes, so popular in the 1980s and part of the 1990s, will perhaps give way to needed "investment attitudes" (1993). The importance of the early childhood education profession and the reasons for its importance in shaping the future of the world and preventing early "brain drain" through lack of early developmentally appropriate stimulation will therefore receive increasing attention as a valuable investment.

◇ ◇ ◇ ◇ ◇ ◇ ◇ ◇ ◇ ◇ ◇ ◇ ◇ ◇ ◇ ◇ ◇ ◇ ◇ ◇

SUGGESTED CLASS ACTIVITIES AND DISCUSSIONS

1. *Professional Association Survey.*   Survey the professional associations in early childhood education, and if possible, interview members of each. Survey questions about or for the organizations should include the goals and purpose, the history, the member services, the size, and the proudest accomplishment to date. Other questions can be developed by the class.

2. *Professional and Effective Listening Practice.*   Using the Guidelines for Effective Listening and Observing in the Instructor Manual (or in Appendix I), divide the class into groups of three. Assign one person as the problem-owner, one as the listener and one as the observer of the interaction. Discuss the guidelines with the class and then have the problem-owner present the problem (selected from staff and parent problems turned in from the class) to the listener, most often the role of the director. The observer takes notes and reports back to the class. This can be done three times with each group mem-

ber taking a turn at each role. Discuss the interaction of professionalism and effective listening.

3. *Teacher Burn-out Project Presentation.*   A small group can research and present current information on teacher burn-out and possible remedies that an individual could use. The presentation might include a stress self-analysis and additional solutions and remedies brainstormed by the class. Handouts to the class on the information and the remedies would be useful. A skit showing right and wrong approaches to the development and to the resolution of teacher burn-out can add insight.

4. *Director-Teacher Role Play.*   A small group can role play "wrong" and "right" examples demonstrating the principle that the way administrators treat the teachers is often the way teachers treat the children. Discuss how a professional would behave in each role.

5. *Professionalism and Public Relations Role Play.*   Students can role play a director or a teacher answering questions about his or her center out in the community. Do a "right way" and a "wrong way" and discuss the implications for early childhood education and for the center.

◇ ◇

BIBLIOGRAPHY

Ade, W. (1982). Professionalism and its implications for the field of early childhood education. *Young Children, 37*(3), 25–32.

Alschuler, A. S. (Ed.). (1982). *Teacher burnout.* Washington, DC: National Education Association.

Benham, N., Miller, T., & Kontos, S. (1988). Pinpointing staff training needs in child care centers. *Young Children, 43*(4), 9–16.

Bittel, L. (1985). *What every supervisor should know.* New York: McGraw Hill.

Bowsher, C. A. (1993, May). *Major issues facing Congress and the new administration.* Speech given at the American Society for the Public Administration, Washington, DC.

Bredekamp, S. (Ed.). (1987). *Developmentally appropriate practice in early childhood programs serving children from birth through age 8.* Washington, DC: National Association for the Education of Young Children.

Bredekamp, S., & Shepard, L. (1989). How best to protect children from inappropriate school expectations, practices and policies. *Young Children, 44*(3), 14–24.

Caldwell, B. (1983). How can we educate the American public about the child care profession? *Young Children, 38*(3), 11–17.

Cedoline, A. J. (1982). *Job burnout in public education.* New York: Teachers College Press.

Dresden, J., & Myers, B. K. (1989, January). Early childhood professionals: Toward self definition. *Young Children, 44*(2), 62–66.

Drucker, P. F. (1991). Don't change corporate culture—Use it! *Wall Street Journal*, March 28, p. A14.

Dumaine, B. (1990, January 15). Creating a new company culture. *Fortune*, pp. 127–131.

Elkind, D. (1990, April). Headshakers and mindbinders. *Child Care Information Exchange*, p. 28.

Feeny, S., & Chun, R. (1985). Effective teachers of young children. *Young Children, 41*(1), 47–52.

Fullan, M. (1993a). *Change forces: Probing the depths of educational reform*. London: Falmer Press.

Fullan, M. (1993b, March). Why teachers must become change agents. *Educational Leadership, 50*(6), 12–17.

Fuller, F. F., & Brown, O. H. (1975). Becoming a teacher. In K. Ryan (Ed.), *Teacher education* (pp. 25–52). Chicago: University of Chicago Press.

Greenberg, G. F. (1984). *Managing stress*. Dubuque, IA: William C. Brown.

Hamburg, D. A. (1990). *A decent start: Promoting healthy child development in the first three years of life*. New York: Carnegie Corp.

Hellriegel, D., Slocum, J. W., & Woodman, R. W. (1998). *Organizational Behavior*. Cincinnati, OH: South-Western College Publishing.

Hostetler, L., & Klugman, E. (1982). Early childhood job titles: One step toward professional status. *Young Children, 37*(6), 13–22.

Hue, J. (1993). "How McKinsey Does It." *Fortune*, November 1, pp. 56–81.

Jones, E. (1973). *Dimensions of teaching-learning environments: Handbook for teachers*. Pasadena, CA: Pacific Oaks College.

Jones, E. (1990). Creating environments where teachers, like children, learn through play. In *Developing staff skills* (reprint collection no. 7), pp. 3–6. Redmond, WA: Child Care Information Exchange.

Jorde, P. (1986). Early childhood education: Issues and trends. *The Educational Forum, 50*(2), 171–181.

Jorde-Bloom, P. (1998). Assess the climate of your center: Use the early childhood work environment survey. *Day Care and Early Education, 15*(4), 9–11.

Kamii, C. (1985). Leading primary education toward excellence. *Young Children, 40*(5), 3–9.

Katz, L. (1984). The education of preprimary teachers. In L. Katz (Ed.), *Current topics in early childhood education*, (Vol. 5, pp. 209–228). Norwood, NJ: Ablex.

Katz, L. G. (1972a). Condition with caution. *Young Children, 27*(5), 277–280.

Katz, L. G. (1972b). Developmental states of preschool teachers. *The Elementary School Journal, 23*(1), 50–54.

Katz, L. G. (1975, October). Some generic principles of teaching. *Second collection of papers for teachers*. Urbana, IL: Univ. of Illinois, College of Education. (ERIC Document Reproduction Service No. 119 807)

Katz, L. G. (1987). The nature of professions: Where is early childhood education? In L. Katz & K. Steiner (Eds.), *Current topics in early childhood education* (Vol. 7, pp. 1–16). Norwood, NJ: Ablex.

McDonough, F. (1998). "Government 2010." Speech given at the Association for Federal Information Resource Management Seminar, March 19, Washington, D.C.

Moore, P. (1985). *Public personnel management: A contingency approach* (Chapter 2). Lexington, MA: DC, Heath.

Mosher, F. (1968). *Democracy and the public service*. New York: Oxford Press.

Mosher, F. (1982). *Democracy and the public service* (2nd ed.). New York: Oxford Press.

Naisbitt, J., & Aburdene, P. (1983). *Megatrends*. New York: William Morrow.

Naisbitt, J., & Aburdene, P. (1990). *Megatrends 2000*. New York: William Morrow.

National Association for the Education of Young Children. (1982). *Early childhood teacher education guidelines for four- and five-year programs*. Washington, DC: Author.

Peters, T. (1992). *Liberation management*. New York: Alfred Knopf.

Raquepaw, J., & deHass, P. A. (1984). *Factors influencing teacher burnout* (Report No. CG 018 202). Chicago: Paper presented at the annual meeting of the Midwestern Psychological Association. (ERIC Document Reproduction No. ED 256 980)

Schein, E. H. (1985). *Organizational culture and leadership*. San Francisco: Jossey-Bass.

Seefeldt, C. (1988). Teacher certification and program accreditation in early childhood education. *Elementary School Journal, 89*(2), 241–251.

Southern Association on Children Under Six. (1985). *Position statement on quality four year old programs in public schools*. Little Rock, AR: Author. (ERIC/ECE Document Reproduction Service No. ED 272 272)

Southern Association on Children Under Six. (1986a). *Position statement on supporting parents*. Little Rock, AR: Author. (ERIC/ECE Document Reproduction Service No. ED 272 272)

Southern Association on Children Under Six. (1986b). *Position statement on quality child care*. Little Rock, AR: Author. (ERIC/ECE Document Reproduction Service No. ED 272 272)

Spodek, B., & Saracho, O. N. (1990). Professionalism in early childhood education. In B. Spodek, O. N. Saracho, & D. L. Peters (Eds.), *Professionalism and the early childhood practitioner* (pp. 59–74). New York: Teachers College Press.

Staley, L. (1998). Beginning to implement the Reggio philosophy. *Young Children, 53*(5), pp. 20–25.

Swick, K. J. (1989). *Stress and teaching*. Washington, DC: National Education Association.

Taylor, F. W. (1947). *Scientific management*. New York: Harper and Row.

Toffler, A. (1980). *The third wave*. New York: Bantam.

Toffler, A. (1990). *Powershift*. New York: Bantam.

Wade, B. (1977). Initial teacher education and school experience. *Education Review*, pp. 58–66.

Winklestein, E., and others. (1976, June). *In-service training models for early childhood education programs* (Report No. PS 008647). Urbana, IL: Univ. of Illinois, College of Education. (ERIC/ECE Reproduction Service No. ED 125 754)

Leadership and Helping Children in their Environment

Families play a very important role in their children's early care and education. Recent studies done on early brain development show just how significant that role can be. As leaders and agents for change—in the home, the community and the child care setting—parents are critical players and consumers in a service-to-the-citizen, consumer-driven economy, and remind early childhood leaders that parents have a primary place in their children's development. A positive attitude towards parents is an essential element of a child care program's supportive environment for children and reduces barriers to full parent participation. The professional staff's commitment to the concept of the parent as the child's first and most important teacher (and person) in the child's life, helps to embody an "architect's paradigm" of helping parents in developing the child, keeping the best interests of the child in mind. Understanding parents as developing adults (at a variety of adult life-stages) also helps staff to assist them as key partners and in building their confidence with their own children.

Empowering parents and helping them to see themselves as change agents both in their children's learning and in the child care setting, yields benefits for all involved. The new collaborative models of community based governance for child and family services include user-planning in planning new services and in deciding how resources are to be used. The commitment parents make to their children constitutes their strength and perseverance with policy makers; advocating on behalf of children sends a message to policy makers. While the recent trend of older, professional, first-time parents demonstrates that experience enables them to be heard "at the table" in both education and social services, younger parents with less professional experience will benefit from training to make this partnership with professionals more effective. The focus in early childhood education has shifted from being on merely the child to include a consideration of the child's whole context: the family, parent education available, parent involvement possible and available, and, in tuition-based programs, professionals as parents, all with a shared commitment to the healthy development of children.

Many early childhood staff members are not comfortable with building equal relationships with parents. Encouraging parents as leaders requires staff, as they become more professional, to understand issues of adulthood and parenthood as well as they understand childhood. The understanding that parents are the primary people supporting a child's life underlies early childhood care and education, and requires building bonds with parents as well as with children.

Developing this attitude in early childhood staff will require preservice and inservice training. In preservice training and education, little emphasis has been placed on forming relationships with parents or insuring their voice in the organizational governance and structure, regardless of the income group to which parents belong. (The poor were considered too poor and busy, and the well-off were considered too well-off and busy). However a knowledge base in adult development would enable early childhood professionals in this regard to be more skilled and confident (Langford and Weissbourd, 1997). Studies on adult development in general and relationship building with adults and parents in particular, might begin with Erickson's stages of development, for instance.

Parent leadership training has long been a foundation of parent cooperative nursery school governance and materials from these programs and others (such as Head Start) can be a referral source for early childhood educators attempting to build relationships with parents. Targeting the child and the family, not just the child alone, is a new conviction and one that is not widely accepted yet. But just as the importance of education and an understanding of the first three years of life was once considered insignificant and was a relatively unknown concept until recently, viewing the child as inseparable from the family must move into being a widely accepted concept (Langford and Weissbourd, 1997). Parents of all income levels have a desire to be involved in their children's education. However, there is still a need for more parent education on the subject of child development. Policy and program reform can both benefit from parent leadership voices which have been developed with the help of early childhood educators, who provide an environment that is supportive and enhancing to children and parents alike. However, in every program there are special issues in helping children overcome problems, both medical and legal, which also interact with their environment.

◇ ◇

HELPING CHILDREN OVERCOME PROBLEMS

The more knowledge and power early childhood professionals have to impact and help children and parents with a variety of problems, the more effective their child care centers and programs will be. Knowledge *is* power. This section includes chapters on parent education and involvement, legally related problems such as divorce, foster care, adoption, legislation, child advocacy, and child abuse—which of course extends into medically related problems and issues.

Some of the medically related issues discussed will include child mental health, hyperactive (ADHD) children, the inclusion of children with various health challenges and disabilities, hospitalized children and children and death. Some of these issues have been much discussed through federal government programs and whole master's degree programs addressing them. Some issues, such as children and death and hospitalized children, are rarely discussed.

Inclusion is not new in early childhood programs. Analysis, diagnosis and planning are new for children with (formerly) undiagnosed challenges, problems and disabilities. Screening of two-, three- and four-year-olds is also relatively new and is not always accurate. All of these issues, as well as legal issues related to foster care and adoption that are addressed less often than other legally related issues such as divorce and, again, child abuse, can come across a child care director's desk. Since every director and most teachers in early childhood education have found themselves in a counseling and referral role, a brief review of many of these topics is included in this section.

Understanding the Environment of the Child

First let's take a look at families, communities and resources *available*. How many children in the community are in some kind of child care? What do their communities look like both at home and in the child care setting?

Is the child care facility substandard? Is the home? Due to lack of construction funding many child care facilities are in need of renovation or upgrading simply to bring them up to licensing standards.

Child Care Statistics

In 1995 there were 21 million children aged five or younger. About 41 percent were cared for by parents, 21 percent by relatives, 4 percent by sitters, 31 percent in center based programs, and 14 percent in family child care homes.

Some children were cared for in different settings at different times. Single mothers and lower socio-economic status parents are not the only ones that need child care. In 1994, 62 percent of married mothers were in the workforce, versus 30% in 1970 according to a Department of Labor study (Mann, 1998).

Communities

What are the attributes of a good community for children? Quality schools? Churches? Community health and welfare services? Adequate police and fire protection? Postal service? Make a list of about 20 items: include space, parks, room to play and playgrounds, safety, lighting and more.

In understanding one's own community, look at the commercial structure, government input and regulations (federal, state and local), resources for children and parents and for those with special needs, and welfare and community action resources. Consumer protections might fall under this category also and can range from child care regulation and licensing on the local and state levels, to federal protections on toy and playground safety, and television censorship efforts. Police protection, fire, post office and library availability, safe play spaces and sidewalks contribute to the total environment of the child. Medical care, public transportation to it and other resources such as recreation and social services, are included. And, lastly, the ethnic, age, and general socio-economic diversity of a neighborhood all contribute to the child's expectations about the world he or she will live in. New housing developments without "age diversity" or that do not portray a picture of reality or other diversity, for example, may not contribute quite as much to children's perspective of the world. All of these help early childhood professionals understand the environment of the child and the family.

◇ ◇

BIBLIOGRAPHY

Comer, J. P. (1984). Home-school relationships as they affect the academic success of children. *Education and the Urban Society, 16,* 323–337.

Fisher, R. (1984). *Let the people decide: Neighborhood organizing in America.* Boston: G. K. Hall.

Langford, J., & Weissbourd, B. (1997). New directions for parent leadership in a family-support context. In *Leadership in early care and education* (pp. 147–155). Washington, DC: NAEYC.

Mann, J. (1998, May 29). A modest child care proposal. *The Washington Post,* p. E3.

Zigler, E. G., & Muenchow, S. (1992). *Head Start: The inside story of America's most successful educational experiment.* New York: Basic.

Parent Education and Parent Involvement

Being supportive of children means involving their parents. Parent education precedes and then goes hand-in-hand with parent involvement as a vital part of any child-care center's efforts on behalf of children. As parents try out ideas and materials with their children, they become involved and want to learn more, whether through parent education meetings, study groups, or send-home papers. (See Appendix A for Home Learning Enablers and Appendix B for Parent Papers.) As parents learn more about their children, such as how they develop and think, parents often become more interested in being active and involved with their children (Figure 10.1).

Research shows the tremendous positive impact that even the smallest efforts on the part of parents can have on children. When parents are given help in supporting their children's learning, it has been found that children hold their gains longer (Clark, 1983; Henderson, 1987; Linney & Vernberg, 1983; Moles, 1982). In a review of 37 studies, the most clearly positive results were found when parent participation of almost any kind was a critical ingredient in the program. In follow-up studies 10 years later, these children were still performing at higher levels both academically and socially (Henderson, 1987), as shown in Figure 10.2.

These studies also showed that the more intensely and longer the parents supported their children, the better the children did (Linney & Vernberg, 1983; Henderson, 1987). When parents were involved in activities with their own young chil-

FIGURE 10.1
Parent Education and Parent
Involvement Develop Together

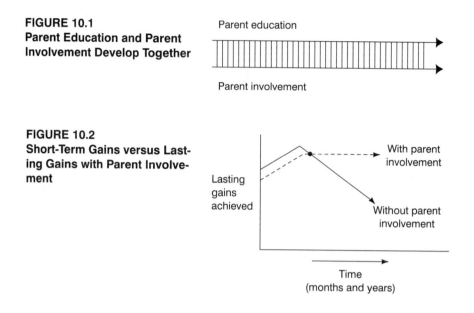

Parent education

Parent involvement

FIGURE 10.2
Short-Term Gains versus Last-ing Gains with Parent Involve-ment

Lasting gains achieved

With parent involvement

Without parent involvement

Time
(months and years)

dren, although a small additional cost to the center was involved (for example, the cost of one ream of paper for send-home activities, which actually could be charged to the parents), the impact of state, federally funded, and any well-organized early childhood programs in some cases almost doubled (Jones, 1981). Susan Gray (1971) found that, along with the gains of the children involved in the child-care program, the I.Q.s of younger and older siblings also went up when home visits and parent activities were part of the program. It has been stated that the least expensive way to reach every child is to reach every parent as they often represent more than one child.

◊ ◊

PARENT-CHILD INTERACTION

Rich empirical and philosophical literature has existed for many years describing the deep and lasting benefits of parent-child interaction. This literature includes concepts about the nature and development of infant learning, insight into the ways children develop thought processes, and new interpretations of the structure of knowledge and early learning.

Environmental influences on learning, the effects of the family upon achievement, and the effect of early stimulation upon later life have also been studied. It has been noted that the most familiar sound to a baby or young child is the sound of his or her mother's voice. Babies can distinguish the timbre and pitch of their own mother's voice from the day of birth, partly because they heard her voice before they were born (Friedman, 1978). The impact of the mother-child bond on learning, and of the father-child bond (since his voice is usually the second-most familiar) on learning, has only been peripherally explored. However, it seems that family members who were present during the pregnancy have the most direct impact on learning, and all family members have a very strong impact (Bornstein and Tamis-Lemonda, 1989).

Professional educators who work directly with children, especially children over six years of age, have much less influence on children's learning than was previously thought, according to Burton White (1974). With this perspective in mind, the family must receive increasing priority as the first educational delivery system.

Hamburg (1990), as well as White and many others, lists three main obstacles confronting families as they attempt to educate their young children: ignorance (not knowing what is helpful), stress (economic stress and physical stress, such as tiredness from coping), and a lack of assistance from local, county, state, or federal resources. Many programs for parents have been designed to help parents overcome at least the first and last of these obstacles—ignorance and lack of assistance. Parent education and assistance programs might benefit from addressing four areas that make up the foundation of educational capacity: language development, curiosity, social development, and cognitive intelligence (White, 1974).

Clark (1983) isolated some characteristics of families whose children do well in school; these qualities appeared in both single and two-parent homes, and in both poor and middle-class families:

- Clearly expressed valuation and support of education and achievement;
- Parents' sense of self-mastery and control over their own lives;
- Frequent discussions, positive expectations, and support and reinforcement of interests and schoolwork; and
- A family climate that includes regular routines and mealtimes and encourages purposeful use of time and space.

Providing support to families, with two-way communication being a key ingredient, can help more of these characteristics to occur.

Bloom's studies (1964, 1981) also support the critical importance of the home and of parents as teachers of their children. The findings confirm the statements of Goodson, Swartz, and Millsap (1991) that parent involvement produces the most lasting retention of gains made. Bloom (1981) indicated that differences in children's academic and cognitive development can be traced to the value placed on education by the family and specifically to parents' reinforcement of the child's activities in school. Bloom (1964) also found that one-half of all intellectual differences that exist at age 17 can be found in the range of differences seen in that child at age 4.

Parent–Child Interaction and Intelligence

A significant group of early education projects emerged following the publication of Benjamin Bloom's book *Stability and Change in Human Characteristics* (1964), which introduced the importance of early education. Earl Schaefer, who was part of the Infant Education Project at Catholic University in Washington, D.C., was a leader in one of the first of these projects. Schaefer was knowledgeable about the differences in mental test scores that emerge in the second and third years of life. In a presentation entitled *Parenting and Child Behavior Predictors of Retention in Grades K, 1, 2* (1986), he revisited these important concepts.

Schaefer believed in the importance of early education, and designed an experiment in which tutors visited the homes of disadvantaged boys between the ages of fifteen months and three years. This was a child-centered tutoring program in which the tutor worked with the children one hour a day, five days a week. The children did very well, confirming the experimenter's hypothesis on the benefits of early education.

After tutoring stopped at three years of age, follow-up testing showed that the I.Q.s of the experimental children began to decline, while the I.Q.s of the control group began to rise. The parents of the children in the control group had seen only the testing activities, but had not seen the tutoring used with the experimental group. About these parents Schaefer (1974) says:

> To some extent they grew interested in their child's intellectual development. I think it is conceivable that our control groups' parents grew more interested in helping their child develop than our experimental groups' parents were when we tutored their children—we are the experts; we have the competence; we have the skills; we will take responsibility for educating your child. And that's always wrong. Professionals can't do it. They are there for only a limited time each day. And a limited time isn't enough. So this dialectic process started out—the need for early education, which was confirmed. Then the drop in test scores after we stopped lead to an antithesis—the need for continuing education. The only synthesis and antithesis is to develop the family as an educational institution right from birth to maturity. (p. 18)

Schaefer (1974) then went on to examine studies that did involve the family. He says:

> Look at Phyllis Levenstein's early study, don't look at my study. The I.Q.s of the children in the Mother's Home Training Program went up 17 points in 7 months, whereas the I.Q.s of the children in my study went up 17 points in 21 months and then dropped. (p. 18)

In addition to the Mother's Home Training Program (Levenstein, 1975), Schaefer also recommended Susan Gray's study (1971), which shows the impact of parents' interaction with their children on lasting improvement in I.Q. scores, as do many other studies (Clark, 1983; Epstein, 1984a, 1986, 1987b, 1987c, 1988b; Hess & McDevitt, 1984; Lazar, 1977).

In Levenstein's Mother's Home Training Program, the decline in I.Q. scores did not appear, suggesting that this project's model of verbal interaction between parent and child (in contrast to the tutor-child model in the Schaefer project) shows that parent participation is a crucial factor in the maintenance of long-term effects.

The Family Development Research Program at Syracuse University (Honig, 1978) in reporting their longitudinal findings obtained from observing families with normal and special needs children interacting at home, found many benefits in helping families to improve parenting skills, as did many of the other studies already mentioned. A summary of Honig's findings indicated that mothers who planned and organized their infants' experiences and routines produced the most competent babies. Her studies also indicated that those children exposed to typical nursery-school toys, such as crayons, paper, and puzzles, appeared more competent than those lacking this exposure (Honig, 1989).

Another positive factor connected with competent children was that they were allowed to help with household chores, such as dusting, hammering, raking leaves, and sorting the laundry. Other factors contributing to the children's level of competence (according to Honig, 1978) included limiting television viewing time, reading to the children, and allowing the children to delve into "messy" and perhaps even slightly dangerous processes. In other words, the most competent children had parents who (1) severely limited and supervised television viewing; (2) read to them regularly on a daily basis; and (3) allowed them to experiment with blunt scissors, for example, or wash dishes.

The mothers of the competent children modeled appropriate activities; were good observers; praised, encouraged, suggested options, and served as facilitators; and behaved as teachers. The fathers in these families inject a positive aspect also. The study indicated that the fathers of the competent babies also spent more positive interaction time with their children. The competent children's parents had firm, consistent household rules, for which they provided explanations. They engaged in role-playing games as well as other games and entertainment with their children that provided intellectual content. As a result of these findings, Honig suggested that some children have a higher level of competence which results from their relationship with their parents (Honig, 1978).

Lally and Honig (1977) reported the results of a comprehensive "omnibus" program of family services that included home visits plus center child care for 2 1/2 years to 108 families low in income and education. Data indicated that families in this program saw their participating children, in comparison with siblings and peers, as more likely to ask questions, make their own choices, teach other children, try new and difficult tasks, and fight less often.

In 1981, Jones conducted a study that tracked I.Q. changes that occurred after using parent-involvement send-home papers (see Home Learning Enablers, Appendix A) weekly for 14 weeks with 127 three-year-olds in 15 federally funded child-care centers. Overall, the treatment children (those whose parents were given the Home Learning Enablers) gained an average of almost 4 points more than did the control children, and the children in both groups gained an average of 5 points just from being in a well-organized child-care program (with some variation across the centers, of course). Thus, nearly 9 points were gained in the 14 weeks for the treatment children.

One negative development also appeared in the study: The children with higher I.Q. levels *lost* I.Q. points over the 14-week period. The more-able treatment children receiving parent enabler papers weekly lost an average of 5 points *less* than did the more-able control children, but both groups lost points since there were no provisions for gifted children in the centers. Children undergoing traumatic experiences during the 14-week period (e.g., one child stated, "The police come and take my Mommy away.") experienced fluctuations in their I.Q. scores. These children's scores dropped, but started to regain ground before the end of the study, showing that generally even traumatized children can continue to learn. Some children showed extremely high gains.

Overall, however, the study results backed the current research findings, showing that by implementing 14 weekly home-learning, send-home papers per child, the gains sought by the center's program could be nearly doubled (Jones, 1981).

Parent–Child Interaction and Language

A number of studies and programs have focused specifically on the impact of the parent-child relationship on language development. Studies have ranged from naturalistic home observations of behaviors that encouraged children verbally, to quite structured approaches aimed at changing a mother's syntax and grammar and thus improving her child's verbal skills.

Many writers have focused on ways to help parents during the crucial years of their children's language development. Larrick (1976), for example, concentrates on ways parents can help their children develop oral language facility and build positive attitudes toward the printed language so they will learn to read easily and happily. Reading aloud to children from an early age (4 to 24 months and up) continues to be supported by study after study (Fredericks & Rasinski, 1990; Hess, Holloway, Dickson, & Price, 1984; Mavrogenes, 1990; Norman-Jackson, 1982). The parents' reading level seems to be less important than the activity itself. Language learning researchers are finding that language literally "sculpts" and reorganizes the brain as a child grows, and talking and reading to infants and young children is of prime importance in language and brain development (Brownlee, 1998).

Thus, in summing up current research results, the importance of the home environment in language development cannot be emphasized enough (Anderson, Fielding, & Wilson, 1988; Brownlee, 1998; Clay, 1987; Jenson, 1985; Silvern, 1985).

Parent–Child Interaction and School Achievement

To understand the role of parents in schools today, it might be useful to look at how parents' interaction with schools came into being. According to Hobbs (1976), at one time many schools regarded parents as a nuisance and many parents regarded schools as forbidden places in which they should have no legitimate interest. The view of "let the experts do it" was prevalent among parents and was encouraged by schools (Schaefer, 1974). However, in the past two decades, families and programs for young children have been coming together in many interesting ways as the importance of the relationship of parent-child interaction to later school achievement has been realized (Council of Chief State School Officers, 1989).

Schools at one point followed the industrial model. They removed the children from the family, set up a system of authority based on state-level sanctions and expertise, and instituted a "work" discipline similar to that of adult organizations. Teachers were treated as "interchangeable parts" in different classrooms. As time has progressed, the relationship between educational settings and parents, and between teachers and parents, has improved, but not to its fullest extent.

As we have seen, there is a need to build stronger parent-child interaction in the early years of a child's life, not only to help later school achievement, but also for other reasons. As many researchers are beginning to document, perhaps strengthening the parent-child relationship is the answer to teachers' frustrations of not being able to bring about the results they want from the children in their classrooms. Perhaps this is also the answer for those frustrated and disappointed parents who blame the schools for the fact that their children are not achieving satisfactorily. These attitudes can be seen spilling over into the classrooms of child-care programs.

It has been said that achievement starts and builds at home (Rich & Jones, 1978; Schaefer, 1974). From parents, children learn basic attitudes toward learning and develop the values that will later be infused into academic tasks. Parent-child interaction is important in the educational process because children's first and most important teachers are their parents (Taylor, 1967). It is not the sole responsibility of schools and child-care centers to educate children, nor should they try to do it alone. In order to maximize the learning process, it is necessary for schools and centers to seek the aid of parents.

Coleman et al. (1966, 1973) demonstrated that reading achievement is more fully an outgrowth of home influences than it is a function of what takes place in school. Moore and others (1976) discuss research into the role of in-home and out-of-home early childhood education and the effects of both on later academic achievement. In this discussion, the importance of the role of the family and home environment in early education is emphasized, and it is suggested that providing education in parenting skills and in improving the home environment should be primary goals of early childhood education (Gordon, 1977; Henderson, 1987; Swap, 1987).

Research suggests clearly that the home has as much or more influence on child learning as do teachers and the educational setting. The most effective children's program, therefore, will be one in which the home and the school or center work together on behalf of the child. Even with this knowledge, parent involvement still has not entered into the mainstream of teacher education but remains on the edges. This may continue to be the case unless teacher educators, teachers, administrators, parents, and politicians see the need to change the situation. If they choose the path of greater parent involvement, the child is likely to emerge the winner (Greenwood & Hickman, 1991).

◇ ◇

INSTRUCTIONAL MATERIALS

An emphasis on children's interaction with specific learning materials has a long tradition in early childhood education, beginning with Frederich Froebel (1782–1852). Froebel (1902) created a variety of toys, or "gifts" as he called them, designed to help children learn about the world and about themselves. Froebel's ideas greatly influenced programs for young children in the late 1800s, especially his emphasis on the importance of children's play.

Maria Montessori (1870–1952) also designed an elaborate set of materials (1968). Her goal was to increase children's abilities to discriminate among stimuli and to order stimuli among various dimensions, such as height, weight, and color. In the Montessori system, the critical relationship is that between the child and his or her learning materials.

According to Dewey (1938), thinking is best promoted by allowing children the opportunity to engage in experiences that suggest problems to be solved. Most interpretations of this position suggest that such experiences need to be concrete in nature. For example, field trips and excursions into the immediate community provide experiences and thinking activities.

Piaget (1973), in studying the way children come to understand their world, concluded that early sensorimotor experience with concrete objects plays a crucial role in the development of thought. This belief suggests that children younger than age five need to have a variety of experiences with concrete manipulatives, both at home and in group settings.

Most child-care centers provide opportunities for a wide range of experiences. The typical materials found in early learning settings show a high level of consistency. This array of materials provides a range of opportunities to develop or build upon skills and concepts. Children in these programs are encouraged to explore and experiment with these materials in a variety of ways.

Science, math, language, and other academic subjects can be the basis of a host of learning activities involving manipulation, observation, and record-keeping that are developmentally appropriate. Cooking and nutrition-oriented activities also make use of sensorimotor experiences as a means for learning.

Each type of manipulative material requires a slightly different combination of skills and competencies. When using these manipulatives, children are also required to answer different questions that help them build on the skills and competencies they are learning. Helping adults understand the purpose of these questions can help them, as parents or teachers, to make full use of the materials as mediums or catalysts in children's thinking and learning. The Home Learning Enablers in Appendix A provide this type of help in a send-home format for parents.

Instructional Materials and Programs for Parents

Many kinds of instructional programs and materials are available to parents. Some—such as study groups, books and manuals for improving parenting skills, home visits and parent participation opportunities in early childhood programs—do not focus, except peripherally, on the parents' use of instructional materials with their own children. Some parent involvement or outreach efforts, however, do provide activities and materials, often combined together in a book or packet, for parents.

A literature search reveals very little information about the types of materials prepared by instructional programs that are meant to be used by parents. There is minimal description of these materials in terms of time needed, complexity, attractiveness, or adaptability to individual home situations. There are a few exceptions, however. For example, the *Family Math* book (Stenmark, Thompson, & Cossey, 1986) contains specific activities for kindergarten and older children. Another simple yet effective program for sending home materials, developed by Carol Rountree for a class project in 1992, is the PAL (Parent Assisted Learning) bag. This canvas tote bag, containing a book the child selects along with specific activities related to the book, is sent home for one to two weeks by the center or program. (A software program disk or CD ROM disk could also be sent home this way.) If funds are available, a blank tape can be included in the bag with a request for parents to record the reading of the story and the child's innovations. Parents are also asked to keep a journal of activities.

It is a developmentally appropriate practice, according to Bredekamp (1990), "to view parents as integral partners in the educational practice." However, many parents neither appreciate nor understand the critical role they play in literacy development (Jewell & Zintz, 1990). Egawa (1990) encourages adult participation in activities that connect a child with a book; it is often through an adult's reaction to a given book that a child's perceptions and emotional responses are born, thus building purposefulness into the literacy activity. Jacqueline Norman-Jackson (1982) found that successful readers in second grade differed from unsuccessful ones in the amount of verbal interaction that took place with family members during the pre-elementary school years. Thus, active participation by parents and families in a child's education is as essential for academic success as are multisensory activities that address a child's individual learning style (Carbo, Dunn, & Dunn, 1986; Hess & McDevitt, 1984; Kennedy, 1991).

Epstein (1989) reported that when teachers encouraged parents, parents' involvement in their children's education increased. Many programs utilize a number of strategies to encourage parents, including newsletters that suggest home activities for parents to do with their children. The goals for such programs are to promote a home environment that reinforces the school or center environment, and to help the program director assist parents with their expectations of their children.

A newsletter, in addition to home learning activities, is a must for a well-run center or program. Child development information and current curriculum topics make good columns to include, as do ideas for activities parents can do with their children. (These ideas can even include cooking recipes.) Many directors and teachers find it helpful to share samples of their program's Parent Newsletters at professional meetings or at local Director/Teacher Council meetings. Directors or teachers who do not have time or do not have a committee to produce a monthly newsletter can buy or subscribe to inserts for newsletters; for example, the Parent Papers in Appendix B make good newsletter inserts. The sample newsletter in Figure 10.3 can be used as a model, with different news items printed or typed in the boxes. A sample of a kindergarten weekly newsletter is shown in Figure 10.4. A prepared insert could then be stapled to this type of "cover sheet," and communication is under way. The Parent's Helping List shown in Figure 10.5 is another sample newsletter insert appropriate for kindergarten programs. A one-page weekly note to tell general things, like what the group is investigating, is another "newsletter" approach. Leave a blank space at the bottom for the teacher to write a specific note about what *that* child was observed doing, such as "Heidi and her friend Blake built an airport in the block corner Wednesday. Heidi made a sign that said "Oakland Airport." A parent send-home monthly calendar is helpful for programs that meet less than five days a week, to convey daily activities on a monthly basis.

Training manuals are available to instructors of parent study groups whose members are interested in learning new parenting skills. It is hoped that with this assistance, these study groups will foster home-based early childhood education. Although no materials are provided specifically for parent members, many study groups suggest ideas for nonconcrete activities, such as games and songs for parents and children to enjoy together. Group discussions in these study groups might include topics such as using behavior modification techniques and helping children develop self-control. Parent Papers (Sets 1 and 2) in Appendix B also provide a springboard for discussions on a variety of topics with a child-development focus, including discipline.

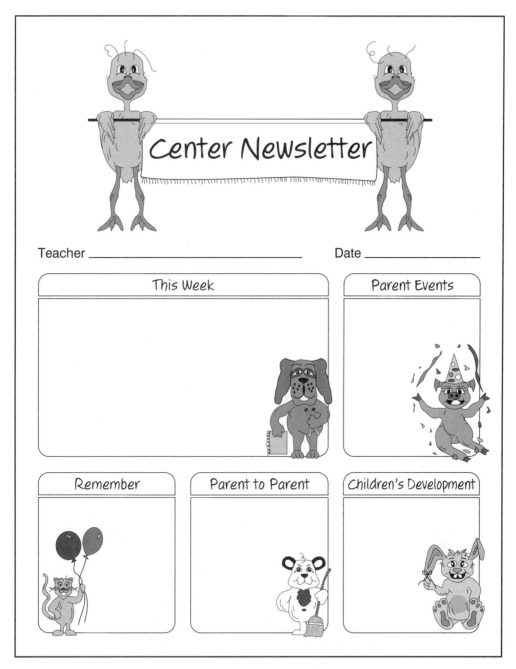

FIGURE 10.3
Sample Newsletter Cover Sheet

Monday We practiced counting to 10 this week. Ask your child to do this at home. Count backwards, next. We also started to fill in a 0–10 number chart by attaching the correct number of small objects in each row. Some children finished weighing/comparing apples and other objects. Music with Mr. Holden.	*Tuesday* Story <u>Five Little Monkeys</u>. During circle time the 5 pattern block shapes (square, triangle, trapezoid [larger blue block] and hexagon) were named and described. Art Invitation—children cut out the cover page of their Apple booklet. Large-muscle room with Mrs. Sapper and Mrs. Smith.
Wednesday During circle time we discussed shades of colors. The children then sequenced color squares from dark to light shades. We visited the library with Mrs. Roberts and almost everyone remembered to bring back his/her library book! The game Skyscrapers was introduced. Music with Mrs. Holden	*Thursday* The children met a puppet, and he led them in thinking about what they like to do in school during the Fall. Thank you to Mrs. McCord and Mr. Erle who assisted us. The children paired up and played Skyscrapers. We had a surprise snack of goldfish crackers and "ate down to 0" (zero).
Friday Thank you to Mrs. Emerald who helped us make applesauce! Art Invitation—the children illustrated a short apple poem. Reading Invitation—each child read/talked his or her Apple story to me. Computer Lab—we worked in Kid Pix.	*NOTICES* The children are doing a good job of learning the routine. Thank you for your support! We will continue talking about color next week. Next Thursday each child should wear his or her favorite COLOR.

FIGURE 10.4
Sunshine (Public) Kindergarten News

Home Visits as Instructional Programs/ Opportunities for Parents

Regardless of the socioeconomic status of the home, all parents want their children to achieve in education, but often they do not know how to help their children attain that goal (Kennedy, 1991); many of these parents desire teacher or center direction in this endeavor (Mavrogenes, 1990). Home visits are one way of helping parents achieve educational goals for their children. One example of a research program that included home visits is the Family Development Research Program (Honig, 1979). This program offered a quality infant daycare service that incorporated home visitation. The goals of the home visit program were to maximize family functioning, contribute to parental knowledge of child development, and foster parent involvement in their children's cogni-

Parent's Helping List

1. *Kitchen/Cooking Parent (need at least 2)*
    To bring to class the prepared food items needed for class projects (i.e., celery washed and cut).

2. *Art Room Parent (need at least 2)*
    Assist weekly in the Art Room from 9:30 to 10:30 a.m. Take home art smocks and wash weekly so they are clean and fresh for next class project.

3. *Field Trip Parents (need at least 5)*
    Accompany class of approximately 22 students on field trips throughout the year to make it enjoyable and safe for the children.

4. *At Home Projects Volunteers*
    Prepare classroom items as needed (i.e., cut out pictures, gather colored leaves, etc.).

5. *Class Party Parents (need 4)*
    To set up, make materials for, and clean up after the classroom parties.

6. *Woodworking Parent*
    Collect and donate wood.

7. *Typing (2nd semester) (need 2)*
    To prepare students' stories into finished products. Another parent should be available to work directly with children in our room. (Flexible hours)

8. *Garage Sale Parents*
    All parents can participate in this area. The class needs at least 4 diligent parents to actively search for safe, inexpensive roller skates, small bikes, and Big Wheels to help upgrade the dwindling classroom supply.

9. *Computer Volunteers*
    Volunteer to help directly with kids in our room with our computer as needed. Prior computer skills needed. We supply software and computer.

Name:

Phone #:

Child's name:

FIGURE 10.5
A Parent's Helping List

tive and psychosocial development. Materials were not given directly to the parents, but instead provided to the home visitors.

Another project that utilized home visits is the Houston Parent-Child Development Center, which developed a program to meet the needs of low-income Mexican-American families with preschool children. The program included home visits and family workshops in its agenda, as do many similar programs.

During instructional home visits, parents often are given or shown educational activities to participate in with their children. To make sure that these brief home activities are used in developmentally appropriate ways, it is important for the program representative to model the activities during the home visits, as well as in the program setting. This is best accomplished after establishing trust with the parents and perhaps other family members. Many other examples of successful home visit models are listed in this chapter. Head Start and other federally funded programs use home visits as a vital part of building the home-school link that, according to Bronfenbrenner (1979), helps a child feel secure and successful. Developing and using self-evaluation checklists for home visitors may be useful in helping participating programs meet their goals for home visits.

Parental Participation in the Classroom as Instructional Opportunities for Parents

The Compensatory Education Program for Preschoolers in Fresno, California, offered a school setting for two-, three-, four-, and five-year-olds with the requirement that parents in the program participate one day a week. Advice was given to parents about how to interact with the children during the one-day period per week the parents would spend participating in the program. Parents learned about the specific needs and abilities of preschool children, and materials helpful to parents also were listed in the newsletter. Cooperative nursery schools offer many of these same benefits. One program for young children had staff act out the program's philosophy in skits at a parent orientation meeting showing what might happen at the program and how they would handle it. This "modeling" approach was very successful. They continued using skits in parent meetings at night during the year as a supplement to the written philosophy in the parent handbook, to dramatize and promote discussion of the philosophy. If this approach is used, issues can then be discussed at parent coffees along with tips (instruction) about participating in the classroom. A photo and work sample album updated by each classroom also can show the philosophy in action, with pictures of parents participating in daily life with the children in the classroom. Teachers can use the album during conferences, also, as a sort of portfolio for the whole class.

Parent participation is almost always helpful in "engaging" disengaged families. Actually doing something with a child or children yields concrete examples and results with a formerly disengaged parent, leading to a (small, perhaps) sense of accomplishment. More tips on using parents in the classroom can be found in Appendix G, "Volunteer Program Papers."

A few programs combine some of the characteristics previously discussed, such as group discussions, home visits, classroom participation, and activities for parents to use with their children as a follow-up to training sessions. Head Start, Home Start, and Even Start are some programs that combine approaches and that provide suggested home activities.

Home Instructional Materials Used by Parents

Activities that parents actually engage in with their children, whether for the purpose of building social or cognitive skills, fall into several categories depending on the type of instructional materials needed. The first category includes activities that make use of common household items; the second category includes activities organized around specific instructional materials either provided to the parent or carefully described; and the third category includes activities such as reading stories, playing games, or taking part in general art projects that either build language or positive self-concepts.

Activities with Common Household Items

Gray and Ruttle (1976) designed a longitudinal study in which 51 low-income families, each with two children under the age of five, participated in a 5-year home-based intervention study designed to help mothers become more effective educational agents. One group of families received a 9-month treatment based on the needs and characteristics of the specific families; another group received a treatment that focused on materials the mothers were to use in the homes with their children; a third group was made the control group. When mothers and children were pretested and posttested on a range of instruments relating to maternal and child competency, the results of the first two groups were positive and above those of the control group (Gray, 1984; Gray & Ruttle, 1976).

The Demonstration and Research Center for Early Education (DARCEE), in a report compiled by the Far West Laboratories (1971), described a training program designed for three groups of parents. One group would participate in the training program within the environment of a demonstration center; the second group would be given the training by a home visitor; the third group of parents and children were in a school setting that did not incorporate parent involvement or parent training (this was the control group). The training consisted of teaching parents to use common household items as teaching tools and to take advantage of everyday home situations as opportunities for teaching specific skills, such as using laundry to teach children about colors and sorting. Parents participating in the training also received instructional materials used by the teachers and samples of the work done by the child for use with their child.

Gray and Klaus (1970) and Gray, Ramsey, and Klaus (1981), who worked closely with this project, reported that the results for the group attached to the center were superior to those for the home visitor group and for the control group. The target children and their younger siblings in the home visitor group did show significant gains in I.Q. levels, but their gains were not as high as those of target children whose parents were trained in the center. After two years of public school, all three groups were again tested, and it was found that in the two target groups, the children's I.Q.s had remained stable. In the group in which the mothers were not involved, however, there was a decline in I.Q. levels. As a result of these findings, Gray suggests that perhaps working with parents is not only highly economical from the standpoint of immediate cost efficiency, but also has long-lasting cost benefits and benefits for the child.

Hess and McDevitt (1984), in their longitudinal study of maternal intervention techniques and their effects on cognition, also found lasting benefits to working with parents, but found that the method in which a mother interacted with her child in learning situations had a direct influence on the child's performance. The more controlling the mother's directions were, the poorer the child's outcome. The authors found that children who were guided and encouraged to discover solutions for themselves were more likely to see themselves as capable problem-solvers and to transfer that sense of competency to other settings (Hess & McDevitt, 1984). Suggestions by professionals for appropriate parental and family responses to children's efforts, and guidance for implementing these responses, are therefore also needed when setting up training programs for parents.

An English-Chinese program in California, called "Parents Helping Children to Learn" (Fuduka, 1976), suggested activities for parents to do with their children to supplement the school program. Twelve monthly "letters" were sent home that contained four to six ideas for each month. These ideas included practical exercises such as setting the table, sorting the laundry, and cooking, as well as other activities such as outings to the library and to the park, playing games, making handicrafts, coloring and painting, and reading picture stories with simple words.

Shoemaker, in *Home Learning Enablers and Other Helps* (1996), suggests activities categorized by age and subject matter for parents to do with their children. These activities make use of common household materials or daily routines. Cooking, making trips to the supermarket or the gas station, and using materials such as newspapers, toilet paper, kitchen cans, and jars are just a few suggestions specific to ages three, four, five, six, and seven; third, fourth, fifth, and sixth grades; and middle school/junior high. A section in each activity is devoted to adapting the activity for older or younger children, the parents' evaluation of the success of the activity, and space for "new ideas" from the parent or the child. While these Home Learning Enablers suggest specific materials to use in each activity, the materials are common to most homes. These Home Learning Enablers are to be sent home weekly, biweekly, or monthly. Infant-Toddler Home Learning Enablers and Program Enrichment papers are also available. (See Appendix A for Home Learning Enabler samples for ages three, four, and five.)

Activities with Specific Instructional Materials

One well-documented project that made use of specific instructional materials was Phyllis Levenstein's Mother's Home Training Program. This study utilized specific curriculum materials composed of 12 books and 11 toys, which were all carefully selected based on well-defined criteria. All components of the curriculum were designed to promote verbal interaction between mother and child, and family and child. Between 1967 and 1974, more than 300 children and their mothers participated in the program, accomplishing both its cognitive and affective objectives. Over a period of seven months and 32 home visits, Levenstein reported a 17-point gain in I.Q. levels in her population (Levenstein, 1975).

One of the most valuable aspects of the program, reports Hess and Goodson (1975), is that its design allowed for specification of some of the variables. For example, situations that did not involve the mother/child dyad or the specified toy or book were not nearly as effective as were situations involving three variables: a toy demonstrator, the mother and child, and the toy or book. Follow-up results support the active role of the parent as teacher in a child's development.

Fourteen years after the beginning of her project, Levenstein was able to say that the effects of the Mother's Home Training Program last into the third grade (Russell, 1979). Learning takes place, according to Levenstein, because the child is *in* the mother-child relationship. Those aware of the mother-child bond often are tempted to try to intensify it—to give mothers child-rearing advice when listening to their troubles. Levenstein views this as an invasion of privacy and favors a "light touch," or a nonintrusive approach. This strategy, she feels, ensures respect for families, and promotes the learning that occurs in the constant reciprocal process between mother and child, which is the heart of this program. Father-child and family-child programs have also shown gains. Levenstein is dismayed by programs that show disdain for the people with whom they are working. She also deplores programs that do not give top-quality curriculum materials to the families as a long-lasting focus of verbal stimulation and a bridge to later school experience.

Instructional materials need not be commercial, of course, to be beneficial. For instance, parent education manuals for parents of preschool children with disabilities describe specific instructional materials or toys that can be made at home. Some of these toys include spools for stringing, spools of graduated sizes, graduated cans, a lacing shoe, a sandpaper alphabet, a lotto game, sequence cards, lacing cards, and rough and smooth cards. Children without disabilities would also enjoy these activities.

Early childhood is a time ripe with opportunities for instruction. Burton White (1975b), in describing the last half of a child's second year and the child's third year, states that this is a time for nurturing the roots of intelligence—the learning to learn skills—as well as a time for development of language, social skills, and curiosity. He gives general suggestions for encouraging competence and suggests specific materials that he especially recommends for the 2- to 3-year-old. White's list includes commercial toys and household materials such as cans, pots and pans, and plastic refrigerator containers with lids of all sizes. He does not, however, suggest activities or skills that might be developed with these materials.

Gordon, Guinagh, and Jester (1972) state that "the years between two and four are special because so much happens in the child's use of speech and language" (p. 1). They go on to say that the way in which parents and adults play and work with children at these ages is of special importance.

Activities to Build Language and Self-Concept at Home

Newsletters or handouts for parents of preschool children can be used to provide ideas for play experiences that are informal learning activities. Language games, mathematical concept games, and creative activities can be suggested and explained in detail. Such activities have the potential to enhance the social, emotional, cognitive, motor, and language development of preschool children. No materials need be provided, although any materials needed for creative activities can be listed in that section. Hints for parents on interacting with their children also could be included. A section on traditional art projects for children, as well as science, cooking, gardening, drama, and woodworking, can be worked into the newsletter schedule also. Family outings, pet care, and chores are also good topics.

Preparation of Instructional Materials for Parent Use

While so much has been written on preparing instructional materials for use by educators, very little has been written on preparing instructional materials that might be used especially by parents. Indeed, a great many of the parent education programs and handbooks provide parents with instructional activities involving only spoken words to use as instructional tools, despite the evidence that preschool children learn best through concrete experience.

The Home Learning Enablers (Shoemaker, 1992, 1994, 1996; see also Appendix A) and *Family Math* (Stenmark, Thompson, & Cossey, 1986) are two resources written with parents in mind. They both use formats for each activity that are easy for adults to scan; each activity lists the components of the exercise, and leaves plenty of white space to visually separate the logical sequence of needed steps.

The following steps are included in the Home Learning Enablers: (1) name of activity, (2) materials needed, (3) how to do it, (4) time needed, (5) age of child, (6) evaluation, and (7) adaptation. Many of the Learning Enablers also list subject-matter categories for areas in which an activity builds skills.

The "time needed" step is a unique feature of the Home Learning Enablers in that many programs do not incorporate the variable of time into their procedures. White's (1975) extensive research in the Harvard Preschool Project points to the importance of time as a learning variable, noting that 30- to 60-second "brief enrichments" are most beneficial to young children since their attention span is short. The time length of the Home Learning Enabler activities starts with two or three minutes for toddlers, and works up to 15 minutes for children of junior high age.

The *Family Math* activities are all math-related, of course, but do list objectives and explain how to do each activity, which is very helpful. These activities are for kindergarten age and older. Some of these might be very useful as send-home resources from child-care programs for school-age children.

The Home Learning Enablers and *Family Math* both feature brief one-page activities for easy assimilation by parents. Many activity books cram several activities onto each page. Another drawback to such activity books is that while many of the materials are suggested for use by parents or are given to the parents, the simple language meant to make these materials accessible is often lost in the paragraph-style writing and in the small print.

When preparing instructional materials for parents, videos for parent groups also might be included. The usefulness of these materials is somewhat limited, however, since they rely on the spoken word and visual impact rather than on concrete materials parents can use with their children.

In conclusion, it seems that very little material is available for parents to use with their children. Those materials available for parents of children with disabilities or for bilingual children are quite specific to families in those particular situations, and are also specific in terms of the suggested concrete materials to be used. There are a few programs for parents, however, that benefit a wider range of families, and that are unique in utilizing common household items in a specific, logical way that is easy for most parents to follow.

◇ ◇

INVOLVEMENT OF PARENTS WITH LIMITED ENGLISH PROFICIENCY

In order to promote the healthy self-esteem and success of each and every young child, early childhood programs must be thoughtfully designed to serve both parents and children. This is a particularly challenging task when the families to be served speak a language other than English at home. Programs for young limited English proficiency (LEP) children need to be designed to reinforce the strengths of the individual child and his or her family. Because families are the groups of greatest importance to young children, programs must serve the whole child within the context of the family (Derman-Sparks & A.B.C. Task Force, 1989).

According to Dixon and Fraser (1986), having parents of LEP students participate is a reliable way to gain information about children's family traditions and attitudes, particularly when the cultural backgrounds of these children are unfamiliar to the teacher.

Early intervention is key to the academic success of educationally and economically disadvantaged students, many of whom are LEP students. Research has found that a combination of early intervention and parent involvement increases children's educational achievement (Vargas, 1988).

Research in the field of early childhood education indicates that parental involvement is a necessary condition to ensure the success of all children in early childhood programs (Nissani, 1990). Parents provide the needed link between home and school or center. Much of the research involving bilingual/multicultural education in early childhood emphasizes the role of parents, either directly in the classroom or in auxiliary programs. Data gathered from several programs shows that in programs where children make the greatest gains, parents have been actively involved (Arnberg, 1983). In a review of 20 bilingual preschool education programs around the world, almost 70 percent of them reported parental involvement as a major component of their program (Arnberg, 1983).

Overall, research has demonstrated that even a modest degree of parental involvement has a positive effect on a child's later academic achievement and promotes a generally improved attitude towards learning. The effects are even more powerful among children from lower socioeconomic groups and minority students. Studies undertaken in New Haven, Connecticut, between 1969 and 1984 indicated that parent participation activities improved parent-teacher relations, energized both the parents and the teachers, and had a favorable impact on the children (Ornstein & Levine, 1989).

The focus or goals of a program can be more easily understood and learned by a parent who is visiting the classroom, with an interpreter when necessary. In addition to observing, parents also can be directly involved in working in the classroom. In some programs, parent involvement may be gained through home visits, which encourage and support parents as they work with their children at home.

Social events, such as a potluck supper or a Saturday flea market/yard sale, are often a first step in making parents feel comfortable and involved, since eating and socializing together in this context just naturally brings about conversations about children and school. A special parent education committee could be organized to compile a list of possible activities, from which the most popular ideas could be selected and voted on. Two or more parents might be put in charge of each event, which could occur monthly or at times and intervals convenient to parents. One center felt its surrounding neighborhood was unsafe for evening events, and held parent gatherings at breakfast or supper times to coordinate with drop-off and pick-up times.

Parent involvement opportunities should be made available to all parents. Often language-minority parent involvement in their children's education is inhibited by language barriers, lack of knowledge about the program, high mobility rates, insufficient incentives to become involved, and shortage of staff time to encourage and nurture parental involvement while trying to fulfill the basic curriculum objectives. Early childhood programs that serve language-minority students should employ staff familiar with the needs of the families they serve. This includes bilingual and culturally sensitive personnel who are trained in parent involvement concepts and methods and so are able to attract parent participation. A responsive staff will make a parent feel welcome and important, and this will affect the parent's decision to respond to and partici-pate in the program's activities. It is critical that early childhood education programs communicate with parents in a language and form the parents understand (Vargas, 1988).

Issues of sociocultural differences and the importance of teacher attitudes in establishing home/child-care program interdependence are certainly very rele-vant to the education of language-minority children. To date, neither parents nor centers and schools have taken full advantage of the benefits of parent involvement.

Parental involvement in the classroom ultimately benefits children, because by observing teachers and the ways in which children learn and interact at school, parents can become aware of ways in which they can help their chil-dren learn (Arnberg, 1983). Programs that incorporate home visits, particu-larly if the professional involved in the visit is bilingual and/or is a member of the parents' minority group and so is not seen as a threat by the parents, can demonstrate ways in which parents can stimulate their children's growth in the home. Parents are not uninterested in their children's development and education, but often lack skills and knowledge concerning how they can posi-tively influence their children's growth. It has been demonstrated that home visits increase parent involvement, enhance children's self-esteem, support the curriculum, and help alleviate communication problems for some bilingual families (Fox-Barnett & Meyer, 1992). The visits give parents an opportunity to communicate with the teacher without the boundaries of an institution. When such visits are not judgmental or critical, the parents may in turn feel that the center or school is a more approachable place (Fox-Barnett & Meyer, 1992).

Another commonly used method for involving parents in the classroom is to provide workshops or classes on ways to develop children's skills at home and to reinforce what is learned at the center or nursery school. With this goal in mind, the focus of early childhood education for parents should be topics such as emergent literacy and whole-language skills, ways to reinforce basic number concepts, oral language development, the role of self-concept, and the use of games for skills development. Since the most common reason given for seeking parent involvement is that it improves academic achievement, it may be argued that a crucial focus of parent involvement should be on activities that relate directly to academic tasks (Cervantes, Baca, & Torres, 1979). One center points out the daily activities involving math to all interested parents. These include counting the days on the calendar and putting in the correct date (children write the numerals and say the number in their own language), counting place settings for snack, one-to-one correspondence, setting the table, counting things so people have an equal number, measuring when doing cooking projects, and finding their own numbered mat to lie down on for rest time. This particular center also tells parents about theme projects involving math, such as measuring how many children it takes to equal a dinosaur length (Stegosaurus, 20 feet), drawing a life-sized Tyrannosaurus footprint, and tracing the children's feet to see how many of them would fit inside it (24). The teachers tell parents about the toys that involve math, such as measuring spoons and cups in the sand area, blocks for three dimensional building, parquetry blocks for shape recognition and patterns, and board games that require counting or spinning a spinner and recognizing the next number. Children enjoy songs with counting forwards *and backwards* in English or the language of a child in the class. Adults talk about things that will happen "in five minutes" or "in three days" and compare times to something the children are familiar with, like "that's about how long it takes us to eat our snack."

While the role of language-minority parents in the classroom is often limited to such activities as cooking or making music, some more academic programs have been established with these families in mind. For example, programs have been developed to enhance language-minority parents' and children's reading attitudes as they participate in a series of instructional sessions. Activities for building communication skills as well as methods of reading aloud to children are modeled for parents, and the parents have an opportunity to practice the activities in the classroom as well as at home. Researchers have concluded that modeling is an effective method for training parents in skills for working with their children at home as well as at the program (Ovando & Collier, 1985).

Parents want the best for their children, and they rely on educational programs to enable their children to succeed. Although parents may not always have the time, self-confidence, or clear understanding of the program's goals to demonstrate that concern in a fashion that is recognizable to the school or center, language-minority parents, as well as other parents, must make it a priority to be an active and integral part of the center's program. The success and strength of parent-center relationships in multilingual communities will depend on parents reinforcing their children's cognitive development at home. Ethnic parents, like all parents, will appreciate and help work toward community and center efforts that value their contributions, yield positive academic results, and encourage positive interpersonal and intercultural relationships.

One way to foster positive community participation is to allow parents to plan a day or days in which emphasis is placed on their particular culture. This event could involve activities such as reading brief stories to the children in parents' native languages (other than English), bringing artifacts or pictures from home to share, preparing a typical dish with the children, bringing music and/or clothing from their country, or teaching the children a typical game, song, or craft. This not only increases parents' self-esteem, but also reflects positively on their children, since this is an opportunity for the children of this particular culture to play an important role by having their parents share something that is such an important part of their lives. In addition to exposing children to artwork and materials from different cultures, by integrating the cultures that are represented in the classroom *into* the classroom throughout the year, a mere "tourist curriculum" approach is prevented.

When incorporating home visits into a program, it is beneficial to locate community bilingual volunteers to accompany the program representative on the visits, so that the parents and educators are certain to communicate. An even better situation would be to encourage other family members (aunts, uncles, etc.) who are bilingual to act as interpreters, thereby decreasing the parents' anxiety at having so many strangers in their home.

◇ ◇

INVOLVEMENT OF PARENTS WITH SPECIAL NEEDS CHILDREN

When dealing with children who have special needs and their parents, provide parents with general developmental guidelines and activities that are not age-graded. The Home Learning Enablers in Appendix A, with the age section blocked out, are useful for send-home activities, since they move sequentially from easier to more difficult and can be used with older children who are delayed for a variety of reasons. For instance, an activity specified for a three-year-old could be sent home with a five-year-old with little or no adjustment necessary. However, remind parents that they are responsible for making the final judgment on the care of their children. Parents of special needs children should consult with their pediatrician and developmental specialist regarding the most appropriate activities for their children. In other words, suggestions from a center should not be used as a replacement for recommended therapy (Baker & Long, 1989).

◇ ◇

SUMMARY

Mother-child and family-child communication has been found to be a central factor in a child's scholastic ability, and the lack of it a central factor in the effects of cultural deprivation. Obviously, there seems to be great benefit in encouraging more family-child and mother-child interaction and verbal communication (Lazar, 1977).

An emphasis on children's activities and interactions with specific materials has a long tradition in early childhood education. Piaget (1952), in studying the way children come to understand their world, concluded that early sensori-motor experiences with concrete objects play a crucial role in the development of thought. This suggests that children younger than age seven need to have experiences with concrete manipulatives both at home and in a group setting. However, parents often are not provided with materials or suggestions about materials for their children. If educators need instructional materials, it is reasonable to assume that parents need materials too. Parents of bilingual and special needs children especially need to be involved in early learning programs and in parent-child activities that make use of concrete instructional materials.

◇ ◇

SUGGESTED CLASS ACTIVITIES AND DISCUSSIONS

1. *Role Play a Home Visit.*   Role play a home visit using suggestions given. Other conferences that lend themselves to role play include a parent-teacher conference at the center. Cover this seven-point outline:

   a. What is the child's place in the family?

   b. Is there anything the teacher should know about, such as a family member who is ill, that might affect the child's behavior?

   c. What is something the parent is proud of that the child does at home?

   d. What is something the parent is concerned about?

   e. Tell something the teacher is proud of that the child does at preschool or the center.

   f. Ask about something (if any) that the teacher is concerned about at the center and discuss it. (If there is more than one concern, have more than one conference).

   g. Tell about activities in the child's curriculum at present. Suggest parent ideas to build on the current curriculum at home, as appropriate.

2. *Role play a conference with an abusive and/or difficult parent.*   Using the same seven-point outline just given, students can role play a conference (of course, opening with "How are you?") with an abusive or difficult parent. Take the "parent" aside and describe a set of problems this parent has in order to give context, such as: She is pregnant, has 4 or 5 children, two younger than the four-year-old, her husband is in jail, she has chronic back problems and money problems. (Based on real case studies).

Generally, the role play gets "stuck" about half way through with the "teacher" feeling that she is not "getting through" and that it is hopeless to try to talk to this parent about their child being too noisy in circle time (or whatever). At this point, the role play can be stopped and each participant asked to describe how they feel. The parents often say that they appreciate the interest and feel more trusting but verbally all they have told the teacher is that their back hurts! Some parents say that they will be more cooperative with their *next* child in the program. Occasionally, the "teacher" will become very resourceful and offer original types of help such as part-time work for the thirteen-year-old in the family. Classes have found this opportunity to stop and analyze difficult conferences as a useful memory-link when they are in real-life situations.

3. *Survey Parent Education and Parent Involvement in nearby centers.*   Students can survey 3 to 4 nearby centers either in person or by mail on issues and questions they design, about the types and practices of parent education and parent involvement done in centers. If the survey is done by mail, suggest including a stamped self-addressed envelope and perhaps a pencil as a "thank you" gift to encourage returns.

4. *Write a policy that outlines state commitment to parent involvement.*   Students can write a sample policy that outlines and discusses your state's commitment to parent involvement in publicly-funded child care programs and public schools. This can be aimed at state funding of many sorts as part of a state policy that recognizes the importance of a comprehensive program of parent involvement for children of all ages. Students can send them to the Governor or legislators and report what responses they get.

5. *Role play family members as volunteer aides in the classroom.*   After a discussion and presentation on parent volunteers, an interested group of students can prepare and demonstrate parent involvement as volunteer aides in the classroom—perhaps as a final project. This should be accompanied by handouts describing the Volunteer Aide Orientation Program; the Volunteer Aide Schedule; and the Volunteer Aide On-Going Training Meeting Schedule and Topics (See also Appendix G). Meeting and greeting the volunteer aides and teaching them to meet and greet the children is also important, and this can be a full and complete role play.

6. *Make It—Take It Family Workshop.*   A final project group can design and present a "Make It—Take It" workshop with centers for parents to make home-learning materials for their children in such areas as nutrition, math, language arts, and music. A bilingual center might offer bilingual activities and an interpreter for family members with limited English. The workshop for parents can include name tags and a "getting to know you" warm-up and refreshments. Other parent workshop ideas could feature one subject matter area only such as Art or Nutrition with centers around that subject.

◇ ◇ ◇ ◇ ◇ ◇ ◇ ◇ ◇ ◇ ◇ ◇ ◇ ◇ ◇ ◇ ◇ ◇ ◇ ◇

BIBLIOGRAPHY

Ainsworth, M. D. S. (1969). Object relations, dependency, and attachment: A theoretical review of the infant-mother relationship. *Child Development, 40,* 969–1025.

American Speech and Hearing Association. (1981). *Partners in language: A guide for parents.* Rockville, MD: Author. (Available from ASHA, 10801 Rockville Pike, Rockville, MD 20850; Telephone 301-897-5700)

Anderson, R., Fielding, L., & Wilson, P. (1988). The growth in reading and how children spend time outside of school. *Reading Research Quarterly, 23,* 285–303.

Andrews, S. R., Blumenthal, J. B., Johnson, D. L., Kahn, A. J., Ferguson, C. J., Lasater, T. M., Malone, P. E., & Wallace, D. B. (1982). The skills of mother: A study of parent-child development centers. *Monographs of the Society for Research in Child Development, 6* (Serial No. 198), 47.

Anselmo, S. (1978, November). Improving home and preschool influences on early language development. *Reading Teacher, 32,* 139–143.

Arnberg, L. (1983). *Bilingual education for preschool children.* Sweden: Department of Education, Linkoping University. (ERIC Document Reproduction Service No. ED 245 535)

Baker, C., & Long, T. (1989). *Tips from tots: A resource guide for your infant and toddler.* Los Angeles: Vort Corporation.

Baratta-Lorton, M. (1972). *Workjobs.* Menlo Park, CA: Addison-Wesley.

Baratta-Lorton, M. (1975). *Workjobs . . . for parents. Activity centered learning in the home.* Menlo Park, CA: Addison-Wesley.

Barber, B. K., & Buchler, C. (1996). Family cohesion and psychological control: Different constructs, different effect. *Journal of Marriage and the Family, 58,* 433–441.

Barth, R. M., & Parke, R. D. (1993). Parent-child relationship influences on children's transition to school. *Merrill-Palmer Quarterly, 39,* 1173–1182.

Bauch, P. (1985, April). *Parent involvement: Exploring roles for parents in curriculum and school improvement.* Paper presented at the annual meeting of the National Catholic Education Association, Washington, DC.

Bell, K. (1991). *Home visits revisited.* New York: National Center for Children in Poverty, School of Public Health, Columbia University.

Benaisch, A. A., & Brooks-Gunn, J. (1996). Maternal attitudes and knowledge of child-rearing: Association with family and child outcomes. *Child Development, 67,* 1186–1205.

Bernstein-Tarrow, N., & Lundsteen, S. W. (1981). *Activities and resources for guiding young children's learning.* New York: McGraw-Hill.

Bettelheim, B. (1987). *A good enough parent.* New York: Knopf Books.

Black, B., & Logan, A. (1995). Links between communication patterns in mother-child, father-child, and child-peer interactions and children's social status. *Child Development, 66,* 255-271.

Blank, S. (1987). *Contemporary parenting education and family support programs: Themes and issues in an emerging movement.* New York: Foundation for Child Development.

Bloom, B. (1964). *Stability and change in human characteristics.* New York: Wiley.

Bloom, B. S. (1981). *All our children learning: A primer for parents, teachers and other educators.* New York: McGraw-Hill.

Bolger, K. E., Patterson, C. J., Thompson, W. W., & Kuperschmidt, J. B. (1995). Psychosocial adjustment among children experiencing persistent and intermittent family economic hardship. *Child Development, 66,* 1107–1129.

Bornstein, M., & Tamis-Lemonda, C. (1989). Maternal responsiveness and cognitive development in children. In M. Bornstein (Ed.), *Maternal responsiveness characteristics and consequences.* San Francisco: Jossey-Bass.

Bowlby, J. (1988). *A secure base: Parent child attachment and healthy human development.* New York: Basic Books.

Bowman, B. T. (1989). Educating language minority children: Challenges and opportunities. *Phi Delta Kappan, 71*(2), 118–121.

Bradley, B. (1988, March). School: The parent factor. *Parents,* pp. 111–114. Bredekamp, S. (Ed.). (1987). *NAEYC position statement on developmentally appropriate practice in programs for 4- and 5-year-olds.* Washington, DC: National Association for the Education of Young Children.

Bredekamp, S. (Ed.). (1990). *Developmentally appropriate practice in early childhood programs serving children from birth to age 8.* Washington, DC: National Association for the Education of Young Children.

Bronfenbrenner, U. (1979). *The ecology of human development.* Cambridge, MA: Harvard University Press.

Bronfenbrenner, U. (1986). Ecology of the family as a context for human development: Research perspectives. *Developmental Psychology, 22,* 723–742.

Brown, D., & McDonald, P. (1969). *Learning begins at home: A stimulus for a child's I.Q.* Los Angeles: Lawrence Publishing.

Brownlee, Sharon (1998). Baby talk: Learning language is an astonishing act of brain computation. *U.S. News and World Report, 124*(3), 48–55.

Bruner, J. (1960). *The process of education.* New York: Vintage Books.

Bruner, J. (1964). The course of cognitive growth. *American Psychologist, 19,* 1–15.

Bruner, J. (1966). *Studies in cognitive growth.* New York: Wiley.

Burket, L. L. (1981, April). *Positive parental involvement in the area of reading during preschool years and primary grades.* (Report No. CS006658) Bloomington, IN: Resources in Education. (ERIC Document Reproduction Service No. ED 216 324)

Burleson, B. R., Delia, J. G., & Applegate, J. L. (1995). The socialization of person-centered communication: Parents' contributions to their children's social-cognitive and communication skills. In M. A. Fitzpatrick & A. L. Vangelisti (Eds.), *Explaining Family Interactions,* pp. 34–76. Thousand Oaks, CA: Sage.

Caldwell, B. M., & Smith, L. E. (1970). Day care for the very young—Prime opportunity for primary prevention. *American Journal of Public Health, 60,* 690–697.

California Department of Education. (1991). *Parent involvement programs in California public schools: Families, schools and communities working together.* Sacramento, CA: Parent and Community Education Office, California Department of Education.

Canter, L. (1991). *Parents on your side materials workbook.* Santa Monica, CA: Lee Canter & Associates.

Canter, L., & Canter, M. (1991). *Parents on your side.* Santa Monica, CA: Lee Canter & Associates.

Carbo, M., Dunn, K., & Dunn, R. (1986). *Teaching children to read through their individual learning styles.* Upper Saddle River, NJ: Prentice Hall.

Cervantes, H. T., Baca, L. M., & Torres, D. S. (1979). Community involvement in bilingual education: The bilingual educators parent trainer. *NABE Journal, 3*(2), 73–82.

Chamberlain, P., & Patterson, G. R. (1995). Discipline and child compliance in parenting. In M. H. Bornstein (Ed.), *Handbook of Parenting: Vol. 4, Applied and Practical Parenting,* pp. 205–225. Mahwah, NJ: Lawrence Erlbaum.

Cherlin, A. J. (Ed.). (1988). *The changing American family and public policy.* Washington, DC: The Urban Institute Press.

Children's Defense Fund. (1989). *A vision for America's future.* Washington, DC: Author.

Chrispeels, J., Boruta, M., & Daugherty, M. (1988). *Communicating with parents.* San Diego, CA: San Diego Office of Education.

Chud, G., & Fahlman, R. (1985). *Early childhood education for a multi-cultural society.* British Columbia, Canada: Pacific Educational Press.

Cicchetti, D., & Carlson, V. (Eds.). (1989). *Child maltreatment: Theory and research on the causes and consequences of child abuse and neglect.* New York: Cambridge University Press.

Clark, R. (1983). *Family life and school achievement: Why poor black children succeed or fail.* Chicago: University of Chicago Press.

Clay, M. (1987). *Writing begins at home.* Portsmouth, NH: Heinemann.

Cole, M., & Cole, S. R. (1989). *The development of children.* New York: W. H. Freeman.

Coleman, J. S. (1973, November). *Effects of school on learning: The IEA findings.* Paper presented at the Conference on Education Achievement, Harvard University, Cambridge, MA.

Coleman, J. S., Campbell, E., Mood, A., Weinfeld, E., Hobson, C., York, R., & McPartland, J. (1966). *Equality of educational opportunity.* Washington, DC: U.S. Government Printing Office.

Comer, J. P. (1988, November). Educating poor minority children. *Scientific American, 259*(5), 42–48.

Comer, J. P. (1990). Home, school, and academic learning. In J. I. Goodlad & P. Keating (Eds.), *Access to knowledge: An agenda for our nation's schools.* New York: New York College Entrance Examination Board.

Council of Chief State School Officers. (1989). *Family support, education, and involvement: A guide for state action.* Washington, DC: Author.

Council of Chief State School Officers. (1991). *Families in schools.* Washington, DC: Author.

Covell, K., Grusee, J. E., & King, G. (1995). The intergenerational transmission of maternal discipline and standards for behavior. *Social Development, 4,* 32–43.

Crouter, A. C., & McHale, S. M. (1993). The long arm of the job: Influences of parental work on childrearing. In T. Luster & L. Okagaki (Eds.), *Parenting: An ecological perspective* (pp. 179–202). Hillsdale, NJ: Lawrence Erlbaum.

Darling, N., & Steinberg, L. (1993). Parenting style as context: An integrative model. *Psychological Bulletin, 113,* 487–496.

Das Eiden, R., Teti, D. M., & Corns, K. M. (1995). Maternal working models of attachment, marital adjustment, and the parent-child relationship. *Child Development, 66,* 1504–1518.

Davies, D. (1991). Schools reaching out. *Phi Delta Kappan, 72*(5), 376–382.

Denham, S. A., Renwick-DeBardi, S., & Hewes, S. (1994). Emotional communication between mothers and preschoolers: Relations with competence. *Merrill-Palmer Quarterly, 40,* 488–508.

Derman-Sparks, L., & A. B. C. Task Force. (1989). *Anti-bias curriculum: Tools for empowering young children.* Washington, DC: National Association for the Education of Young Children.

Dewey, J. (1938). *Experience and education.* New York: Collier.

Dix, T., & Gruesec, J. E. (1983). Parent socialization techniques: An attributional analysis. *Child Development, 54,* 645–652.

Dixon, G. T., & Fraser, S. (1986, March/April). Teaching preschoolers in a multilingual classroom. *Childhood Education,* pp. 272–275.

Douglas, J. W. (1964). *The home and school: A study of ability and attainment in the primary school.* London: MacGibbon and Kee.

East, P. L. (1991). The parent-child relationships of withdrawn, aggressive, and sociable children: Child and parent perspectives. *Merrill-Palmer Quarterly, 37,* 425–444.

Education Research Service. (1990). Effects of open enrollment in Minnesota. *ERS Research Digest.* Arlington, VA: Author.

Egawa, K. (1990). Harnessing the power of language: First grader's literature engagement with "Owl Moon," *Language Arts, 67,* 582–588.

Emery, R. E., & Tuer, M. (1993). Parenting and the marital relationship. In T. Luster & L. Okagaki (Eds.), *Parenting: An ecological per-*

spective (pp. 121–148). Hillsdale, NJ: Lawrence Erlbaum.

Epstein, J. L. (1984a). A longitudinal study of school and family effects on student development. In S. A. Mednick & M. Harway (Eds.), *Handbook of longitudinal research.* New York: Praeger.

Epstein, J. L. (1984b). *Single parents and the schools: The effects of marital status on parent and teacher evaluations* (Report 353). Baltimore, MD: The Johns Hopkins University Center for Social Organization of Schools.

Epstein, J. L. (1986). Parents' reactions to teacher practices of parent involvement. *The Elementary School Journal, 86,* 277–294.

Epstein, J. L. (1987a). Parent involvement: State education agencies should lead the way. *Community Education Journal, 14,* 4–9.

Epstein, J. L. (1987b, February). Parent involvement: What research says to administrators. *Education and Urban Society,* 119–136.

Epstein, J. L. (1987c). Toward a theory of family-school connections: Teacher practices and parent involvement across the school years. In K. Hurremann, F. Kaufmann, & F. Losel (Eds.), *Social intervention: Potential and constraints.* New York: de Gruvter.

Epstein, J. L. (1988a). Effective schools or effective students: Dealing with diversity. In R. Haskins & D. MacRae (Eds.), *Policies for America's public schools: Teachers, equity, indicators.* Norwood, NJ: Ablex.

Epstein, J. L. (1988b). How do we improve programs for parent involvement? *Education Horizons, 66*(2), 58–59.

Epstein, J. L. (1991, January). Paths to partnership: What we can learn from federal, state, district, and school initiatives. *Phi Delta Kappan,* 344–349.

Far West Laboratory for Educational Research and Development. (1971). *Demonstration and Research Center for Early Education program report.* Nashville, TN: George Peabody College for Teachers.

Ferber, R. (1986). *Solve your child's sleep problems.* New York: Simon and Shuster.

Field, T. (1995). Psychologically depressed parents. In M. H. Bornstein (Ed.), *Handbook of parenting: Vol. 4, Applied and practical parenting* (pp. 85–99). Mahwah, NJ: Lawrence Erlbaum.

Finnie, N. R. (1975). *Handling the cerebral palsied child at home.* New York: E. P. Dutton.

Fitzpatrick, M. A., & Badzinski, D. (1994). All in the family: Interpersonal communication in kin relationships. In M. L. Knapp & G. R. Miller (Eds.), *Handbook of interpersonal communication* (2nd ed., pp. 726–771). Thousand Oaks, CA: Sage.

Flaxman, E., & Inger, M. (1991). Parents and schooling in the 1990s. *The Education Digest, 57*(4), 3–7.

Fox-Barnett, M., & Meyer, T. (1992). The teacher's playing at my house this week! *Young Children, 47*(5), 45–50.

Fraiberg, S. (1981). *The magic years.* New York: Macmillan.

Fredericks, A. D., & Rasinski, T. V. (1990). Working with parents: Factors that make a difference. *The Reading Teacher, 44*(1), 76–77.

Friedman, R. (1978, Fall). First cry of the newborn: Basis for child's future musical development. *Journal of Research in Music Education, 21,* 264–269.

Froebel, F. (1902). *Pedagogies of the kindergarten.* (J. Jarvis, Trans.). New York: D. Appleton and Company.

Fuduka, A. (1976). *Parents helping children to learn.* San Francisco: Chinese Bilingual Pilot Program.

Furman, W. (1995). Parenting siblings. In M. H. Bornstein (Ed.), *Handbook of parenting: Vol. 1, Children and parenting* (pp. 143–162). Mahwah, NJ: Lawrence Erlbaum.

Galinsky, E., & David, J. (1983). *The preschool years.* New York: Random House/Time Books.

Garcia-Coll, C. T., Meyer, E. C., & Brillon, L. (1995). Ethnic and minority parenting. In M. H. Bornstein (Ed.), *Handbook of Parenting: Vol. 3, Status and social conditions of parenting* (pp. 189–209). Mahwah, NJ: Lawrence Erlbaum.

Garland-Burtt, K., & Kalkenstern, K. (1994). *Smart toys*. St. Paul, MN: RedLeaf Press.

Ge, X., Conger, R. D., Cadoret, R. J., Neiderhiser, J. M., Yates, W., Traughton, E., & Stewart, M. A. (1996). The developmental interface between nature and nurture: A mutual influence model of child antisocial behavior and parent behaviors. *Developmental Psychology, 32,* 574–589.

Gelfer, J. (1991). Teacher-parent partnerships: Enhancing communication. *Childhood Education,* pp. 164–167.

Gesell, A. (1945). *The embryology of behavior: The beginnings of the human mind.* New York: Harper.

Goldsmith, S. (1984). *ABC123—A teacher/parent resource for teaching beginning concepts.* Nashville, TN: Incentive Publications.

Goldstein, R. (1990). *Everyday parenting: The first five years.* New York: Viking/Penguin.

Goodnow, J. J. (1995). Parents' knowledge and expectations. In M. H. Bornstein (Ed.), *Handbook of parenting: Vol. 3, Status and social conditions of parenting* (pp. 305–332). Mahwah, NJ: Lawrence Erlbaum.

Goodson, B. D., Swartz, J. P., & Millsap, M. A. (1991). *Working with families: Promising programs to help parents support young children's learning.* Cambridge, MA: Abt Associates.

Gordon, I. J. (1969). Developing parent power. In E. Grotberg (Ed.), *Critical issues in research related to disadvantaged children.* Princeton, NJ: Educational Testing Service.

Gordon, I. J. (1977). Parent education and parent involvement: Retrospect and prospect. *Childhood Education, 34,* 71–77.

Gordon, I. J., & Breivogel, W. F. (Eds.). (1976). *Building effective home-school relationships.* Boston: Allyn & Bacon.

Gordon, I. J., Guinagh B., & Jester, R. E. (1972). *Child learning through child play.* New York: St. Martin's Press.

Gotts, E. E., & Purnell, R. F. (1986). Communications: Key to school-home relations. In R. P. Boger, & R. T. Griffore (Eds.), *Child rearing in the home and school.* New York: Plenum.

Gray, S. T. (1984). How to create a successful school/community partnership. *Phi Delta Kappan, 65*(6), 405–410.

Gray, S. W. (1971, January). Home visiting programs for parents of young children. *Peabody Journal of Education, 48,* 106–111.

Gray, S. W., & Klaus, R. A. (1970, December). The early training project: A seventh year report. *Child Development, 41,* 909.

Gray, S. W., Ramsey, B., & Klaus, R. (1981). *From three to twenty: The early training project.* Baltimore, MD: University Park Press.

Gray, S. W., & Ruttle, K. (1976). *The family-oriented home visiting program: A longitudinal study.* Bethesda, MD: National Institute of Child Health and Human Development.

Greenberger, E., O'Neill, R., & Nagel, S. K. (1994). Linking workplace and homeplace: Relations between the nature of adults' work and their parenting behaviors. *Developmental Psychology, 30,* 990–1002.

Greenwood, G. E., & Hickman, C. W. (1991). Research and practice in parent involvement: Implications for teacher education. *The Elementary School Journal, 91*(3), 279–288.

Grusee, J. E., & Goodnow, J. J. (1994). Impact of parental discipline methods on the child's internalization of values: A reconceptualization of current points of view. *Developmental Psychology, 30,* 4–19.

Halpern, R. (1989). Community-based early intervention: The state of the art. In J. Shonkoff & S. Meisels (Eds.), *Handbook of early intervention.* New York: Cambridge University Press.

Halpern, R., & Weiss, H. B. (1990). Family support and education programs: Evidence from evaluated program experience. In *Helping families grow strong: New directions in public policy* (Papers from the Colloquium on Public Policy and Family Support). Washington, DC: Center for the Study of Social Policy.

Hamburg, D. A. (1990). *A decent start: Promoting healthy child development in the first three years of life*. New York: Carnegie Corp. (Annual Report).

Harkness, S., & Super, C. (1995). Culture and parenting. In M. H. Bornstein (Ed.), *Handbook of parenting: Vol. 3, Status and social conditions of parenting* (pp. 211–234). Mahwah, NJ: Lawrence Erlbaum.

Hart, C. H., Blurts, D. C., & Charlesworth, R. (1997). Integrated developmentally appropriate curriculum: From theory and research to practice. In C. H. Hart, D. C. Blurts, & R. Charlesworth (Eds.), *Integrated curriculum and developmentally appropriate practice: Birth to age 8*. Albany, NY: State University of New York Press.

Hayes, C. D., Palmer, J. L., & Zaslow, M. J. (Eds.). (1990). *Who cares for America's children: Child care policy for the 1990's*. Panel on Child Care Policy, Committee on Child Development Research and Public Policy, Commission on Behavioral and Social Sciences and Education. Washington, DC: National Academy Press.

Hechinger, F. M. (Ed.). (1986). *A better start: New choices for early learning*. New York: Walker and Co.

Hedrick, V. (1977, July). The winning play at home base. *American Education, 13*, 27–30.

Henderson, A. T. (1987). *The evidence continues to grow: Parent involvement improves student achievement*. Columbia, MD: National Committee for Citizens in Education.

Henderson, A., Marburger, C., & Ooms, T. (1986). *Beyond the bakesale: An educator's guide to working with parents*. Columbia, MD: National Committee for Citizens in Education.

Hess, R. D. (1969). Parental behavior and children's social achievements. In E. Grotberg (Ed.), *Critical issues in research related to disadvantaged children*. Princeton, NJ: Educational Testing Service.

Hess, R. D., Beckum, L., Knowles, R., & Miller, R. (1971). Parent training programs and community involvement in day care. *Day care: Resources for decisions*. Washington, DC: U.S. Government Printing Office.

Hess, R. D., Block, M., Costello, J., Knowles, J. R., & Miller, R. (1971). Parent involvement in early education. *Day care: Resources for decisions*. Washington, DC: U.S. Government Printing Office.

Hess, R. D., & Goodson, B. (1975, May). *Parents as teachers of young children: An evaluative review of some contemporary concepts and programs*. Palo Alto, CA: Stanford University.

Hess, R. D., & Holloway, S. D. (1984). Family and school as educational institutions. In R. D. Park (Ed.), *Review of child development research* (Vol. 7). Chicago: University of Chicago Press.

Hess, R. D., Holloway, S. D., Dickson, W. P., & Price, G. G. (1984). Maternal variables as predictors of children's school readiness and later achievement in vocabulary and mathematics in the sixth grade. *Child Development, 55*, 1902–1913.

Hess, R. D., & McDevitt, T. M. (1984). Some cognitive consequences of maternal intervention techniques: A longitudinal study. *Child Development, 55*, 2017–2030.

Hetherington, E. M. (1989). Parents, children and siblings six years after divorce. In R. Hinde & J. S. Hinde (Eds.), *Relationships within families*. Cambridge, England: Cambridge University Press.

Hetherington, E. M. & Stanley-Hagan, M. M. (1995). Parenting in divorced and remarried families. In M. H. Bornstein (Ed.), *Handbook of Parenting: Vol. 3, Status and social conditions of parenting* (pp. 233–254). Mahwah, NJ: Lawrence Erlbaum.

Hobbs, N. (1975). *The future of children*. San Francisco: Jossey-Bass.

Hochschild, A., & Machung, A. (1989). *The second shift: Working parents and the revolution at home*. New York: Viking Publishing.

Hoff-Ginsburg, E., & Tardif, T. (1995). Socioeconomic status and parenting. In M. H. Bornstein (Ed.), *Handbook of parenting: Vol. 2, Biology and ecology of parenting* (pp. 161–188). Mahwah, NJ: Lawrence Erlbaum.

Honig, A. S. (1972). *The family development research program: With emphasis on the children's center curriculum.* Syracuse, NY: The New York College for Human Development.

Honig, A. S. (1978). *Parent involvement and the development of children with special needs.* Syracuse, NY: Syracuse University.

Honig, A. S. (1979). *Parent involvement in early childhood education.* Washington, DC: National Association for the Education of Young Children.

Honig, A. S. (1989). Quality infant/toddler caregiving: Are there any magic recipes? *Young Children, 44*(4), 4–10.

Hoover-Dempsey, K. V., Bassler, O. C., & Brissie, J. S. (1992). Explorations in parent-school relations. *Journal of Educational Research, 85*(5), 287–293.

Horowitz, J., & Faggella, K. (1986). *Partners for learning.* Weston, MA: First Teacher Press. (Parent-teacher involvement suggestions and reproducible letters are featured in this early childhood book.)

Hunt, J. M. (1961). *Intelligence and experience.* New York: The Ronald Press.

Hunt, J. M. (1972). *Human intelligence.* New Brunswick, NJ: Transaction.

Jenson, M. A. (1985). Story awareness: A critical skill for early reading. *Young Children, 41*(1), 20–24.

Jewell, M. V., & Zintz, M. G. (1990). *Learning to read and write naturally.* Dubuque, IA: Kendall/Hunt.

Johnson, D. L., and others. (1976). *Houston parent-child development center.* Houston, TX: Houston University.

Jones, C. C. (1981). *The relationship of selected instructional materials used by parents and intelligence of three-year-old day care children from lower socio-economic families.* Ann Arbor, MI: UMI.

Kagan, J. (1977). The effect of day care on early development. In B. Persky & L. Golubchick (Eds.), *Early Childhood.* Wayne, NJ: Avery.

Kagan, S. L. (1990). *Excellence in early childhood education: Defining characteristics and next-decade strategies.* Office of Education Research and Improvement, U.S. Department of Education. Washington, DC: U.S. Government Printing Office.

Kahn, A. J., & Kamerman, S. B. (1987). *Child care: Facing the hard choices.* Dover, MA: Auburn House Publishing.

Kalt, B. R., & Bass, R. *The mother's guide to child safety.* New York: Grosset and Dunlap.

Kamii, C., & Radin, N. (1967). *The Ypsilanti early education program.* Ypsilanti, MI: Ypsilanti Public Schools.

Karnes, M. B. (1969). *A new role for teachers: Involving the entire family in the education of preschool disadvantaged children.* Urbana, IL: University of Illinois.

Katz, L. F., & Gottman, J. M. (1994). Patterns of marital interaction and children's emotional development. In R. D. Parke & S. G. Kellam (Eds.), *Exploring family relationships within other social contexts* (pp. 49–74). Hillsdale, NJ: Lawrence Erlbaum.

Kennedy, C. (1991, March). Parent involvement: It takes PEP. *Principal,* 25–28.

Kochanska, G. (1995). Children's temperament, mother's discipline, and security of attachment: Multiple pathways to emerging internalization. *Child Development, 66,* 597–615.

Kuczynski, L., & Kochanska, G. (1995). Function and content of maternal demands: Developmental significance of early demands for competent action. *Child Development, 66,* 616–628.

Lally, J. R., & Honig, A. S. (1977). *The family development research program: A program for prenatal, infant and early childhood enrichment.* Syracuse, NY: The New York College for Human Development.

Lancy, D. F., & Nattiv, A. (1992, Summer). Parents as volunteers. *Childhood Education,* pp. 208–212.

Larrick, N. (1976). From "Hands off" to "Parents, we need you!" *Childhood Education, 52,* 134–137.

Lazar, I. (1977). *The persistence of preschool effects: A longterm follow up of fourteen infant and preschool experiments.* Washington, DC: Administration for Children, Youth and Families.

Levenstein, P. (1975). *The mother-child home program.* New York: Carnegie Corp.

Linney, J., & Vernberg, E. (1983). Changing patterns of parental employment and family-school relationships. In Hayes and Kamerman (Eds.), *Children of working parents: Experiences and outcomes.* Washington, DC: National Academy Press.

Maring G. H., & Magelky, J. (1990). Effective communication: Key to parent/community involvement. *Reading Teacher, 43*(8), 606.

Marzollo, J. (1987). *The new kindergarten full day, child centered academic.* New York: Harper & Row.

Mavrogenes, N. A. (1990). Helping parents help their children become literate. *Young Children, 45*(5), 35–40.

McKay, D. (1981). *Introducing pre-school children to reading through parent involvement* (Report No. PS0123708). Paper presented at the Annual Meeting of Parents and Reading Conference, New York. (ERIC Document Reproduction Service No. ED 206 406)

Melson, G. F., Ladd, G. W., & Hsu, H. (1993). Maternal support networks, maternal cognition, and young children's social and cognitive development. *Child Development, 64,* 1401–1417.

Minnesota Department of Education. (n. d.). *Minnesota early childhood family education: Answers to commonly asked questions.* St. Paul, MN: Author.

Moles, O. C. (1982, November). Synthesis of recent research on parent participation in children's education. *Educational leadership.*

Montessori, M. (1968). *Dr. Montessori's own handbook.* New York: Schocken Books.

Moore, R. S., and others. (1976). *The balanced development of young children.* Berrien Springs, MI: Hewitt Research Center.

Morgan, E. L. (1989, October). Parent-teacher communication techniques. *Education Digest,* p. 32.

Mosteller, F., & Moynihan, O. P. (Eds.). (1972). *On equality of educational opportunity.* New York: Random House.

Nardine, F. E., Chapman, W. K., & Moles, O. C. (1989). *How involved are state education agencies in parent involvement?* (Report No. 17). Boston: Institute for Responsive Education.

Nardine, F. E., & Morris, R. D. (1991). Parent involvement in the states: How firm is the commitment? *Phi Delta Kappan, 72*(5), 363–366.

National Association for the Education of Young Children. (1972). Parents as educators: Evidence from cross-sectional, longitudinal, and intervention research. In W. Hartrup (Ed.), *The young child: Reviews of research.* Washington, DC: Author.

National Association for the Education of Young Children. (1986, May). Accreditation: A new tool for early childhood programs. *Young Children,* pp. 31–32.

National Association for the Education of Young Children. (1991). *Accreditation criteria and procedures of the National Academy of Early Childhood Programs.* Washington, DC: Author.

National Commission on Children. (1991). *Beyond rhetoric: A new American agenda for children and families.* Washington, DC: Author.

Nevius, J. R., & Filgo, D. J. (1977). *Home start education: A guideline for content areas* (Report No. PS009645). Washington, DC: U.S. Educational Resources Information Center. (ERIC Document Reproduction Service No. ED 147 013)

Nissani, H. (1990). Early Childhood Programs for Language Minority Children. *Focus, 2.* (ERIC Document Reproduction Service No. ED 337 033)

Norman-Jackson, J. (1982). Family interactions, language development, and primary reading achievement of black children in families of low income. *Child Development, 53,* 349–358.

Ornstein, A. C., & Levine, D. U. (1989). *Foundations of education*. Boston: Houghton Mifflin.

Ovando, C. J., & Collier, V. P. (1985). *Bilingual and ESL classrooms*. New York: McGraw-Hill.

Parents and schools make a difference! (1989). Sacramento, CA: California State Board of Education Policy on Parent Involvement.

Piaget, J. (1952). *The origins of intelligence in children* (M. Cook, Trans.). New York: International University Press.

Piaget, J. (1973). *To understand is to invent*. New York: Viking Press.

Radke-Yarrow, M., & Zahn-Waxler, C. (1986). The role of familial factors in the development of prosocial behavior: Research findings and questions. In D. Olweus, J. Block, & M. Radke-Yarrow (Eds.), *Development of antisocial and prosocial behavior*. Orlando, FL: Academic Press.

Raines, S. C. (1990). *The whole language kindergarten*. New York: Teachers College Press.

Ramsaur, M. C. (1992). From teacher to parent to child. *Teaching K–8*, pp. 78–84.

Rich, D., & Jones, C. (1977). *A family affair: Education*. Washington, DC: The Home and School Institute.

Rich, D., & Jones, C. (1978). *The three R's plus: Teaming families and schools for student achievement*. Washington, DC: The Home and School Institute.

Rogers, D. E., & Ginzberg, E. (Eds.). (1990). *Improving the life chances of children at risk*. Boulder, CO: Westview Press.

Roopnarine, J. L., Bright, J. A., & Riegraf, N. B. (1994). Family dynamics and day care children's peer group participation. In H. Goelman & E. V. Jacobs (Eds.), *Children's play in child care settings* (pp. 53–68). Albany, NY: State University of New York Press.

Roopnarine, J. L., & Lamb, M. E. (1978). The effects of day care on attachment and exploratory behavior in a strange situation. *Merrill-Palmer Quarterly, 24,* 85–97.

Rose-Krasnor, L. Rubin, K. H., Booth, C. L., & Coplan, R. J. (1996). Maternal directiveness

and child attachment security as predictors of social competence in preschoolers. *International Journal of Behavioral Development, 14,* 309–325.

Rothbaum, F., Rosen, K. S., Pott, M., & Beatty, M. (1995). Early parent-child relationships and later problem behavior: A longitudinal study. *Merrill-Palmer Quarterly, 41,* 133–151.

Rubin, K. H., Rose-Krasnor, L., Bigras, M., Mills, R. S., & Booth, C. L. (1996). Predicting parental behavior: The influences of setting conditions, psychosocial factors, and parental beliefs. In G. M. Tarabulsy & R. Tessler (Eds.), *Social-emotional development of children*. Quebec, Canada: University of Quebec Press.

Russell, A. (1979, Fall). Hidden curriculum in the mother-child home program: Update from Phyllis Levenstein. *Human Ecology Forum, 10,* 8–12.

Rutter, M. (1985). Family and school influences on cognitive development. In R. A. Hinde, A. N. Perret-Clermont, & J. Stevenson-Hinde (Eds.), *Social relationships and cognitive development*. Oxford, England: Clarendon Press.

Schaefer, E. S. (1974). New perspective in learning—The parent centered approach. In *Proceedings*. Rockville, MD: Conference of the Montgomery County, Maryland, Parent Cooperative Preschools.

Schaefer, E. S., Hunter, W. M., & Watkins, D. B. (1986). *Parenting and child behavior predictors of retention in grades K, 1, 2.* Paper presented at the annual meeting of the American Education Research Association, San Francisco.

Schoumacher, S., & Cadden, V. (1989, September). Preparing your child for the 21st century. *McCall's*, p. 41.

Schweinhart, L., & Weikart, D. (1983). The effects of the Perry preschool program on youths through age 15—A summary. *Consortium for longitudinal studies: As the twig is bent . . . lasting effects of preschool programs*. Hillsdale, NJ: Erlbaum.

Scott-Jones, D. (1984). Family influences on cognitive development and school achievement. In E. Gordon (Ed.), *Review of research in education* (Vol. 11). Washington, DC: American Educational Research Association.

Seefeldt, C., & Barbour, N. (1990). *Early childhood education: An introduction.* New York: Merrill/Macmillan.

Seitz, V. (1977, February). *Long term effects of intervention: A longitudinal investigation.* Paper presented to AAAS Conference, New Haven, CT.

Seitz, V., Apel, N., Rosenbaum, L., Zigler, E., & Abelson, W. (1983). *Long term effects of projects Head Start and Follow Through: The New Haven project.* Hillsdale, NJ: Erlbaum.

Seitz, V., Rosenbaum, L. K., & Apfel, N. H. (1987, April). *Long term effects of the Yale-New Haven family support intervention project.* Paper presented at the biennial meeting of the Society for Research in Child Development, Baltimore, MD.

Shaw, J. W., & Schoggin, M. (1969). *Children learning: Samples of everyday lives of children at home.* Nashville, TN.: Demonstration and Research Center for Early Education.

Shoemaker, C. J. (1996). *Home learning enablers and other helps* (3rd ed.). Marbury, MD: ECEA Institute.

Shonkoff, J. P., & Meisels, S. J. (Eds.). (1990). *Handbook of early childhood intervention.* New York: Cambridge University Press.

Sigel, I. E., & McGillicuddy-Delisi, A. V. (1984). Parents as teachers of their children: A distancing behavior model. In A. D. Pelligrew & T. D. Yawker (Eds.), *The development of oral and written language in social contexts* (pp. 71–92). Norwood, NJ: Ablex.

Silvern, S. (1985, September/October). Parent involvement and reading achievement: A review of research and implications for practice. *Childhood Education, 62*(1), 44–50.

Skeels, H. M., & Dye, H. B. (1939). A study of the effects of differential stimulation on mentally retarded children. *Proceedings of American Association of the Mentally Deficient, 44,* 114–136.

Smetana, J. G. (1994). Parenting styles and beliefs about parental authority. *New Directions for Child Development, 66,* 21–36.

Solomon, Z. P. (1991, January). California's policy on parent involvement. *Phi Delta Kappan, 72*(5), 359–362.

Spewock, T. (1991). Teaching parents of young children through learning packets. *Young Children,* pp. 28–30.

Sroufe, L. A. (1988). The role of infant-caregiver attachment in development. In J. Belsky & T. Nezworski (Eds.), *Clinical implication of attachment.* Hillsdale, NJ: Erlbaum.

Stenmark, J., Thompson, V., & Cossey, R. (1986). *Family math.* New York: Carnegie Corporation.

Stevens, J. H., Jr., & Matthews, M. (1978). *Mother/child, father/child relationships.* Washington, DC: National Association for the Education of Young Children.

Swap, S. (1980). *Parent involvement and success for all children.* Boston, MA: Institute for Responsive Education.

Swap, S. (1987). *Enhancing parent involvement: A manual for parents and teachers.* New York: Teachers College Press.

Taylor, K. W. (1967). *Parents and children learn together.* New York: Teachers College Press.

Tizard, J., Schofield, W. N., & Hewison, J. (1982). Collaboration between teachers and parents in assisting children's reading. *British Journal of Educational Psychology, 52,* 1–15.

Trelease, J. (1998). *The new read-aloud handbook.* New York: Penguin Books.

U.S. General Accounting Office. (1990, July). *Home visiting: A promising early intervention strategy for at risk families* (Report GAO/HRD 90–83). Washington, DC: Author.

Vandegrift, J. A., & Greene, A. L. (1992). Rethinking parent involvement. *Educational Leadership, 50*(1), 57–59.

Vargas, A. (1988, June). *Smart start: The community collaborative for Early Childhood*

Development Act of 1988. Paper presented before the Senate Committee on Labor and Human Resources, Washington, DC.

Vermulst, A. A., DeBrock, A. J., & Van Zutphen, R. A. (1990). Transmission of parenting across generations. In P. K. Smith (Ed.), *The psychology of grandparenthood: An international perspective* (pp. 100–122). New York: Routledge.

Warner, I. (1991, January). Parents in touch: District leadership for parent involvement. *Phi Delta Kappan,* 372–375.

Weikart, D., & Lambie, D. (1967). Preschool intervention through a home teaching program. In J. Hellmuth (Ed.), *The disadvantaged child* (Vol. ii). Seattle, WA: Special Child Publications.

Weiss, H., et al. (1991). *Raising our future: Families, schools, communities joining together.* Cambridge, MA: Harvard Families Research Project.

Wherry, I. (1992, April). Getting parents involved. *Educational Digest,* pp. 49–50.

White, B. L. (1974). *Reassessing our educational priorities.* Paper presented to the Education Commission of the States, Boston, MA.

White, B. L. (1975a). *Experience and environment.* Upper Saddle River, NJ: Prentice Hall.

White, B. L. (1975b). *The first three years of life.* Upper Saddle River, NJ: Prentice Hall.

Wikelund, K. R. (1990). *Schools and communities together: A guide to parent involvement.* Portland, OR: Northwest Regional Educational Laboratory.

Williams, D., & Stallworth, J. (1983/1984). *Parent involvement in education project.* Austin, TX: Southwest Educational Development Laboratory.

Wittes, G., & Radin, N. (1969). *Two approaches to group work with parents in a compensatory preschool program.* Ypsilanti, MI: Ypsilanti Public Schools.

Zigler, E. F., & Lang, M. E. (1991). *Child care choices: Balancing the needs of children, families and society.* New York: The Free Press.

Zigler, E. F., & Weiss, H. (1985). Family support systems: An ecological approach to child development. In R. N. Rappaport (Ed.), *Children, youth, and families.* New York: Cambridge University Press.

Legal Issues in Early Childhood

Legal issues affecting young children include divorce and single-parent homes, foster care, adoption, and child abuse, which is also a medical issue. There are other legal issues as well and an aware director needs to have access to legal counsel of some sort, perhaps through a church or community Board of Directors, to understand the possible implications and ramifications of such situations. The discussion here is limited to these few, but major, issues.

◇ ◇

DIVORCE

With the number of divorces increasing in families with children under age five, it is important to review the problems related to divorce, the child's perception of it, legal ramifications for the child, and the choice of strategies that can be used to help a child deal with these difficult psychosocial problems. The many spill-overs from this one, basically legal, children's issue show up in (almost) every program for young children.

More than 1,000,000 children under the age of 18 cope with divorce every year (CCWD, 1997) and, unfortunately, the rate of divorce continues to soar. These are children from all walks of life and socio-economic groups, but more often they are those at the lower end of the economic ladder (Prokop, 1986).

Behind each statistic is the dissolution of a family. With this transition comes many emotions and adjustments (Diamond, 1985). Many parents think that since they don't talk to their children about problems in the marriage, the children are unaware of what is going on. In truth, even infants and certainly children of three, four and five know very well when parents are having marital trouble (LeShan, 1978; Wallerstein, 1989, 1990).

When parents make a decision to divorce, it is recommended that they tell their child together. This gives children a feeling of closeness with both parents and other siblings. It also conveys the parents' willingness and availability to discuss the separation and divorce further. Discussions with each parent separately sometimes creates a secretive and distrustful atmosphere.

It is best to tell children of the decision to divorce several days in advance, rather than give no advance warning or have children wake to find that dad or mom has left during the night (Barnes & Coplon, 1980). Divorce should not be discussed if the parents are still ambivalent or haven't made definite decisions about living arrangements.

When the time comes, children need to be given concrete details about upcoming changes in order to minimize their anxiety. Parents should be honest, simple and brief and avoid giving details or placing blame on the other parent (Hillowe, 1989). Use words that the children are able to understand. Ask, "Am I making myself clear?" and "Tell me what I'm saying" (Rogers & O'Brien, 1987).

It is important for children to realize that this is a grown-up matter and has nothing to do with them. They should know that their parents did love each other once and that they are the product of that love. In order to give children a feeling of self-worth, they should be reminded that they were wanted once and are still wanted. While the marriage is now a mistake and parents have imperfections, the failure is NOT the children's fault (Barnes & Coplon, 1980).

According to Wallerstein (1989), parents should explain that they are separating because they don't want to fight anymore and don't want the children to be sad when they fight. Letting children know that parents are disappointed, angry or hurt that the marriage is ending, but that these feelings are not directed at them, is a way of easing some of the children's pain. Wallerstein's (1990) continued work emphasizes the serious harm experienced by children from divorced families grown to adulthood and advises serious reluctance in taking this path. The Children Cope With Divorce (CCWD) seminars programs run by Families First in Atlanta, Georgia, help families deal with many of these issues. Some attorneys and judges even require divorcing parents to attend such seminars (CCWD, 1997).

Preschoolers need to know where they will live, how often they will see each parent and that they'll have plenty to eat and a place to live (Barnes & Coplon, 1980). Acknowledge the children's sadness as they grieve the loss of their family. "Repeated discussions may be needed as an emotional desensitization, and to reassure the children of their parents' continuing interest" (Hillowe, p. 2).

Children cannot handle too many changes at once and it is less stressful if they can live in the same house and attend the same preschool or child care program. The early childhood program can be a safe haven when so many drastic changes are occurring at home (Hillowe, 1989).

According to Wallerstein (1989), preschoolers need to know that the parent who is leaving is not disappearing for good. Children at this age are very dependent on their families and need to be reassured that parents still will be there to take care of them. In her earlier work, Wallerstein found that 80% of four-year-olds had not been told of the divorce beforehand. Some weren't even sure where the other parent went, and thought they (the children) might be sent away next. This approach can cause feelings of separation anxiety in children. The children need to know where the parent who is leaving will be living. This second home should be set up so that children will have their own space with their own belongings. Let them become familiar with the house or apartment and the neighborhood and establish a routine. In both homes, order and rules are necessary to show the children that the parents are coping and remain in control (Hillowe, 1989).

Preschoolers will have different reactions to the news that their parents have separated. The fear of abandonment is especially prevalent at this age. Babies love to play peek-a-boo because it reinforces the idea that, even though loved ones disappear for a second, they always come back. The reason toddlers often cry loud and long when left with a sitter is because they are not sure their parents are coming back. This fear of abandonment is also the reason most children feel frightened when they go to child care.

When parents separate, children's fears take over. It doesn't matter how warm and loving parents are—most children have this fear sometimes. Quite simply, children know they need grown-ups to take care of them. (One said "Who will keep track of me?") They know that if abandoned they could not survive (LeShan, 1978).

Divorce can lead to even stronger feelings of abandonment than those that follow the death of a parent. A bereaved child usually receives support from family and friends. In the case of divorce, however, neighbors, friends and even grandparents may keep their distance to avoid taking sides in the conflict (Segal, 1989).

Youngsters may be anxious about their relationship with their parents after a divorce, because their logic tells them that, if the marital tie can be broken, then so can the parent-child bond. Parents should stress that the feelings between a man and woman are very different from the feelings a parent has for a child (Rogers, 1987).

Many young children feel neglected after a divorce. Their parents are engulfed in their own problems and simply don't pay as much attention to them. In this period directly after divorce, mothers and fathers are more likely to ignore their children and communicate less effectively with them, show less affection and even make fewer demands (Segal, 1989). Unfortunately, this can be true after the death of a spouse as well, the reason being that the remaining parent is preoccupied processing his or her own feelings.

It is sometimes difficult for parents to show their love for their children when they themselves are so upset. While parents are feeling overworked and unappreciated, they need to make certain that their children feel loved before, during and after the divorce. By helping their children to cope, parents continue to be competent and attentive parents.

Children adapt best when the conflict of their parents' relationship is minimized and when they are allowed to maintain contact with both parents. Children should be encouraged to feel that they now have two families and two homes. They need to be reassured that both parents love them and are committed to being their parents forever (Hillowe, 1989). Wallerstein's work in *2nd Chances: Men, Women, and Children a Decade after the Divorce* (1990), reminds readers that divorce damages children and its effects sometimes last for decades.

Prokop (1986) states that many children of divorced parents feel anxious, angry, confused, lonely and depressed. Some of those unhealthy feelings may come from false beliefs children have about themselves and divorce. Children sometimes worry that their inappropriate thoughts or actions were the cause of their parents' breakup.

According to one five-year-old, "Mom and dad would have stayed in love if I didn't act up." This results in a lingering sense of guilt. Another child thought his father left because he had made him angry when he played in the street. Children may feel that the departure is aimed at them, not the other parent (Hillowe, 1989), and need to be reminded over and over that they are NOT the cause of the divorce.

Many preschoolers become anxious and "clingy" during the divorce. Their concepts of dependability and personal ties have been deeply shaken. They may not want to attend their early childhood program. They may look for a security blanket that they gave up some time ago. Some common reactions to the stress of divorce include regressive behavior such as thumb sucking, wetting the bed, needing help with feeding, having physical complaints and tantrums. These and other developmental regressions usually disappear after a few weeks as children gain some strength and learn to cope with this transition and deal with their anxiety.

Children's sadness during divorce can diminish the capacity to play for awhile. They may not be able to concentrate, and play could revolve around looking for lost loved ones. This grief will gradually subside if the children have regular involvement with the absent parent. In this way, at least some threads of continuity are not disturbed (Segal, 1989).

Some older preschoolers may have no apparent emotional reaction but will start to imitate adult behavior by scolding and lecturing younger siblings and friends. They may adopt these "pseudo-adult behaviors" as they worry about their parents' welfare and their parents' distress. Their whole idea of parents and adults may change as they see them as "vulnerable" individuals and not a unit. These super-children may try hard not to display any painful feelings of their own.

Wallerstein (1989) advises that children should not be overburdened with adult responsibilities. Children enjoy and are proud to feel they can be of help to their parents. While helping a parent can ease a child's adjustment, making so many demands that they take over a major part of the child's life, or asking for adult-level emotional support, can be damaging to a child's well-being. Children should not be expected to become "grown-up" or take the place of a missing parent. In reacting to the stress of divorce, one fourteen-year-old said, "I don't want to be the 'man of the family' now."

Many children deny that the divorce is occurring, live in a fantasy of a restored family or fantasize that their parents will get back together. Others may fantasize that children take care of children and that adults are unimportant and uninvolved. Youngsters need to realize that their parents will probably not reunite and that they can be happy living with one parent.

Children sometimes feel pulled in opposite directions by parents. Divorce can be a time of conflicted loyalty and children may feel that by moving closer to one parent, they betray the other. Some choose aloneness and try to avoid being close to either parent out of love for both. If parents are in open conflict, others may resolve this difficulty by siding with one and becoming angry with the other (Hillowe, 1989; Wallerstein, 1989). Parents need to avoid making children take sides.

While normal distress can be comforted, open distress that manifests itself in nightmares, sleepless nights, inattentiveness at preschool, and aggression on the playground can last six months to a year. When it becomes chronic or interferes with development, help should be sought (Wallerstein, 1989).

If a child is unable to share his or her feelings with a special person, the feelings will not go away. It is normal to need a parent, grandparent, teacher or even a counselor or social worker to talk to. When the problems are recognized and understood, they often do not seem so overwhelming, and the healing process can begin (Prokop, 1986). Self-confidence is restored and coping skills can develop once again.

In the end, what seems to matter the most is the way the mother and father handle the divorce and where they place their values. Children of divorce need what children in all families need: The devotion of parents who, despite their preoccupations, place the long-term interest of their young at the top of their priorities (Segal, 1989).

While the rate of divorce has escalated in contemporary America, more research has been done over time to explore the effects this stressful event has on children. While the majority of the research indicates that divorce does have a negative impact on the development and functioning of children, there are inconsistencies regarding the extent of the impact and the long-term effects on children's development.

The divorce process poses a series of stressful experiences and demands, which often require the entire family to reorganize roles and responsibilities. These events cause a disruption in family relationships and render the child more psychologically vulnerable. According to Hetherington (1981) and Wallerstein (1983), the child goes through two phases during this vulnerable time. Initially, there is a short *crisis phase,* when the child suffers the greatest, characterized by separation phobias, anxiety reactions, ego repression, sleep disturbances, and acute mourning reactions. This acute emotional upheaval is usually followed by an *adjustment phase,* when conflict begins to subside and the child strives to adapt to the new environment and obtain some type of balance. This phase may take up to several years (or decades) until resolution (Wallerstein, 1983, 1990; Schaffer, 1988).

Children of divorce are forced to face an additional burden as compared to children from intact families. Therefore, it is not surprising that Kalter (1987), in his study, found that nearly one-third of the children referred for psychiatric evaluation were from divorced families. These children had a higher rate of delinquent problems, depression and enuresis and there was a greater incidence of this group acting out aggressively, particularly towards parents. Children of divorce seemed to have increased moodiness, and lower academic and social competencies than children from intact families. The socio-emotional problems found in these children seem to be the result of an interaction between familial, social, and cultural factors, and the economic, legal and psychological systems affecting their experiences and the effects of the divorce (Portes, Haas, & Brown, 1991).

All children do not appear to be equally at risk for the problems frequently associated with divorce, however. Some of the research suggests that the sex and age of the child have a strong impact on their adjustment. Boys seem to have a more difficult time with the experience than girls. Schaffer (1988) reviews two studies in which the girls were shown to have recovered from the divorce two years later, while the boys thereafter continued to experience emotional distress and difficulties with interpersonal relationships.

The age of the child during the marital separation seems to have an effect on the meaning of the loss for the child and the means a child has for coping with the loss. Children who were under two years of age when their parents divorced displayed a range of reactions. Some of the children showed intensive searching for the absent parent followed by increased separation anxiety. Other children showed no outside indications of distress and quickly accepted a substitute parent. Children between the ages of two and three during the onset of the divorce seemed to experience periods of distress before and after visits with the absent parent. These were combined with repeated questions regarding the reorganization of the family which most likely were not answered to the child's satisfaction. If children in this age group did not receive proper support, feelings of loss began to make their appearances in the form of hyperactivity and pseudo-maturity. Children who experienced the loss at age four or five tended to develop a set of fantasies explaining why the separation happened and secretly wished for the reuniting of the family. While children in this age group tended to feel compassion for their parents, there were also feelings of guilt and mourning. Children who were in the latency period (ages 6–12) during their parents' divorce reacted differently depending on the role they had played in the family and the continuing relationships they had with both parents (Tessman, 1978; Wallerstein, 1983).

Children aged six and seven at the time of divorce experience pervasive sadness. They are unable to use the defenses of denial by fantasy to alleviate some of their suffering. Most of these children become fearful of their present and future family situation and worry about not having a protective family structure. Feelings of deprivation are also common among this age group. Children aged 6 to 12, unlike preschool children, seem to deny feelings of responsibility for the divorce; however, they do strongly wish for the reconciliation of their parents. The sense of loss is very strong for this age group as well. Many feel abandoned and rejected by the missing parent. This is especially true among boys if the absent parent is the father. These boys also tend to express considerable anger toward their custodial parent for "driving the father off." These outbursts in behavior often are carried over into the school setting, into the after-school child care setting, as well as with friends and other siblings (Kelley and Wallerstein, 1976).

Sex and age do appear to have some impact on the child's adjustment. However, several other factors seem to be a greater determinant of the child's adjustment. The following factors seem to impact adjustment: (a) quality of parent-child relationship, (b) amount of quality time with the custodial parent, (c) consistency of discipline, (d) interpersonal conflicts, and (e) the quality of the child's non-parental relationships (Zaslow, 1988; Portes, Haas, Brown, 1991). In a study done by Kelly and Wallerstein (1976) on the impact of parental divorce in early latency children (6–7 years old), the psychological condition of the child one year after the divorce depended greatly on the post-divorce family structure. This included such things as the amount of disequilibrium, quality of parent-child relationships, and the interaction of these factors with the developmental needs of the child at that particular time. In a study that followed these children after one and two decades, Wallerstein (1990) found that the now-grown children still mind the disruption in their lives.

All of the family factors do have an impact on the child's long-range adjustment. However, one area that has not been addressed is children's ability to master coping strategies in order to readjust to their new family structures. Wallerstein (1983) found six psychological tasks the child needs to master in order to cope and maintain integrity and development. These tasks are all in addition to the normal developmental load a child carries throughout the growing-up process. The six tasks are interrelated, hierarchical, and begin during the onset of marital conflict and continue throughout adolescence. The first task is to acknowledge the reality of the marital rupture. This is seen as the simplest task for the child, and requires the child to comprehend family changes and separate them from any fantasies about the parents reuniting. Most children are capable of accomplishing this task one year after the divorce. Figure 11.1 shows these psychological tasks.

The second task for the child is the disengagement from the parental conflict and distress and assumption of customary pursuits. At this time, the child needs to separate himself or herself from the family crisis and resume normal roles in school/center and play. This will require the child to psychologically distance himself or herself from the parents. For the older child, this is a somewhat more difficult task. After a year and a half, most youngsters were able to resume their friendships and concentration in school. However, it should be noted that a significant number of children at every age had difficulty resuming their own agenda after the family crisis.

The third task is the resolution of the loss. This task is perhaps the most difficult and forces the child to mourn for the multiple losses and come to terms with the restructuring of the family. The child also must overcome his or her feelings of rejection and unlovability. Unfortunately, many children are unable to overcome their feelings of unworthiness, and, year in and year out, continue to feel disappointed and unlovable.

The fourth task is resolving anger and self blame. Children must forgive themselves for having wished for the divorce and/or having failed to restore the intact marriage. Wallerstein seems to believe that there is a profound connection between the children's ability to forgive themselves and the ability to forgive the parents.

The fifth task is accepting the permanence of the divorce. Developmental factors play a key role in resolving this task since younger children may have a difficult time giving up their fantasies of parental unification.

The final task is to achieve realistic hope regarding (other) relationships. This appears to be the most important task for the child and society, since it is concerned with the child's ability to view relationships realistically and think of himself or herself as a lovable person capable of sustaining relationships with others. Wallerstein believes that the resolution of these tasks will enable the child to reach closure with the divorce and live an independent life with the capacity to trust and love (1983).

TASK: Understanding the Divorce
- to acknowledge the reality of what divorce means in their family and what its concrete consequences will be
- the more mature task of understanding what led to the marital failure awaits the perspective of the adolescent and young adult

TASK: Strategic Withdrawal
- disengaging from parental conflict and distress and resuming customary pursuits
- to get physically and emotionally to the normal tasks of growing up

TASK: Dealing with Loss
- absorbing loss is probably the single most difficult task imposed by divorce
- the task requires children to overcome the profound sense of rejection, humiliation, unloveability, and powerlessness they feel with the departure of a parent

TASK: Dealing with Anger
- divorce, unlike death, is always a voluntary decision for at least one partner in a marriage
- children know that their unhappiness has been caused by the very people charged with their protection and care
- children get angry at their parents

TASK: Working Out Guilt
- children often feel responsible for divorce, thinking that their misbehavior may have caused one parent to leave —they need to separate from guilty ties that bind them too closely to a troubled parent and to go on with their lives with compassion and love

TASK: Accepting the Permanence of the Divorce
- in accepting permanence, the children of divorce face a far more difficult task than children of bereavement. Death cannot be undone but divorce happens between living people who can change their minds.

TASK: Taking a Chance on Love
- children of divorce must grow, become open to the possibility of success or failure, and take a chance on love.
- they must hold on to the realistic vision that they can both love and be loved

FIGURE 11.1
Psychological Tasks of Divorce for Children

Minimizing the Trauma of Divorce for Children

Divorce tends to be a very disruptive experience for all those involved. A variety of factors influence the child's adjustment to the divorce experience. The child must learn a myriad of coping mechanisms in order to acclimate himself or herself to the changed environment. Tactics such as open communication and support from a parental figure help to decrease the negative long-term effects divorce has on the child. Many will have to adjust to living in a single-parent home. Most importantly, children need to be told repeatedly that the divorce does not weaken the bond between parent and child. Geographical distances should not be equated with emotional distance or less love. Parents divorce each other, not their children. Children must be made to realize the importance of working to maintain connections. Finally, children need to be permitted to love both mother and father regardless of the circumstances and should not be asked to side with one parent against the other. This is an unfair and cumbersome burden that no child should be asked to bear. Parents can protect their children from unnecessary pain by remembering that even though the marriage is over, they are still Mom and Dad.

Single-Parent Families

In the last decade, the number of single-parent households has increased tremendously. In 1985, 22% of families with children were headed by a single parent; by 1994 this number had increased to 26% (Kids Count Project, 1997). Furthermore, it is thought that 50 to 60 percent of all American children may reside at some point in a single-parent home. Single-mother households, particularly, are increasing rapidly, and are a growing family situation in U.S. society. Many mothers today are working women. Due to an increase in divorces and to their unmarried status, many are forced to raise their children alone, relying on support from family members and friends. In many cases, paternal involvement may exist only on a part-time basis (Worrell, 1991).

According to Norton (1987), single-parent families are characterized by high minority representation, low education and high residential mobility. About 60 percent of the children under 18 years of age in single-parent households live in poverty, compared to 25 percent of the total under-18 child population. Bearing the financial responsibility of finding adequate housing, child care and maintaining full-time employment creates more ongoing stress than that experienced by most married mothers. Thus, these single parents experience a higher rate of psychological distress, daily economic, family and health frustrations (Compas & Williams, 1990). In comparing single and married mothers, the decreased family income constitutes the most important source of ongoing stress in these families.

When examining a single-parent household, it is important to determine the impact this family situation has on the emotional development of the child. Until recently, the major focus was on the father's absence as the principal variable affecting the social development of children in single-parent families. Weinraub and Wolf (1983) show that father absence is a variable that can affect children in a number of direct and indirect ways.

The direct effects of father absence include those relating to reduced social attention, stimulation and modeling resulting from the absence of a second, particularly male, parent. Many single mothers use grandfathers and uncles to help fill in the void from the absence of the biological father. Indirect effects of father absence include those resulting from the increased social, emotional and financial stresses on the mother.

In a single-parent household, there is often a greater closeness between the parent and the children than before the parents divorced (Weiss, 1981). Since other adults may not be present, only the children are left to confide in, and to depend on for advice and companionship. Children of single mothers are often more responsible, and develop a partnership routine with the parent. The parent thus may share worries with the children because they have some understanding of the responsibilities of running the household. According to Weiss (1981), allowing the children to be junior partners in the management of the household grants them new rights and authority and requires them to have new responsibilities. Often an older child is asked to be responsible for younger children in the family, and delegation of parental responsibility may occur even though the older child is still quite young. Sometimes a child is asked to assume responsibilities that would have been assumed by the spouse. This "faster growing-up" can cause these children to have special strengths but also special vulnerabilities when they become adults. Though they may work well autonomously, they are vulnerable to dissatisfaction, no matter how well they do on the job. Nothing on the job seems to satisfy their need for care and investment of a nurturant figure.

The experience of growing up in a single-parent family can affect the later functioning of children and adolescents, but for many children the demands on them for autonomy and responsibility will lead to growth. It is important for the single mother to have social, emotional and, if possible, financial support. There are many organizations that provide the first two. Even though these children grow up a little faster than their peers in intact families, with support they can grow up to be well-adjusted adults. One goal of centers can be to provide this additional support to families, and help them obtain the most out of life. Some children of divorce end up in foster care, however, and the next section discusses this little-understood phenomenon.

◊ ◊

FOSTER CARE

Foster children enter Court Supervised Care under a state or city Department of Human Resources or Development (formerly called the Child Welfare Department in many jurisdictions) for several reasons. The most prevalent reasons are: abandonment, neglect of the child, parental abuse, mental illness, and parental substance abuse affecting the newborn as well as the older child (Lawder, 1961; Clinton, 1996). Divorce can be a contributing factor in many of these cases. In 1996 there were 450,000 children in the nation's foster care system, and in 1997 over 500,000. Of these, some 100,000 would not return to their original homes, according to President Clinton (1996, 1997). In an initiative to double the number of adoptions among these foster-care children from 27,000 currently to at least 54,000 by the year 2002, the president said, "No child should be trapped in the limbo of foster care, particularly when there are families with open arms waiting." It is interesting to note that adoptions in general have dropped from 89,000 20 years ago to 60,000 in 1997.

Most children who are placed in foster care are under three years of age. Some children are placed in a temporary or long-term foster home. Other children are adopted. With more awareness of the ramifications of foster care, some positive changes have occurred within the system. Yet most children are deeply affected, many throughout their entire lives.

Some short-term cases in foster homes have been successful. Others have not attained any success due to the child's background and lack of adaptability skills. Other reasons for lack of success include the foster care home, the caretakers, the system itself, and the court system which determines the child's fate.

The life experiences of foster children have been different, and they have needs that are individually unique. However, the trauma of separation from family is a common experience for children placed in foster care. No matter what the reasons, or what the child's life experiences have been, being placed in foster care means a change in environment. Children placed in foster care are separated from the people they know and trust, and on whom they've learned to depend, and the environment in which they are placed is different and strange to them. While it may be similar, it is still not the same.

Between the ages of three months and two years (usually three to nine months), the child forms an "attachment" to the mother or other person (caregiver) in this environment who is most stimulating to him or her and most responsive in meeting his or her needs. Usually this person is the mother because she is most often responsible for feeding, clothing, and caring for the child. However, merely meeting the child's physical needs does not seem to be the characteristic that will cause the child to form an attachment. Stimulating the child by looking at him or her, smiling, and talking, seems to be the most important characteristic. It is also important that the mother or caregiver be sensitive to the child's capacity for stimulation. The child who receives too much stimulation may develop methods for shutting out the environment, and the child who does not receive enough stimulation may withdraw and become listless.

In order to form an attachment, the child must have developed the ability to distinguish the mother from other persons in the environment. The child must be able to recognize when the mother is present and when she is not. The child must have the ability to follow the mother's movements at least visually, and often the child is able to follow the mother by crawling or walking about at the time the attachment is formed. Children have individual needs and ways of interacting with their environment. Because of the individual differences in children, it seems important that a mother be responsive to the individual needs of her child. The child may form attachments to other persons in the environment, but usually the attachment to the mother is the strongest.

The closer the child comes to being two years old without having formed an attachment, the less likely it becomes that he or she will ever form an attachment successfully. It is possible for a child to form an attachment after two years of age, but the prospect becomes very slim. This heightens the importance of careful placement in foster care following a divorce (or for any other reason).

If the foster child has never formed an attachment, there may be little reaction to being separated from his or her birth parents. However, the child who has formed normal attachments to members of his family is likely to display a variety of reactions to separation. A period of mourning may be one way a child copes, although this process will be unique to each child. It is important that the foster parents be sensitive to the child's reactions to separation.

Foster parents can help the child by recognizing and accepting the feelings experienced and then by helping the child verbalize those feelings. This means the foster parent must be able to pick up cues from the child. For example, when the child says "my old man is a drunken bum," he may be expressing more than a description of his parent. Under that description lies the feelings of affection for his father and the disappointment he feels because his father's drinking problem has caused him to live with another family instead of with the parents he loves.

The child may also harbor feelings of "my father is a drunk so that's why I am no good." The foster parent (or in some cases, an early childhood professional), could help the child express the hidden feelings by saying "You're disappointed about your father," "You are feeling hurt because you have to live with us (the new home) instead of with your parents," or "You're angry when you see your father drinking and you feel the drinking has caused you to be separated."

Foster children may not know how to relate to foster parents because of the poor relationship with their own parents. They may expect to be punished severely for minor transgressions or may expect that adults do not care about what they do as long as they don't get in the way. Children may feel hostile toward foster parents or teachers because they feel they are conspiring to keep them from their families, or perhaps because they cannot deal with the anger, fear and hurt feelings felt toward their own parents. Children may turn these feelings of hostility inward, or toward any adult, and do things that are self-defeating or self-destructive. They may try to hide or deny feelings by becoming withdrawn from or over-placating toward the foster parents or the caregiver.

Furthermore, foster children may feel guilty for the behavior of the birth parents, especially if the parents have been involved in some kind of criminal behavior. The children may feel unlovable because of what the parents have done and may feel that they need to be punished over and over again. The confusion children feel between loving and missing their families on the one hand, and hating them and themselves for what they think or imagine they have done must be terribly painful. In this pain, children often choose to strike out at those nearest. There may be a need to pick on other children in the family or the center, or argue with foster parents or teachers, to hide or relieve the pain. Children may withdraw from all interaction in order to protect themselves from feeling the pain of what has happened or to prevent being hurt again. With over 500,000 children in foster care today (Clinton, 1997) the chances of these children being in caregiver care are very great.

The child's sense of trust in relationships, especially with adults, may be broken. There may be a fear of forming a close relationship with another person because of the anticipation of the pain of losing that person. In helping the foster child, the adult caregiver has three major tasks: (1) to anticipate various reactions he or she might have; (2) to help him or her become aware of and accept these feelings; and (3) to be sensitive, understanding and accepting of him or her as a person.

One adult student, who had been a foster child, described her feelings about religion as "the only love I knew and the substitute parents I didn't have." This woman, now aged 60, happily married with three grown children, finally felt able to talk about her experiences, and was studying to be a counselor. She told stories of going to a pay telephone from age 10 or 11 on, and calling her social worker to change her placement if the physical or sexual abuse had gotten too bad. This person felt that adoption would have been far better for her, but her mother refused to release her for adoption. The next section sheds some light on this system.

◇ ◇

ADOPTION

The number of adoptions of unrelated persons has actually declined in the U.S. over the last 20 years from 89,000 to 60,000. There is a heightened interest in adoption, however, due to media coverage of contested adoptions, international adoption and an increase in the demand for children. Many children in high-quality programs for young children are adopted, and little is ever known about it. However, adoptive parents may have some specialized questions and support needs.

An interesting service has been developed on the Internet, the AdoptioNetwork, that can answer many of these questions. It was created to help increase the rate of adoption and to improve the availability of information about adoption, thus encouraging the placement of more children in families. The URL address for this service is www.adoption.org/adopt. Prior to this web page with its tremendous breadth, the information was only available through the federal government's National Adoption Information Clearinghouse (NAIC), sponsored by the U.S. Department of Health and Human Services. This clearinghouse was known to many adoption professionals, but not to the general public, including adoptive parents, adoptees and birthmothers. The web page has the name, address and telephone number of all public and private adoption agencies and all adoption support groups in the U.S. Also, the site contains the only Internet-based current digest of the adoption laws of every state, a comprehensive list of national adoption organizations, international adoption information, a statistics and speakers section, and a legal resources section.

The Network provides adoptive parents and birthmothers with basic information so they are more aware of the process and their options before contacting government or private agencies. The Network is also a demonstration of a new paradigm of how volunteer organizations can complement government efforts by using new and innovative tools to achieve common objectives. The information is available at no cost, and there is no wait caused by ordering the information by mail.

The Network purchased the electronic version of the NAIC data and made all of this government information available freely. Congress established the NAIC in 1987 to disseminate information related to adoption, such as the name of licensed adoption agencies, state laws relating to adoption and intercountry adoption information to professionals and the general public. The telephone number of the NAIC is on the Adoption Network and the Clearinghouse is planning to create a web page to distribute additional information. The Clearinghouse receives about 1,000 calls a month, and the Network receives 5,000 to 7,000 queries a month. Both organizations have been asked to exhibit at national adoption meetings.

The Network permits users not only to find adoption agencies and support groups, but also to become better informed before they contact an agency. The Network also carries information concerning all aspects of infant adoption and the adoption of children with special needs. This saves time and money and allows the agencies to concentrate on providing specialized services. Internet access is available at most public libraries.

Information on telling children they are adopted and helping them handle this knowledge is available in the literature, on this Internet network, and in the parent literature and children's books. Disclosing this information appears to be the current trend. Frequently, the most suitable time and manner in which to inform children of their adoptive status is the earliest time possible. After that, it is wise to proceed to talk about adoption during the growing up years. In a matter-of-fact, accepting manner, conversations or discussions should take place keeping the adoptee's changing emotional and developmental level, needs, and abilities constantly at the forefront.

The adoptive parent's own comfort in talking about the subject is, perhaps, the most important factor in telling a child about his or her adoption. A lack of open, honest communication has frequently been cited as a major cause of difficulty between adoptive parents and their children. A child may sense the parents' reluctance to discuss his or her origins and therefore refrain from raising embarrassing questions which, in turn, may lead the parents to conclude that the child is not really interested in the subject. Often an adopted child would learn nothing about the adoption from parents during childhood, but because all the relatives knew of the situation, the truth would sometimes slip out. As an adult applying for a passport or marriage license the shock of learning the truth from an amended or "birth by adoption" birth certificate can be very painful and destructive. Consequently, adoptive parents are impressed with the importance of telling their children early in life and in a natural way, that they are adopted. In fact, if the adoption isn't discussed, the child might feel that there is something dreadful about it. Some agencies even require the parent's agreement that the child be raised with knowledge of the adoption, and told that he or she was a "chosen" child, perhaps.

Informing a child in babyhood, before the child has any idea of what a parent is talking about is recommended. Infants can sense love in a voice, and in such endearing terms as "our sweet little adopted baby" the baby associates "adoption" with happy words like mommy and daddy. As the child grows older, parents should naturally read books about adoption. Some parents even make a "Chosen Child" scrapbook, with snapshots and stories showing the child coming home, and even getting off the plane in the case of a foreign adoption.

Children then grow up thinking of the adoption as a special event and they feel the privilege of being chosen. It is important, however, that the adopted child feel comfortable with the adoption itself, not the specific details surrounding it. Children who are adopted in second marriages, by stepparents, may undergo a similar but different experience. If the "new" parent has children of his or her own, a child can be quite selfish when it comes to seeking attention and not getting it. Openness and love, and possibly counseling for all the family, help with some of these adjustments.

◊ ◊

CHILD ABUSE AND NEGLECT

U.S. Health and Human Services Secretary Donna Shalala noted that the report by the National Center on Child Abuse and Neglect (1994), "Child Maltreatment 1994: Reports from the States," showed that 1,012,222 children in 48 states were victims of substantiated child abuse and neglect in 1994, a 27 percent increase since 1990. Furthermore, the Third National Incidence Study of Child Abuse and Neglect estimates that almost three times the state-reported number of children are maltreated. This would mean more than 2,000,000 other cases are not reported to the agencies whose responsibility it is to protect children from further abuse. The 1994 report showed that nearly half of the 1,012,000 children were under six years of age, and more than 25% were under three years of age. Of the total, 53 percent suffered neglect, 26 percent physical abuse, 14 percent sexual abuse, five percent emotional abuse and 22 percent suffered other forms of maltreatment. Loss of life is the severest form of child abuse and neglect and the report (1996) indicates that 1,111 children were killed in 1994 and 5,400 children were killed over the five years, 1990–1994. These severe statistics again remind childcare professionals that being informed of maltreatment reporting procedures in their local and state jurisdictions is of prime importance. Teachers of young children are an essential part of the professional team that can prevent abuse and neglect. The National Clearinghouse on Child Abuse and Neglect Information, at 1-800-FYI-3666, or mailing address at P.O. Box 1182, Washington, D.C. 20013-1182, offers considerable information and practical suggestions (even kits) to help communities combat this insidious epidemic.

The Internet provides a wealth of resources and information can be accessed on a variety of topics (for example, try URL *www.*hhs.gov and choose the Government Information Locator Service).

A 1983 report stated that only 13% of child abuse reports were made by teachers or school personnel (The American Humane Association, 1983). Teachers are reluctant to report suspected cases, especially when physical neglect or emotional abuse and neglect are involved. A hesitation to interfere in child-rearing techniques and sensitivity to social and cultural differences contributed to this low percentage of reporting. However, social services agencies seek a minimum of care for all children, so they are free from harm, and these incidents need to be reported. Teachers have a legal and ethical responsibility to combine their knowledge of child development and their observation skills to identify children in need of protection (Meddin & Rosen, 1984).

For those children who cannot safely remain with their families, prompt placement into a loving, adoptive home is crucial to their stability and well-being. Foster care is another usual alternative. The Adoption Opportunities Program is one of the many federal initiatives for child abuse prevention and treatment. Parents Anonymous, a 12-step program approach, seems to have the longest track record of success for changing the behavior of parents whose abused children stay in the home. Among other things, parents are assigned a "buddy" in this program, to call when they feel tempted to abuse a child. First names only are used in these groups, which are available, and in the telephone book, nationally.

The Pattern of Parental Child Abuse and Neglect

As early as January 31, 1974, when the Child Abuse Prevention and Treatment Act (P.L. 93–247) was signed into law, a pattern of neglect and abuse in parents had been identified. Parents who abuse often have the "potential to abuse," i.e., they were abused themselves (up to 90% of abusers were abused). Abusive parents often are isolated and distrustful persons (an effect of abuse), have a poor self-image, and have unrealistic expectations of their child or children.

Spanking a nine-month-old baby for crying is an example of these unrealistic expectations. For these reasons, every effort should be made to convey child development information to those parenting young children.

Abuse sometimes occurs when a child, often a single child in a family, looks like a hated parent or ex-spouse, or who behaves and responds differently. This usually perfectly normal child may be seen as bad, willful, spoiled, slow, stubborn, or demanding.

Often there is some sort of "crisis" that sets the abusive action in motion, usually not related to the child but to adult frustrations (e.g., job, car, household responsibilities). Many abusive parents are "needy" and expect to derive comfort from the child, rather than the reverse. Many have missed their own childhood due to abuse by their own parents (Helfer & Kempe, 1987).

Common Signs of Abuse of Neglect

What is child maltreatment and neglect? Child abuse is any action or inaction that results in the harm or potential risk of harm to a child. It includes:

- physical abuse (cuts, welts, bruises, burns);
- sexual abuse (molestation, exploitation, intercourse);
- physical neglect (medical or educational neglect, and inadequate supervision, food, clothing, or shelter);
- emotional abuse (actions that result in significant harm to the child's intellectual, emotional, or social development or functioning); and
- emotional neglect (inaction by the adult to meet the child's needs for nurture and support).

Teachers of young children often observe bruises or wounds that are in various stages of healing on children. This indicates that the injuries occurred at different times and may have been inflicted on a regular basis. Physical abuse can be suspected, for example, if injuries appear a day or so after a holiday or long weekend (bruises take a day to show up). Injuries that occur on multiple places of the body or that leave a mark that looks like a hand or tool should also be considered nonaccidental.

Children who take food from others may be suffering from neglect. One agency investigated a case in which a preschool child constantly took food from other children's lunches. The child was receiving one-half of a peanut butter sandwich a day at home and needed the additional food for survival. Another common sign of neglect is seen in children who come to school inappropriately dressed for the weather. The child who wears sandals in the winter or who doesn't wear a coat on a cold snowy day meets the definition of neglect and may be considered at risk of harm.

Regression often indicates that children are attempting to protect themselves or to cope with a difficult situation. A typical example of such a behavior change might be seen in the 5-year-old child who develops toileting problems. Likewise, the child who strives to do everything exactly right, or fears doing anything wrong, may be trying to avoid incurring the anger of adults.

Burns often leave clues as to their origin. Oval burns may be caused by a cigarette. "Stocking" or doughnut-shaped burns may indicate that the child was put into a hot substance. Any burn that leaves an imprint of an item, such as an electric stove burner on a child's hand, may indicate that the injury was not accidental. The natural response of children is to withdraw when a body part comes in contact with a hot object; thus, if the burn is accidental, only a small section of skin is usually burned.

Another possible clue to abuse or neglect lies in the behavior of the child who always stays in the background of activities. This child usually watches intently to see what adults are doing—possibly to keep out of their way in order to prevent being harmed.

Children who are abused frequently expect such abuse from all adults. Do you, as a teacher, know children who cower when you lift your hand in the air? Are there children in your group who hide broken crayons rather than asking for tape to repair them? Discussion, stories written by the children, drawings, or sharing time may also reveal episodes of abuse and neglect.

Parent (or other prime caregiver) behavior may also give clues that children are at risk of harm. Most preschool program staff see parents twice a day, and occasionally during parent conferences or home visits as well. Teachers of primary-age school children have fewer occasions to observe parents, but can still be aware of parent behaviors through responses to notes, questionnaires, or phone calls.

Long-Term Effects of Abuse

Parents who abuse their children do not follow one particular pattern. It is difficult to predict which parents will abuse. A significant indicator of whether or not a parent will abuse is if they have been abused themselves. Although those adults who were maltreated as children are more likely to maltreat their own children, compared to those who were not maltreated, it must be emphasized that the majority of parents who were maltreated as children do not maltreat their own children (Helfer, 1975). However, it seems that adults who were abused as children are often not aware of other ways of disciplining their children. As noted earlier, a history of abuse is a large factor in whether or not a parent abuses children, especially those children who exhibit some kind of "conduct disorder."

As mentioned previously, the literature shows that there is not one life situation that causes parents to abuse their children. Because it is difficult to know who will abuse or what child is being abused, it is necessary for programs, centers and schools to provide teachers with training to identify the subtle warning signals that children give, as discussed earlier.

Both clinical studies and research evidence demonstrate that abuse suffered in childhood has serious long-term effects that can be identified years after the occurrence of the abuse, especially child sexual abuse. Long-term effects range from depression, low self-esteem, anger, and hostility to difficulties in forming sexual and other relationships. There also appears to be a correlation between child sexual abuse and later substance abuse, particular types of pathology, revictimization and victims later becoming abusers themselves (Bard et al., 1983).

Providing support groups for parents who are recently unemployed or who are in need of financial assistance is one way that counselors and centers can perhaps help to lessen the incidences of child abuse. Offering workshops on nonphysical ways to discipline children might be another helpful tactic. Professionals who are armed with the warning signs of child abuse and the factors that possibly cause it, can better serve the children who are at risk of being abused.

A Model of Processes Followed in One County's Child Abuse Prevention Program

While many counties and states have instituted well-organized child protection and abuse prevention departments, when thinking about how to work with and improve services in the local area child care as an advocate for children, it is interesting to review at least one model. The name of the county (and the state) have been purposefully omitted.

The County Department of Human Development is mandated by State law to investigate reports of abuse and neglect. The reports may be made to the County's Child Abuse Hotline during the hours of 8:00 A.M. to 5:00 P.M. or to the 24-hour State toll-free Hotline after working hours.

County Child Protective Services are made up of six units each comprised of a supervisor and seven social workers. Three intake units have primary responsibility for the investigation of allegations of abuse and neglect. Another intake unit specializes in the investigation of child sexual abuse. The remaining two units provide on-going treatment in cases where abuse and neglect have been established, or where preventive services are indicated and accepted by the family. Services offered include counseling, parenting classes, temporary housing, transportation, foster care, and other support. In addition, the on-going treatment workers are involved in monitoring compliance with court orders and determining that every effort is made to avoid a repeat of the prior abuse and neglect.

Child Protective Services interviews the child within twenty-four hours of the reported abuse. Afterwards, the caseworker interviews the parent and/or child care provider or teacher to obtain further information. The caseworker compares the information and determines whether the case is founded, suspected, or not founded. If founded, a record is kept on the abuser for ten years in the central state register. The founded case can be given to a social worker for treatment purposes, is taken to court, and is occasionally closed. Children are only removed from the home when a life-threatening situation exists.

Treatment options are provided through social services. Some families are referred to county mental health centers and others are sent to treatment at the State Family Services. The social service department contracts out to home services for non-English speaking families. Many cases are referred to Alcohol and Drug Services.

If the abuse occurs in a family day care home, the provider must notify the parents of the other children in their care that a complaint has been made to Child Protective Services. If founded, the provider loses his or her permit. If the abuse occurs in a child care center, State Licensing, the regulatory agency, also conducts an investigation. NAEYC has a clear statement opposing child abuse occurring in child care centers.

If the case is not founded, the complainant is sent a letter to that effect and files are destroyed within 30 days, unless personal legal action is pursued. If the child abuse is a "suspect case," then a social worker will monitor the family.

Cases of neglect are treated in the same way as abuse. Many neglect cases occur with regard to teenage parents who are unable to handle parenting responsibilities. Special parenting classes and health and child care resources are available to teenagers. Financial aid for child and health resources are also available to low-income families who neglect children due to lack of funds.

In conclusion, child abuse is a serious problem in the U.S. Child care professionals, parents, and the community, working together, can reduce the problem. Prevention by public awareness and cooperation is essential. In the future, more funding and community interest in continuing prevention programs will educate potential abusers and victims. Also, the current trend is for victims to talk about their experiences openly, thus helping others to come forward and receive treatment. The most effective prevention is in helping people before the abuse occurs.

◇ ◇

SUMMARY

Of the many legal issues that impact the environment of the child, a few have been reviewed here. Issues involving divorce, foster care, adoption and child abuse affect children profoundly, and early childhood professionals therefore need to be aware of the basic issues and symptoms that might result from these concerns.

Children's wounds, physical as well as emotional, need to be attended to, acknowledged and cleansed, sometimes with the help of someone who will listen to and talk with them. Whether this is an early childhood professional or a counselor, helping children overcome problems that may appear in their lives, is a path with many future rewards for developing happy, competent individuals in society.

Setting children free of these past hurts, if only little by little, helps them move forward with their lives. While the topics discussed in this chapter, divorce, foster care, adoption and child abuse, tend to be ongoing, so is child advocacy and the work toward better protection against and prevention of some of the problems caused by these issues. As more women become lawyers and judges and these issues are viewed more sensitively by men and women alike, these problems can be appropriately addressed.

Child advocacy will always be a part of the role of early childhood professionals, especially directors. Being aware of child care legislation and advocating for children at every opportunity gives children MORE adult voices on their behalf. If there is any opportunity for enactment of "stork and stroller" policies, regulations or laws in the state or federal government, or even in the local shopping mall, child care professionals should make their voices heard.

The bibliography at the end of this chapter is extensive to provide early childhood personnel many different kinds of resources. Being knowledgeable about *all* of the problems children may face may seem daunting, but being aware of what one doesn't know, and knowing where to look it up, is a first step. Issues for children that are medically related, such as child mental health (including the effects of television), hyperactivity, inclusion, hospitalized children, and children and death will be discussed in the next chapter.

◇ ◇ ◇ ◇ ◇ ◇ ◇ ◇ ◇ ◇ ◇ ◇ ◇ ◇ ◇ ◇ ◇ ◇ ◇ ◇

SUGGESTED CLASS ACTIVITIES AND DISCUSSIONS

1. *Attributes of a good community—Understanding your own community.* Write a short paper on the attributes of students' own communities. Include commercial resources; government resources and input; children's resources of all kinds; welfare and community action resources; and religious resources. Include demographic information and age and income ranges. Summarize with the effects of the community on parents and children.

2. *Child Abuse.*   Students can do a small group project on child abuse, including laws regarding reporting in your jurisdiction, community resources, known parent help groups such as Parents Anonymous, and a bibliography plus handouts to be given out in class.

Have small group discussions on the following real questions from teachers, and report back: (Add other questions from class members)

   a. What do you do when a child in your center comes in with strap marks on his body?

b. What do you do when a child leaves the center on Friday, seemingly okay, but returns Monday morning very, very hungry?

3. *Legislation and Child Advocacy.* Small groups can research different aspects of legislation affecting different ages of children on the Internet and through traditional means, and report back to the class. Materials from various advocacy groups such as the Children's Defense Fund and NAEYC should be included.

4. *Write to Congress.* Write letters or e-mail members of Congress about current legislation or issues of concern about children. Bring copies and printouts to class. Share any responses. (Usual e-mail addresses for Congress are: name@senate.gov or name@house.gov).

5. *Foster Children.* Invite a former foster child (or adult) or present foster child to come to class or to give an interview, taped with permission, discussing their experiences and how they feel about them.

6. *Single Parent Survey.* Survey one or more preschool classes to find out the number of children living in single parent homes. Discuss the percentage of the total in the class, and the implications of single parent homes.

◊ ◊

BIBLIOGRAPHY

American Humane Association (1983). *Highlights of official child neglect and abuse reporting.* Denver, CO: Author.

Bard, L., Carter, D., Cerce, D., Knight, R., Rosenberg, R. & Schneider, B. (1983). Assessing the long-term impact of child sexual abuse: A review and conceptualization. In D. Finkelhor, & A. Browne, *Family abuse and its consequences: New directions in research*, pp. 270–284. CA: Sage Publications.

Barnes, B., & Coplon, J. (1980). *The single-parent experience.* New York: Macmillan.

Berger, S., Shoul, R., & Warschauer, S. (1989). *Children of divorce.* Washington, DC: National Education Association of the U.S.

Bolles, E. (1969). *Adopted children.* New York: Adama Books.

Bolles, E. (1984). *The penguin adoption handbook.* New York: Viking Press.

Burgess, L. (1981). *The art of adoption.* New York: W. W. Norton & Company.

Cartney, A. (1976). *No more here and there.* Chapel Hill, NC: North Carolina Press.

Children Coping with Divorce (CCWD). (1997). http://www.familiesfirst.org/CCWDO.htm

Clinton, W. J. (1996). Clinton Stresses Adoption of Children in Foster Care. Radio Address, Dec. 14, 1996. *USA Today*, 12/14/96.

Compas, B., & Williams, R. (1990). Stress, coping and adjustment in mothers and young adolescents in single- and two-parent families. *American Journal of Community Psychology, 18*(4), 525–543.

Coulton, C. J., Korbin, J. E., Su, M., & Chow, J. (1995). Community level factors and child maltreatment rates. *Child Development, 66,* 1262–1276.

Craft, J. L., & Staudt, M. M. (1991). Reporting and founding of child neglect in urban and rural communities. *Child Welfare, LXX*(3), 359–369.

Crockenberg, S. B., & Forgays, D. K. (1996). The role of emotion in children's understanding and emotional reactions to marital conflict. *Merrill-Palmer Quarterly, 42*, 22–47.

Cummings, E. M. (1994a). *Children and marital conflict: The impact of family dispute and resolution*. New York: Guilford.

Cummings, E. M. (1994b). Marital conflict and children's functioning. *Social Development, 3*, 16–36.

Diamond, S. A. (1985). *Helping children of divorce*. New York: Schocken Books.

Erickson, E. L., McEvoy, A. W., & Colucci, N. D. (1984). *Child abuse and neglect: a guidebook for educators and community leaders*. Florida: Learning.

Friedrich, W. N., Einbender, A. J., & Luecke, W. J. (1983). Cognitive and behavioral characteristics of physically abused children. *Journal of Consulting and Clinical Psychology, 51*(2), 313–314.

Gardner, R. A. (1977). *The parent's book about divorce*. New York: Doubleday.

Gelles, R. J., & Cornell, C. P. (1983). *International perspectives on family violence*. Lexington, MA: Lexington Books.

Greenberger, E. (1989). Contributions of a supportive work environment to parents' well being and orientation to work. *American Journal of Community Psychology, 17*(6), 755–779.

Grych, J. H., & Fincham, F. D. (1990). Marital conflict and children's adjustment: A cognitive-contextual framework. *Psychological Bulletin, 108*, 267–290.

Grych, J. H., & Fincham, F. D. (1993). Children's appraisals of marital conflict: Initial investigations of the cognitive-contextual framework. *Child Development, 64*, 215–230.

Helfer, R. (1975). *The Diagnostic Process and Treatment Programs*. Washington, DC:

National Center for Child Abuse and Neglect, DHEW.

Helfer, R. E., & Kempe, R. S. (Eds.). (1987). *The battered child*. Chicago: The University of Chicago Press.

Hetherington, E. M., Stanley-Hagan, M. M., & Anderson, E. R. (1989). Marital transitions: A child's perspective. *American Psychologist, 44*, 303–312.

Hillowe, B. (1989). Helping preschoolers cope with divorce. *Parent and Preschooler Newsletter. 4*(9), 1–3.

Jenkins, J. M., & Smith, M. A. (1991). Marital disharmony and children's behavior problems: Aspects of a poor marriage that affect children adversely. *Journal of Child Psychology and Psychiatry, 32*, 793–810.

Johnson, M., & Hutchinson, R. (1989). Effects of family structure on children's self-concepts. *Journal of Divorce, 12*, 129–138.

Jones, L. (1990). Unemployment and child abuse. *Families in Society: The Journal of Contemporary Human Services, 7*, 579–585.

Kalter, N. (1976). Children of divorce in an outpatient psychiatric population., *American Journal of Orthopsychiatry, 47*, 40–51.

Kalter, N. (1987). Long-term effects of divorce on children: A developmental vulnerability model, *American Journal of Orthopsychiatry, 57*, 587–600.

Katz, L. F., & Gottman, J. M. (1993). Patterns of marital conflict predict children's internalizing and externalizing behaviors. *Developmental Psychology, 29*, 940–950.

Kelley, J. B., & Wallerstein, J. S. (1976). The effects of parental divorce: experiences of the child in early latency. *American Journal of Orthopsychiatry, 46*(1), 20–32.

Kids Count Project (1997). www.accf.org

Lawder, E. (1961, December). Some psychological determinants in the foster child's development. *Child Welfare, XL*, 7–11.

LeShan, E. (1978). *What's going to happen to me?* New York: Four Winds Press.

Meddin, B. J. & Rosen, A. L. (1987). *Child abuse and neglect prevention and reporting.* In Reducing Stress in Young Children's Lives, pp. 78–82. Washington, DC: NAEYC.

National Center on Child Abuse and Neglect. (1994). *Child Maltreatment 1994: Reports from the States.* Washington, DC: Author, HHS.

Norton, A. (1987, July–August). Families and children in the year 2000. *Children Today*, 6–9.

Pardeck, J. T. (1989). *Child abuse and neglect: Theory, research and practice.* New York: Gordon and Breach Science Publishers.

Portes, P. R., Haas, R. C., & Brown, J. (1991). Identifying family factors that predict children's adjustment to divorce: An analytic synthesis. *Journal of Divorce and Remarriage, 15*, 87–103.

Prokop, M. S. (1986). *Divorce happens to the nicest kids.* Warren, OH: Alegra House Publishers.

Quamma, J. P., & Greeenberg, M. T. (1994). Children's experience of life stress: The role of family social support and social problem-solving skills as protective factors. *Journal of Clinical Child Psychology, 23,* 295–305.

Rogers, F., & O'Brien, C. (1987). *Mister Rogers talks with families about divorce.* New York: Berkley Books.

Sack, W. H., Mason, R., & Higgins, J. E. (1985). The single parent family and abusive child punishment. *American Orthosychiatric Association Inc., 55*(2), 252–259.

Salk, L. (1978). *What every child would like parents to know about divorce.* New York: Harper & Row.

Schaffer, D. R. (1988). *Developmental psychology, childhood, and adolescence* (2nd ed.). Pacific Grove, CA: Brooks Cole Publishing Co.

Schnayer, R., & Orr, R. (1989). A comparison of children living in single-mother and single-father families. *Journal of Divorce, 13,* 171–183.

Segal, J., & Segal, Z. (1989, September). Dealing with divorce. *Parents Magazine, 64*(9), 201.

Tessman, L. H. (1978) *Children of parting parents.* New York: Jason Aronson.

Trickett, P. K., Aber, J. L., Carlson, V., & Cicchetti, D. (1991). Relationship of socioeconomic status to the etiology and developmental sequelae of physical child abuse. *Developmental Psychology, 27*(1), 148–156.

Wallerstein, J. S. (1983). Children of divorce: the psychological task of the child. *American Journal of Orthopsychiatry, 53*(2), 230–243.

Wallerstein, J. S. (1989, May 29). Wallerstein's advice on damage control. *People Weekly, 31*(21), pp. 87–91.

Wallerstein, J. S. (1990). *2nd chances: Men, women and children a decade after divorce.* New York: Houghton Mifflin.

Weinraub, M., & Wolf, B. (1983). Effects of stress and social supports on mother-child interactions in single- and two-parent families. *Child Development, 54,* 1297–1311.

Weiss, R. (1981, May-June). Growing up a little faster: Children in single-parent households. *Children Today*, pp. 24–25.

Worell, J. (1991). Single mothers: From problems to policies. *Women and Therapy, 7*(4), 3–14.

Zaslow, M. J. (1988). Sex differences in children's response to parental divorce: Research methodology and post-divorce family forms. *American Journal of Orthopsychiatry, 58,* 355-378.

Medical Issues
in Early Childhood

Chapter contributed by Victoria Youcha,
*Director, Early Childhood Special Education
Program, AGEC, George Washington University*

The medical issues discussed in this chapter are by no means all-inclusive, but are, instead, an overview of issues frequently inquired about by directors, teachers and elementary school principals involved in programs for young children. Children's mental health, including that of children with disabilities, hospitalized children and children and death will be discussed here. More resources than can be listed are available in course work and, now, on the Internet also.

◇ ◇

CHILDREN'S MENTAL HEALTH

Helping children grow positively in social, emotional, physical and intellectual ways will always be a cornerstone of child mental health for teachers and for parents. Developmentally appropriate practices with suitable intellectual extensions and challenges by age or ability go a long way to insure that growth in these four areas will happen in a positive manner. However, raising healthy, well-adjusted children is a challenge in today's society.

Self-esteem of the child and the development of self-concept will continue to be central to programs for young children, in terms of developing their mental health. Since a child is not born with an image of self, many theorists assume that some form of interaction takes place that affects this developing outlook of a young human being. The responses the child receives from his or her parents and caretakers will help determine the child's ability to love and to think well of himself or herself. This places a great deal of responsibility on the adult world—the parents, the family, the early childhood professional and caregiver, and social agencies that may come in contact with this developing human child.

Self-concept can be defined as the individual's total evaluation of his or her abilities, appearance, background and feelings which act as a directing force in his or her behavior. This includes physical as well as psychological self-image. In addition, a charming definition of attachment says:

> Attachment is the process by which the child becomes passionately loving of the mother or other main caregiver and devotes uniquely powerful energy to retaining visual and auditory contact with her, shows severe disorganization and emotional distress at separating and unlimited joy at reunion (Sears et al., 1965, p. 18).

The bonds of attachment can be ruptured during the critical period of 3 to 9 months of age, producing children who have been deprived of elements vital to developing a positive self-concept. It is important that those concerned with the importance of attachment and parent-bonding in the emergence of the self-perception be aware of this important issue and *not* rotate caregivers for children under 18 months of age, and encourage responsiveness and stimulation of infants and toddlers by those giving them care.

Furthermore, television and movies today expose children to violence at a very young age. Large numbers of children have experienced their parents' divorce and others have experienced the illness or death of a family member. The presence of substance abuse or domestic violence also threaten the emotional well-being of a significant number of young children. Young children face a variety of serious stressors that can adversely affect their development. The administrator's role in assuring children's mental health means designing programs for young children that:

1. promote the healthy emotional development of children,
2. support family strengths,
3. identify early signs of emotional and behavioral difficulties, and
4. assist families with special needs.

There are some basic components that help make programs emotionally healthy for young children. First, children need materials and activities appropriate for their developmental level. Second, they need adequate and safe space. Finally, they need sensitive and caring adults who understand the developmental sequences and challenges of childhood, recognize and respect children's feelings and provide opportunities to communicate those feelings through actions and words.

Programs can support family strengths by providing opportunities for them to become involved in program activities, making them aware of available community resources such as parenting programs, and helping families under stress find mental health supports.

Children and TV, Videos, and Movies

Impacting today's young children and their mental health are television and the VCR tapes that they watch. In recent years, child developmentalists and the public at large have become very concerned about the potentially negative impact of television and movies on children's interpersonal behavior. Even Plato said in *The Republic* "shall we simply allow our children to listen to any story anyone happens to make up, and so receive into their minds ideas often the very opposite of those we shall think they ought to have when they grow up?"

The Facts.   Why is the study of television's effect on young children and their development deemed so important? The statistics speak for themselves. These statistics show that most children will have watched 5,000 hours of television before they start their formal public education (Gortmaker et al., 1990). A child born today by age 18 will have spent more time watching television than in any other single activity except sleeping. These incredible statistics of viewing time during the crucial years of cognitive development surround the question: How could television not have some effect?

Hypotheses.   Hypotheses concerning the effects of television on cognitive development fall into three categories: (1) a positive effect (facilitation hypothesis), (2) a negative effect (inhibition hypothesis), and (3) no effect at all. The positive, facilitation effect is generated by both educational programming such as Sesame Street, and by the mere presence of words which appear on the screen such as titles and credits. Educational programming itself provides a beneficial effect by teaching, supplementing, or overlapping center and school content.

Under the inhibition hypothesis, television has negative effects on cognitive development and social interaction skills and models. These can include displacement, passivity, hemispherical specialization, concentration deterioration and anti-school attitudes. In the early 1960s, increased aggressive behavior in preschoolers was studied (Bandura, Ross, & Ross, 1961, 1963). The children's behavior was observed and recorded in a playroom setting immediately following a viewing period of aggression-stimulating film projected onto a television screen. The goal was to identify the processes by which children learn by observing and imitating behavior of others. In these famous studies, a plastic "Bobo" doll in the corner of the playroom was repeatedly hit by the children who watched the aggressive films, but not by the control group who watched peaceful shows. Articles on the impact of TV violence upon children ignited firestorms of social concern in 1963 (Bandura, Ross & Ross, 1963).

The displacement hypothesis claims that television impairs children by taking the place of other activities like imaginary play that would foster cognitive development. There is also a diluting effect when children combine activities such as doing something else while watching television. The passivity hypothesis states that television induces children to become mentally lazy and less prepared to engage in activities involving books and art materials that require more mental energy. The hemispherical specialization argument delineates that effect, charging that over-stimulation of the right brain by high doses of television reduces the left brain functions.

The concentration-deterioration hypothesis argues that television weakens a child's ability to concentrate due to its fast pace. Some experts believe that this effect is manifested in impulsive thought and a shortened attention span which precludes persistence later in academic tasks. At an extreme, this effect could produce an anti-school attitude because school can't compete with the amusement provided by television.

The third main hypothesis is that there is "no effect" (Beentjies & Van der Voort, 1988). There can be three reasons for this: (1) the effects are simply not there, (2) the positive and negative effects cancel each other out, having no net effect, and (3) the research could not locate the effects.

However, correlational surveys paint a similar picture: children (and adolescents) who watch a lot of televised violence at home tend to be more aggressive than their classmates who watch little violence on television (Eron, 1980, 1982). So it appears that heavy exposure to televised violence (which proliferated in the late 1990s) during early and middle childhood may promote the development of aggressive habits and dispositions that persist over time.

Television violence may also instigate aggression in that children younger than 6 or 7 cannot easily distinguish appearance from reality and much of what they see on television is quite realistic and likely to be believed.

In summary, learning is a relatively permanent change in a behavior that occurs as a result of practice or experience according to one definition (Schaffer, 1988). It is the process by which children (and all people) acquire new information, attitudes, abilities and behaviors. It is therefore important to carefully assess which of these attitudes and behaviors parents and early child-hood professionals want young children to learn from television and movie experiences, limit this exposure and substitute other (live) experiences that *do* provide information, attitudes, abilities and behaviors they would like to see develop and nurture, to promote positive child mental health for a long life.

Negative Effects of Television Violence on Children

Children grow up watching an average of four hours of television a day or 28 hours a week (Levin & Carlsson-Paige, 1994). By age 18, the average American child will have viewed about 200,000 acts of violence on television alone (Levin, 1998). Many young children spend far more time watching TV than they do playing or interacting with others. There is a growing body of research that shows the negative effects of so many hours spent in front of the television.

"Children who are exposed to violence often and at an early age grow desen-sitized to the pain of others. Violence becomes a normal means of resolving conflict or stress" (NAEYC, 1995). Even though children may grow immune to the pain of others, they grow more fearful of their own vulnerability. Exposure to media violence can increase aggressive and anti-social behavior and lead to an appetite for more violence in entertainment and in real life.

"Children have been shown in many controlled studies to exhibit more aggressive behavior after being exposed to visual depictions of dramatic vio-lence" (Harvard Mental Health Letter, 1996, p. 5). Children often imitate the violent behavior of their favorite television heroes. Since television often fails to show the consequences of the violence it portrays, children may learn that there are few repercussions for aggressive behavior. They will often act out the scenarios they have witnessed, taking on the role of their favorite action hero. Young children may not be able to clearly distinguish between cartoon fan-tasies and real life. They don't necessarily understand that their pretend play could hurt a friend. Instead of banning action figures, teachers and adminis-trators can use the television heroes to explore alternative pro-social behav-iors. By asking children what their hero would do if someone was hurt or needed help, teachers can lead the group in a discussion of problem-solving behaviors and they can begin to talk about the consequences of violent behav-ior. Then the children can generate peaceful solutions and talk about how they handle conflicts with their friends. It is important that children learn to take another's perspective. By putting themselves in someone else's shoes, they begin to develop an understanding of the consequences of their actions. This is empathy, and it helps children control their aggressive impulses and come to the aid of their friends.

The National Association for the Education of Young Children recommends that parents watch television with their children and evaluate the program-ming. Parents need to be aware that most of the television watched by children was designed for adults. If parents watch with their children, they can help their children distinguish between fantasy and reality. They can discuss the violent acts and images and ask children to think about what would happen in real life. Would anyone die or go to jail? Would anyone be sad or hurt? Would the violence solve problems or create them? As an administrator, you can help by educating parents about this "media literacy" issue through your newsletter and parent meetings.

Other Stresses

As an administrator, you will confront situations where a child is exhibiting disruptive or unusual behavior and the cause is unclear. Remember that children are communicating important information through their behavior. A sudden change in behavior may indicate the presence of stress in a child's life. For example, a two-year-old who begins biting and pinching other children may be experiencing some changes at home. The presence of a new baby or the illness of a family member may be the underlying cause. Of course, the aggressive behavior must still be managed, but understanding the entire picture can help you provide the appropriate supports.

Other situations may also contribute to aggressive behavior or unusual play patterns. Substance abuse and domestic violence are two circumstances that will almost certainly have an impact on children's behavior in your program. In both situations, children are exposed to dangerous and often violent behaviors of the adults they depend on for safety and well-being. Although children may exhibit a variety of symptoms, often their play will reveal the stresses at home. Children may act out hitting, shouting and swearing, calling the police, and hiding using dolls or puppets. They may play out similar scripts on the playground with their friends. Listen carefully to the words they use. If you are concerned, set up a time to meet with the parents. Describe the behaviors you have noticed and give the parents some examples of the play you have observed. Your concern must be for the child's well being. If the parents can see that their child is suffering, they may be more open to seeking help. Seek out resources in your community so you can refer parents in need.

◇ ◇

INCLUDING CHILDREN WITH DISABILITIES

Increasing numbers of young children with disabilities are enrolling in community early childhood programs. This move towards serving children with and without disabilities in the same setting is called *inclusion*. Research has shown that inclusion, when carefully planned and implemented, offers benefits to teachers, families and children. Teachers and parents report unexpected developmental gains made by children with disabilities. They also talk about the benefits to the typically developing children in learning to appreciate individual differences and take on the roles of helper, leader, and friend. The following section describes the legislative basis for including children with disabilities alongside their non-disabled peers.

Overview of Federal Disability Laws

Until the 1970s, children with disabilities had often been denied access to public education. Both the civil rights movement and the efforts of parents of children with disabilities contributed to the passage of legislation which assured their rights and children with disabilities gained a mandate for education when federal legislation was enacted. Section 504 of the Rehabilitation Act of 1973, The Americans with Disabilities Act (ADA) and Public Law 105-17, the Individuals with Disabilities Education Act (IDEA Amendments of 1997) prohibit discrimination solely on the basis of a disability. IDEA guarantees a *free and appropriate, publicly supported education* (FAPE) in the *least restrictive environment* (LRE) to all children with disabilities. The Americans with Disabilities Act (ADA) is the most recent of the federal laws ensuring the civil rights of children with disabilities and prohibiting discrimination.

The related laws helped shape current thinking and programming for young children with disabilities. They have an impact on the children with identified disabilities that you may serve in early care and education programs. Knowing about these related laws can help you understand what you need to offer the children and to locate the resources and services available for any child with a disability in your program.

As many as one out of ten children in your program may have a disability. At least half of young children with disabilities will have difficulties with speech and language skills. Other children may have genetic disorders such as Down's syndrome, neurological disorders such as cerebral palsy or epilepsy, or sensory disorders such as vision or hearing impairments. Many of these children are entitled to special education and related services. The following section describes each federal law. Later sections explain how to obtain special education services for children in your program who may qualify.

Section 504

P.L. 93-112, The Rehabilitation Act of 1973, Title V, Section 504, mandates that programs receiving any federal monies be nondiscriminatory. Section 504 ensures equal and accessible transportation, architecture, educational programs, and nonacademic services for children and adults with disabilities. Any child care programs receiving federal assistance, such as those on military bases or supported by the General Services Administration or USDA food programs, may not discriminate against children, families, and employees with disabilities. All physical spaces (e.g., entrances, corridors, classrooms, play spaces, bathrooms) must be accessible and barrier free. Any transportation provided, such as buses or vans, also must be accessible for all users. Even if services to people with disabilities are separate, the quality of the services cannot be substantially different. Physical surroundings and transportation services must be comparable. For example, if a child with a disability comes to your center on a separate school bus, you can work to assure that the child arrives and departs with the other children and that he uses the same entrance as everyone else.

IDEA

IDEA states that children with disabilities, ages birth through twenty-one, have the right to a free appropriate public education. This is the law that provides the mandate for special education services in the public schools. It strongly supports the right of children with disabilities to be educated in the least restrictive environment. It also provides for the identification and assessment of children who might have disabilities. For children under the age of five, this service is called Child Find. Child Find screens and evaluates young children when there is a concern about their development. As an administrator, this is a valuable resource. Parents must make the actual referral and give written permission for the assessment, but all services are provided at no cost.

Eligible children receive services based on their Individualized Education Program (IEP). This document states the precise services a child will receive. A child may receive a range of services including special education, physical, occupational, or speech therapy, and/or vision/hearing services, depending on his individual needs.

ADA

The ADA, IDEA and Section 504 are closely related. All three laws say that people with disabilities should be with their peers who are not disabled as much as possible.

The ADA requires early childhood programs to be as physically accessible as possible and to make modifications in their policies, practices and procedures to assure that these do not discriminate against people with disabilities. The requirements of the law are closely tied to the resources of the individual program and will vary from center to center. Centers must assess each potential change or modification and decide on a case-by-case basis which changes are realistic at the present time. Under the ADA, early childhood programs may not exclude children solely on the basis of a disability. Child care settings that receive Federal aid must make every effort to accommodate any child with a disability who applies for admission. Early childhood programs and family day care homes must have nondiscriminatory enrollment procedures and must assure that children with disabilities can participate fully in all activities. If your program requires that children be toilet-trained prior to admission, you should review this policy to be certain that it does not discriminate against children whose disability may interfere with this skill. One might also consider ways to accommodate a child with a physical disability. For example, if a child who uses a wheelchair is enrolled and the lunch area is upstairs, the routine might be changed to serve lunch to everyone in a downstairs classroom.

According to the ADA, no one with a disability should be made to choose a setting that completely separates him or her from others without disabilities. Segregated programs are not prohibited but their existence may prevent a person with a disability from participating in a more integrated setting. The creation of separate programs is actively discouraged.

If a parent wants his or her child with a disability to attend a community program, the child cannot be denied enrollment because a separate program for children with disabilities is available. Within a building, the existence of separate special education classrooms for children with disabilities should not keep a child with disabilities from being included in a classroom with children without disabilities if that is the desired and appropriate placement.

All three laws, the Americans with Disabilities Act, the Individuals with Disabilities Education Act, and Section 504 combine to prevent discrimination, ensure equal rights and provide appropriate programs for all people with disabilities. Figure 12.1 compares the major features of these laws.

Initial Contact with Parents

Try to approach each initial contact with an open mind. When a parent begins to describe his or her child's disability, you may begin to worry about whether you can meet all of the child's needs. Can your staff provide an appropriate program for the child? Does the child have extensive needs that will require special equipment or expensive adaptations? Will staff and other families have questions and concerns about the child's presence?

As your list of concerns grows, write them down, but don't voice them to the parents yet. At this first stage you and the parents are just getting to know each other. They are evaluating you and your center and trying to decide if their child will be welcomed.

You will have plenty of time to discuss your concerns if the parents decide to enroll. Right now you want to put them at ease and begin to gather information. Your goal is to communicate your willingness to discuss the issues and work together to find ways to meet both their needs and your program's needs.

When a parent calls your center, remember what she is looking for. First, she wants to know if your program will be a good place for her child. As you talk she may be asking herself these questions:

	Section 504	ADA	IDEA
Setting	Integrated Settings	Integrated Settings	Least Restrictive Environment
Definition of disability	General and comprehensive definition of qualified individual with a disability (same as ADA)	General and comprehensive definition of qualified individual with a disability (same as Section 504)	Specific disabling conditions defined
Applies to	Federally-funded grants and activities	Transportation State and local government services Public Accommodations Telecommunications Employment	Public Education
Enforcement	Office of Civil Rights U.S. Department of Education	U.S. Equal Employment Opportunity Commission U.S. Department of Justice U.S. Department of Transportation Federal Communications Commission	U.S. Department of Education

FIGURE 12.1
Comparison of the Laws

- Will my child be safe?
- Will the people here like and accept my child?
- Will my child make friends and be happy?
- How will my child get along here?
- Will my child learn new skills?

Parents need information to decide if the program is right for them and their child. Specifically, they need to know about:

- Location
- Program cost
- Program philosophy
- Program hours
- Group size
- Child-staff ratios
- Curriculum
- Staff experience
- Registration procedures

Parents of a child with a disability may also be interested in the center's physical accessibility, the training and experience the staff has had with children with disabilities, and the availability of special education or other therapeutic services.

When parents come to visit the center, this may be the first face-to-face meeting. It is a time for parents to see the center and for you to gather more in-depth information about what they want and what their child needs. This first visit might include the following steps:

1. Tour the center first.
2. Find out if the parents wish to pursue enrollment.
3. If they do, go to a quiet area to finish giving them information and answering questions about the program.
4. Ask them to describe their child and find out what kind of program they are seeking for their child.
5. Talk about the match between what your program provides and what they are seeking for their child.
6. If you have concerns about the match, do not hesitate to voice your concerns honestly but sensitively. Put yourself in the parents' place—how would you like to be treated in a similar situation?
7. Finally, clearly and carefully explain the enrollment procedures, including all fees.

Remember that you should not ask directly about the presence of a disability. If a parent offers this information, it may be included in the discussion about the type of program that the parents are seeking for their child. This is one way that you can get information about what special needs the parents expect your center to meet.

Ask only for the information you *need to know* to make the best possible admission/placement decision. Respect the parents' and the child's right to privacy. If you need to press for further information, explain how and why it would be helpful to know more about the child and his needs. Ask about the child's current program and services. Find out if people currently working with the child would be a helpful resource.

If Your Program Can't Accommodate the Child

A positive relationship with the parents is in your best interest whether or not the child ever enrolls in your program. If you reject a child because he is disabled and you are worried about caring for him, you risk angering parents who may decide to file a discrimination complaint or talk poorly of your center to others.

If you are concerned that you won't be able to accommodate a child, give the parents some specific information about how your program operates. Describe the class size, the ratios, and some typical activities. Talk about the amount of time and supervision that staff can provide each child. This information will help parents decide if your center is right for their child.

Feel free to talk about your experience or lack of experience serving children with disabilities. If your staff has not had special training, let the parents know. If you have never enrolled a child in a wheelchair, say so. At the same time, you should communicate your willingness to try new approaches.

Even if your main concern is cost, try not to rush into a discussion of what changes you can and cannot afford to make. Keep reminding yourself that these conversations are just a beginning. An unanticipated solution may present itself if you keep an open mind.

Checkpoints for Dealing with Parents

The following set of questions can remind you of the areas to address when a parent of a child with special needs calls your program.

1. Have I conveyed a program philosophy that is accepting and flexible?
2. Have I clearly communicated important program information?
3. Have I gathered the necessary information about the family's wishes and the child's needs in a non-judgmental and supportive manner?

4. Have I openly discussed expectations about enrollment and placement?

5. Have we agreed upon and scheduled the next step in the process?

6. Have I set a positive tone for future conversations?

These are only the first steps. Building a relationship takes time. As the parents get to know and trust you and your staff, this relationship will strengthen. Open and frequent communication are the keys to this process.

Making Adaptations for Children with Disabilities

Equipment and materials in the environment should be flexible enough to be used by children with a wide range of abilities. For any age child, the equipment and materials should foster independence. Blocks, sand and water tables can suit children of many developmental levels. For toddlers, equipment also needs to support motor development. Preschoolers need materials invitingly displayed with visual cues about how and where to use them. For example, areas defined by tape on the floor and pictures of block constructions show where and how to build with the blocks. Of course, all equipment and materials should support the development of new concepts and skills in children with diverse developmental levels. Well-conceived activities are:

- flexible enough to meet a variety of developmental learning needs for individualization
- designed to meet multiple learning objectives
- motivating and interesting to the children.

Environments for all children, including those with special needs, should provide many opportunities for them to be the best that they can be. Simple adaptations and sensitivity to individual needs can make all the difference.

Adaptations for Children with Physical Disabilities

The addition of a child with physical disabilities to your program may require some special equipment. Such equipment might include:

- Chairs to help a child sit better (e.g., a corner chair, or a bolster chair with head and back support)
- A standing apparatus for a child who cannot stand alone (e.g., a prone stander)
- Wheelchairs and walkers
- Body, hand or leg braces to keep the trunk, arms and legs in good positions or help make the limbs more functional.

Often, the largest pieces of equipment in the classroom are the furniture. One of the most important things you can do for a child with physical disabilities is to make sure that there is enough room to maneuver around the furniture in the room.

Ask the child's parents for an explanation of the equipment he or she needs. Learn when and how it is to be used. The parents can demonstrate what needs to be done and you can try it yourself while the parents are observing. Check to see if the child's physical or occupational therapist can consult with the teachers about the use of the equipment. If you are uncomfortable about using the equipment, keep working with the parents, ask for clarification, and try different alternatives until the best situation for you and the child has been found. Teachers should be encouraged to write the procedures down if equipment and use are complicated.

Adaptations for Children with Hearing or Language Disabilities

Children with hearing or language impairments may also need special devices. Some children may need hearing aids or amplifiers. Language boards, and augmentative communication devices can help other children communicate about what they want and help them initiate and sustain conversations. (Augmentative communication devices amplify or *augment* the sounds of language.)

For children with hearing impairments, the environment needs to include additional clear and noticeable visual cues to help them function independently and understand what is happening in the classroom. For example, teachers can switch the lights on and off to signal an activity change, rather than ringing a bell. Staff can use manual signs to sing the song marking clean-up time. Make certain that the child can see the person giving instructions.

Again, ask the parents to explain and demonstrate the techniques they use. Also ask for guidance from the child's speech therapist or audiologist.

Adaptations for Children with Visual Impairments

To assist a child who is visually impaired, large furniture will need to remain in the same place. Prepare all the children for room changes or include them in the planning of the changes. If the furniture or room arrangement is going to change, make sure that the child who is visually impaired gets to explore and learn the new arrangement.

Tactile cues help children who are visually impaired locate equipment and materials independently. The name on the child's cubby can be marked with a textured sign that the child can feel. Small objects or toys can be taped on the outside of bins to help the child identify where each piece of equipment belongs.

Modifying the Schedule

As you help your staff adjust routines to include children with disabilities, think about the events in the daily schedule in terms of the following characteristics: structure; grouping; activity level; time; purpose; and the role of the teacher. Staff can then make adjustments based on each child's needs and level of development.

These questions can guide your discussions about scheduling for children with disabilities:

- Is there a schedule that is predictable for the children and reflects little waiting or "down" time?
- Is the classroom schedule flexible enough to accommodate programming changes?
- Are the blocks of time in the classroom schedule developmentally appropriate for the group?
- How and when do children move from one activity to the next? Is there a clear signal or do they have to wait any length of time to begin the next activity?
- How will you assure access to special program events, such as field trips?

For each child with a disability, consider the balance between child-initiated and teacher-directed activities. Can the child work in large groups or does he or she need more individualized attention? What is the child's activity level tolerance? And finally, what level of independence does the child show during transitions and waiting times? Does the child understand the cues for activity changes?

Sometimes adaptations require several adjustments. For example, Justin is a very active, visually impaired child who attends his neighborhood preschool. At first the director was concerned because she had never enrolled a child like him before. She talked to his mother and did some reading. Working with the teacher, she reviewed the classroom arrangement and had his mother help introduce him to the areas of the room. The teacher used very bright tape to mark different areas. She also added a fuzzy sticker to Justin's cubby, carpet square and chair so he could find them. Yet, even after two weeks, Justin was having frequent outbursts during transitions between activities. The other children knew when it was time to change activities and what would happen next. Justin didn't seem to understand.

What made the difference were a few simple adjustments. These included a schedule board with tactile cues so that Justin could make a plan for his one long play time and could refer back to it on his own, keeping Justin with the same small group of children for two weeks, and also giving him his own timer so that he would have a few minutes of extra warning before it was time to change activities.

Well-planned and balanced schedules often give children the security and predictability to function independently.

Disability Definitions

This section describes the disability definitions included in the IDEA and gives an example of each. Under the IDEA, a disability must adversely affect educational performance for a child to receive special education services.

Remember that the disability is only one piece of information. A child with a disability is a child first, and shares the same feelings, needs and interests as typical children. This child also has some needs that are different from those of typical children, but knowing the name of the disability tells you very little about how the child learns or how best to teach him or her. It does not tell you what his or her later abilities might be. Applying a diagnostic label may be necessary to determine a child's eligibility for services, but learning about who a child is and what he or she needs must go beyond that label or diagnosis.

Autism is a developmental disability that significantly affects verbal and non-verbal communication and social interaction. It is a neurological disorder that is generally evident before age three. Other characteristics often associated with autism are engagement in repetitive activities and stereotyped movements, resistance to environmental change or change in daily routines, and unusual responses to sensory experiences.

> *Peter is three years old and has been attending preschool since he was eighteen months old. The first thing his teacher noticed was that he preferred to play alone and took very little notice of the other children. When she held him, he tended to pull away. When upset, he was difficult to comfort and holding him didn't help.*
>
> *Now, at age three, Peter doesn't talk to other people, and often repeats what is said to him. He gets upset and cries if the routine of the day is changed or if one of the classroom staff is absent. He likes to line up all of his toys and will not allow anyone to move them. Peter is good at putting puzzles together and loves to look at books. He always notices the new library books and goes through each one of them. He has just started to name some toys in the classroom.*

Deafness is a hearing impairment that is so severe that a child is unable to hear and understand spoken words, with or without amplification.

> *Samantha was born quite prematurely and only weighed three and three quarters pounds. She spent a lot of time in the "preemie nursery" before she could go home. Although very tiny, she developed well and her parents were pleased until they noticed that she didn't seem to turn toward the sound of their voice or notice when the dog was barking. When Samantha was nine months old, the pediatrician sent the family to an audiologist who diagnosed a severe hearing loss. The audiologist also recommended a program for children who have hearing impairments. A teacher began coming to the*

house and to the family day care provider to teach Samantha, her parents, and her child care provider sign language.

Deaf-blindness means concomitant hearing and visual impairments, the combination of which causes such severe communication and other developmental and educational problems that they cannot be accommodated in special education programs solely for children with blindness.

> *Tia's mother had a mild cold and sore throat when she was two months pregnant, but she did not notice anything unusual in her pregnancy. When Tia was born, the doctor immediately noticed that the baby had difficulty breathing and that she was stiff and irritable. She nursed poorly and lost a lot of weight. After a thorough examination, it was determined that Tia was both deaf and blind and had delayed motor development. The infection Tia's mother had is called cytomegalovirus which can cause severe damage to the development of a fetus if contracted in the first trimester of a pregnancy.*

Hearing impairment means that an individual has a hearing loss, whether permanent or fluctuating.

> *Jason wore a hearing aid to school. When the other children asked about it, Jason's mother came to class to talk about hearing aids and let the other children try some on. She reminded the children that it was important for Jason to see the face and mouth of the person talking to him because sometimes he could "see" what they were saying. She also said that sometimes they would have to show him how to do something rather than explain it to him. She said that Jason sounded funny when he talked because he couldn't hear what he said very well.*

Mental retardation is significantly below average general intellectual functioning existing concurrently with deficits in adaptive behavior. Adaptive behavior refers to the ability to meet the demands of the environment through age-appropriate, independent skills in self-care, communication and play.

> *Melissa was born with Down's syndrome. The doctor was very helpful and supportive when explaining that the condition was the result of an extra chromosome. Both of Melissa's parents were very upset, but they began to read books about Down's syndrome. They visited an early intervention program for infants with disabilities and talked to other parents of children with Down's syndrome. One thing that they learned was that children with Down's syndrome almost always have some degree of mental retardation.*

Melissa's parents weren't sure what this meant or what to expect. At the age of six months, Melissa started in the early intervention program and they realized that her development was like that of her older brother, but much slower. She walked much later and didn't begin to talk until she was three. Learning new things took Melissa a long time and she needed lots of practice until she was able to perform skills independently.

Multiple disabilities means concomitant impairments such as mental retardation-blindness, mental retardation-orthopedic impairment, hearing loss-blindness, etc., the combination of which causes such severe educational problems that they cannot be accommodated in a program solely for one of the impairments.

Ms. Freeman had a very difficult delivery and her baby Latavia did not get enough oxygen. The lack of oxygen caused brain damage which resulted in cerebral palsy and cortical blindness. At age 2 she could not roll over or reach for toys. The doctor said that Latavia would always need someone to care for her. She now attends a special education program in the mornings where she receives occupational, physical and speech therapy, and a child care center in the afternoon where she has the opportunity to play with her peers.

Orthopedic impairment is any condition that involves muscles, bones, or joints and is characterized by difficulty with movement. The term includes impairments caused by congenital anomaly (e.g., clubfoot, absence of a body limb, etc.), impairments caused by disease (e.g., poliomyelitis, bone tuberculosis, etc.), and impairments from other causes (e.g., cerebral palsy, amputations, and fractures or burns that cause contractures.) In educational or non-educational settings it affects the ability to perform small or large muscle activities, or to perform self-help skills.

John is a very sociable child who loves to talk with his friends and teachers. He was born with an opening in his spinal cord which had to be surgically closed. This condition is called spina bifida. The nerves were damaged below the opening in his spine and he does not have any feeling in his legs and can't move them. Shortly after birth he also had increased pressure in his brain and the doctor inserted a device called a shunt to help drain the extra spinal fluid and relieve the pressure. John wears braces on his legs to support his weight when he walks with crutches. He recently got a motorized wheelchair for school since walking is so difficult for him.

Other health impairment is any condition that limits strength, vitality or alertness due to a chronic or acute health problem. Examples are cancer, some neurological disorders, rheumatic fever, severe asthma, uncontrolled seizure disorders, heart conditions, lead poisoning, diabetes, AIDS, blood disorders (hemophilia, sickle cell anemia), cystic fibrosis, heart disease, attention deficit disorder.

> *Jarron is a very active four-year-old with attention deficit disorder. He is constantly in motion and loves to run, climb, and chase. In the classroom, he wiggles at group time and often annoys the children sitting next to him. He shouts out answers and has a very hard time waiting his turn. During center time, he can't seem to focus on one activity and is easily distracted by noise around him. He is a very intense child and is either very happy, or very upset. Jarron does not like art activities. He holds the scissors awkwardly and gets frustrated and angry when he can't cut on a line.*

Severe emotional disturbance describes a child who has behavioral or emotional responses that are extremely different from other children with the same ethnic or cultural background. These extreme behaviors impair social relationships, self-care skills, and are very disruptive in the classroom.

1. The term means a condition that includes one or more of the following characteristics over a long period of time and to a marked degree that adversely affects a child's educational performance—

   a. An inability to learn that cannot be explained by intellectual, sensory, or health factors;

   b. An inability to build or maintain satisfactory interpersonal relationships with peers and teachers;

   c. Inappropriate types of behavior or feelings under normal circumstances;

   d. A general pervasive mood of unhappiness or depression; or

   e. A tendency to develop physical symptoms or fears associated with personal or school problems.

2. The term includes schizophrenia. The term does not apply to children who are socially maladjusted, unless it is determined that they have a serious emotional disturbance.

It is unusual for young children to be given this diagnosis. Usually, extreme behaviors in young children are related to autism, mental retardation, acquired brain injury, or general developmental delay. Sometimes these behaviors result from early trauma such as abuse or neglect.

Specific learning disability is a disorder in one or more of the basic *psychological* processes involved in understanding or using spoken or written language. Children may have difficulty listening, thinking, speaking, writing, spelling, or doing mathematical calculations. The term includes such conditions as perceptual disabilities, brain injury, minimal brain dysfunction, dyslexia, and developmental aphasia. The term does not apply to children who have learning problems that are primarily the result of visual, hearing, or motor disabilities, of mental retardation, or emotional disturbance, or of environmental, cultural, or economic disadvantage. Although this definition does not usually apply to preschool-aged children, teachers may notice children who have trouble acquiring the *beginning* skills for reading, writing, spelling or doing math.

> *Fred's mother remembers that in preschool his teacher told her that Fred was "all boy" and had no interest in any table or art activities. He preferred physical activities and pretend games like Ninja Turtles. When he participated in "sharing time," he seemed to have a lot of general knowledge and a very good memory.*
>
> *Now Fred was in first grade and handwriting was so frustrating that Fred hated to write anything. Although he could repeat whole stories that were read to him, he couldn't seem to make sense of letters and words. Fred's teacher told his mother that he just didn't seem motivated. His mother didn't understand how Fred could easily do his math problems and put together complicated models, but was unable to recognize simple words. One day the reading teacher called and said she suspected that Fred might have a learning disability. The subsequent testing proved her to be right. Now with the help of a resource teacher who works on visual perception and fine motor skills, all of Fred's school work has started to improve and he seems much happier.*

This category is very broad and it may be difficult to distinguish a learning disability from other learning problems especially in a young child. Each school system develops its own criteria for determining if a child has a learning disability. Contact your local special education department in the public school for their definition.

Speech or language impairments are communication disorders such as stuttering, impaired articulation, or voice impairment. This category also includes the inability to express oneself or an inability to understand what is being said.

> *The teacher had a great deal of difficulty understanding what Lydia was saying. She knew that young children often mispronounced some words, but Lydia's trouble seemed more severe. In the classroom she understood everything that was said to her and followed directions well. Much of the time the teacher had to have Lydia*

show her what she wanted because she couldn't figure out what Lydia was trying to say.

Traumatic brain injury[1] is an injury to the brain caused by an external physical force, resulting in total or partial functional disability or psychosocial impairment, or both. The term applies to open or closed head injuries resulting in impairments in one or more areas, such as cognition; language; memory; attention; reasoning; abstract thinking; judgment; problem-solving; sensory, perceptual, and motor abilities; psychosocial behavior; physical functions; information processing; and speech. The term does not apply to brain injuries that are congenital or degenerative, or brain injuries induced by birth trauma.

> ◆ *When Jeffrey was two he discovered an interesting toy in his father's closet. Unfortunately the "toy" turned out to be a gun. The gun went off, shooting Jeffrey in the head. Jeffrey quickly recovered and soon afterwards he started preschool. His teacher noticed that the left side of his body didn't work as well as his right side. He seemed to be learning well and could talk clearly, but he had trouble remembering and using the right words. Most of the time he was very friendly and cooperative, but sometimes he had violent tantrums that seemed to come out of nowhere.*

Visual impairment is any loss of sight that, with or without correction, adversely affects a child's learning. Blindness refers to a condition with no vision or only light perception. Low vision refers to limited distance vision or the ability to see only items close to the eyes.

> ◆ *When Sarah was 3 months old, her mother noticed that she did not seem to focus on objects and follow them with her eyes. An examination by the doctor confirmed that Sarah had cataracts. After an operation and the use of contact lenses, Sarah could see much better. She moved around more and became very excited when she saw her parents and the toys that she liked.*

Additional Definition

IDEA has an additional category for young children of **developmental delay**. It is defined as:

> Children ages birth to five who are experiencing delays, as defined by their state and measured by appropriate diagnostic instruments and procedures, in one or more of the following areas: physical development, cognitive development, com-

---

[1] Although the preferred terminology for this disability has been changed to **acquired brain injury**, traumatic brain injury is used here since it is the term used in IDEA.

munication development, social or emotional development, or adaptive development, and who therefore need education and related services. The extent of the delays may range from mild to severe and may include:

1. children with identifiable conditions that interfere with their learning and development;
2. children with developmental delays but no apparent biological condition; and
3. children who are at risk because of a variety of environmental and/or biological factors.

States may now choose to apply this diagnostic category to children through the age of eight.

Referring a Child to Special Education Services

You are likely to encounter at least three different situations related to children with disabilities and your public school special education services. Each circumstance requires a separate sequence of actions to obtain needed services for the child in question.

In the first situation, you may have a child in your program who already receives special education services. The child may attend a special education classroom in the morning and come to your program in the afternoon. Sometimes the child will be in your program full-time and special education personnel will come to your site to provide services. Sometimes the parents or the public schools will transport the child to another site to receive special education services. The issues in this situation are communication and coordination. Each person working with the child needs to know what the other people are doing.

In the second situation, you may have a child in your program whose development concerns you. If you enroll infants, you may encounter a situation in which one of the babies does not learn to sit up, crawl, or walk as you would expect. With toddlers, staff sometimes become concerned about a child who is not talking as well as the other children her age. At the preschool age, teachers expect children to be able to cut with scissors by age 4½ or 5, play together, and use a variety of outdoor equipment. Staff needs to be well trained in child development and in the offering of developmentally appropriate activities, of course. A child who looks markedly different from his peers in any of these areas will be brought to your attention. The first step in any of these circumstances is a parent conference. The next step may be a referral for a special education evaluation.

The third situation is similar to the second but occurs rarely. You discover a child whose development concerns you and you speak with the parents. In this case, the parents are aware of the concerns but they have decided not to use the special education process. They may not wish to obtain services or they may be obtaining services privately, outside the public school system. Since the final decision does rest with the family, you must respect their wishes. However, if the child continues to attend your program, you may need additional information to successfully provide for that child. The issues in this situation are related to building a trusting relationship with the family as well as obtaining information about appropriate techniques in working with the child.

Most of the situations you encounter will be type one or type two. You may find yourself working with special education personnel to coordinate services for a child with an identified disability or you will be referring a child for an evaluation.

As you go through the required process to refer a child and obtain services, remember that your program and your staff can make important contributions at each step along the way. The director and the staff see the child daily and have a lot of information about his or her abilities and needs. They also see the whole child, and they see other children developing typically. Sometimes child care professionals see the process of obtaining special education services as separate from what they do. It is very important to work closely with your public schools to coordinate services and information and to provide a comprehensive program that will benefit the child and the family, because you and your staff see the child from the widest range of perspectives.

The best advice is to trust your judgment and document your observations. If you suspect a child is having developmental difficulties or if you feel a child needs some change in his or her special education program, speak up. Of course, the first people to speak with are the parents. With their written permission you may also speak directly with personnel from your public schools. It is very helpful to have several people observe the child and write up a brief report that details the observations and specifies your concerns. This report can be shared with the parents and with their permission can be an important contribution to the referral and evaluation process. Remember, your active involvement and participation in the process of obtaining special education services can benefit everyone.

◇ ◇

HOSPITALIZED CHILDREN

Hospitalization is traumatic for any child. Even routine doctor visits are often upsetting. As with any new situation, children are afraid of the unknown. Their fears are often developmentally as well as situationally based. The preschool child who is developing autonomy and independence doesn't want to be told what to do. She doesn't want unfamiliar adults touching her body. In addition, she may fear being separated from her parents. Many young children quickly learn that a visit to the doctor can involve the pain of an immunization or blood test. Children with serious or chronic illnesses may have more intense reactions because of their frequent contact with medical personnel.

Children are less fearful when they feel prepared and know what to expect. Even the very young child can be prepared for a hospital visit by acting out the events with a stuffed animal, doll, or puppet. Although the one-year-old cannot be expected to fully understand, the frequent repetition of the play-acted events will help alleviate her fears. Once she is at the hospital, her parents can use the stuffed animal to demonstrate what the doctor is going to do. The very young child is helped by simple explanations that are repeated frequently.

The preschool child will also benefit from acting out events. His parents and teachers can help by reading books and talking with him about what to expect. Parents will need to decide when to tell their child about an upcoming hospitalization. Since children's sense of time is limited, it is usually best to tell them just a few days in advance. Parents need to balance the time their child will need to get used to this new idea against the potential for their child to become worried and anxious. Of course the classroom teacher can help by reading books about doctors and hospital visits to the whole class. Incorporating this into the classroom curriculum will benefit all of the children in the group.

After the child returns to the program, it is important to provide opportunities for him to talk about his experiences and act them out in play. As an administrator, you can alert the teachers to the importance of allowing children to express their feelings and fears. If a child is seriously ill, she may hesitate to talk with her parents about her fears because she doesn't want to make her mother or father sad. A child with a serious or chronic illness may find it easier to talk with a caring adult who is not a family member. Talking to a familiar adult who will listen non-judgmentally can ease the worries that a sick child may have. Since young children are magical thinkers, they may feel guilty about their illness and think they are in some way responsible. A child may think that if he hadn't eaten that candy, he wouldn't have gotten sick. Another child might wonder if his illness is punishment for his misdeeds. The child needs to know that it is all right to express these fears and that he or she is not responsible for his illness.

◇ ◇ ◇ ◇ ◇ ◇ ◇ ◇ ◇ ◇ ◇ ◇ ◇ ◇ ◇ ◇ ◇ ◇ ◇ ◇

CHILDREN AND DEATH

Young children are learning lessons about death and dying from tragic sources today. Increased violence and poverty and increased exposure to graphic violence in television and movies have made death an everyday part of life. AIDS, cancer, accidents, drugs, and murder are touching the personal lives of children and families in many communities.

Early childhood administrators can be important sources of information and support as families and children confront serious illness and death. How can we help children deal with death? This issue is a difficult one for adults. If we want to learn how to help young children and their families deal with these concerns, we must work to clarify our own ideas about life and death. First, it is important to understand that children's view of death is different from that of adults. There are four components to children's understanding of death: irreversibility, finality, inevitability, and causality (Christian, 1997). These stages are connected to the child's developmental level.

Children as young as three years old experience the emotion of grief (Christian, 1997). Even younger children are sensitive to the stress and react to the emotions of the adults around them. Preschool children often think that death is reversible (Fitzgerald, 1992; Goldman, 1996). They don't understand the meaning of "forever." At this age children often ask questions like, "When is Daddy coming home?" or "My mommy died today. When is she coming back?" They need to hear the same information over and over again until it begins to be real.

Another consideration is that preschoolers are literal thinkers, so adults have to explain death very clearly. If a child is told, "Grandma went to sleep," he may wonder if he will also die when he goes to sleep. Four-year-olds are egocentric and magical thinkers. For them, thinking makes it so. They may feel guilty and think that the death is their fault if they have had negative feelings about the person who died. One four-year-old thought he had caused his grandfather's heart attack because he hadn't liked the birthday present his grandfather had given him the day before.

Young school age children are beginning to learn that death is real and final. A six-year-old may feel guilty because she believes that if she had acted in time, she could have prevented the death. At this stage, children believe that death happens only to old people. They may ask the adults around them if they are old yet.

Children want to know facts. They are trying to understand causality and will ask what, when, and where questions. They want to know what it was that made someone die. Older children often see death as some form of tangible being. They may fear a ghost or bogeyman. By age ten, children know that death can happen to young as well as old. Children this age often fear that a parent might die. Indeed, once a child is reassured that he is safe and his parents are not going to die, the death of someone else's parent is less threatening (Greenberg, 1996). Adolescents begin to ask philosophical questions. They are beginning to integrate death into their belief system and may talk about an afterlife. While they may now understand the concept of death, they still have difficulty comprehending the possibility of their own death. When helping children and their families deal with death, it is important to remember that grieving takes a long time. Children's grief may be cyclical—as they enter a new developmental stage, they may ask questions and revisit concerns that had been discussed and addressed when they were younger (Christian, 1997). Children also grieve sporadically. They can often put their grief aside to focus on more pleasant things (Fitzgerald, 1992).

It is also important to remember how resilient children can be. They "can withstand many difficulties, including war, hunger, dislocation, and death of a parent, and end up emotionally healthy as long as they have at least one caring adult who sees [them] through the hardship" (Greenberg, 1996, p. 76).

Children have a range of reactions to the death of a loved one. It is important to remember that death is a stress and that stress can create all kinds of physical problems. Some children may just say, "I don't feel well." If the death was caused by illness or disease, a child may complain about some of those symptoms, for example, "My chest hurts. I can't breathe." Other common reactions include difficulty concentrating, inability to sleep, anger and separation anxiety. Children may show a need to care for others. They may have dreams or phobias. They may also create fantasies to explain the dead person's absence.

Children take their cues from the important adults around them. They react to the loss of attention, separation, and changes in routine (Christian, 1997). While family members are wrapped up in their own grief, children may need extra attention from their teachers. The familiar adults in the early childhood setting can be the stable constant caregivers in the child's life until the family is able to step back in.

The early childhood program can help by providing consistent structure and minimizing distractions. The child's play will tell you a great deal about how he is dealing with the loss. It is a good idea to talk with the parents about how they would like you to handle information related to the death. They can tell you what the child is comfortable sharing or discussing. You can help by providing clear information and opportunities to talk about feelings. The child with a stomachache can be told that stomachaches may be a sign of feeling sad or lonely. Young children often need an adult to help them make the connection between how they are behaving and how they are feeling.

A director also needs to be concerned about the other children and families in the program. Prepare the other children before the grieving child returns to class. Help the other children think about what to do if Jennifer starts to cry. Children can plan what they want to say when the child first returns. "I was sorry to hear about your grandpa dying." They can make a "welcome back" poster or cards.

Books are another valuable resource. Teachers can read books in the classroom to help answer children's questions. The program can also make books available to teachers and parents to help them respond to children's concerns.

With the parents' permission, you may want to send a letter to all of the families in the program that explains the facts of the death and includes information and resources on children and grief. As the administrator, you will also want to meet with the teachers to discuss appropriate ways to work with the children. It may be helpful to have mental health professionals available for both teachers and families.

In some instances it may be appropriate to plan a memorial service at the program. A planning meeting with parents and teachers can be used to discuss the service and ways to help prepare the children. A memorial service allows children to participate in saying goodbye. Children should be invited to participate but attendance should be voluntary and adults should be prepared to leave with any child who feels uncomfortable. The memorial service should be child-centered. One program planned such a service after one of the children died unexpectedly. The teachers set up tables at which children could draw and paint. There were bubbles and balloons available for those who wanted to stay outside. Children shared stories, artwork, poetry, dances and songs.

After the death, consider aspects of the program that might now have a different meaning for the grieving child and family. Holiday celebrations may be different. Consider how to handle Mother's Day and Father's Day if a child has lost a parent. Plan other celebrations with the family and the teachers.

Once in a while the child and family will need additional supports. Find out if there are any bereavement groups in your community. You should be concerned if the child doesn't want anyone to know about the death. Other causes for concern are signs of regression such as thumb sucking or toileting accidents that do not improve after several weeks.

The most helpful thing you can do is to address the issues of grief directly. Children need the opportunity to ask questions over and over. Adult sadness or discomfort should not prevent the program from providing the support that children and families desperately need.

◇ ◇ ◇ ◇ ◇ ◇ ◇ ◇ ◇ ◇ ◇ ◇ ◇ ◇ ◇ ◇ ◇ ◇ ◇ ◇

SUMMARY

Just as there are many legal issues that affect young children in early childhood programs, there are many medically related issues as well. A child's mental health and development can surmount experiences that seem traumatic much more successfully if the professional adults involved can give support and understanding to the parents and the child, and also can give appropriate community or regional resource referrals.

Television and movies expose children to violence at a very young age. Disabled children face the same challenges as nondisabled children but with the added challenges of their own unique situations. A child who is hospitalized suddenly or without preparation will need time to process and "play-act" the experience in the safety of the classroom. And lastly, a child dealing with the death of a family member or even his or her own terminal illness will need special love and support. Sometimes these situations may also contribute to aggressive behavior or unusual play patterns. Often children's play will reveal stresses at home. Whatever the situation, adequate staff training, perhaps using handouts and guest speakers if possible, can go a long way towards helping these children and the center staff learn about and deal with these various issues. A small number have been discussed here, but more topics and more resources are available in coursework, and on the Internet especially. Next, our focus will shift from issues that come up *in* operations to operational matters that affect the structure of all programs: facilities and finances.

◇ ◇

SUGGESTED CLASS ACTIVITIES AND DISCUSSIONS

1. *Americans with Disabilities Act (ADA)*.   A group or several small groups can research the different implications of the ADA law for young children, and present charts of them to the class. Discuss other laws and their implications for children challenged in a variety of ways.

2. *Hospitalized Children's Bibliography*.   Develop a bibliography of children's books that would be helpful to a child going to the hospital or to one that has been released from the hospital recently. Set up the dramatic play corner as a hospital room in a center in which one student works. Report back observations of the children's play in it.

3. *Children and Death*.   Develop a bibliography of children's books written to help children understand a death of a family member or close relative. Distribute as handouts to the class.

4. *Child Mental Health*.   Research acceptable children's TV shows and develop a rating system as a class or in a small group with criteria based on developmental appropriateness.

5. *Adaptations for Special Needs*.   Class members can research various types of handicaps that preschoolers might bring to a group program and discuss the adaptations that might be needed for each.

6. *Have small group discussions* on the following (real) questions and report back (add other questions from class members):
   a. What do you do with a child who constantly disrupts the classroom by throwing temper-tantrums, by using abusive language, by physically attacking the teacher aides, the social worker and the director? The mother refuses to accept the fact that the child behaves as reported to her.
   b. What do you do about a mother who, after finding out that her child is diabetic and needs to follow a special diet, fails to inform the staff of the center where her child has been enrolled for over a year?

◇ ◇

BIBLIOGRAPHY

Bailey, D. B., & Winton, P. J. (1989). Friendship and acquaintance among families in a mainstreamed day care center. *Education and Training of the Mentally Retarded, 24,* 107–113.

Bailey, D. B., & Winton, P. J. (1987). Stability and change in parents' expectations about mainstreaming. *Topics in Early Childhood Special Education* 7(1), 73–88.

Bandura, A., Ross, D., & Ross, S. A. (1961). Transmission of aggression through imitation of aggressive models. *Journal of Abnormal and Social Psychology, 63,* 575–582.

Bandura, A., Ross, D., & Ross, S. A. (1963). Imitation of film mediated aggressive models. *Journal of Abnormal and Social Psychology, 66*(1), 3–11.

Beentjies, J. W. J., & Van der Voort, T.H.A. (1988). Television's impact on children's reading skills: A review of research. *Reading Research Quarterly, 23*(4), 389–413.

Bricker, D. D., M. B. Bruder, & Bailey, E. (1982). Developmental integration of preschool children. *Analysis and Intervention in Developmental Disabilities, 2,* 207–222.

Christian, L. (1997). Children and death. *Young Children, 52*(4), 76–80.

Cooke, T. P., Ruskus, J. A., Appolloni, T., & Peck, C. A. (1981). Handicapped preschool children in the mainstream: Background, outcomes and clinical suggestions. *Topics in Early Childhood Special Education 1*(1), 73–83.

Dodson, F., & Alexander, A. (1986). *Your child: Birth to age 6.* New York: Simon and Schuster, Inc.

Eron, L. D. (1980). Prescription for reduction of aggression. *American Psychologist, 35*(3), 244–252.

Eron, L. D. (1982). Parent-child interaction, television violence, and aggression in children. *American Psychologist, 37*(2), 197–211.

Fitzgerald, H. (1992). *The Grieving Child.* New York: Fireside.

Giangreco, M. F., Dennis, R., Cloninger, C., Edelman, S., & Schattman, R. (1993). I've counted Jon: Transformational experiences of teachers educating students with disabilities. *Exceptional Children, 59*(4), 359–373.

Goldman, L. (1996). We can help children grieve: A child-oriented model for memorializing. *Young Children, 51*(6), 69–73.

Gortmaker, S., Salter, C. A., & Walker, D. K. (1990). The impact of television viewing on mental attitude and achievement: A longitudinal study. *Public Opinion Quarterly, 54*(4), 594–604.

Green, M., & Widoff, E. (1990). Special needs child care: Training is a key issue. *Young Children, 45*(3), 60–61.

Greenberg, J. (1996). Seeing children through tragedy: My mother died today—when is she coming back? *Young Children, 51*(6), 76–77.

Harvard Mental Health Letter. (1996, June, 12). (12), 5–7. http://ericps.ed.uiuc.edu/nccic.

Levin, D., & Carlsson-Paige, N. (1994). Developmentally appropriate television: Putting children first. *Young Children, 49*(5), 38–44.

Levin, D. (1998). *Remote control childhood: Combating the hazards of media culture.* Washington, DC: National Association for the Education of Young Children.

Miller, L. J., Strain, P. S., Boyd, K., Hunsicker, S., McKinley, J., & Wu, A. (1992). Parental attitudes toward integration. *Topics in Early Childhood Special Education, 12,* 230–246.

National Association for the Education of Young Children. (1995). *Media violence and children: A guide for parents.* Washington, DC: Author.

Neugebauer, B. (Ed.). (1992). *Alike and different: Exploring our humanity with young children.* (Rev. ed.). Washington, DC: NAEYC.

Odom, S. L., & McEvoy, M. A. (1988). Integration of young children with handicaps and normally developing children. In S. L. Odom and M. B. Karnes (Eds.), *Early intervention for infants and children with handicaps: An empirical base* (pp. 241–268). Baltimore, MD: Paul H. Brookes.

Odom, S. L., & McEvoy, M. A. (1990). Mainstreaming at the preschool level: Potential barriers and tasks for the field. *Topics in Early Childhood Special Education, 10*(2), 48–61.

Peck, C. A., Odom, S. L., & Bricker, D. (1993). *Integrating young children with disabilities into community programs: Ecological perspectives on research and implementation.* Baltimore, MD: Paul H. Brookes.

Plato. (1992). *Republic.* Indianapolis, IN: Hackett.

Rab, V. Y., & Wood, K., (1995). *Child care and the ADA: A handbook for inclusive programs*. Baltimore, MD: Paul H. Brookes.

Ross, H. W. (1992). Integrating infants with disabilities. Can "ordinary" caregivers do it? *Young Children, 47*(3), 65–71.

Schaffer, D. R. (1988). *Developmental psychology, childhood and adolescence* (2nd ed.). Pacific Grove, CA: Brooks Cole Publishing Co.

Sears, R., Rau, L., & Alpert, R. (1965). *Identification and child rearing*. Stanford, CA: Stanford University Press.

Slaby, R., Roedell, W., Arezzo, D., & Hendrix, K. (1995). *Early violence prevention. Some things you should know about media violence and media literacy*. (www.aap.org/advocacy/childhealthmonth/media.htm)

Templeman, T. P., Fredericks, H. D., & Udell, T. (1989). Integration of children with moderate and severe handicaps into a day care center. *Journal of Early Intervention, 13,* 315–328.

White, B. P., & Phair, M. A. (1986). It'll be a challenge! Managing emotional stress in teaching disabled children. *Young Children, 41*(2), 44–48.

Wolery, M., Holcombe, A., Venn, M. L., Brookfield, J., Huffman, K., Schroeder, C., Martin, C. G., & Fleming, L. A. (1993). Mainstreaming in early childhood programs: Current status and relevant issues. *Young Children, 49*(1), 78–84.

Wolery, M., Strain, P. S., & Bailey, D. B. (1992). Reaching potentials of children with special needs. In S. Bredekamp and T. Rosegrant (Eds.), *Reaching potentials: Appropriate curriculum and assessment for young children: Vol. I.* (pp. 92–111). Washington, DC: NAEYC.

www.aap.org/advocacy/childhealthmonth/media.htm

◇ ◇ ◇ ◇ ◇ ◇ ◇ ◇ ◇ ◇ ◇ ◇ ◇ ◇ ◇ ◇ ◇ ◇ ◇

RESOURCES FOR PARENTS

Fitzgerald, H. (1992). *The grieving child*. New York: Fireside.

Grollman, E. (1970). *Talking about death: A dialogue between parent and child*. Boston: Beacon Press.

◇ ◇ ◇ ◇ ◇ ◇ ◇ ◇ ◇ ◇ ◇ ◇ ◇ ◇ ◇ ◇ ◇ ◇ ◇

RESOURCES FOR CHILDREN

Davison, M. (1992). *Rita goes to the hospital*. New York: Random House.

Dooley, V. (1996). *Tubes in my ears*. Mondo Publishing.

Smith, D. B. (1988). *A taste of blackberries*. Reprint, New York: Harper Collins.

Viorst, J. (1987). *The tenth good thing about Barney*. Reprint, New York: Simon & Schuster.

White, E. B. (1952). *Charlotte's web*. New York: Harpers.

Leadership, Operational Issues and Evaluation

Operational issues are ongoing, but their efficient implementation depends on leadership, planning, decision-making, and problem-solving. All of these processes, when used well by the human resources team, benefit the motivation level, the team building efforts, and the skills of the entire staff. They also lead to a feeling of professionalism throughout the center. As parents receive education and become knowledgeable about what a good early childhood program includes, involving them in a center's operation can help a program meet the challenges facing young children and early childhood education.

Issues such as facility usage, room arrangement, and scheduling all allow opportunities for discussion as to why a center does things in a certain way and how this philosophy benefits children. Rethinking these areas every year or so during parent-staff orientation meetings keeps the program fresh and up to date. One center that housed an awkwardly placed closet for years found that by sharing the problem, a committee of parents and community volunteers rebuilt it, adding a deck and an interesting play space on top. Fresh thinking yields many more ideas than can be used at first, but by listing them on a bulletin board in some central location, as circumstances change, the list will generate thinking about possible solutions.

Finances, record-keeping, and proposal writing also lend themselves to sharing the load and sharing the power; thus, as seen in Chapter 2, Understanding Leadership and the Use of Power, the total power of the program increases. As problems in these areas are shared with a specific committee that is devoted to that particular topic, more ideas and expertise are brought to bear and better solutions emerge. For example, a parent who feels less-than-expert in dealing with his or her toddler may have expertise in the management information systems of the center or the center's administration. By participating in this area, the parent can gain a sense of esteem for having helped the center. By having parents participate in pricing or budgeting for equipment and supplies, parents can learn what equipment and supplies benefit children. With or without writing a proposal, much of the thinking needed provides a good evaluation tool for your center, who it serves and how well. Add to this teacher self-evaluation as described in chapter 8 and a Portfolio Review (or similar evaluation as described in numerous materials) for children as they progress through the year, and a more complete picture of your center emerges. This will allow your center to assess where it is, and begin to plan where it wants to go (see chapters 2–7).

Finally, recognition for a job well done is rare in many job situations, and is valued by volunteers as well as staff. Successful child-care centers make sure to recognize participants' efforts. Part five moves from issues that arise in the environment of the child to matters of the center: facilities management and finances.

Facilities, Equipment, Room Arrangement, and Scheduling

W hen visiting different child-care programs, one can see many similarities and variations in programs, some of which are very good and some of which are not quite as good. All good programs, however, have the common goal of providing growing experiences for children.

Children's growing experiences require a sound underlying philosophy of developmentally appropriate early childhood education, upon which teachers and parents agree. From this foundation follows a better understanding of children's needs, good programming, and good relationships among the center staff and with parents. When considering early childhood programming, key issues, in addition to curriculum choices, are facilities and the use of space, equipment and room arrangement, and scheduling.

◇ ◇

FACILITIES AND THE USE OF SPACE

It is essential for children to be physically active in mastering their world. They become mentally alert as they develop the ability to move with purpose. The facilities chosen to house a particular center, then, need to allow this type of activity—providing opportunities for indoor and outdoor large-muscle play as well as meeting local fire and zoning regulations. When beginning a new center, it should be remembered that to a certain extent, the layout of an existing facility dictates its usage. The situation can be very different when a director and Board have an opportunity to design and build a new space in a housing area, office complex, or shopping area.

Developing and realizing a vision is achievable but takes several steps. Interesting, appealing and attractive space as a work environment for staff helps reduce turnover, and contributes to a setting in which children develop appropriately and are at ease (Sussman, 1998).

Daily surroundings are very important; a well-planned child-care environment can be one of a child's most valuable teachers. The environment introduces the child to the colors, shapes, smells, and sounds of the world. Infants and toddlers grow and learn by interacting with their environment, so the environment must be one that is safe and interesting. Indoor and outdoor areas need to be free of dangerous conditions or hazardous materials. The playground equipment must be checked often to ensure its safety. A first-aid kit also must be kept and staff should be well-trained in administering first aid during an emergency. In addition, the child-care setting should accommodate the needs of the caregiver as well as the infants, toddlers, and preschoolers (Lally & Stewart, 1990).

Renovating an existing facility calls into play broad issues of center design as well as particular challenges. Obtaining technical assistance early is important, just as in building a new center, since a good architect experienced in child care development can help predict hidden structure and systems costs, which traditionally are borne by the property owner. In addition, financing and grants packages can be pulled together with professional advice. Innovative funding approaches might include various state funds being developed for child care such as those in Maine, Massachusetts, New York, Illinois, North Carolina, and even more when community development funds are accessed. For a more complete list of child care lenders, write to the Center for Policy Alternatives in Washington, D.C., the Child Care Action Campaign in New York City, and the National Association of Community Development Loan Funds in Philadelphia (Sussman, 1998).

When setting up a child-care environment, there are ten concepts to remember (Lally & Stewart, 1990). The ideal infant/toddler/preschooler care-giving environment should:

1. ensure safety
2. promote health
3. provide comfort and a homelike "feel"
4. be convenient
5. be child-sized (e.g., bathrooms and furnishings; have pictures, mirrors and large numbers made of sandpaper, at child's eye level)
6. maximize flexibility
7. encourage movement
8. allow for choice (e.g., be relaxing yet stimulating)
9. be colorful and cheerful (have pastels and bright colors that blend)
10. have character and charm that adds uniqueness in classrooms (pp. 7–16).

Because space requirements are calculated on a per-child basis, the number of children that will be in a group or classroom has important implications for facility design. The best-planned indoor and outdoor physical environment fosters optimal growth and development through opportunities for exploration and learning.

Outdoor Play

Play facilities for children must provide room for two things: action and contemplation (Stone, 1970). The proof of a good outdoor play yard is in its use. Will children have room to move and the opportunity to affect their environment—feel it and mold it? Can they put together a playhouse or clubhouse or at least improve on one that already exists? Can they try out new ideas, make rules, discuss possibilities, experience success and failure, learn to try again? Is there room for water play? For sand play? One center met the children's need to use their hands to shape, mold, and feel a medium by setting up a water table on wheels, so it could be used indoors or rolled outdoors for warm-weather play. A similar table could be used as a mobile sand table, or the water table could double as a sand table or a sensory table during a different week.

Even large pieces of equipment can be moved and set up in new places to give an outdoor space a new look. Slides can be added to a jungle gym or a path for tricycles built to extend children's play in new ways. Good equipment invites departures from routine; for example, it can make possible a morning snack out-of-doors (Stone, 1970).

Children learn and relearn as they play with common materials such as water, sand, and even mud (provided in some sort of container, perhaps). Children are discovering and learning when they have the opportunity to control this small piece of their environment. Outdoor equipment and structures should be selected to allow creative expression and imaginative interpretation by children. If possible, the outdoors should be an extension of indoor space; doors that are readily accessible and windows that allow plenty of outside views are ideal.

A child needs to be able to react more energetically and quickly to his or her environment than does an adult. Discovering space—distance, height, width, level and inclined planes, and how one's body fits into and around space—is part of the physical development of childhood (U.S. Dept. of Health, Education and Welfare, 1969). Outdoor space may be large or small, flat or hilly, grassy or paved, shaded or unshaded. A brook is nice, but a hose or buckets of water will do in the summer. Whatever the available space offers, imagination can be used, just as it is indoors, to provide the active play children need: running, jumping, climbing, and throwing. Providing for outdoor activity and children's large muscle development makes it less likely that this energy will all be expended indoors in ways that are wearing on the staff and that the staff or classroom is less-equipped to handle.

Age Grouping

Traditional age-grouped classes, such as those for toddlers, three-year-olds, four-year-olds, and five-year-olds, are found in most programs for young children. This allows for grouping equipment and materials according to the same developmental level or, as in the case of chairs and tables, the same size. For example, two-year-olds need different-sized chairs than do five-year-olds.

A further benefit of traditional age grouping is that teachers need only be expert with a particular age, or at least be highly focused on one age group each year. Of course, even children who are the same age will present a range of abilities, from the youngest in the group to those who are more advanced than average, so a wide knowledge of child development will always be needed. However, age grouping is more suitable for beginning teachers or for centers that have a relatively inexperienced staff or that have staff members involved in on-the-job training. Another variation on this is called "looping" in which the teacher is "promoted" along with the children to the next year (or grade in public schools), such as from the 3-year-old class to the 4-year-old class.

Activity Grouping and Multi-age Groups

Some centers must work with a particular space that dictates that the large muscle room, the creative activities room, and the story/quiet room be dedicated exclusively to these kinds of activities. In such a situation, use of the rooms by mixed-age groups results. Some programs choose a multi-age group approach for many reasons other than space, and public schools use this approach on occasion, establishing grades like K–1, 1–2, or 5–6.

Multiple ages like costumes.

The educational benefits of mixed-age grouping have been discussed by reformers such as Montessori, Pestolozzi, and Dewey. Since the 1930s, educators have become increasingly aware of the limitations of a rigidly age-grouped system. Educators have found, in contrast, that nongraded organizational systems can allow for recognizing and planning for a wide range of child abilities. It also allows for differential rates of progress and makes it easier for the teacher to adjust to individual emotional and social needs.

What, then, is multi-age grouping? This particular philosophy opposes the restriction of individual age-grouped levels and instead offers flexible groupings that encompass a two- to four-year span, allowing movement between levels for those children ready to advance or needing more help. The multi-age classroom concept is based on vertical grouping, meaning that children can have the same teacher or teaching team for more than one year. Also, mixed-age grouping compels educators to organize learning activities and curriculum so that individuals and small groups of children can work on different tasks together. The benefits of mixed-age grouping include:

- Children have a wide selection of models from whom they can learn; it provides older children with leadership opportunities and younger ones with more complex pretend play opportunities.

- Mixed-age grouping seems to result in greater cooperation and less competitive pressure and therefore seems to lead to fewer discipline problems.
- Mixed-age grouping can be an effective strategy for dealing with different levels of cognitive maturity so intellectual growth is stimulated.

The disadvantages of mixed-age grouping include:

- Same-age, same-sex children may have difficulty in developing friendships, if the group is small.
- Older children often have fewer challenges than do younger children.
- Younger children, especially if they are very competitive, may be frustrated by the perceived gap between their "work" and that of older children.
- Scheduling special enrichments or field trips can be difficult.
- Teachers are required to do more planning for a wider range of children, and therefore an experienced teacher is needed (Lodish, 1992).

The external organization of age-grouped or multi-age classrooms is less significant than is the quality of the classroom environment and the learning opportunities made available. Because children respond differently to different situations, it is important to have some choices in possible groupings and to operate with flexibility.

Architectural and Legal Requirements

The architectural design of a child-care facility should be in keeping with the program's philosophy. For example, a teacher-directed philosophy may require less space than would an interaction-with-the-environment or learning-through-play philosophy, which would require room to move about and provision for physical and psychological comfort.

When planning for direct or indirect federal assistance of any kind, programs must be accessible to disabled children and employees. Section 504 of P. L. 93–112 describes the requirements of making programs accessible to the disabled. Money in the form of grants may be awarded by Congress to pay for all or part of the costs for remodeling buildings to eliminate barriers for disabled children; this funding is authorized in P.L. 94-142, and is dependent upon Congress's determination of appropriateness for funding this part of the law (Decker & Decker, 1992). With full inclusion of all children being required by federal legislation, all programs serving all families will need to be well-informed and ready to serve the physically challenged population. More detail on this can be found in chapter 12 on medically related issues for young children.

States vary in their requirements for indoor and outdoor space per child. Some states do not even have an outdoor space requirement. Thirty-five square feet per child for indoor space is an average, but some states require less; as children get older, providing more space per child is more appropriate. Poor arrangement can reduce the usefulness of large amounts of square footage per child, so careful planning and attention need to be addressed to indoor and outdoor space layout and equipment layout.

Lighting

Lighting affects physical well-being; seasonal affective disorder (SAD), a condition that occurs when there is less daylight during the shortened winter days, affects some adults and may also affect children. Making the best use of available light, then, is very important. The brightness and attractiveness of centers can be increased by using local or spotlight lighting, and reflective surfaces in the room can greatly increase the efficiency of the lighting that is chosen. Light-colored walls, light-colored tables and countertops, and even light-colored floors can add brightness and cheerfulness to rooms. Glare can be controlled by using blinds, louvers, curtains, and flat finishes. Ideally, the window area should be about 20 percent of the floor area, and windows should be low enough so that children can see out.

Heating/Cooling

A comfortable temperature of around 68° to 72°, whether through heating or cooling, needs to be maintained at the *children's* level. Thermometers that are placed low on the walls, or even a thermostat placed at the children's level, can monitor this zone for temperature. Good ventilation is also a requirement, and it is important not to close spaces in and reduce ventilation when air conditioning is installed in child-care centers. If there is no humidifier installed, humidity can be added to the rooms through open fish tanks or a water table.

Acoustical Control

Since young children make noise, attention to acoustical control and sound absorption is important. Rugs are the least expensive approach to acoustical absorption, and centers can ask parents or the community for donations. Rugs must be kept clean, so placement must be a consideration. Some centers may use rugs or carpets only for certain areas, such as the block area and the story area. Long flat walls reflect sound; to counteract such a design, decorations, bulletin boards, and children's pictures might be hung on clotheslines to help break up wall space and sound waves as they hit the walls. Padding on furniture legs can also reduce noise.

Legal Requirements and Agency Regulations

Licensing in most areas is handled by local and state agencies who inspect nursery schools, preschools, and child-care centers. Although licensing takes time, an interim permit is often issued to allow the program to get under way while awaiting health, fire, and safety inspections. A center may need to alter buildings if they fall short of any requirements necessary for licensing. (One example of a necessary alteration is the need to install fire doors.) The cost of many alterations may be covered by specific grants or funds, or they might be shared with the landlord in some instances.

It may be necessary to deal with regulations or standards in any or all of the following areas:

- Zoning
- Business licensing
- Safety issues, including fire extinguishers, smoke alarms, fire alarms, exits, and escape plans
- Educational standards, including teacher/pupil ratio; indoor space/child ratio; outdoor space/child ratio; staff qualifications; and health requirements
- Equipment
- Parking
- Building codes, including those for electricity, plumbing, heating capacity, and access, as well as environmental requirements, such as whether or not lead paint or asbestos is present
- Health regulations, including food preparation, food storage, number of bathrooms, lighting, and ventilation
- Transportation regulations or licenses

Most high-quality early childhood programs establish educational standards that far exceed any regulations that may be required by legislation. When beginning a new center, a valuable early step in considering architectural and legal requirements is to visit several similar early childhood programs and observe their different housing arrangements. Interview teachers and administrators regarding the regulations they must meet in their city, county, state, or province. It might also be helpful to consider the information in the *Early Childhood Environmental Rating Scale* (Harms & Clifford, 1980). To aid in such information gathering, many national early childhood conferences provide opportunities to visit excellent early childhood programs that have interesting layouts.

Outdoor Space

Since outdoor space and indoor space flow together in a developmental program, many of the same considerations should be used when setting up both areas. There should be time to use and explore the space; it should demonstrate flexibility and adaptability; and it should be safe and secure for children, day and night.

Playground and Layout

Many states and licensing authorities have requirements about the amount of average outdoor space available to each child, with suggested space ranging from 75 to 250 square feet per child. In general, more is better, as long as supervision can be carefully accomplished. Fencing with gates is required, and enclosing outdoor play areas is one of the first major expenses for a center that is just starting up.

Many wonderful materials are available on the subject of playgrounds and playground layout, as well as catalogs from different equipment suppliers. Some programs earmark their initial registration fees to go to a "large muscle equipment fund," since the necessary large playground equipment can include expensive items, such as a jungle gym, that are difficult to acquire on a tight budget. Researching the selection of large muscle equipment is a wonderful task to delegate to a committee made up of parents, since much parent education can occur while the committee pours over catalogs (which the director can provide), and checks and compares prices, delivery options, and set-up plans.

The playground can include a tricycle path, an area for sand play, an area for water play, and even a garden. Lovell and Harms (1985) developed a rating scale that can serve as a useful checklist for designing or improving an outdoor play space.

Outdoor Storage

Outdoor storage is essential to a rich and varied outdoor play program, because it enables the housing of tricycles, movable equipment, and seasonal items. A wide door and a ramp to the outside of the storage building (perhaps removable) allows children to come in and help bring out the equipment. Whether the storage building is a shed or an outbuilding attached to the main building, or just a garage, it can serve as a windbreak for the children's play space. Raised flooring in the storage room is a must to prevent dampness and rust. Some programs even fence the roof of a storage building, if the roof is flat, and allow the children to use it as a "tree house," perhaps attaching a slide and cargo net. Imaginative use of, and changes to, the outdoor play area are as important as they are for indoor play area(s).

◇ ◇

EQUIPMENT AND ROOM ARRANGEMENT

Because all children have a great deal of potential and because there is such an infinite variety of individual differences among children, it is important that a child-care center offer to its children rich and varied opportunities through its curricula and equipment so that the needs of each child will be met.

Even the most inspired and experienced staff members have limited time and energy. Requirements of the staff can be eased if the spaces for children are carefully planned and arranged. In spaces properly designed for child development, the doors, walls, windows, floors, furnishings, and fixtures can motivate a child's curiosity, encourage the potential for learning, and provide assistance to the staff. When the staff can focus on the children's activities rather than on the deficits in the indoor or outdoor spaces, a better program results.

Equipment

Activities and moods can shift rapidly in a program for young children. Indoor spaces that promote quiet, perhaps equipped with soft items such as large pillows on the floor maybe even inside a cloth tunnel, are just as important as the block corner and the truck run area. Making use of movable shelving units, rolling storage bins for blocks and small toys, and work tables and painting easels that can be used in new locations at different times all help provide the adaptability and flexibility that enhance a program. Materials or items that are disorganized, or are stored in such a way that a child must always ask for them, are frustrating for both children and adults.

Too much single-purpose furniture can also restrict activities and the use of imagination. There should be room for the unexpected: a grocery-box train, a large box made into a house, and frequent changes in the dramatic play area. The scene changes in the dramatic play area can range far and wide: a veterinarian's office, a dentist's office, a library, a styling salon, a pizza restaurant, a gas station, and whatever else the children propose and agree upon. A project curriculum approach might do "group research" (e.g., take field trips, read books, etc.) and planning, as well as review and follow-up, for each one of these areas that (some of) the children choose to develop. Stocking these play areas with receipt pads, note pads, and writing tools can encourage a print-rich environment for older preschool children, and also adds realism to their play. Joining related play areas, such as the block area and the dramatic play corner, can expand children's play as they find ways to combine the materials from both areas (Dodge, 1988; Seefeldt & Barbour, 1990; Trawick-Smith, 1992).

Adults are aware of the need for privacy at one time or another, but often there is a tendency to overlook this same need in young children. A classroom is an extraordinarily stimulating place, so children will frequently wish to take a break, catch their breath, and enjoy solitude in a quiet area. This private space should be respected by both the teacher and other children (Cherry, 1976; Miller, 1990; Seefeldt & Barbour, 1990; Trawick-Smith, 1992).

Throughout the years, one of the most effective ways teachers have provided for play is through the use of *learning centers*, which usually occupy separate areas within the classroom. Some of the most common learning centers used are areas for a library (books), woodworking, art, music, sand/water, blocks, manipulatives/table toys, and dramatic play (Cherry, 1976; Dodge, 1988; Miller, 1990; Seefeldt & Barbour, 1990; Trawick-Smith, 1992).

The library/book area is a quiet, cozy spot where children can retreat and read a favorite book or look at pictures. Books are displayed in an interesting and accessible manner, with the covers visible. Old magazines, parts of a newspaper, and catalogs can also be included. By providing comfortable chairs, pillows, and bean bag chairs, the teacher creates a very inviting atmosphere. Obviously, this area should be situated away from noisier activities in order to minimize distractions.

Woodworking can be an extremely popular activity, especially for those children who have never had such opportunities before, and the benefits abound (Cherry, 1976). As children manipulate materials, improved eye-hand coordination occurs; both imagination and memory are exercised as children construct different objects; children also can practice measuring and approximating distance as they build objects. The teacher can stock the woodworking center with such items as glue, toothpicks, styrofoam, pipe cleaners, tape, glitter, wood scraps, and paper strips. When more sophisticated materials (such as hammers, nails, and saws) are introduced, an adult must supervise the activity closely, and goggles may be required when certain materials are in use. Because of the nature of this center and to minimize danger, a limit should be placed on the number of children who may participate at the same time (Seefeldt & Barbour, 1990).

Art is another popular activity. Typically, children of all ages love to explore and create with different types of media and materials. By providing a well-planned art center, the teacher demonstrates awareness of the cognitive importance of art. The use of open-ended art activities, not patterns, promotes creativity and instills pride in achievement. The manipulation of the media allows children to develop small motor skills as well as eye-hand coordination. The art area should be located close to a water source for cleanup, and might include easels and tables as work areas (Dodge, 1988; Miller, 1990; Seefeldt & Barbour, 1990).

Children enjoy music enormously, yet too frequently it is offered only at certain times of the day. It is important to allow children opportunities to experiment with instruments and recordings on their own. A music center, which allows such exploration, could be located in a quiet part of the room or in a noisier area, depending on the teacher's expectations (Seefeldt & Barbour, 1990). In either case, limits should be set as to how loud the instruments and music can be played. Tape recording the songs children naturally make up and sing adds interest for the children. (These tapes can also be shared with parents.)

Often sand and water are ignored as learning tools because they are messy, but many mathematical concepts, such as measuring and comparing, can be learned through the use of these materials. Children can use these substances to observe cause and effect and to practice problem-solving. Sand and water areas are another type of learning center where eye-hand coordination and small motor skills are strengthened. The sand and water area should be in a quiet, secluded place and children should be encouraged to keep the materials in the appropriate containers (Dodge, 1988).

Manipulatives and table toys include such items as Legos, Lincoln Logs, Bristle Blocks, snap beads, and other similar hands-on materials. They can be used on the floor or on a table, by one child or by several. Table toys can be categorized as self-correcting, open-ended, or collectible (Dodge, 1988). Self-correcting toys are ones that fit together in one particular manner, such as puzzles, lotto games, nesting boxes, and self-help skill frames. Open-ended toys can be put together in many creative ways and include Legos, colored cubes, Lincoln Logs, and attribute blocks. Collectibles consist of groups of similar items, such as buttons, seeds, rocks, and shells. By using all of these different types of table toys, children practice fine motor skills and eye-hand coordination. They learn about relationships as they practice sorting and classifying objects. This type of learning center usually works best in a quiet area where children can concentrate, but if some manipulatives are occasionally placed close to the unit blocks, children can combine materials from the two areas (Dodge, 1988; Miller, 1990; Seefeldt & Barbour, 1990).

Blocks are some of the most valuable teaching tools, as well as some of the most forgotten. Teachers rarely incorporate blocks beyond first grade, yet there are many developmental benefits when they are used in later years. Children can acquire numerous mathematical concepts, including shape, size, length, height, weight, and balance through their play with blocks. As they create, children's eye-hand coordination and small motor control are developed as well. They can take pride in their constructions and experience a sense of accomplishment. Children working as a group on blocks practice many social skills, such as sharing and cooperating (Dodge, 1988; Seefeldt & Barbour, 1990).

Dramatic play areas are usually very lively. Teachers can provide props related to specific themes, such as a fast-food restaurant, a hospital, or other community establishments as mentioned previously. Housekeeping and dress-up equipment might also be kept in this area; children can create wonderful dramatic play situations with such materials. By changing the materials occasionally, as was mentioned earlier, the teacher will encourage use of the area (Miller, 1990). A fast-food chain or community service organization might be willing to donate materials that could be used in the dramatic play area.

The "ambiance" of the classroom includes such elements as lighting, texture, and noise. Each of these features affects play in various ways.

Lighting

A sunny, naturally lighted room is considered vital to the development and health of young children as mentioned earlier. A room brightened by sunshine provides the opportunity to observe the daily passage of time and to see objects at different stages of daylight (Trawick-Smith, 1992). Therefore, having large, uncovered (but coverable) windows is the ideal arrangement, with full-spectrum lighting used in the absence of windows (Cherry, 1976; Trawick-Smith, 1992).

Texture

A variety of textures tends to promote more frequent and varied use. Providing rugs, quilts, pillows, bean bag chairs, and cushions gives the room a "soft" feel. Trawick-Smith (1982) concludes from a study done in 1979 by Weinstein that a "soft and warm environment creates security and comfort and reduces stress in young children" (p. 27). Other textures may include messy, manipulative and sensory items such as sand, finger paint, shaving cream, water, grits, rice, oatmeal, birdseed, dried corn kernels, different sizes of pinecones, shells, chunks of ice, dirt, moss, and sticks, snow (with or without food coloring), leaves, rocks and pebbles, cornstarch, clay, play dough, carpet squares, sheepskin, and tile (Dodge, 1988; Miller, 1990).

Noise

Controlled acoustics and comfortable surfaces promote quiet play. The environment for any classroom needs to provide for noisy group activities as well as for quiet individual pursuits. When a classroom is basically box-shaped—with a flat ceiling and a flat floor—then color, texture, and lighting, in addition to acoustical controls, need to be employed to provide the best possible environment for children. Too small a space can interact with noise in such a way that children may react by withdrawing or by increasing physical aggression (Weinstein, 1979).

A "quiet center" can be made from a refrigerator box, stood vertically, with a door made from a cut across the halfway point of the front. Remove the portion above the door to allow staff to look in over the top to check on the child (and to let in light). Put in a bean bag chair, add a DO NOT DISTURB sign for the door (that can be turned around) and decorate the "quiet center" box. This idea from a child-care center in Washington state was very popular with the children *and* the staff.

Equipment Summary

In equipping a child-care center, it is necessary to be clear about its aims. If the center is to emphasize the development and self-fulfillment of the whole child socially, emotionally, physically, and intellectually, this goal will be seen in the center's choice of equipment. Some suggestions include:

Equipment to provide for emotional release

- Messy: finger paint, clay, sand, water, mud
- Creative: paints, posters, scissors, glue
- Pets
- Sensory: table with alternating materials from nature and the kitchen (especially appropriate for a Reggio curriculum approach)

Equipment to provide for social development

- Dramatic play and housekeeping corner
- Adequate quantity and kinds of items in high demand, such as telephones, doll strollers, irons, wagons, tricycles

Equipment to provide for physical development

- Large muscle equipment
- Materials that promote sensory experiences
- Facilities for meeting bodily needs, including sleeping arrangements that are soft and maybe even curtained off
  (Idea: Place a picture of the baby or young child on each to help them find their beds).

Equipment to provide for intellectual development and stimulation (This category includes all of the above plus some activities specifically aimed at challenging mental growth.)

- Books, puzzles, lotto games
- Puppets, dolls, trucks, blocks
- Science and other subject materials appropriate for early childhood

Room Arrangement

In arranging rooms for children, it is important to remember that children are small, and because in general the world seems just too large to manage, they want to feel stronger, bigger, and more competent. Through imagination and make-believe, children create situations that they can control. A child's problem-solving and creative planning sometimes come from the ability to imagine the idea and to imagine the possible steps to achieving goals. Children need opportunities to think about and weigh the consequences of their actions. To provide for all of these diverse requirements, room arrangement should accommodate the following:

1. Housekeeping/dramatic play
2. Table activities
3. Paints
4. Blocks
5. Equipment for indoor large muscle activity
6. Music
7. Books
8. Science

◇ ◇

SCHEDULING

Scheduling to meet the main objectives of the program and its philosophy helps to provide continuity of development and is the backbone, along with planning, of any child development program. Some of the overall considerations to keep in mind include:

- Does the program include large blocks of time for self-directed play?
- Are there only a few times when all the children will be doing the same things at the same time?
- Are there provisions made for children who do not want to listen to a story or participate in music or science activities?
- Are the transitions from one activity to another accomplished smoothly?
- Is the atmosphere relaxed and unhurried?
- Is there a good relationship between the teacher, the aides, and the parents?
- Is there respect for the teacher as the leader?
- Is support provided for the child who needs help with a puzzle? Who needs more suggestions in the block area? Who needs a role in the housekeeping/dramatic play corner? Who needs help sharing and taking turns? Who needs help with the hammer or saw?

Sample Schedules

Child-Care Centers

Child-care centers, which often must plan for a day that begins at 6:30 or 7:00 A.M. and does not end until 6:00 or 6:30 P.M., can benefit from a flexible schedule at the beginning and end of the day. Children often arrive and depart at different times during these flexible transition periods. A possible sample day is shown in Figure 13.1.

Infant and Toddler Programs

With infants and toddlers, it is especially important that a secure attachment bond be allowed to form with one caregiver and that the bond not be ignored or harmed by routinely rotating caregivers. The scheduling may have to be adjusted to accommodate this arrangement. The secure bond that is formed at this particular age lasts a lifetime (Erickson, 1963) and also yields immediate benefits in the child's well-being throughout the year and in the caregiver's retention at the center (Honig, 1993). When setting up a schedule, keep in mind that, in general, infants set their own schedule and pace; toddlers can follow the all-day sample format shown in Figure 13.1, with provisions for morning and afternoon naps as needed individually.

Half-Day and Preschool Programs

The traditional preschool half-day program, as shown in the sample schedule in Figure 13.2, does not include a nap, unless an "extended day" program is offered two or three days a week or more. In an extended day program, children bring their lunch, have a nap, and participate in additional indoor and outdoor supervised play.

Kindergarten

Kindergarten programs follow a schedule similar to the one for a half-day program, with variations due to the curriculum in the particular school system. Usually an opening group time begins the day. All-day kindergartens sometimes use two classrooms (alternating two groups), setting one room up with subject matter and other centers, and the other room with "choosing-time" centers (see Figures 13.3 and 13.4). The room arrangements shown in Figures 13.3 and 13.4 contain many useful ideas for other age groups as well.

6:30–9:00 a.m.	Welcome time, breakfast, free choice time in the center areas. Provision is made for children who want sleeping time.
9:00–11:30 a.m.	Active play and free choice time including finger plays, stories, songs, and art activities. Toileting and snack provided mid-morning integrated with the activities.
11:30 a.m.–12:00 p.m.	Quieter activities and preparation for lunch (toileting and hand washing).
12:00–1:00 p.m.	Lunch
1:00–3:00 p.m.	Nap and quiet playtime for children who do not take naps or who take short naps.
3:00–3:45 p.m.	Mid-afternoon snack and toileting time.
3:45–6:00 or 6:30 p.m.	Indoor and outdoor supervised play until departure.

FIGURE 13.1
Child-Care Sample Schedule

9:00–9:30 a.m.	Welcome time, free choice activities with a collage table and a science table in addition to centers as children gather.
9:30–10:30 a.m.	Indoor play with child-selected activities and a teacher invitation for an art or other activity (finger painting, making play dough, etc.). Discussions about the theme of the day (week or unit). Toileting begins at the end of this period and clean-up time.
10:30–11:00 a.m.	Snack time with finger plays and conversations. Discussions about food and recent experiences.
11:00–11:45 a.m.	Outdoor play.
11:45 a.m.–12:00 p.m.	Return indoors for story time and preparation to go home. Clean up, reflect on the day's learnings, plan for tomorrow.
12:00 p.m.	Departure time.

FIGURE 13.2
Half-Day Program

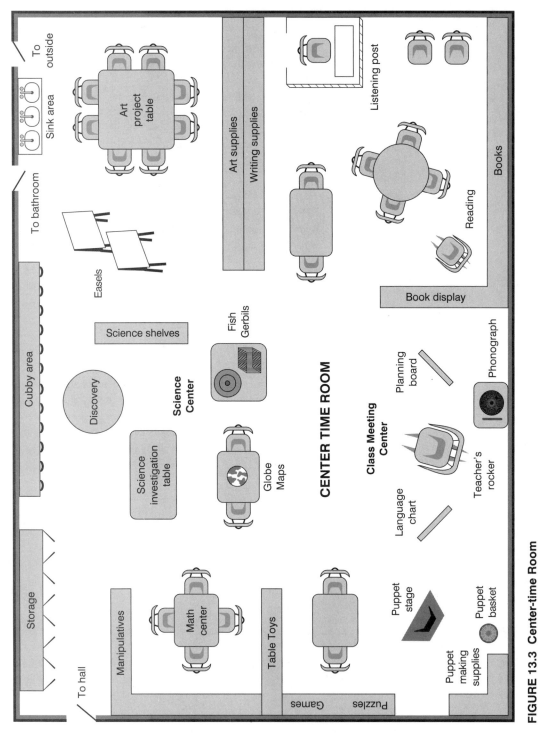

FIGURE 13.3 Center-time Room
Courtesy of Harriet Hougland.

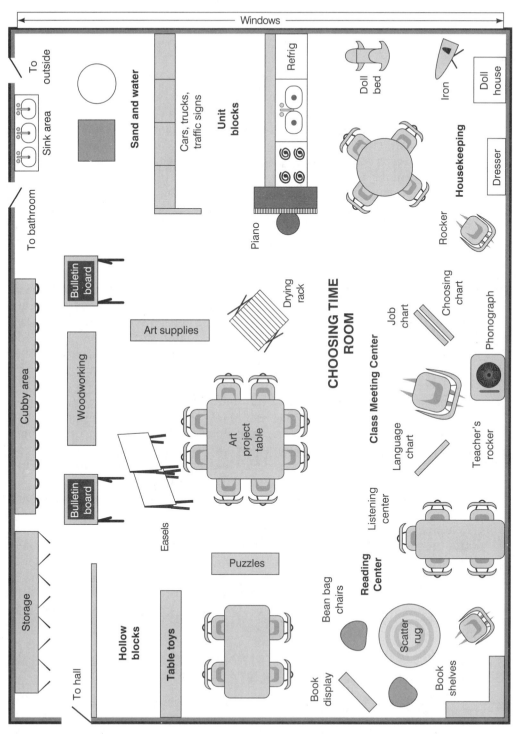

FIGURE 13.4 Choosing-time Room
Courtesy of Harriet Hougland.

◇ ◇

SUMMARY

How facility spaces, equipment, room arrangement, and scheduling are used is an important area of discussion for early childhood educators. A program staff may need to discuss several issues related to their particular situation or plans for expansion, such as same-age grouping versus multi-age grouping, activity grouping versus space available, as well as other issues. As these concerns are discussed among the staff, Board, and parents, a practical (concrete) spring- board is developed for learning about what excellent programs for young chil- dren might and can include. Realizing that quality space is achievable and important is a first step. Developing a vision of what an ideal center would look like and working backwards from that, using imagination and color to provide uniqueness, and charm to provide a comfortable and "non-institu- tional" environment is a next step. Depressing conditions and acceptance of low facility and equipment standards drains both the children and the staff. These conditions may even contribute to high staff turnover and (certainly) counter efforts to deliver high quality care (Phillips, 1987). Being desensitized and having chronically low expectations of a center environment is the oppo- site of nurturing a vision of the way things ought to be. Working towards a vision that translates the staff's child care experience and expertise yields much better results and a play environment clearly suited to children.

The growing demand for child care and the potentially harmful impact of poor and mediocre child care, has lead to a "national brain drain" as described in the media, in which children are not helped to develop and grow appropri- ately. Avoiding this impact requires new thinking (and funding approaches) for appealing, attractive child-centered play and learning environments for today's children, who may spend most of their waking hours in these facilities.

As mentioned earlier, the adaptations used to make space, equipment, room arrangement, and schedules work for a particular center can vary over time. Adapting spaces and routines to a particular facility and demographic area cre- ates uniqueness and pride of achievement. Color, for instance, can be a striking feature that is often the least costly possibility. As children are nurtured, they grow and develop; a well-run center that is nurtured will also grow and develop. To help create a well-run center, the next chapter deals more fully with operational issues such as finances, record keeping, and proposal writing.

◇ ◇ ◇ ◇ ◇ ◇ ◇ ◇ ◇ ◇ ◇ ◇ ◇ ◇ ◇ ◇ ◇ ◇ ◇ ◇

SUGGESTED CLASS ACTIVITIES AND DISCUSSIONS

1. *Practice with Child Development Principles.*   Students can choose to work individually with children of particular ages that are unfamiliar to them.

Use one or more age-appropriate Home Learning Enabler activities in Appendix A or look at www.homelearning.net for infant/toddler or school-age Home Learning Enablers. Students can report back to the class and relate the child's behavior to needs for equipment, scheduling, or even room arrangement. This activity can be combined with an observation exercise, and is especially good for pre-service students with limited access to children.

2. *Awareness of Obstacles to Open Space Arrangements.*   Draw a diagram of a classroom on the board or use Figure 13.4 or 13.5 and ask the class to brainstorm possible strengths and weaknesses using the following parameters: Promotes safety? Promotes health? Provides comfort and softness? Convenience? Is it child-sized? Flexible? Does it encourage movement? Allow for choice?

After strengths and weaknesses have been identified for a particular age of children, brainstorm further for "how to avoid" weaknesses and possible solutions. Age of children is important as a room for two-year-olds might need more softness than a room for five-year-olds, and so forth.

3. *Learning Centers and Stations.*   Divide the class into small groups and have each group brainstorm items to include in a learning center they select as a group. These can include a wide variety of choices: a library; a veterinarian's office; a dentist's office; a store; a beauty shop; an auto shop, all with a print-rich environment and writing materials perhaps. Try math, science, music, art and other subject matter centers for older children. If possible, set up the centers and let the student group rotate through them. If this is acted out, the "teacher" addresses the "role" the person/child is in, for each center.

4. *Kindergarten Curriculum Comparison.*   Examine three kindergarten curriculum guides available at the college library or at a school system central office. Using different curriculum approaches such as those described in chapter 1, do the following:

- Present the underlying philosophy
- Identify and discuss contributions of at least two authorities associated with this approach.
- Plan an opportunity for a learning experience for three- four- or five- year old children based on this approach (i.e. part of a day's activities). Be sure to include:

  1. Objectives
  2. How the student would initiate the activity
  3. Learning opportunities
  4. Materials and equipment needed
  5. Evaluation (can be somewhat based on observation of behavior)

6. Scheduling needs

7. Limitations and future suggestions

If time permits, present some of these "Learning Opportunities" to the class.

5. *Redesign of a Classroom.*   A student currently working in a center can draw a model of his or her own classroom on the board, and ask the class for ideas for design—or a hypothetical classroom can be used. Consider individual teacher preferences as well as research. Consider also the following questions:

- Where do children play?
- Where are the adults?
- What is the flow of traffic?
- What else is going on at the same time?
- Are there changes from September to January for developmental reasons? For change of season reasons?
- What areas do children go to?
- Does one teacher want more animals in the room?

Discuss findings and redesign the room in one or more layouts.

◇ ◇ ◇ ◇ ◇ ◇ ◇ ◇ ◇ ◇ ◇ ◇ ◇ ◇ ◇ ◇ ◇ ◇ ◇

BIBLIOGRAPHY

Bingham-Newman, A. M., & Saunders, R. A. (1977). Take a new look at your classroom with Piaget as a guide. *Young Children, 32*(4), 62–72.

Bloom, P. J. (1982). *Avoiding burn-out: Strategies for managing time, space, and people in early childhood education.* Lake Forest, IL: New Horizons.

Bredekamp, S. (1987). *Developmentally appropriate practice in early childhood programs serving children from birth through age 8.* Washington, DC: National Association for the Education of Young Children.

Cherry, C. (1976). *Creative play for the developing child.* Belmont, CA: David S. Lake.

Christie, J. F., & Wardle, F. (1992). How much time is needed for play? *Young Children, 47*(3), 28–32.

Decker, C. A., & Decker, J. R. (1992). *Planning and administering early childhood programs.* Upper Saddle River, NJ: Merrill/Prentice Hall.

Dodge, D. T. (1988). *The creative curriculum for early childhood.* Washington, DC: Teaching Strategies.

Dodge, D. T., & Colker, L. J. (1992). *The creative curriculum for early childhood.* Washington, DC: Teaching Strategies.

Eddowes, E. A. (1991). The benefits of solitary play. *Dimensions, 20*(1), 31–33.

Eisenberg, J., & Jalongo, M. (1993). *Creative expression and play in early childhood education.* New York: Macmillan.

Eisenberg, J., & Quisenberry, N. L. (1988). Play: A necessity for all children. A position paper of the Association for Childhood Education

International. *Childhood Education*, *64*(3), 138–145.

Elkind, D. (1987). *Miseducation*. New York: Knopf.

Elkind, D. (1989). Developmentally appropriate practice: Philosophical and practical implications. *Phi Delta Kappan*, *71*(2), 113–117.

Elliott, S. (1986). The role of the teacher in children's play. In J. S. McKee (Ed.), *Play: Working partner of growth*, pp. 42–46. Wheaton, MD: Association for Childhood Education International.

Erickson, E. H. (1963). *Childhood and society* (2nd ed.). New York: Norton.

Fein, G., & Rivkin, M. (Eds.). (1986). *The young child at play: Reviews of research* (Vol. 4). Washington, DC: National Association for the Education of Young Children.

Greenman, J. (1988). *Caring spaces, learning places: Children's environments that work*. Redmond WA: Exchange Press.

Harms, T., & Clifford, R. M. (1980). *Early childhood environment rating scale*. New York: Teachers College Press.

Honig, A. S. (1993). Mental health for babies: What do theory and research teach us? *Young Children*, *45*(6), 30–35.

Kritchevsky, S., & Prescott, E. (1977). *Planning environments for young children: Physical space* (2nd ed.). Washington, DC: NAEYC.

Lally, J. R., & Stewart, J. (1990). *A guide to setting up environments*. Sacramento, CA: California Department of Education.

Lodish, R. (1992, May). The pros and cons of mixed-age grouping. *Principal*, *71*, 20–22.

Loughlin, C. E., & Suina, J. H. (1982). *The learning environment: An instructional strategy*. New York: Teachers College Press.

Lovell, P., & Harms, T. (1985). How can playgrounds be improved? A rating scale, *Young Children*, *40*, 3–8.

Maslach, C. (1982). *Burnout: The cost of caring*. Upper Saddle River, NJ: Prentice Hall.

McKee, J. S. (1986). Play materials and activities for children birth to 10 years: People, play,

props and purposeful development. In J. S. McKee (Ed.), *Play: Working partner of growth* (pp. 15–28). Wheaton, MD: Association for Childhood Education International.

Miller, K. (1990). *More things to do with toddlers and twos*. Chelsea, MA: TelShare Publishing.

Morrison, G. S. (1991). *Early childhood education today*. New York: Macmillan.

Myers, B. K., & Maurer, K. (1987). Teaching with less talking: Learning centers in the kindergarten. *Young Children*, *42*(5), 20–27.

Papalia, D. E., & Olds, S. W. (1990). *A child's world: Infancy through adolescence*. New York: McGraw-Hill.

Pattillo, J., & Vaughan, E. (1992). *Learning centers for child-centered classrooms*. Washington, DC: National Education Association of the United States.

Phillips, D. A. (1987). *Quality in child care: What does research tell us?* Washington, DC: NAEYC.

Rogers, C. S., & Sawyers, J. K. (1988). *Play in the lives of children*. Washington, DC: National Association for the Education of Young Children.

Rubin, K. H. (1977). Play behaviors of young children. *Young Children*, *32*(6), 16–23.

Rubin, K. H., & Howe, N. (1986). Social play and perspective taking. In G. Fein & M. Rivkin (Eds.), *The young child at play. Reviews of research* (Vol. 4) (pp. 113–125). Washington, DC: National Association for the Education of Young Children.

Seefeldt, C., & Barbour, N. (1990). *Early childhood education: An introduction*. New York: Macmillan.

Seifert, K. L., & Hoffnung, R. J. (1991). *Child and adolescent development*. Boston: Houghton Mifflin.

Sherman, G. (1977). *Restructuring a kindergarten classroom to include more developmentally appropriate activities*. (Ed. Dept. Practicum Report). Ft. Lauderdale, FL: NOVA University. (ERIC Document Reproduction Service No. ED 350 097)

Singer, D. G. (1986). Make-believe play and learning. In J. S. McKee (Ed.), *Play: Working partner of growth* (pp. 8–14). Wheaton, MD: Association for Childhood Education International.

Smilansky, S. (1971). Can adults facilitate play in children? Theoretical and practice considerations. In G. Engstrom (Ed.), *Play: The child strives toward self-realization* (pp. 39–50). Washington, DC: National Association for the Education of Young Children.

Spodek, B., Saracho, O. N., & Davis, M. D. (1987). *Foundations of early childhood education: Teaching three-, four-, and five-year-old children*. Upper Saddle River, NJ: Prentice Hall.

Stone, J. G. (1970). *Play and playgrounds*. Washington, DC: National Association for the Education of Young Children.

Sussman, C. (1998). Out of the basement: Discovering the value of child care facilities. *Young Children*, 53(1), 10-17.

Torelli, L., & Durrett, C., with Chan, M. (1995). *Landscapes for learning: Designing group care environments for infants, toddlers and two-year-olds*. Berkeley, CA: Torelli/Durrett Infant and Toddler Childcare Furniture.

Trawick-Smith, J. (1992). The classroom environment affects children's play and development. *Dimensions*, 20(2), 27–30, 40.

U.S. Department of Health, Education and Welfare. (1969). *Designing the child development center*. Washington, DC: Author.

U.S. General Services Administration. (1993). *GSA child care center design guide*. Public Buildings Service, Office of Child Care and Development Programs, Washington, DC: GSA.

Weinstein, C. S. (1979). The physical environment of the school: A review of research. *Review of Educational Research, 35*(49), 577–611.

14

Finances, Record-Keeping, Proposal Writing, and Evaluating

Running a center and keeping its budget "in the black" requires good management practices. In part, good management results from paying close attention to the financial aspects of a center, the record-keeping processes, and any plans for future income that may necessitate proposal writing. Since child-care is essentially a service, qualified personnel are key to a successful center, and more attention is given elsewhere in this book to training and performance objectives for child-care staff. In addition to overseeing the training and performance of staff, however, budgets and records need to be kept, and all these tasks need to be done well. The responsibilities of maintaining the budget and records are given to the director, who can then hire a person especially because he or she has these capabilities. To understand the foundation for the financial part of center operations, this chapter will begin with a start-up plan. A center that is already in operation can adapt the following activities as appropriate.

◇ ◇

STARTING UP: DEVELOPING A MANAGEMENT PLAN

Many publications and free materials are available to help persons develop a management plan. Local bookstores and the United States Small Business Administration (Washington, D.C., 20416) have these materials. Generally, new businesses are advised to allow at least 6 to 12 months for planning for a start-up. This time provides a chance to meet with interested parents and to form working committees, as described in chapter 1, for the following areas:

Developing the program philosophy

Setting up bylaws and filing incorporation papers

Purchasing equipment and supplies

Planning for the hiring of teachers/director

Planning marketing and public relations strategies

Checking on licensing and zoning regulations

External Review

Any start-up plan should carefully review at least three other centers and place the findings on a matrix, as shown in Figure 14.1. Within the matrix, rank each item as better or worse than your own plan, and then note any good ideas or new possibilities that this exercise might yield.

	Equipment	Location	Staff competence and attitudes	Layout
Center A				
Center B				
Center C				
Our center				

FIGURE 14.1
Comparison Matrix

Setting Goals and Establishing a Time Line

Once the external review is complete, other important steps must be taken in a start-up plan: (1) developing a time line to chart beginning and ending dates for various tasks; (2) developing measurable goals and subgoals; (3) establishing an action plan; (4) making allowances for obstacles; and (5) providing for review and resetting of goals. Most centers, in planning for the 12 months before opening day, will have a time line developed by a committee. The time line for the 12 to 24 months prior to opening day, which in this case was spent getting university approvals, would vary with the parent organization and with zoning and other regulations that must be met.

◊ ◊ ◊ ◊ ◊ ◊ ◊ ◊ ◊ ◊ ◊ ◊ ◊ ◊ ◊ ◊ ◊ ◊ ◊ ◊

INCOME ISSUES

Much of a center's success in staying "in the black" will depend on how well the organization sets tuition fees and develops the plan for income. If the cost per child is figured so low that the margin of income does not even cover expenses, the center will not be able to build up a surplus for future growth or to cover emergencies. If the cost per child is set too high, in all likelihood the enrollment will fail to meet the income projections. It is hoped that before the center opens, the tuition and other sources of income will have been decided upon, so that the average cost per child that the center expects to maintain will be clear, with adjustments for inflation as needed.

Does the center expect to provide deluxe child care, good-quality child care, or the best possible low-budget child care? Determining which goal the center should aim for will help to decide the best possible location for the center, and will pinpoint which corporate personnel offices should receive information, or where flyers and fact sheets should be distributed. It will also determine, to some extent, the quality of services to be offered, within approved accreditation ranges. Additional programs offering a foreign language or a Saturday computer camp may not be desirable for a low-budget program, but may be very appropriate for a deluxe service program. Ideas for this type of program planning are discussed in chapter 5 on creativity and problem-solving.

Additional income from federal, state, or local grants should be planned at this point, keeping in mind the basic rule: "Don't put all your eggs in one basket." In other words, do not rely on only one grant or even a few grants. Grants need to be renewed, and they do get cancelled, so having several funding sources is always wise. A section on proposal writing is included in this chapter to help your center apply for grants. Another useful tactic is sending proposals to corporations suggesting educational partnerships. If a center is to be housed within a corporation, the outline introduced later in this chapter gives a thorough format to present to decision-makers in the corporation.

After establishing a tuition and income policy that is synchronized with the program's philosophy and overall developmental goals, the director must look at the amount of income and the number of enrollees needed to cover expenses and to build a surplus. If the center has been operating for a year or longer, decision-makers can analyze past records and find out the percentage of income needed for operating expenses and the resulting net surplus. This surplus should be in addition to the amount needed to pay off loans taken to start the center. Surplus funds are necessary for unexpected price increases in supplies and materials, for adding classrooms or teachers, for increasing the hours of operation, or for building more centers.

If the center has just opened, decision-makers will have to estimate the costs and income carefully. A good rule of thumb is to figure the number of enrollees at 10 to 15 percent less than the maximum possible. This underestimating will allow for a surplus in income in good times, and will provide coverage in case of a sudden drop in enrollment. Costs for administration, bookkeeping, tax services, and publicity costs (that is, all of the overhead) should already have been figured into the cost per child on a percentage basis. This planning will enable the director to know how many available child-care slots must be filled for the program to maintain a surplus or contingency fund balance.

Not all child-care slots need to have the overhead percentage attached to them, however. A sliding scale is possible if some slots have a higher percentage and some a lower percentage for overhead. If the income is figured too low, though, the resulting additional children may cost more than the center can support. If this occurs and the center does not have substantial outside grants, raising other center prices should be considered. Decision-makers should keep in mind the overall "mark-up" for tuition and the above-cost percentage needed to pay for overhead and to build a surplus, in addition to knowing about tuition costs of competing centers.

◇ ◇

PURCHASING

While it may not seem that child-care programs need to purchase a great deal, since they are a service provider, some purchasing is necessary to keep a center operating for long hours. Keeping a well-stocked supply of equipment, food, and classroom supplies, as well as keeping up with maintenance services such as housekeeping, depend on a buying schedule. This necessitates careful research into *who* and *where* the best vendors are, including how prices and benefits compare.

When to buy deserves attention, as well. Are there preschool and child-care buying cooperatives in the area, or should the center start one in the next five years? Normally, it is better to avoid speculative buying because it interferes with the normal operations of the center's business. (In other words, don't stock up on green paper unless the amount needed for the year is clear!) Speculative buying can lead to losses and storage problems. As soon as enough time has passed to judge, the center can determine how much of a certain material is necessary by checking the center's records. Obviously, it is important not to overbuy, but it is just as important not to underbuy. If the center does not buy enough food or supplies, these items will not be there when they are needed. To help with these problems of estimating, some records for inventory control are needed. The goal is to keep the inventory in balance—neither too large or too small. There should be a proper proportion and variety both of supplies and food.

While some organizations keep a dollar control system showing the amount of money invested in each category, a unit control record-keeping system is more appropriate for child-care programs. The unit control system tells how much of each item is in the inventory, from whom the items were bought, when orders were placed and when reorders must be made, how much the items cost (receipts), and when the items will be used. These records guide the center in determining what, from whom, when, and how much to buy. A computer spreadsheet software program greatly facilitates this type of record-keeping.

◇ ◇

RECORD-KEEPING

Center failures can often be attributed to inadequate records. Every director needs to be able to foresee impending disaster in time to take corrective action; to develop this kind of foresight, it is important to have records that show trends and highlight possible problems. By keeping up-to-date records, the director can avoid problems that make it difficult to see in advance the direction in which a center might be headed. It may require extra work to keep adequate records, but this work will be well worth the effort and expense to any center. Many record-keeping tasks can be delegated to an administrative assistant.

When developing a record-keeping system, it is very important to keep records to substantiate the following:

1. Returns filed under federal and state tax laws, including income tax and social security laws;

2. Requests for credit from equipment manufacturers or for bank loans; and

3. Claims about the center, should it become necessary to transfer ownership.

In addition to these records, and perhaps most important, are records that plan for, and outline the distribution of, surplus funds allocated for growth and improvement.

With an adequate yet simple record-keeping system, questions such as the following can be answered:

1. How much are the income and expenses?
2. What are the expenses? Which expenses appear to be too high?
3. What is the center's gross surplus margin? The net surplus?
4. How much are we collecting on our delayed billings (if any)?
5. What is the condition of the working capital?
6. How much cash is on hand and in the bank?
7. How much is owed suppliers?
8. What is the net worth of the center; that is, what is the value of the center when liabilities are subtracted from assets?
9. What are the trends in receipts, expenses, surplus, and net worth?
10. Is the center's financial position improving or growing worse?
11. How do the assets compare with debts owed? What is the percentage of return on the original investment (also called ROI)?
12. How many cents out of each dollar of income are net surplus? (Metcalfe, 1973)

By preparing and studying balance sheets and profit-and-loss statements, and by detailing this information and keeping it in an orderly fashion, these and other questions can be answered. The following is a list of records grouped according to their use. Not every center will need every record; perhaps only a few records will be necessary for a particular center. However, these lists may call attention to some records that can be used to great advantage. When deciding which records to use, one should first answer the questions: How will this record be used? How important is the information kept likely to be? Is the information available elsewhere in an equally accessible form?

Inventory and Purchasing Records (These records provide facts to help with buying and selling.)

Inventory control record

Item/unit perpetual inventory record

Out-of-stock sheet

Open-to-buy record

Purchase order file

Supplier file

Accounts payable ledger

Income Records (These records reveal facts to determine income trends.)

Record of monthly/weekly tuition receipts

Summary of monthly/weekly tuition receipts (also quarterly summary and half-year summary)

Promotion plan and plan for dissemination of center information and publicity (to increase income)

Cash Records (These records show what is happening to cash.)

Daily cash reconciliation (tuition receipts and other income)

Cash receipts journal

Cash disbursements journal

Bank reconciliation

Accounts Receivable Records (These records keep track of who owes the center and whether payments are made on time.)

Accounts receivable ledger

Accounts receivable aging list

Employees' Records (These records maintain information legally required and are helpful in the efficient management of personnel.)

Record of employee earnings and amounts withheld

Employees's withholding exemption certificate (Form W-4)

Record of hours worked

Record of expense allowance

Employment applications

Record of changes in rate of pay

Record of reasons for termination of employment

Record of employee benefits

Job descriptions

Crucial incidents records

Fixtures and Property Records (These keep facts needed for taking depreciation allowances and for insurance coverage and claims.)

Equipment records

Insurance register

Bookkeeping Records (These records, in addition to some of those listed previously, are needed if you use a double-entry bookkeeping system.)

General journal

General ledger

For efficient operation, a center needs information from records to observe trends and for tax purposes. Furthermore, centers should use records to plan. With a well-thought-out plan as a guide, chances for success are strengthened. A budget is a record that shows the finances of such a plan. Planning a budget helps to determine just how much increase in surplus is reasonably within reach. The budget will answer such questions as: What income will be needed to achieve the desired surplus? What fixed expenses will be necessary to support this income? What variable expenses will be incurred? A good budget enables administrators to set goals and then determine what steps to take to reach those goals.

Periodically, administrators should compare budget projections with actual operations. Using contingency planning and responsiveness planning (described in chapter 3) at least quarterly or every six months is also a good idea. With effective records, one can do these comparisons. Then, when discrepancies appear, corrective action may be taken before it is too late. Choosing the right corrective action will depend upon knowledge of management techniques in buying, setting tuition, selecting and training personnel, and handling other management problems as described throughout this text. In addition, the Budget Priorities Worksheet in Figure 14.2 can be a useful staff workshop/orientation tool, or a mid-spring yearly planning tool, to help integrate good ideas with goal development.

◇ ◇

PROPOSALS TO HELP YOUR CENTER GROW

Since presenting proposals for many reasons (funding, grants, support) is frequently asked of nonprofit and service organizations, it is hoped that this section will serve as a useful outline. A positive attitude and careful attention to detail are two key ingredients for successful proposal writing.

A well-written proposal describing an idea that will help one's center improve and/or serve more children can be written by following a few guidelines. The first step is to write a letter introducing the idea. Check your idea(s) against the following questions:

• Does your idea fit within your organization's mission?
• Does your idea address elements of need in your community?

FIGURE 14.2
Budget Priorities Worksheet

Please list all items you would like to see in the budget next fiscal year. This is not a guarantee it will come to pass, but it will help us to give priorities to certain items. Try to give an estimated dollar amount. Thank you.

Item	Price

- Can you document this need?
- Does your program have a specific population that will receive this service? Can you incorporate user-planning?
- Does your idea meet the needs of those funding the program?
- Does your idea support future center development and long-range plans?

As a first submission, most groups or foundations usually want a two- to four-page letter introducing an idea. This letter should cover all the areas of concern that will be addressed at greater length in a later, longer version of the proposal. Other funding sources may require a brief summary as well as the complete proposal or application at the time of submission.

For either document, at a minimum, the following main points must be covered:

1. Why the project should be undertaken. (Why should this organization be awarded funds?)
2. How you will carry out the project's implementation. (What steps will it entail? How will these steps be organized?)
3. How the project will be managed. (What is the staffing? What are the qualifications of staff members? How will they be managed? How will the time line be followed to ensure all intended activities take place?)

4. How the project fits into what the organization is already doing. (What are the institutional qualifications for doing it? How will other on-going program activities make for a better project result by serving as (no-cost) resources? This is another way of underscoring the question in number 1.)

In addition to these topics, the budget must be considered. This item must be treated separately because of the many different situations of grantees and grantors. Suffice it to say that it should indeed be included and should match the other items in the document in proportion. For example, in a three-page proposal, a half-page of budget information should be sufficient to give the reader the general categories of expenditure envisioned, the total amount involved, and some sense of whether the estimates seem reasonable. A longer proposal will require substantially more detail. Some of the steps and the differences between public and private funding source sequences can be seen in Figure 14.3, "Funding Sequences."

Why Should the Project Be Undertaken?

Regardless of how much administrators know about a potential funding source's interest areas—whether through explicit statements in application guidelines or other means—it is important to lay some general groundwork for establishing the value of the proposed work. This first section of a proposal also serves to introduce the organization making the proposal. By showing an awareness of the context in which it operates, the organization lets the funding source assess its credibility and also, therefore, the credibility of the project.

FIGURE 14.3
Funding Sequences

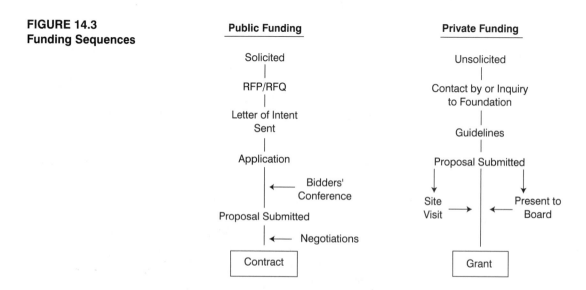

This section of the proposal is often called "Understanding the Problem." This implies that an understanding of the problem or need must be reached, and that this understanding must be mutual. After establishing an understanding of the problem, this section then should include a description of the situation that the proposed project will address. This section might also be titled "Background Statement" or even "Introduction."

At this point, the proposal might include statistics on the number of children in the city and other relevant facts that in concert establish the need for continued provision of the services offered (such as mentioning recent cutbacks in local public programs). If the project proposed involves any improvements in the way services are presently provided, note here the problems that exist, and how the project would resolve them.

To show what the organization's role has been in services to date, it is necessary to describe the organization somewhat in this section. This is the first opportunity to show the reader how important the organization's services have been and thus how important it is that they continue and expand. Note that this is different from the *description* of the organization, which comes later.

In concluding this section, the most effective way to lead the reader into the next section, which describes the project, is to bring together the problem described and the organization's ability to address it now. In other words, describe why this organization should be funded to carry out this particular program; let the reader know that this organization can do the job better than anyone else, whatever that job may be. The point to get across, although this language may be too strong, is: "And thus it is clear that our organization is ideally situated to address this pressing need." The final sentence in this section should lead the eager reader into the proposal: "The following section describes exactly how we will carry out this important project."

Description of the Project: How the Project Will Be Carried Out

This section establishes in the reader's mind whether or not the applicant *should* be allowed to carry out this project. In other words, is the planning sound? Does the project really address the need identified earlier? Has the project been thought through step by step, and described in enough detail to make it clear that the applicant already has some idea of how to cope with problems, should they arise?

Writing this section of the proposal is actually an organization's chance to do this planning. While the idea of the project should be clear before writing, the opportunity presented here to think through the details allows the writer to make it clear to the reader that the applicant can manage the project, and that the project makes sense. This goal is accomplished by the following components:

1. an introductory section that briefly states what the project is, and, if appropriate, describes the theory behind the project;

2. the nuts-and-bolts section (i.e., the rest of this section of the proposal), which shows how this organization will *do* the project; and

3. the descriptions of the elements of the project that are left for more terse presentation in the management plan, which will be discussed in the following section.

There are two basic ways to present how you will *do* the project, and they can be used separately or together. Both require a presentation of some sort of time line for the project—how long the project is expected to last, what important steps happen at what points in the time line, when results (such as reports) can be expected, and so forth. (Some summary of this time line should go in the introduction to this section as well.) The two presentation techniques are (1) by task or activity (or month), and (2) by job or function (e.g., staff positions). Which technique is used depends on the nature of the project. If an organization is seeking funds for ongoing operations, with no major events occurring during the proposed time period, a description of staff activities might best describe the project. It is important that the work be quantified in this section, however—the number of children served by each staff member per month, the number of homes visited, the number of meals served—whatever the project concerns. This permits the reader to get a "feel" for the project and its impact relative to the size of the problem.

The other technique for describing activities is basically chronological—what will happen first, what will happen next, and so forth. This method of description is useful when there are activities that cannot begin until earlier project steps have been completed, such as selecting teaching/testing materials, seeking enrollments through community outreach, and so forth. Planning in this manner is invaluable to the applicant because it helps him or her foresee potential problems if things do not get done in time for other things to start. Using this foresight, it becomes possible to develop approaches around these problems, and to adjust the project plan at this stage or to modify one's thinking so that these problems will never arise (or if they do, to be prepared for them).

Because this element alone does more than any other part of a proposal to convince the reader that an organization knows what it is talking about and will spend the funding group's money wisely, even if the "function" method of describing the project is chosen, the applicant should give examples of possible situations that may arise, or demonstrate how the different staff functions will interrelate. For example, illustrate how outreach and health workers will visit the same families at the same time, or how meetings and parent-home visits will occur in a certain sequence. If the proposed project is designed to continue an ongoing service but on an expanded scale, the proposal writer probably should choose the chronological approach of presentation to demonstrate how each new element required will be put in place before services are needed, such as preparing food, expanding space, hiring aides, buying materials, and upgrading record-keeping. Expanding an established center might include adding more slots, hiring senior citizens or teenagers as aides, adding slots for handicapped children, adding a component of the Head Start program in a geographic area previously unserved, or opening a second center across town.

Building the reader's confidence in the applicant's planning ability aids the successful reception of the proposal. It also underscores the applicant organization's value in furthering the funding organization's own objectives. The organization can show its suitability for carrying out the proposed project by noting in this section past projects that have been executed by the applicant organization and by mentioning related activities that demonstrate similar management requirements as those now being proposed. By providing such examples, the applicant is saying to the reader, "We will do this well because we have a record of doing such things well, and we will continue to do so in the future, with or without your funding." This confident attitude tells the reader that this is an organization of merit and stability (Cavenaugh, 1993).

A useful approach to assemble the "building blocks" of your proposal can be seen in Figure 14.4. As the proposal develops in your mind, jot down notes in each square. Then, when you begin to write the actual proposal, go back and double check your notes to be sure you have included all the elements of a good project description.

Management Plan

Those who award grants need to have some sense of how a potential recipient is going to spend the money it is given. One way this information can be presented, which reinforces both the plans for project activities and the detailed budget, is in the form of a discussion of management controls. While this need not include pages of detailed charts and graphs, it should contain at least the following:

1. A section on staffing, which includes an organizational chart for the project, a brief statement explaining how the project fits into the larger organization administratively, and, for each staff position, a description of the duties of the position. For professional staff, enclose a description of the person you plan to hire to fill each position. Résumés should also be included, appended to the end of this section.

2. A project time line (if appropriate). A chart similar to the one shown in Figure 14.5 might be helpful. In this chart, months are listed across the top and activities are listed down the side. Horizontal lines of appropriate length are used to indicate when each activity occurs and how long it is expected to last.

Understand the Problem	Brainstorm Solutions	Select Solutions	Describe Expected Results and/or Benefits	→
				→

	Steps/Tasks to Achieve Solutions	Resources Needed: People Time/Non-Personnel Money	Review and Reassess Solutions	→
			Modify as needed	→

	Review and Reassess Results and Benefits	Outcome Measures	Five Years from Now: Next Steps	Interaction with Present Programs
		(What changes will take place: what will have to happen to whom as a result of each component*		

FIGURE 14.4
Proposal Worksheet
*Use numbers and statistics where possible. Tell what indicators of change you will use.

3. A second section on staffing that describes when different staff positions begin and end, if these time frames are different from the start and end of the project period. Also indicate which positions are part-time and which are full-time. This staffing section also can be shown in chart form, with months across the top, positions down the side, and horizontal lines depicting the active periods of each position. This type of visual planning can help in arranging short-term services, such as the hiring of testing consultants, and, when used with the earlier project activities time line, can give a better idea of which months will be your busiest. (At this point, for example, you can begin by saying, "Oh, that falls too close to the Christmas holidays; let's change it." Other

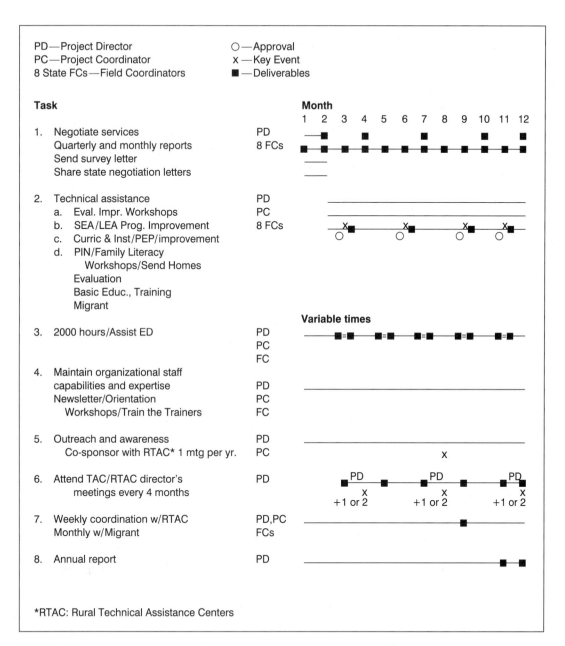

FIGURE 14.5
Project Time Line Example

conflicts and time pressures become apparent when using this tool to consider how the project fits in with the outside world.)

Institutional Qualifications and Competency

The last section of a proposal presents a fuller description of the applicant's organization, and is less specifically oriented to the particular project being proposed than is any other section. This section might be similar in a number of proposals. Here the applicant might:

1. give a brief history of the organization, citing its growth in the number of services provided since it was formed;
2. mention significant qualifications of staff members other than those who will be working on the proposed project directly, pointing out their value as resources to the project;
3. describe other areas of work the organization is involved in, whether related to the proposed project or not; and
4. list some specific past projects, including, where appropriate, the funding agencies and the names and phone numbers of contact people within those agencies who documented the work. Depending on your organization's size and scope, this could be a lengthy list; while it need not be exhaustive, it should provide several different references that can be contacted—three to eight independent sources connected to an organization's more recent projects is sufficient.

◇ ◇

SUMMARY

If a funding application covers all four areas discussed in this chapter, a potential supporter will gain a good idea of what an organization is, what it wants to do, why the project should be done, and how the organization proposes to do it. And you will have a good evaluation of where your center is and where it is headed in an applied sort of way. Doing several proposals leads to evaluating your center in several ways. Answering the questions in the proposal guide for your center as it exists at present is a useful evaluation exercise to do alone or with the staff. After a proposal has been compressed into a three-page letter, along with the all-important budget, close with, "We await your early reply and are eager to begin this important project. Thank you for your consideration." The proposal format given in this chapter, including the materials listed and in the appropriate sequence, almost ends on this note automatically, with or without the final reminder.

In planning to prepare an application for funding, allow enough time (working backward from the due date to the time you *should* start and the time you *must* start) to cover all of the points described in this chapter. Very few funding applications are successful, and most of those rejected are done so because they lack completeness. There is no reason for this, especially considering that in choosing to prepare such an application, you must take time away from other duties and responsibilities. To justify the time spent preparing the proposal, it should therefore at least be complete.

To keep all of these proposal sections in mind, remembering that one is competing for money against other organizations and so should persuasively argue one's case, use the following outline:

I. Understanding the Problem

We know all about this.

II. Description of the Project

We will do this project exactly like successful ones should be done, only better, because we know so much about the problem. (See Section I.)

III. Management Plan

We'll plan; we'll manage.

IV. Institutional Qualifications

We have been doing this for years. (See Section I.)

Of these reminder comments, only the one under Section III should be taken tongue in cheek. It might say "we'll get by," and foundations and agencies certainly do not want to fund organizations that take a casual view of management. Consider this comment instead as a reminder that there *must* be planning and management control evident in and discussed in your application.

The process of making group decisions involving one's staff and parents, and of then writing down the ideas and illustrating them with a time line (preferably also in a group situation), is a useful planning device even if no funding source is involved. The budget and record-keeping sections at the beginning of this chapter further facilitate this planning. Many of the ideas provided in the scenario section in chapter 3 will generate income on their own. However, if there are national, state, or community funding sources that might be interested in the project or in part of it, add Steps I and IV from the previous outline to develop a more complete proposal. The following Proposal Development Guide is offered as a further aid. Both sets of guidelines, the one above and the one to follow, were developed by persons who have separately been awarded several million dollars for their organizations in early childhood, education, and human services fields.

This guide has been prepared to assist in preparing technically valid, fundable proposals.

Answer all questions that apply to the program.

Include all supportive and illustrative materials available.

Anyone who reads the proposal should clearly understand the program purpose, the plan to operate, what the objectives are, and what will occur on a day-to-day basis.

A. *TITLE*
Name of the program.

B. *SPONSOR*
1. Name of the sponsoring agency, organization, or group.
2. Name and title of responsible person.
3. Brief outline of sponsor's background as to type of agency, organization, or group; include any activities sponsor may now participate in or programs currently operated by sponsor.

C. *BACKGROUND AND OVERVIEW* (including needs assessment)
Support the request for funds for the program being applied for.

D. *CHARACTERISTICS OF POPULATION TO BE SERVED*
1. Who is this program expected to reach?
2. Outline eligibility requirements (if any).
3. How many persons will be served during the first year of operation?

E. *PROGRAM MISSION* (Purpose)
What is the purpose of the program?

F. *STATEMENT OF THE PROBLEM*
Why is the program needed? Be sure to state specific problems involved.

G. *PROGRAM OBJECTIVES* (Planned activities to fulfill mission)
What are the specific objectives of the program? (What is it you are trying to do?)

H. *LOCATION* (include map)
1. What are the geographical boundaries of the total area to be served?
2. Indicate the census tracts.
3. Indicate on a map prospective site(s) where program is expected to operate (include addresses when possible).

I. *PROGRAM OPERATION*
Describe in detail how the program will operate. The following questions will assist you.

How will the program operate?

How is the operation related to the objectives of the program?

How will the program work in relation to staff members?

How will the program work for the population to be served?

How will the program work in relation to the other activities, if any, of the sponsor?

J. *RESIDENT PARTICIPATION*
1. What part do residents play in the operation of your present organization? Parents? Parent-Residents?
2. What part did residents have in developing the plans for this program?
3. Describe other ways in which local residents will be involved (subcommittees, local corporations, etc.).

K. *ADMINISTRATION*
1. How is this program administered?
   Briefly describe the staff structure and the role of the policy-making and advisory boards involved in running the program.
2. How will the program be connected to other community programs operated in the same neighborhood(s)?
3. Include two organizational charts, each of which clearly illustrates the supervisory relationships (1) of the staff and (2) of the policy-making and advisory boards.

L. *PERSONNEL*
1. List each staff position and furnish a detailed job description for each job title (include non-professionals, aides, volunteers, etc.). Be as specific and complete as possible.
   Follow this outline:
   a. Job title:
   b. Reports to:
   c. Supervises:
   d. Duties and responsibilities
   e. She/he would work closely with:
   f. Qualifications necessary for the job:
2. Volunteers—Give the following information:
   a. Title of staff persons who will be assigned to supervise volunteers. (This responsibility should be included in the position description for this person.)
   b. Title of staff person who is assigned responsibility for the administrative collecting and reporting of volunteer time. (This responsibility should be included in the position description for this person.)

      c.   Approximate number of volunteers and volunteer hours planned, per month, for this program.

      d.   What responsibilities and duties, and in what components of your program, will volunteers be assigned?

      e.   How do volunteer activities implement your program operation and objectives?

3.   Guidelines for training:

In preparing proposals for programs to be funded, you should be aware that most proposal readers, in reviewing requests for funding, will consider whether an adequate program of staff training will be conducted during the grant period.

Therefore, include in proposals a brief outline of plans for an in-service training program. This training program should be designed to:

a.   improve the ability of staff to relate; and

b.   increase the technical skills needed by staff to work at maximum capacity.

As part of the process of developing an in-service training program, an in-service training committee should be established. This committee should be broadly representative of staff, including both professional and non-professional employees.

In the proposal, training plans for the following three groups should be discussed separately:

a.   Office and clerical workers;

b.   Non-professional employees; and

c.   Professional staff.

Please indicate also the resources on which you plan to rely for training (e.g., your own professional staff, consultants).

Training plans that comprise only routine supervision or weekly staff meetings will not be acceptable. Training time need not necessarily be extended evenly throughout the grant period. If desirable, it may be concentrated within a relatively short period, e.g., daily for several weeks. College courses and requirements for taking them can be listed in this section.

M. *BUDGET*

Use the worksheet in Appendix D (p. 474) in preparing the budget for this program. Special things to look for are the following:

1.   In "Personnel," *fringe benefits* should be computed. Breakdown percentages of fringe components (FICA, health insurance, etc.).

2.   In "Travel," local travel should be based on actual *need*; any out-of-town travel must be justified in a budgetary footnote.

3. In "Space costs and rentals," write in the actual cost and actual square footage wherever possible.
4. In "Consumable supplies:"
    a. *Office supplies*—budget on a per person, per annum formula based on actual cost.
    b. Postage.
    c. *Publications*—to be kept to an absolute minimum.
    d. *Non-federal share* (for federal funding)—The amount of non-federal share to support the proposed program must be at least 20% of the total program cost. This 20% may be in the form of cash (to pay for some specific budget item, e.g., personnel, equipment, consultant services, etc.), or use of volunteers, donations of free use of space, equipment, etc. All non-federal share items must be itemized in the budget and become a part of the total program costs.
5. In "Equipment," determination on the basis of anticipated need:
    a. determine what equipment is owned;
    b. determine what equipment is rented, the monthly rental, and the feasibility of purchasing; and
    c. estimate the cost of servicing machines.
6. In "Other costs:"
    a. *Telephone:* Cost should be estimated on a per person formula based on actual cost experience.

N. *EVALUATION*
    1. How will this program be evaluated?
    2. Who will conduct the evaluation?
    3. What type of information will be gathered?
    4. How do you expect program evaluation to affect program operation?

O. *PLANS FOR NEXT YEAR* (usually used for refunding)
    1. What modifications will be made in the present programming and operation?
    2. What new methods, approaches, or components will be added to help achieve program objectives?
    3. What old methods, approaches, or components will be discontinued? Why?
    4. What staff changes, if any, will be needed because of program change or modification? (Fowler, 1982)

◇ ◇

SUGGESTED CLASS ACTIVITIES AND DISCUSSIONS

1. *Compare budgets vs. curriculum needs.*   In small groups, students can gather three to four budgets from centers in the surrounding area. In addition, the small groups of students can illustrate these centers' programs with pictures, slides or videos of the child-care program and the classroom. Show the pictures in class and discuss impacts on the program that differences in the budget could possibly make. One report might compare the percentage of the total budget spent on supplies and materials in the different centers. This ranged from 3% to 10% with 7% to 7.5% as an average spent on materials in one review by students. Often centers will disclose one line item or percentage of the total for items such as materials or outdoor equipment while not disclosing the entire budget.

Another report, for example, might use pictures of the dramatic play corner and the books in several centers and compare them with information about budgets for these areas.

2. *Budgeting for different seasons.*   Students can construct budgets for the same center in summer and in winter, and for the after school program. Do a cost per child analysis and see if each program pays for itself.

3. *Schedule and staffing exercise.*   Students can schedule the following employees for a center of 50 children and cost out their salaries for each hour of the day. The center has:

13 three-year olds; with a required ratio of 8 to 1

13 four-year olds; with a required ratio of 10 to 1

24 five-year olds; with a required ratio of 15 to 1

The staff includes:

3 Teachers; 4 Aides full-time; 1 Nurse; 1 Cook and 1 Assistant Cook; 1 Custodian; 1 Director; and 1 Administrative Assistant.

Develop a matrix with the hours of the day down one side and the staff members across the top to analyze the cost per hour. There are also volunteer parents, teenagers and grandparents involved in the program. This can be done as a group exercise or as individual assignments. A later activity might be to write a job description for all or some of the staff described in this activity.

4. *Classroom observations and budgeting.*   Students can do classroom equipment observations in nearby child-care centers and then analyze how a low budget, a medium budget and a high budget might affect these particular classrooms. Is there adequate storage? Are there areas for quiet, semi-quiet and noisy activities? Are there any multi-level areas? Is it attractive and "child-friendly?" What would a higher budget add? Generate more questions in

a large group and then divide into small groups that discuss observations and the questions generated, and report back.

5. *Budgeting and the job of the director.*   The class can brainstorm inexpensive helps that can save the center money in a role play: first as a group of parents; then as a staff group; and third as a group of volunteers. Or, the class can be divided into three groups, with one group taking each role and reporting back to the class. Ideas generated can include helps that group members could make or do including everything from saving grocery coupons and comparing prices, to making homemade toys with inspiration from catalogs or books. (E.g., a lotto game can be made from two copies of the same children's toy catalog, covering the pieces with clear plastic contact paper or laminated. Other "puzzles" can be homemade, and thrown away when worn out. See Parent Papers "Toys to Make" in Appendix B for more ideas.)

◇ ◇

BIBLIOGRAPHY

Assistance with child care expenses. (1990, May). *Employees Benefit Plan Review*, pp. 21–22.

Auerback, J. D. (1988). *In the business of child care.* New York: Praeger.

Ballenger, J., & Franklin, G. M. (1991). Perceptions of rural small business owners and managers toward child care assistance. *Proceedings, Small Business Institute Directors Association*, pp. 148–153.

Berney, K. (1988, May). Child care by consortium. *Nation's Business*, p. 23.

Bredekamp, S. (Ed.). (1987). *Developmentally appropriate practice in early childhood programs serving children from birth through age 8.* Washington, DC: National Association for the Education of Young Children.

Bryce, H. J. (1987). *Financial and strategic management for nonprofit organizations.* Upper Saddle River, NJ: Prentice Hall.

Cavenaugh, D. N. (1993). *Personal interview.* Washington, DC: National Association of Community Health Centers.

Cherry, C., Harkness, B., & Kuzma, K. (1987). *Nursery school & day care center management guide.* Belmont, CA: Fearon Teacher Aids (a division of David S. Lake Publishers).

Clay, J. M. (1989, September). The child care issue: Benefits required by a changing workforce. *Employee Benefits Journal*, pp. 32–34.

Coley, S. M., & Scheinberg, C. A. (1990). *Proposal Writing.* Newbury Park, CA: Sage.

Conrad, D. L. (1980). *The quick proposal workbook.* San Francisco: Public Management Institute.

Early childhood teacher education: Traditions and trends. (1988). *Young Children, 44*(1), 53–57.

Fowler, A. (1982). *How to write a proposal.* Speech given at the Administering Day Care and Preschool Seminar, July 14, 1982, Trinity College, Washington, DC.

Galinsky, E. (1989). The staffing crisis. *Young Children, 44*(2), 1–4.

Galinsky, E., & Friedman, D. (1986). *Investing in quality child care: A report to AT&T.* Basking Ridge, NJ: AT&T.

Gotts, E. E. (1988). The right to quality child care. *Childhood Education, 64*, 268–275.

Hall, M. (1988). *Getting funded: A complete guide to proposal writing* (3rd ed.). Portland, OR: Continuing Education Publications.

Highlights from Council on Foundations Convention. (1988). *The grantsmanship center whole nonprofit catalog*. Los Angeles, CA: Grantsmanship Center.

Hildebrand, V. (1984). *Management of child development centers*. New York: Macmillan.

Huth, S. A. (1989, September). Corporations provide variety of child care options. *Employee Benefit Plan Review*, pp. 49–51.

Kiritz, N. J. (1980). *Program planning and proposal writing*. Los Angeles: Grantsmanship Center.

Lauffer, A. (1984). *Grantsmanship and fundraising*. Beverly Hills, CA: Sage.

Leavitt, R. L., & Krause-Eheart, B. (1985). Maintaining quality and cost effectiveness through staffing patterns. *Child Care Information Exchange, 45*, 31–35.

Lefferts, R. (1982). *Getting a grant in the 1980s* (2nd ed.). Upper Saddle River, NJ: Prentice Hall.

Levin, R. (1989, January). Child care: Inching up the corporate agenda. *Management Review*, pp. 49–51.

Metcalfe, W. O. (1973). Starting and managing a small business. In *Starting and managing series* (Vol. I). Washington, DC: U.S. Small Business Administration.

Morgan, G. G. (1987). *The national state of child care regulations*. Watertown, MA: Work Family Directions.

Morgan, G. G. (1982). *Managing the day care dollars: A financial handbook*. Cambridge, MA: Steam Press

Morris, L. L., & Fitz-Gibbon, C. T. (1978). *How to design a program evaluation*. Beverly Hills, CA: Sage.

Morris, L. L., & Fitz-Gibbon, C. T. (1978). *How to measure program implementation*. Beverly Hills, CA: Sage.

National Association of State Boards of Education. (1988). *Right from the start: The report of the NASBE task force on early childhood education*. Alexandria, VA: Author.

Need for child care. (1988, August). *Supervision*, pp. 10–11.

Overman, S. (1990, August). Plant workers, families find not all time created equal. *HR Magazine*, p. 38.

Overman, S. (1990, August). Wizards program work-family solutions. *HR Magazine*, pp. 40–41.

Overman, S. (1990, August). Workers, families cope with retail's irregular schedules. *HR Magazine*, p. 44.

Pecora, P. J., & Austin, M. J. (1987). *Managing human services personnel*. Newbury Park, CA: Sage.

Peters, T. J., & Waterman, R. H. (1982). *In search of excellence*. New York: Harper & Row.

Ritter, A. (1990, March). Dependent care proves profitable. *Personnel*, pp. 12–16.

Schaefer, M. (1987). *Implementing change in service programs*. Newbury Park, CA: Sage.

Schweinhart, L. J., Koshel, J. J., & Bridgman, A. (1987). Policy options for preschool program. *Phi Delta Kappan, 68*, 534–530.

Snow, C. (1983, November). *As the twig is bent: A review of research on the consequences of day care with implications for caregiving*. Paper presented at the Annual Conference of the National Association for the Education of Young Children, Atlanta, GA.

Townsend, T. H. (1974) Criteria grantors use in assessing proposals. *Foundation news*, 15(2), 33–38.

Travis, N., & Perreault, J. (1981). *Day care financial management: Considerations in starting a for-profit or not-for-profit program*. Atlanta, GA: Child Care Support Center.

Tringo, J. (1982). Learning from failure: Resubmitting your rejected proposal. *Grants Magazine*, 5(1), 18–22.

Vinter, R. D., & Kish, R. K. (1984). *Budgeting for non-profit organizations*. Atlanta, GA: Georgia State University.

Wacht, R. F. (1984). *Financial management in non-profit organizations*. Atlanta, GA: Georgia State University.

York, R. O. (1982). *Human service planning*. Chapel Hill, NC: University of North Carolina Press.

Home Learning Enablers

These 10 to 15 week supplies of activities are ideal for building parent involvement. All activities utilize common household items if any materials are needed. These Home Learning Enablers will help parents learn, with a minimum of effort, new ways of talking to and interacting with their children. In addition, parents can learn these skills with little guidance from teachers. The activities are specific, sequenced from less difficult to more difficult, and related to the curriculum—three factors found to be of top importance in maintaining the gains early childhood programs work so hard to achieve. The activities can be sent home with children and feedback sheets can be returned to the center in the same way. Teachers then can review returned feedback sheets to see which areas of learning might need further emphasis, and to review parents' comments.

Parent Involvement

In a review of 28 studies, it was found that, in order to *maintain* the gains young children made in early childhood programs, parent involvement was a necessity. It was also found that if parents were given specific, curriculum-related activities in a sequence, these gains were maintained the most effectively. The following Home Learning Enabler (HLE) activities will help you provide just such a service to your parents (and your children), and also will help to ensure that the efforts made at your center to really help children will have a lasting effect.

The following five features were evident in the 28 programs that showed immediate and lasting gains for children due to parent involvement:

1. The importance of the teacher-to-parent instruction phase in building trust.
2. The curricular emphasis in materials used for home teaching.
3. The ratio of parent to teacher for instruction in home teaching activities (one-to-one was best).
4. The structure (or sequence) of the home teaching activities, from easier to harder, was found to be of top importance for the most stable gains.
5. The specificity or detail and definition of the home teaching activities.

The Home Learning Enabler series involves numbers two, four, and five of these features that help guarantee lasting effectiveness. Building trust in one-to-one situations also occurs in most good centers.

We are particularly proud of the Home Learning Enablers Set I; in a recent study of 127 three-year-old children (60 treatment children and 67 control children), the Home Learning Enablers were linked to significant IQ increases for those children who used them compared to those who did not, at the 95 percent confidence level. Our research showed gains of 1 to 36 IQ points for children using Home Learning Enablers Set I. The Stanford-Binet IQ test was given to all of the 127 children before and after the 14-week period, during which time the treatment children received the HLE activities. We found that children's IQ scores increased even if the parents did only a few of the activities. We are projecting similar gains for children who use HLE Set II, which is meant for four- and five-year-olds, and similar but less dramatic gains for children in kindergarten, first, and second grades. These activities can be used as "send-homes" in school-age child-care programs, as well as by schools.

The Home Learning Enablers are an attempt to encourage home learning by providing instructional materials in the homes of children to prepare them for later school achievement. This goal is an outgrowth of studies done by Levenstein (1975), which suggested that if mothers were given an attractive, relatively simple tool to help their children learn, these mothers in turn assumed some responsibility for their preschool children's verbal growth.[1] A relatively inexpensive form of encouraging parents' interaction with their own children is sending home, weekly, one-page Home Learning Enabler activities that suggest brief, enjoyable parent-child interactions in the home. Learning then occurs in the reciprocal process between parent and child, which is the heart of this program.

There is obviously a need for bridging the gap between the formalized learning that occurs in educational program settings and the informal learning opportunities that parents can take advantage of at home. If educators need instructional materials, it is reasonable to assume that parents need materials too. Additionally, there seems to be a need to encourage more parent-child interaction and verbal communication. Thus, the home learning activities described in this appendix are designed to encourage verbal responses between parent and child.

Home Learning Enablers: Set I

After Home Learning Enabler activities were developed, they were tested weekly by parents and their children who were enrolled in federally funded day-care centers in Maryland. As a result, the parents became actively involved with their children, and returned feedback sheets even in centers that previously did not have a strong parent involvement program. The following is a copy of one of the feedback sheets received from a parent. It is designed so that parents can tear off the form along the perforation and return it to their child's teacher.

- -

For: ___*Kimberly Peters*___
(Child's Name)

1. Did you or someone else do the activity with the child?   Yes _____ No _____

   If yes,

2. How many times did you do the activity?   Once ___   More than once _2_

3. How much time did the activity take?   - - - - - ✓ - - - - - - -
                                           0   15 mins.   More than 30 mins.

4. Did you enjoy this activity with your child?   Yes _✓_ No _____

5. Do you feel your child understood it?   Yes _✓_ No _____

6. Do you feel your child needs more help in this area?   Yes _____ No _✓_

7. Please share any adaptation you may have of this activity, or describe a new activity. (Write on the back, if necessary.)
   Thanks for cooperating!

___*Julia A. Griffith*___   ___*Mrs. Hall*___
Signature   Teacher's Name

Kim especially enjoyed the game.
Especially when played to the tune
of the "Mulberry Bush."

As mentioned before, the activities in HLE Set I are appropriate for children who are older two-year-olds or young three-year-olds through age four and a half. Set II is developed for young four-year-olds through age five and a half. This appendix includes a complete set of activities for children in preschool through second grade. Feedback sheets similar to the one shown should be included on the back of every activity sent home. (See p. 000 for a blank copy.)

The step-by-step Home Learning Enablers are unique in that they utilize household objects as systematic instructional materials. This has proven to be an easy, inexpensive mechanism for involving parents.

A distinct sequence is followed in each activity. First, the *name* of the activity gives the parent a hint as to the content, and is usually colloquial if at all possible. The *"Reason"* section tells the objective or purpose of the activity and provides a line or two of explanation about what the activity teaches. An attempt is made here to be as specific as possible without using educational jargon, long words, or long sentences. Activities have been purposefully written at an eighth-grade reading level.

The *"What You Need"* section lists needed materials. These lists are meant to suggest items that are simple, inexpensive, and already available in the home. Another unique feature of these Enablers is the *"Time Needed"* section, in which the time requirement is always shown clearly; beginning activities, especially, are kept short, about 3 to 10 minutes each. Parents are tired after a day's work, and two-, three-, four-, five-, six-, and seven-year-olds have short attention spans. The activities have been timed, so they are as close in approximation to the times listed as possible.

The *"What To Do"* section gives a simple step-by-step approach to the activity. An effort is made to be brief and clear in this section. The *"Did It Work?"* section provides the parent with some evaluation information by describing observable signs of the success of the Enabler activity. Finally, the *"Easier and Harder Ideas"* section provides ways to adapt the activity by making fairly minor changes. An easier adaptation for younger children is provided in number 1, and a harder adaptation for older or more able children is given in number 2. These ideas also encourage parents and children to creatively adapt Enabler activities and then share these suggestions with the teacher.

Sending Home HLEs

Classroom teachers should send home an HLE with every child each week, along with a cover letter/feedback sheet, perhaps using a safety pin to fasten the activity to the child's clothing. The parents will have seven days to do the activity with their children, one or more times, before returning the feedback sheet and receiving another activity. Participation each week, as well as the degree of participation, is entirely voluntary on the part of parents.

Return of the Feedback Sheets

Children will return the tear-off feedback sheet to their classroom teacher. If the original copy is lost, parents can complete another copy of the feedback sheet either at home or in the classroom. Teachers then review the feedback sheets to see which areas of learning might need further emphasis. Centers that have used the Enablers have found that many parents take pride in checking the blank stating that their child does NOT need more help in that particular area. Parents also respond with other interesting and useful written comments that build the communication link between parent and teacher.

Bibliography

Levenstein, P. (1975). *The mother-child home program.* New York: Carnegie Corp.

HOME LEARNING ENABLER (#1)

◇ ◇ ◇ ◇ ◇ ◇ ◇ ◇ ◇ ◇ ◇ ◇ ◇ ◇ ◇ ◇ ◇ ◇ ◇ ◇

My Homework

Reason

To help your child understand that many things can be red

What You Need

Anything red in your home or outside

"red!"

Time Needed

3 to 5 minutes anytime

What To Do

1. Talk about 3 or 4 things that are red: a toothbrush, a stop sign, a plastic toy, a book, etc.
2. Ask your child to point out things that are red. Tell the child that this is his or her "red" homework.
3. Do this for several days until the child can always correctly tell you what is red. Then go on to "green" homework.

Age of Child

2, 3, 4

Did It Work?

Can your child name things that are red, even if they are quite different, for example, a bowl and a chair? If not, repeat "red" homework.

Easier and Harder Ideas

1. Go on to do other colors, but always do just one color at a time.
2. Ask your child to point out the color red in storybook pictures or magazines. Have your child look for red in the American flag, in other flags, or in cars or trucks.
3. Give your child a red object to keep.

◇ ◇ ◇ ◇ ◇ ◇ ◇ ◇ ◇ ◇ ◇ ◇ ◇ ◇ ◇ ◇ ◇ ◇ ◇ ◇

Stacking Cans

Reason

To help your child develop eye-hand coordination

What You Need

2 groups of 3 matching cans: soup cans, tuna fish cans, soda cans, or any cans that are not too heavy

Time Needed

3 to 5 minutes

What to Do

1. Put all the cans in front of the child.
2. Build a bridge with three of the cans. Then say, "Look, I made a bridge."
3. Ask your child to make a bridge. If you have more sets of cans, the child can make towers on top of the bridge if desired.
4. Make bridges out of other matching items, such as throw pillows, cereal boxes, pudding boxes, or empty milk cartons.

Age of Child

2, 3, 4

Did It Work?

Does the bridge hold up or fall down?

Easier and Harder Ideas

1. Make a set of blocks for your child from empty milk cartons that have been washed out. Stuff them with crumpled newspaper and tape the pointed ends down flat. Perhaps a brother or sister might help by doing a few each week. Keep the blocks in a box or a paper bag.
2. Let your child glue grocery boxes together for a permanent "bridge," and then run cars or have dolls walk over it.

HOME LEARNING ENABLER (#3)

◊ ◊ ◊ ◊ ◊ ◊ ◊ ◊ ◊ ◊ ◊ ◊ ◊ ◊ ◊ ◊ ◊ ◊ ◊ ◊

Wiggle Your Nose

Reason

To help children learn the names of parts of the body

What You Need

None

Time Needed

A few moments any time during any day.

What to Do

1. Choose a part of the body: hand, arm, leg. Tell the child the name and touch child's hand, arm, or leg.
2. Ask him to wiggle his hand or whatever part is selected.
3. Repeat this with other parts of the body: nose, finger, ear, elbow, knee. Use fingers to wiggle nose or ears back and forth.
4. Let child tell you a part to wiggle.

Age of Child

2, 3

Did It Work?

Can child wiggle a part of the body without you touching it first? Can child tell you body parts to wiggle?

Easier and Harder Ideas

1. Make up a song for this activity. To the tune of "Mulberry Bush," or any other tune, sing:

   "Mommy says wiggle your foot

   wiggle your foot

   wiggle your foot

   Mommy says wiggle your foot

   Now can (child's name) do it?"

2. Do some of these in the car.

◇ ◇ ◇ ◇ ◇ ◇ ◇ ◇ ◇ ◇ ◇ ◇ ◇ ◇ ◇ ◇ ◇ ◇ ◇ ◇

Flower Power

Reason

To help children use words to describe things they see and smell

What You Need

Flowers in a garden, a supermarket, or a floral shop

Time Needed

5 minutes

What to Do

1. Ask your child to choose a flower to smell.
2. Ask her to put her nose close to the flower, close her eyes, and smell the flower.
3. Ask your child to tell you what it smells like. (Like Grandma? Like perfume? Is there no smell?)
4. Ask your child to compare the smells of two different flowers. Talk about the colors of the flowers. Are any yellow? Red? etc.
5. Talk to your child about why people give flowers to each other: To show love and caring, to celebrate special events, etc.

Age of Child

3, 4

Did It Work?

Can your child use more and more words to tell you about flower smells or other smells?

Easier and Harder Ideas

1. Help your child gather a bunch of real flowers to give to a friend, neighbor, or relative. (Dandelions are fine.) Let her draw a flower picture for the gift if no flowers are available. Flower pictures from magazines could also be used. Paste them on cardboard or paper.
2. Help your child decorate cookies to look like flowers. Smell things in the kitchen and talk about what the smells remind you of. Does mustard remind you of hot dogs and picnics?

◇ ◇

Outdoor Fun Bag

Reason

To help your child learn by using the senses to touch and feel and talk about nature items found outdoors

What You Need

Paper lunch bags or grocery bags

Time Needed

5 to 10 minutes

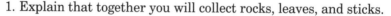

What to Do

1. Explain that together you will collect rocks, leaves, and sticks.
2. Go for a walk and fill the bags. Talk about the trees from which leaves have fallen.
3. Talk about other things you see outside. Does an airplane fly over? Do you hear a truck? Talk about these and other things you see and hear.

Age of Child

3, 4, 5

Did It Work?

Could the child tell you the names of leaves, sticks, and rocks (that is, call a leaf a "leaf," a stick a "stick," and a rock a "rock")?

Easier and Harder Ideas

1. Did you see any animals on your walk? Talk about them.
2. Go for another walk and look for different nature items: acorns, smooth rocks, weeds.
3. Make a collage by gluing the nature items on a piece of paper. Give it as a gift to someone special.

◇ ◇ ◇ ◇ ◇ ◇ ◇ ◇ ◇ ◇ ◇ ◇ ◇ ◇ ◇ ◇ ◇ ◇ ◇

Jump, Hop, Skip

Reason

To help your child listen more carefully

What You Need

Nothing

Time Needed

3 to 5 minutes

What to Do

1. Tell your child you are going to play a game. Ask him to listen carefully while you (or another child) hop on one foot, then jump on two feet.

2. Ask him to close his eyes. Then you (or the other child) hop or jump a second time. Ask him to tell you if he heard hopping or jumping.

3. Ask him to hop and jump while you have your eyes closed. Tell him what he is doing.

4. Add a skip for a third sound for him to name.

5. Ask him to close his eyes while you make other sounds for him to describe. Then reverse roles and let him do this for you.

Age of Child

3, 4

Did It Work?

Can your child tell you correctly what motion you are making?

Easier and Harder Ideas

1. While driving in the car, ask your child to close his eyes. Then tap on the steering wheel. Ask him to guess what you did. Tell him the words for noises he can't describe. At home, tap a spoon on a glass or plate to play the same game.

2. Jump or clap several times and have your child tell you the number of times you jumped or clapped. Or, jump or hop to demonstrate an addition problem for him to solve (for example, 2 + 2). Let him do one for you.

◇ ◇ ◇ ◇ ◇ ◇ ◇ ◇ ◇ ◇ ◇ ◇ ◇ ◇ ◇ ◇ ◇ ◇ ◇

Circle Time

Reason

To help children recognize the basic shapes of a circle or square

What You Need

2 grocery bags, crayon or marker

Time Needed

5 to 10 minutes

What to Do

1. Lay out the grocery bags. Draw a circle on one of them.
2. Ask your child to draw a circle on her grocery bag. Ask the child to draw more circles.
3. Talk about which circles are big and which are small.
4. Talk about other things in the room that are in the shape of circles, such as plates, glasses, or cans.
5. Draw a square on your bag. Ask her to draw a square too. Use a new bag, or turn over the circle bag if needed.
6. Talk about other squares, such as a table, a box, or a piece of paper. Which squares are big? Which are small?

Age of Child

3

Did It Work?

Can the child make a mark that looks anything like a circle? A square? Can she identify and talk about objects that are these shapes?

Easier and Harder Ideas

1. Buy crackers shaped like circles, squares, and triangles. Let the child spread peanut butter, jam, or butter on them. Play a matching game with the shapes to make sandwiches. Use cut-up bread if crackers are not available.
2. Cut shapes out of paper and ask your child to match them. Start with circles and squares. Then add triangles and rectangles.

◇ ◇ ◇ ◇ ◇ ◇ ◇ ◇ ◇ ◇ ◇ ◇ ◇ ◇ ◇ ◇ ◇ ◇ ◇

Learning from Water

Reason

To help your child learn math words and phrases such as *how much, too much, half full, part full, needs more,* and *full*

What You Need

Tub of bath water or kitchen sink with 2 or 3 inches of water in it; 5 or 10 plastic cups, bottles, and measuring cups

Time Needed

5 or 10 minutes

What to Do

1. Gather plastic cups, bottles, measuring cups, and a plastic pitcher if you have one.
2. Ask your child to pour water from one cup into another until the second cup is *full*.
3. If water spills out of the container, explain that it was *too much* water. If he fills it *part full* or *half full*, tell him that.
4. Ask your child *how much* water is in another cup. Then ask if it *needs more* to be *full*.
5. Do these steps as many times as your child wants to.

Age of Child

2, 3

Did It Work?

Can your child tell you when a cup is *full*? When there is *too much*?

Easier and Harder Ideas

1. Ask your child to tell you which bottles are large and which bottles are small.
2. Using measuring cups, ask your child how many ¼ cups it takes to fill 1 cup. (With spilling, it may take more than 4, but the process is still fun.) How many ½ cups to fill 1 cup?

◇ ◇

"Put Away" Words

Reason

To help your child match words with objects

What You Need

Bag of grocery items

Time Needed

3 to 5 minutes

What to Do

1. Tell your child that together you are going to put the groceries away while using words to tell about the items.
2. Describe an item to your child; for example, "find a can with red on it," or "find a big box of soap." Ask your child to bring the item to you *while* describing it; for example, "this is a can of chicken soup," or "this soap is for washing clothes."
3. Repeat the activity for other items.
4. Ask your child to group together items that look alike. Then identify the grouped items for your child: "Oh, I see you have two cans of beans."

Age of Child

3

Did It Work?

Can your child tell you the names of more grocery items than before?

Easier and Harder Ideas

1. Let your child tell you items to put away.
2. At mealtime, talk about the foods that are being served. Talk about who likes them, and whether you use a fork or spoon to eat them.

◊ ◊.◊ ◊

Laundry Lotto

Reason

To help your child notice when things are alike or different

What You Need

Laundry that needs sorting

Time Needed

5 or 10 minutes

What to Do

1. Explain how to match two laundry items such as two towels.
2. Let your child match other laundry items, such as tee shirts, handkerchiefs, underwear, or socks.
3. Ask your child to match some laundry items by color.
4. Ask your child to make a separate pile of clothes for each member of the family.

Age of Child

3

Did It Work?

Can your child match some laundry items correctly?

Easier and Harder Ideas

1. Arrange sets of objects such as two forks and a spoon or table knife; two plates and a cup; or two sticks and a rock. Talk about which things are alike and which are different in each set. Ask your child to hand you the item that is different.
2. Let your child sort and match some nickels, pennies, and dimes. Buttons can also be used—let your child sort buttons according to their different colors.

◇ ◇

Stairs and Chairs

Reason

To help your child learn the meanings of some new words and to help your child learn to follow and give directions

What You Need

Some stairs, either indoors or out; a chair; an object, such as a rock or a stick or toy, to place on the stairs or on the chair

Time Needed

5 to 10 minutes

What to Do

1. Ask your child to go *up* the stairs.
2. Ask your child to go *down* the stairs.
3. Ask your child to walk *across* one stair.
4. Ask your child to stand *in front of* the stairs.
5. Ask your child to place an object *on top of* a stair.
6. Now use the chair and ask your child to sit *on* the chair and then get *under* the chair. Next, ask your child to put an object *in back of* the chair and then walk *around* the chair.

Age of Child

2, 3

Did It Work?

Can your child follow the directions at least part of the time?

Easier and Harder Ideas

1. Trade places with your child and let him direct you.
2. Ask an older child to count the stairs. When the child can do that, give him more difficult directions, such as "go up four steps and come back down two"; "go up one step, walk across it, and then go up three more"; etc. Place a small reward on the stairs.

HOME LEARNING ENABLER (#12)

◇ ◇ ◇ ◇ ◇ ◇ ◇ ◇ ◇ ◇ ◇ ◇ ◇ ◇ ◇ ◇ ◇ ◇ ◇ ◇

The Three Bears

Reason

To help your child learn new words; to help her tell a story; to help her enjoy doing things with an adult

What You Need

Any story book that repeats certain words, such as "Goldilocks and the Three Bears," "The Three Little Pigs," "The Three Billy Goats Gruff," or others

Time Needed

5 or 10 minutes

What to Do

1. Read one of the stories to your child. Stop before the most familiar lines and let the child say the words with you: "Someone's been eating my porridge!" "Who's been sleeping in my bed?"
2. Say the words in different tones of voice. For example, use a deep voice for the father, a squeaky and high voice for the baby. Let your child say the words in the same voice that you use.
3. Stop more frequently while reading the story. As you stop, let your child repeat the line with you.
4. When your child learns the words, let her say them alone.

Age of Child

3, 4, 5

Did It Work?

Does your child ask you to read the stories over and over? Can she say some of the words with you?

Easier and Harder Ideas

1. Read other books with your child. Always have your child "help" with the reading. Ask him or her to make up a new ending.

2. Talk about the pictures with a young child. Don't worry if you only cover about two or three pages.

3. Let your child put together his or her own book. Glue pictures (either magazine pictures or ones your child has drawn) on paper. Punch holes along the side and use wire twists from bread bags to hold the pages together. Make a cover.

◇ ◇ ◇ ◇ ◇ ◇ ◇ ◇ ◇ ◇ ◇ ◇ ◇ ◇ ◇ ◇ ◇ ◇ ◇ ◇

With or Without Mittens

Reason

To help your child learn to describe how things feel; to help your child learn about texture

What You Need

A pair of your child's mittens; some objects to feel such as a marble, a quarter, a cookie, a magazine, and a chair

Time Needed

3 to 5 minutes anytime

What to Do

1. Ask your child to put on his mittens and then touch different objects. Ask him to describe how these things feel. For instance, he might describe them as "lumpy," "flat," or "warm."

2. Then have him take off the mittens and describe how the same items feel. For example, he may say, "Lumpy in some places, smooth in others."

3. Set out five different items at a time. Put on your gloves or mittens and let your child ask you to describe how some items feel.

4. This activity can be done anywhere; in the car is especially good. Have your child feel the seat, the window handle, etc.

Age of Child

3, 4

Did It Work?

Does your child use more words to describe the items when he is not wearing his mittens? Does he use more and more words the longer you play the game?

Easier and Harder Ideas

1. Using several pairs of mittens or gloves, play a matching game.
2. Ask your child to tell you what he can do with his mittens on and his mittens off.
3. Display several pairs of mittens. Ask your child to tell you what is alike about them and what is different about them.

◇ ◇ ◇ ◇ ◇ ◇ ◇ ◇ ◇ ◇ ◇ ◇ ◇ ◇ ◇ ◇ ◇ ◇ ◇

Pick a Toy

Reason

To help your child learn names for objects

What You Need

Bag of small toys, or other small items found in the home

Time Needed

5 minutes

What to Do

1. Pick an item out of the bag and name it.
2. Ask your child to name the object. If she can name it, allow her to keep it; if not, have her return it to the "picking bag."

Age of Child

2, 3, 4

Did It Work?

Can your child name all the items? When she can, start a new "picking bag" that contains different items.

Easier and Harder Ideas

1. Use magazine pictures for this activity too. The pictures last longer when glued to cardboard. Pictures of animals are very good for this activity.
2. Cut into two or four pieces a picture that has been glued to cardboard so that it becomes a puzzle. Keep the picture-puzzles in an envelope.

◇ ◇ ◇ ◇ ◇ ◇ ◇ ◇ ◇ ◇ ◇ ◇ ◇ ◇ ◇ ◇ ◇ ◇ ◇ ◇

Shape Hunt

Reason

To build an awareness of shapes. To develop classification skills.

Materials Needed

None.

Time Needed

5–10 minutes

What to Do

1. Talk with your child about shapes such as circles, squares, rectangles, and triangles.
2. Have a "shape hunt" inside and see how many shapes your child can find. Start with one shape only, such as a circle or a square on a table.
3. Have a "shape hunt" outside. Learn words for new shapes such as oval or hexagon for stop sign.
4. Find shapes in letters on signs outside. Look for these while riding in the car.
5. Look for shapes in storybook pictures.

Age of Child

3, 4, 5

Did It Work?

Can your child identify some shapes correctly?

Easier and Harder Ideas

1. A younger child can stay with the first four shapes. Look for them in food at mealtimes.
2. An older child can learn harder shapes, such as trapezoid, pentagon, parallelogram.

Computer Idea

If you have a computer with drawing software, draw some of the shapes and print them out.

HOME LEARNING ENABLER (#1)

◇ ◇

New Titles for Stories

Reason

To help your child use a few key words to tell about things

What You Need

Nothing

Time Needed

3 to 5 minutes

What to Do

1. Tell or read a familiar nursery story to your child. Ask him what another good title might be for this story.

2. Show your child a picture that seems to tell a story.

3. Ask your child:
   - What is happening?
   - What happened before this in the story?
   - What will happen next?
   - What sounds will the people and the animals make?
   - How do you think this story will end?

Age of Child

4, 5

Did It Work?

Does your child think up new titles for other stories? Can he tell you new endings for stories? Can he make sounds for the stories?

Easier and Harder Ideas

1. Let your child have fun with names. Ask: "What's a good name for some-one who is always happy? What's a good name for a baby who cries a lot?"

2. Take turns telling a story that you start. Next, have your child add a sentence; then you add a sentence, and so forth, until you both like the ending.

◇ ◇ ◇ ◇ ◇ ◇ ◇ ◇ ◇ ◇ ◇ ◇ ◇ ◇ ◇ ◇ ◇ ◇ ◇ ◇

My Grocery List

Reason

To help your child observe carefully and to match pictures and objects

What You Need

A piece of cardboard, magazine pictures of grocery items, scissors, glue

Time Needed

10 minutes to prepare the list, plus the time needed to complete a regular shopping trip

What to Do

1. Talk with your child about the things you plan to buy at the grocery store.
2. Look through magazines or grocery store flyers for pictures of four or five of these items. For example, find pictures of your particular brand of soup, cereal, and soda.
3. Together with your child, cut out these pictures and ask her to glue them onto a piece of cardboard.
4. Tell her, "This is your grocery list." When you get to the store, let her find those items and place them in the cart. The list can be used every week if these are items you buy regularly.

Age of Child

2, 3, 4, 5

Did It Work?

Did your child select the correct items pictured on his or her "grocery list"? Did your child enjoy the shopping trip more?

Easier and Harder Ideas

1. For a young child, start with only two or three items that you glue onto the cardboard.

2. For an older child, print the name of each item, and perhaps the price, under each picture. An older child can work with eight or nine items and then work up to a separate list made for different categories of food. For example, one list might be for fruits and vegetables: lettuce, carrots, potatoes, and apples. Another category might be dairy products: milk, eggs, cheese, and margarine.

◇ ◇

Math Notes

Reason

To help your child recognize numbers; to help your child know "how many" for each number

What You Need

Small scraps of paper, pencil

Time Needed

3 minutes

What to Do

1. Tell your child you will play a game together. Write a number on a piece of paper and have him jump or step that many times.

2. Write the number *2* on a piece of paper and hand it to your child. Ask him to step forward *2* times.

3. Write the number *3* on another piece of paper and hand it to your child. Ask him to step backward *3* times. Write the number *1* on another piece of paper and ask your child to jump *1* time.

4. Stick to the numbers your child knows for sure. Move up to the numbers *4* and *5* after the first week. This activity is ideal to fill time while waiting for appointments.

Age of Child

3, 4, 5

Did It Work?

Can your child step or hop the correct number of times? Is the game enjoyable for your child?

Easier and Harder Ideas

1. Ask your child to bounce a ball _____ number of times.

2. Use a ball to bounce an addition problem for him: Bounce the ball two times, pause, then bounce the ball one time. Ask your child how many times the ball was bounced.

3. Trade places and let your child bounce an addition problem for you to solve.

◇ ◇ ◇ ◇ ◇ ◇ ◇ ◇ ◇ ◇ ◇ ◇ ◇ ◇ ◇ ◇ ◇ ◇ ◇ ◇

Whip It Up

Reason

To help your child learn some basic math concepts; to help your child develop eye-hand coordination

What You Need

Egg beater, instant pudding, milk

Time Needed

10 minutes

What to Do

1. Pour the milk into a bowl according to the directions on the box. Tell your child you are measuring 2 cups of milk (or whatever amount the directions call for). Add the pudding to the milk in the bowl. Start beating.
2. Have your child do most of the beating.
3. When the pudding has been beaten one minute, help your child pour it into bowls. Talk about the concepts of *half full*, *not too full*, *needs more*, and *too full*.
4. After the pudding sets (about 5 minutes), let your child eat some and enjoy her efforts.

Age of Child

2, 3, 4

Did It Work?

Could your child work the egg beater? Is your child beginning to recognize the meanings of the words *full, half full,* etc.? Would your child like to make pudding again?

Easier and Harder Ideas

1. Let your child use a baked frozen pie shell and make a pie using the pudding. Talk about the different amount of milk that is needed to make the

pie filling (if this amount is different from the regular pudding recipe). Encourage the whole family to praise the completed pie.

2. Let your child play with a mechanical egg beater (not electric!) in the bathtub or in a sink filled with soap suds. Have her wear a plastic apron at the sink, or perhaps a trash bag tied at her waist. Your child may also want to use pudding as finger paint. Vanilla pudding makes yummy paint and is less messy than chocolate.

◇ ◇

My House

Reason

To help your child learn to group and organize items, a skill needed in reading

What You Need

Grocery bags; magazines, catalogs, or the magazine section of newspapers; scissors; glue; marker or crayon

Time Needed

15 minutes

What to Do

1. Cut open a grocery bag to make a large sheet of paper.
2. Ask your child what room in the house he would like to choose furniture for.
3. Write the name of the room on the bag.
4. Let the child find pictures of furniture to go in the room. For example, a sofa for the living room, a stove for the kitchen, or a bed for the bedroom.
5. Help your child cut out the magazine pictures and glue them onto the flattened bag.
6. Do other rooms on other days.

Age of Child

4

Did It Work?

Can your child find at least four items for each room? Can he find them in magazines, name them, and put them in the correct room?

Easier and Harder Ideas

1. With your child, glue pictures of rooms on separate grocery bags and label the bags with the name of the room. Ask your child to place pictures of furniture that belong in each of these rooms in the correct bag. When there is time, cut open the bags and glue down the pictures as in the original activity.

2. Make labels for the furniture in one or more of the rooms in your home. Let your child place the labels on the floor in front of the corresponding pieces of furniture.

◇ ◇ ◇ ◇ ◇ ◇ ◇ ◇ ◇ ◇ ◇ ◇ ◇ ◇ ◇ ◇ ◇ ◇ ◇ ◇

Why Do You Like _____?

Reason

To give your child the chance to present his or her own reasons and thinking; to help your child understand that there are reasons for events

What You Need

Nothing

Time Needed

5 minutes

What to Do

1. Ask your child why she likes a certain story. Sometimes you may have to help by saying, for example, "Because Goldilocks ate pancakes?" The child will often say, "Oh, no," and then tell her own reasons.
2. Ask your child why she likes her favorite color. Why does she like her favorite toy?
3. Ask your child what she likes about school and about home. Ask how she would change things if she could.

Age of Child

4

Did It Work?

Can your child give more and more reasons why he or she likes something? Does your child enjoy this activity and smile while doing it? Does she ask other children for reasons?

Easier and Harder Ideas

1. Ask your child why she should do something and why she should not do something. Make it into a game and call it "Yes, I should/No, I shouldn't." For example, let her tell you why she should or should not be allowed to watch certain TV shows.
2. Ask your child why she should or should not go to bed at a certain hour.
3. Try not to disagree with your child; instead, listen to see if she understands two sides to an issue. Ask why she should or should not eat nutritious meals. Together, think up more topics to discuss.

◇ ◇

My Telephone Book

Reason

To help your child practice letter and number recognition; to help your child learn to read numbers in left-to-right order

What You Need

A piece of cardboard, crayon or magic marker

Time Needed

4 minutes

What to Do

1. Ask your child the names of friends and important people she would like to have in the "telephone book."
2. Have him dictate the names of his friends to you while you print them on cardboard. Print the names in letters about one inch tall.
3. Print the telephone number by each person's name. Add parents' work phone numbers, the phone numbers of grandparents and neighbors, and the numbers of the fire department and police station.
4. Keep the cardboard "telephone book" by the phone. Add any other needed numbers. Include the child's own name and number.
5. If your child asks, "What shall I do next?", suggest that she call a friend and invite him to come and play. (That's why friends come first on the list.)

Age of Child

4, 5, 6

Did It Work?

Can your child make a phone call using the numbers on his or her list?

Easier and Harder Ideas

1. Keep a list of two or three friends and one emergency number for a younger child. Or, take pictures of friends and family and paste the pictures on the cardboard next to their phone numbers. This helps the child match the right number with the right person.

2. Help an older child write the names and numbers on the card himself. Use two pieces of cardboard if he prints with large letters.

◇ ◇ ◇ ◇ ◇ ◇ ◇ ◇ ◇ ◇ ◇ ◇ ◇ ◇ ◇ ◇ ◇ ◇ ◇

Comparing

Reason

To help your child learn how things are alike and how they are different; this is a needed skill in both language and math

What You Need

Old magazines

Time Needed

3 to 5 minutes at any time

What to Do

1. Cut out magazine pictures of the following items to compare. Each day, ask your child to compare one of these sets and discuss the differences.
   - a bird and an airplane
   - a sunny day and a rainy day
   - a slipper and a boat
   - something made of wood and something made of glass
2. Ask your child to compare the character of Father Bear in "Goldilocks and the Three Bears" with another bear in another story.
3. Ask your child to compare your work with your spouse's work. Then let her ask you how they are alike and how they are different.
4. Ask your child to compare clothes hung in a warm place with clothes hung in a cooler place.

Age of Child

4

Did It Work?

How many ways does your child compare things? Does the number increase?

Easier and Harder Ideas

1. Put a dish of water in the freezer compartment of your refrigerator. Ask your child to compare this with a dish of water from the tap.

2. Ask your child to compare cooked food with the same food uncooked. Try an egg, a dessert, apples, carrots, or hamburger.

◇ ◇ ◇ ◇ ◇ ◇ ◇ ◇ ◇ ◇ ◇ ◇ ◇ ◇ ◇ ◇ ◇ ◇ ◇ ◇

Play Store

Reason

To help your child learn about money and simple addition

What You Need

Four different items from your kitchen cupboard such as a cereal box, a pudding box, and 2 cans; 20 pennies

Time Needed

5 to 10 minutes

What to Do

1. Play store with your child. Place the four grocery items in front of your child.
2. Make a 5¢ price tag for each item.
3. Ask your child to give you the right number of pennies to "buy" an item.
4. Let your child "buy" all four items; have him count the pennies he has left after each "purchase."
5. Let him sell the boxes back to you now.

Age of Child

4, 5, 6

Did It Work?

Can your child count out the right number of pennies? Does he have enough left to buy the last item? Does he enjoy the game?

Easier and Harder Ideas

1. For a younger child, make a 2¢ price tag for each item and give him 8 pennies.
2. Show your child 4 nickels and explain that they are worth the same as the 20 pennies. Have your child "buy" items with the nickels.
3. For an older child, provide more items and use dimes, nickels, and pennies. Keep the prices at 5¢ each until he understands the right coins to use.

◇ ◇

Learning New Words

Reason

To help your child learn new words

What You Need

Two or three old shoe boxes and an assortment of objects: cotton, a spoon, sandpaper, a book, a bell, a whistle, a stone, a marble, a child's block, a key, a piece of crumpled paper

Time Needed

3 to 5 minutes

What to Do

1. Fill each box with some of the objects.
2. Blindfold your child and let her handle the objects. Ask her to tell you what they are or what they feel like. Encourage her to use new words.
3. Ask her what words each object reminds her of. For example, does the spoon remind her of ice cream? Does the whistle remind her of a policeman? Let the child blindfold you and then you tell her what the objects feel like. Try to use words she has not heard before.

Age of Child

3, 4, 5, 6

Did It Work?

Does your child suggest new items to add to the box? Does she gather her own collection? Is your child able to tell you more things that each object reminds her of?

Easier and Harder Ideas

1. Blow the whistle, ring the bell, and rattle the crumpled paper out of sight (perhaps in a paper bag). Let your child tell you what she hears.
2. Assemble a "smell box" with mustard, cinnamon, and some vinegar. Blindfold your child. Ask your child what these smells remind her of.
3. Assemble a "taste box" with salt, pepper, a piece of candy, a piece of cheese, and a piece of cold cereal. Blindfold your child. Ask her about how these things taste.

◇ ◇ ◇ ◇ ◇ ◇ ◇ ◇ ◇ ◇ ◇ ◇ ◇ ◇ ◇ ◇ ◇ ◇ ◇ ◇

What's It Made Of?

Reason

To help your child learn the words for materials that houses and buildings are made from

What You Need

Pictures of houses; copy of the story "The Three Little Pigs" (either your own copy or a copy from the library)

Time Needed

5 or 6 minutes

What to Do

1. Read the story of the three pigs to your child.
2. Talk to him about the materials they used to build their houses. Which material was the sturdiest?
3. Talk to your child about materials used to build real houses. What are windows made of? Doors? Show him pictures of houses.
4. On another day, talk with your child about what materials other things are made of. For example, ask, "What are books made of? Magazines? Cars? This activity can be done while riding in the car. Show your child pictures of the objects or the actual objects when you get home if he does not see one during the trip.

Age of Child

3, 4, 5, 6

Did It Work?

Can the child talk about what things are made of? For example, can he name the materials used to make houses, windows, and books?

Easier and Harder Ideas

1. Ask a younger child to huff and puff with you when the wolf blows the houses down in the story.
2. Ask an older child what things are made of while you are out in the neighborhood. For example, what are sidewalks, buildings, tires, and toys made of?

◇ ◇ ◇ ◇ ◇ ◇ ◇ ◇ ◇ ◇ ◇ ◇ ◇ ◇ ◇ ◇ ◇ ◇ ◇

My Map

Reason

To help your child learn his or her home address

What You Need

A large grocery bag; crayon or magic marker; old picture magazines; scissors; glue, stapler, or tape; photograph of your home, if possible

Time Needed

10 to 15 minutes

What to Do

1. Help your child cut open a grocery bag so that it will lie flat.
2. Ask your child to draw or glue a picture of your home in the center of the grocery paper.
3. Draw your street and have your child watch as you write the name of the street. Help your child print the number of your home. Together, sing your address to the tune of "Twinkle, Twinkle, Little Star." (For example, "1234 Main Street, St. Louis, Missouri.")
4. Draw an "X" on this map to mark the home of your child's best friend or a helpful neighbor.
5. Add another important place and its name each day. For example:
   - your child's school or child-care center
   - the home of the nearest relative
   - the nearest fire or police station

Age of Child

4, 5, 6

Did It Work?

Does your child know her home address?

Easier and Harder Ideas

1. Talk with your child about which place on the map is nearest to your home and which is farthest away. Mark and label those two locations. Make guesses as to how far the distances are between these places and your home (don't worry about exact distances).

2. Use a phone book to discover street names and addresses of places you wish to add to the map. Write this information in big, bold print on the grocery bag. Then have your child draw or paste a picture of these places on the map.

3. Add the nearest library, your favorite supermarket, the nearest drugstore, the neighborhood post office, and the nearest gas station. Staple or tape another flattened grocery bag to the first one if you need more space.

4. Tape the map to the refrigerator, the washing machine, or a window in your home. Let everyone look at it and use it.

◇ ◇

Opposites

Reason

To help increase your child's vocabulary; to help him better understand the idea of opposites

What You Need

Nothing

Time Needed

3 to 5 minutes

What to Do

1. Tell your child that you are going to play a game. Ask him to supply the missing words in what you say.
2. Say, "A father is a man; a mother is a _____." (Accept *girl*, *lady*, and *woman* as correct answers.)
3. Then say:

   "One rock is big; the other rock is _____."

   "A brother is a boy; a sister is a _____."

   "Soup is hot; ice is _____."

4. Stop and discuss any missing word that he supplies incorrectly. Wait to play the game again until tomorrow.

Age of Child

4, 5, 6

Did It Work?

Does the child respond with reasonably correct answers? Progress to having your child ask you some opposites.

Easier and Harder Ideas

1. When talking with a younger child about opposites, place two objects in front of him. For example, use a rock and a piece of cotton and talk about "hard" and "soft." Or use a long stick and a short stick and talk about "long" and "short." Other opposites might be high and low, black and white.

2. Ask an older child to supply some harder opposites:

    "An inch is short; a mile is _____."

    "A rock is hard; a pillow is _____."

◇ ◇ ◇ ◇ ◇ ◇ ◇ ◇ ◇ ◇ ◇ ◇ ◇ ◇ ◇ ◇ ◇ ◇ ◇ ◇

Reading Stop Signs

Reason

To help your child recognize letters and words in the community around her

What You Need

Nothing

Time Needed

3 to 5 minutes

What to Do

1. Take your child on a walk.
2. When you come to a STOP sign, hold your child up and have her trace the letters with her finger.
3. Tell her the name of each letter as she traces it. Then when she's finished tracing, tell her the word is *STOP*.
4. Follow this procedure with other signs that she can reach, perhaps those found in a shopping center.
5. Talk about the color of the signs.

Age of Child

4, 5

Did It Work?

Can your child recognize STOP signs? Praise her for "reading" them to you. Does she take an interest in the letters on other signs?

Easier and Harder Ideas

1. Ask your child to tell you the color of the STOP sign. Find other signs and ask her to identify at least one color on each.
2. Talk about the shapes of street signs; for example, YIELD signs are triangular in shape, and other signs are round or square. Ask your child to tell you the shape of the signs you pass and tell her what they stand for or say.

HOME LEARNING ENABLER (#1)

◇ ◇

Telephone Number Song

Reason

To help your child recognize and match numbers, and to help him learn his phone number

What You Need

Telephone, seven same-sized pieces of paper

Time Needed

10 minutes

What to Do

1. While showing your child the telephone, talk about your phone number. Write out your phone number and use tape to attach it to your phone if the number is not there already.
2. Sing the first part of "Twinkle, Twinkle, Little Star," substituting the numbers of your telephone number for the words of the song. For example: "7 6 2 - 4 1 0 4, now I know my phone number."
3. Write the individual numbers of your phone number on separate pieces of paper. Ask your child to line them up in order to match her phone number.
4. Mix up the pieces of paper and ask your child to line them up again.
5. Let your child mix them up for you to put in order.

Age of Child

4, 5, 6

Did It Work?

Can your child put the numbers in order? Can she sing her phone number?

Easier and Harder Ideas

1. Write the phone numbers of a relative and three friends on a piece of cardboard for your child. She can use this for her "phone book."
2. Sing the alphabet song, substituting the number and street name of your home address. End the song with "now I know my home address."

◇ ◇

Making a Chart

Reason

To help your child remember to do things daily; to match what he does with pictures

What You Need

Crayons or markers, a piece of paper large enough for a chart (8½" X 11" or larger), magazines, scissors, and tape

Time Needed

10 minutes

What to Do

1. Cut out pictures of things you want your child to use every day or of the activities you want him to take responsibility for. For example, find a picture of a toothbrush, soap, and a hairbrush or comb; or, find a picture of clean white teeth, some clean hands and a face, and some nicely combed hair.
2. Draw a chart with 8 spaces across and 5 or 6 spaces down.
3. Paste the cut-out pictures down the left column. Across the top seven spaces, write the days of the week.
4. Each day when your child brushes his teeth, washes his hands, or combs his hair, allow him to make a check mark or place a sticker in the box for that day.

Age of Child

5, 6

Did It Work?

Does your child enjoy marking his achievements on the chart each day? Does it help him remember to wash his hands and face? Brush his teeth? Comb or brush his hair?

Easier and Harder Ideas

1. For a younger child, use a chart with only two lines, perhaps with a picture of a toothbrush and a picture of soap.

2. Add other chores to the chart for an older child. Cut out pictures of silverware for setting the table, a picture of a bed for making her bed, and a picture of a toy box for putting away toys.

◇ ◇

Paper Bag Fun

Reason

To help your child learn the meanings of prepositions (the little words that tell where things are)

What You Need

A large paper grocery bag

Time Needed

10 minutes

What to Do

1. Stand a grocery bag up on the floor. Ask your child to stand *beside* the bag.
2. Ask your child to stand *in front of* the bag. Now direct him to stand *in back of* the bag.
3. Ask your child to walk *around* the bag.
4. Ask him to put the bag *under* a chair. Then have him place the bag *on top of* the chair, then *beside* the chair.
5. Let your child give you directions to follow with the bag.

Age of Child

4, 5, 6

Did It Work?

Can your child follow the directions, at least part of the time?

Easier and Harder Ideas

1. A younger child can, with help, cut open the bag, lay it flat and lie down *upon* it.
2. An older child can cut open the bag to be flat, and use it to draw a map of the neighborhood or at least of her street.

◇ ◇

Rhythm Clapping

Reason

To help your child listen carefully; to provide her with practice in using words about numbers

What You Need

A radio or tape player

Time Needed

5 minutes

What to Do

1. Clap your hands and count in a rhythm, such as 3 fast claps and 2 slow claps.
2. Ask your child to copy you. Do other sequences and clap in lots of different ways, letting your child copy you each time.
3. Turn on the radio or tape player. Clap to the music. Count your claps to the music.
4. Ask your child to clap while you copy her.

Age of Child

4, 5, 6

Did It Work?

Can your child copy you? Can she count, at least up to five?

Easier and Harder Ideas

1. Even a two-year-old enjoys keeping time to music. Have her jump or bounce to the rhythm.
2. Use other sounds to count: tap on the table, cough, snap your fingers. Ask your child to take turns copying you or another child.

◇ ◇ ◇ ◇ ◇ ◇ ◇ ◇ ◇ ◇ ◇ ◇ ◇ ◇ ◇ ◇ ◇ ◇ ◇ ◇

Describing Objects

Reason

To help your child learn to talk about how things feel; to help him learn about texture

What You Need

Shoebox or similar-sized box, key, steel wool, a coin, small sponge, scrap of material, scrunched up paper, a cookie, and other common objects

Time Needed

5 to 10 minutes

What to Do

1. Ask your child to help you put several objects in a box. Talk about how they feel when you put them in. Are they smooth? Rough? Soft? Hard?

2. Close your eyes and ask your child to close his. Ask him to pick up an object and tell you what it is. See if you can guess what it is. Take turns. Eat the cookie as a treat.

3. Do this activity using other objects in the house.

Age of Child

3, 4, 5, 6

Did It Work?

Does your child use more words to describe the items? Does he use more and more words the longer you play the game?

Easier and Harder Ideas

1. Talk about other objects in your home. The floor is hard. The mirror is smooth. Sandpaper or a nail file is rough.

2. Ask an older child to find and name three things that are hard, three things that are smooth, and three things that are soft.

◇ ◇

Alike or Different?

Reason

To help your child notice and talk about likenesses or differences

What You Need

Several sets of three objects each, with two alike and one different in each set; for example, three coffee cups (two alike and one different), three buttons, three coins (two pennies and a nickel) or three socks

Time Needed

5 to 10 minutes

What to Do

1. Place a set of objects in front of your child. Ask him to pick up the two items that are exactly alike.
2. Ask him to tell you one or two ways they are alike.
3. Ask him to tell you one or two ways they are different from the third object.
4. Pick up the third object that is different and tell your child one or two more things about it.
5. Do this with the other sets of objects.

Age of Child

4, 5, 6

Did It Work?

Can your child tell you one or two ways the objects are alike or different?

Easier and Harder Ideas

1. Ask a younger child to help you match pieces of laundry, such as socks, underwear, or shirts.
2. Ask an older child to tell you three or four ways objects are alike or different.

◇ ◇

Number Clips

Reason

To help your child see that a written number stands for an actual number of items

What You Need

Five clothespins or five hairclips, a magic marker, magazines or newspapers, scissors

Time Needed

10 minutes

What to Do

1. Write the numbers one to five on the five clothespins or hairclips. On the back of the pin or clip, draw the number of dots that represent that number.
2. Look through the newspapers and magazines for pictures of groups of items, such as cars, clothes, or food items.
3. Cut out the pictures. Have your child clip each picture with the clip that has the matching number of dots.
4. Turn the clip over so your child can see the matching number.

Age of Child

4, 5, 6

Did It Work?

Can your child clip the correct number of pictured items with the matching number clip, at least part of the time?

Easier and Harder Ideas

1. Ask a younger child to count to five as she touches individual items. Have her count stairs as she climbs, cans as you put away groceries, fruit as you make a salad, or any other household things.
2. Have an older child make clips representing the numbers 1 to 10, then have her match larger groups of items.

◇ ◇ ◇ ◇ ◇ ◇ ◇ ◇ ◇ ◇ ◇ ◇ ◇ ◇ ◇ ◇ ◇ ◇ ◇ ◇

Everyday Shapes

Reason

To help your child recognize shapes; to help him realize that shapes are all around him

What You Need

Paper, pencil or markers

Time Needed

10 minutes

What to Do

1. Draw and talk about different shapes: a square, a circle, a rectangle, and an oval.
2. Talk about the differences between the shapes. Which have corners? Which are smooth?
3. Ask your child to help you look for shapes in your home. For example, point out the squares in the floor tile, the circles in the top and bottom of a lampshade, the oval kitchen spoons, and the rectangles in the windows.

Age of Child

4, 5, 6

Did It Work?

Can your child identify some of the shapes correctly?

Easier and Harder Ideas

1. Look for shapes wherever you go. For example, point out to your child the shapes in lights, road signs, store windows, and gas stations.
2. Cut out several shapes and ask an older child to combine the shapes to make a house, a wagon, a snowman, and other objects.

◇ ◇

Identifying Sounds

Reason

To help your child understand that words begin with sounds and that alphabet letters represent those sounds

What You Need

Shopping bags filled with various items from a recent shopping trip

Time Needed

5 to 10 minutes

What to Do

1. Ask your child to help you put away the items you bought at the store.
2. Have your child pick out an item that starts with a sound she knows; for example, if your child knows the sound of the letter *m*, ask her to find the milk in the grocery bag. Repeat the sound, then ask your child to bring you other *m* items, such as meat or mushroom soup. Draw an *m* on a piece of paper and explain to your child that this letter stands for the sound she hears at the beginning of *milk, meat,* and *mushroom.*
3. Name other purchases. Ask your child to repeat the name and then bring the item to you. Talk about the beginning sound of the item's name, and write that letter on another piece of paper. Give the paper to your child and have her keep a "book" of letters she knows.
4. Take turns putting away purchases by letting your child ask you for items.

Age of Child

5, 6

Did It Work?

Can your child match sounds and letters for one or two letters? Is her "letter book" getting thicker?

Easier and Harder Ideas

1. At mealtime, ask your child to tell you the sounds each food begins with. Say the sound and the letter, and then write it for her.
2. At bedtime, name the furniture in the room and talk about the sounds the names begin with. Name the letter for your child.

◇ ◇

Helping Wash Dishes

Reason

To help your child see that some things sink and some float; to encourage your child to make predictions and then see if he is right

What You Need

Soapy water in the sink or bathtub, apron (plastic if you have it)

Time Needed

5 to 10 minutes

What to Do

1. When you are washing dishes, give your child an apron and ask him to help. If some dishes are plastic, show him how the lighter ones will float.
2. Show him how the heavy things sink.
3. Give him some plastic containers or lids and have him guess which ones will float. Then ask him to test each one to see if it floats.
4. Give him some heavier items such as a metal spoon or a coin. Ask him to guess if it will float or sink, then have him test it to find out.
5. Let him ask you if you think something will float or sink.

Age of Child

4, 5, 6

Did It Work?

Does your child guess correctly that one or two items will float or sink?

Easier and Harder Ideas

1. A younger child can do this in the bathtub with bathtub toys. Add some heavier items that will be "sinkers."
2. An older child can gather up 5 or 10 items he thinks will float or sink and then test them.

HOME LEARNING ENABLER (#1)

◊ ◊ ◊ ◊ ◊ ◊ ◊ ◊ ◊ ◊ ◊ ◊ ◊ ◊ ◊ ◊ ◊ ◊ ◊ ◊

Listening to the Weather

Reason

To help your child notice the weather and build listening skills; to help her keep track of the weather for a week

What You Need

Radio (the car radio is fine), pencil, paper

Time Needed

5 minutes

What to Do

1. Ask your child to listen to the weather forecast with you. Talk about what the forecast means and what clothes she should wear to be prepared for the weather.
2. On a piece of paper, keep track of sunny days, rainy days, hot days, or cold days.
3. Ask your child to keep track of weather announcement changes from day to day. Ask her if she notices whether different weather forecasters predict different weather.

Age of Child

5, 6, 7

Did It Work?

Does your child notice the weather more? Does she choose the right kinds of clothes to wear for the weather?

Easier and Harder Ideas

1. Read the newspaper's weather prediction to your child.
2. Mount an outdoor thermometer outside a window. Read the temperature together, and see if it differs from the temperature predicted for the day.

◇ ◇

Teaching Sorting Skills

Reason

To help your child notice when things are alike or different; to help him classify things

What You Need

Sewing kit, tool box, gadget drawer, or jewelry box

Time Needed

10 minutes

What to Do

1. Ask your child to find all the things that are round in your tool box or jewelry box.
2. Ask your child to find all the long things or all the short things.
3. If you are using sewing supplies, ask him to sort the buttons from largest to smallest.
4. Have your child pick something for you to sort. Have your child choose the categories you must sort the objects into.

Age of Child

5, 6, 7

Did It Work?

Can your child group together correctly things that are similar, such as things that are round? Can he correctly separate things by category?

Easier and Harder Ideas

1. Have a younger child sort buttons by color.
2. Ask an older child to sort things by sounds, perhaps using a toolbox full of objects. For example, what sound does a nail make when it's dropped? Does it sound the same as or different from a screw that is dropped? From a bolt? This builds listening skills.

◇ ◇ ◇ ◇ ◇ ◇ ◇ ◇ ◇ ◇ ◇ ◇ ◇ ◇ ◇ ◇ ◇ ◇ ◇ ◇

Telling a Story

Reason

To help your child learn about sequence, that is, what comes before or after something else

What You Need

Nothing (This is a good activity to do in a car.)

Time Needed

5 minutes

What to Do

1. Begin a story and ask your child to finish it.
2. Ask her to begin a story and then you complete it.
3. Take turns telling parts of a story that you think up together.
4. Write down your child's story or ask a visitor or family member to write it down. These written stories are fun to read later.

Age of Child

5, 6, 7

Did It Work?

Can your child complete a story you start? Does she ask to do the activity again?

Easier and Harder Ideas

1. Ask other family members to take turns telling a story with the two of you. Stories about family history are good subjects for this activity.
2. When reading a story or a picture book to your child, stop and ask your child to guess what happens next.

◇ ◇

Playing Store

Reason

To help your child learn about money; to help him practice adding and subtracting

What You Need

20 pennies, 4 nickels, 2 dimes, 4 objects from the kitchen, slips of paper, and a pencil

Time Needed

10 to 15 minutes

What to Do

1. Talk about the concept of 5 pennies being worth one nickel. Put these coins in front of your child.
2. Talk about 10 pennies being worth a dime. Put these coins in front of your child.
3. Write the words *5 cents* and *10 cents* on separate pieces of paper. Place each piece of paper near its respective number of pennies. Tell your child that the paper shows the value of each set of pennies.
4. Arrange four objects and then place the slips of paper ("price tags") labeled *5 cents* and *10 cents* beside two of the items. Ask your child to buy one of the objects from you by paying for it with either the dime, the nickel, or the correct number of pennies.

Age of Child

5, 6, 7

Did It Work?

Can your child count out the correct coins for his "purchases" at least some of the time?

Easier and Harder Ideas

1. Ask your child to choose four food items and then tell you the price of each. Write, or have your child write, the number on each price tag and then play store.

2. Use price tags totaling less than 20 cents for all four objects. Ask your child to count out the correct change to buy the objects. Provide more coins to your child if necessary. After he buys the items, let him be store-keeper and give you change after you buy the items.

3. Make price tags for several items around your house. In the beginning, use numbers that end in 5 or 10. Ask your child to play store with you to practice number recognition and money values.

4. When your child becomes comfortable playing store, take him to a real store and allow him to pay for his own popsicle or ice cream.

◇ ◇ ◇ ◇ ◇ ◇ ◇ ◇ ◇ ◇ ◇ ◇ ◇ ◇ ◇ ◇ ◇ ◇ ◇ ◇

Magazine Words

Reason

To help your child talk in complete sentences

What You Need

Magazine or newspaper pictures containing sentences on or near them, scissors

Time Needed

10 minutes

What to Do

1. Read a sentence from the magazine picture to your child. Then cover up one word and ask her what word is missing. Cut out the word and give it to her.
2. Follow this same procedure with two or three more sentences that are located near pictures. Keep the pictures and cut-out words together. Tell your child that these pictures and words are "word puzzles."
3. Show your child each picture, then ask her to find the appropriate cut-out words that will complete the picture's corresponding sentence.
4. Talk about the sentences that you read together. Leave off the last word in each sentence and ask your child to complete the sentence. Take turns.

Age of Child

5, 6, 7

Did It Work?

Can your child correctly arrange the cut-out words in the appropriate sentences? Can she finish a sentence you start?

Easier and Harder Ideas

1. Combine the magazine sentences into a story that you and your child make up together. Staple the pictures together for a "book."
2. For an older child, use longer sentences.

◇ ◇

Homemade Poems

Reason

To help your child hear and discriminate between the sounds at the ends of words; to help your child identify ending sounds that match or rhyme

What You Need

Nothing (This is a good activity to do in a car, on a bus, or while waiting in line.)

Time Needed

10 minutes

What to Do

1. Talk about words that rhyme, such as *bake* and *cake*.
2. Tell your child, or have your child tell you, more words that end with the same sound: *take, lake, rake*.
3. Say another word, such as *hall*. Then ask your child to say a word that rhymes with it, such as *wall* or *fall*.
4. Make up a short sentence that contains two or three rhyming words. Say it aloud to your child. Ask him to tell you which words rhyme.
5. Write down some rhyming words and sentences. For example, "For goodness sake, I'm going to rake." Give these to your child and have him make a "poem book."

Age of Child

5, 6, 7

Did It Work?

Can your child think of one rhyming word to match a word that you say?

Easier and Harder Ideas

1. As you recite a list of words, have a younger child clap whenever you say a word that rhymes with a specific word that you choose.
2. Have an older child jump rope while you say rhyming words. Talk about the sounds in jump rope rhymes.

◇ ◇

Math Puzzles

Reason

To help your child practice adding and subtracting

What You Need

Squares of cardboard or paper plates, scissors, marker or pen

Time Needed

10 minutes

What to Do

1. Write a simple addition problem on a piece of cardboard or a paper plate, such as 2 + 2 = 4.
2. Cut the cardboard or paper plate apart, making a zigzag line between the problem and the answer. The pieces now form a puzzle.
3. Write other problems on other cardboard pieces and cut them apart with curving or zigzag lines.
4. Mix up the problems and answers, then have your child complete the puzzles.

Age of Child

6, 7, 8

Did It Work?

Can your child match up one or two of the puzzle pieces correctly?

Easier and Harder Ideas

1. Make a set of subtraction problems this same way, or, match words and numbers, such as "dime = 10 cents."
2. For an older child, use multiplication problems or tables for the puzzles. Division problems are good, too. As with the other puzzles, have your child match the answer pieces with the problem pieces.

◇ ◇ ◇ ◇ ◇ ◇ ◇ ◇ ◇ ◇ ◇ ◇ ◇ ◇ ◇ ◇ ◇ ◇ ◇ ◇

Waiting for Time

Reason

To help your child practice the skills needed for telling time

What You Need

A watch or clock that displays all 12 numbers (in addition, a digital clock can be used as a learning help)

Time Needed

10 minutes

What to Do

1. Show your child the minute hand on a watch or clock and ask her to see how long a TV commercial is.

2. When the commercial is over, help her figure out the length of time that has passed. One minute? Half a minute? Explain the marks on the clock; for example, tell your child that the five marks between two numbers in a row on a clock represent five minutes of time.

3. Have your child practice counting by fives to 60: 5, 10, 15, 20, 25, and so on. Show your child how this method of counting relates to the marks on a clock's face. (Count by tens if fives are too hard.)

4. Help your child time other things, such as a song on the radio, how long it takes a traffic light to change, how long it takes to read a certain story, or how long her sibling may play with a particular toy.

Age of Child

5, 6, 7

Did It Work?

Does your child understand what "wait 5 minutes" means? Does she talk about time more?

Easier and Harder Ideas

1. Talk to a younger child about the "thirties" and the "o'clocks" on a clock. Tell her that when both hands are at the top it is 12 o'clock. When

the big hand is at the bottom it is 12:30. Explain that the small hand always tells the "o'clocks" and the big hand always tells the "thirties."

2. Use a "time-out" chair when your child misbehaves. Ask her to sit on a chair for 5 minutes and give her a watch or clock to hold and observe while she waits. This is a good way to interrupt a fight or a temper tantrum.

◇ ◇

Home Chart

Reason

To help your child talk about and think about safety habits

What You Need

Piece of paper large enough to make a chart and a marker or pen

Time Needed

10 minutes

What to Do

1. Walk around your home with your child for a "safety inspection tour."
2. Look for electric cords that are frayed and for throw rugs that slide. Look for papers, rags, paint, laundry soap, or anything poisonous that is not stored safely and away from little children.
3. Make a chart of things that need attention. Write the needed safety repairs down the left side of the chart. Then write the days of the week across the top of the chart. Use this chart to record when things get done.
4. Plan a trip to the store to buy any supplies that will help make the needed safety repairs. These might include electrical tape for frayed cords or double-sided tape to secure a throw rug.

Age of Child

6, 7, 8

Did It Work?

Does your child think more about how safe things are? Does he enjoy putting check marks or stickers on the chart when repairs are made?

Easier and Harder Ideas

1. Talk to a younger child about safety rules. For example, "Look both ways before crossing the street. Don't run on stairs. Stay in your seat on the bus." Make a chart of these "safety activities" and allow your child to check them off.
2. Ask an older child to make a chart for another family member, with that family member's help. For example, he could make a chart that relates to the car: Check the tires; check the oil; check the transmission fluid.

◇ ◇

Comparing Lengths

Reason

To help your child build number and comparing skills

What You Need

String or yarn, scissors

Time Needed

10 minutes

What to Do

1. Talk with your child about comparing the lengths of different items.
2. Cut a piece of yarn or string so that it is the same length as a particular piece of furniture, such as the dresser in your child's bedroom.
3. See how many times the piece of yarn is needed to measure the length of your child's bed. How many lengths are needed to measure the rug? The front door? The window?
4. Find out which item in your house needs the most lengths.
5. Measure your child and then yourself with the piece of yarn.

Age of Child

5, 6, 7

Did It Work?

Does your child notice that it takes more lengths of yarn to measure the bed than the dresser?

Easier and Harder Ideas

1. Ask your child to guess how many lengths of yarn it will take to measure an object.
2. Use a tape measure or a yardstick to measure the same pieces of furniture you measured with the yarn. Record the lengths of items and compare the lengths measured in inches.

HOME LEARNING ENABLER (#1)

◇ ◇

A Box for Me

Reason

To help your child make a place that is her very own; she can use this for storing school things and private treasures

What You Need

A cardboard box, crayons or markers, scraps of fabric, comics from the newspaper or a piece of gift wrap, and glue

Time Needed

10 to 15 minutes

What to Do

1. Ask your child to decorate her "Treasure Box" with some of the materials listed.
2. Encourage your child to use the box to keep her things that she doesn't want to lose.
3. Suggest that she use the box to keep the booklets she makes at school and the things you two make together based on these home activities.
4. Explain to the rest of the family that this box is "off limits" to everyone but this child.

Age of Child

4, 5, 6, 7, 8

Did It Work?

Does your child enjoy using her box? Does she keep special toys or gifts in it?

Easier and Harder Ideas

1. A younger child can make a simpler box, perhaps using a shoe box and markers.
2. An older child can decorate boxes especially for each member of the family. These make good gifts.

437

◇ ◇ ◇ ◇ ◇ ◇ ◇ ◇ ◇ ◇ ◇ ◇ ◇ ◇ ◇ ◇ ◇ ◇ ◇ ◇

Love Notes

Reason

To help your child practice writing

What You Need

Pieces of paper, pencil or pen

Time Needed

5 or 10 minutes

What to Do

1. Ask your child to write a short note to each family member. These notes might say, for example, "Good morning" or "I love you" or even "You can play with my blue toy today."
2. Together, have fun deciding where to put these notes so that each family member finds his or hers: in a lunch bag, on a pillow, on the refrigerator, or on a mirror, for example.
3. Encourage family members to write notes back.
4. Keep sending notes. Designate one day a week to be "note-writing day."

Age of Child

6, 7, 8

Did It Work?

Does your child enjoy sending and receiving notes? Does he write longer notes as his writing gets better?

Easier and Harder Ideas

1. Have a younger child draw a picture and tell you (dictate) the message he wants you to write on it.
2. At holiday time, add little gifts to the notes, such as a pencil or a piece of candy. Sign the notes, "From Secret Santa" or whatever name suits your family traditions.

◇ ◇

Problem-Solving

Reason

To help your child use hints and clues to guess the identity of an object or idea

What You Need

Nothing (This activity can be done in the car.)

Time Needed

5 to 10 minutes

What to Do

1. Describe an object that is in another room of the house. If you are driving, describe an object that you can't see in the car.
2. After providing a few hints, ask your child to guess what the object is; provide more and more hints if necessary.
3. If possible, after your child names the object, give her the object to look at and have her tell you how helpful your clues were.
4. Take turns. Have your child give you hints to help you guess an unseen object.

Age of Child

5, 6, 7, 8

Did It Work?

Does your child guess the objects more and more quickly? Does she give you better and better hints when it is her turn?

Easier and Harder Ideas

1. For a younger child, provide simpler clues.
2. With an older child (or adult), play "Twenty questions": Think of an object, then have the player ask you questions about the object. These questions should require either a "yes" or "no" answer. See if the player can guess an object by asking you less than 20 questions. Take turns.

◇ ◇

Puzzle Comics

Reason

To help your child learn sequence skills

What You Need

Color or black-and-white comic strips (comics your child can read are best), scissors, envelopes

Time Needed

10 minutes

What to Do

1. Ask your child to cut apart the blocks of one comic strip. Then have him mix them up and put them in order again.
2. Cut up more comic strips and then put them back in order. Keep each set of comic strip blocks in a separate envelope.
3. Take one block out of one envelope. Ask your child to tell you what's missing. Or, ask him to make up the words or story for the missing blocks.
4. Do this for the other strips, too.

Age of Child

6, 7, 8

Did It Work?

Can your child put the comic strips back together again?

Easier and Harder Ideas

1. Find a comic strip with little or no words for a younger child.
2. Take out the ending block of a comic strip and ask your child to make up a new ending for the story. Ask him to draw the new ending.

◊ ◊

Neighborhood Map

Reason

To help your child learn mapping skills; to help her see that she can draw pictures of places, which is what a map is

What You Need

Newspapers or brown paper grocery bags to make a large piece of paper, marker or pen, tape

Time Needed

15 minutes

What to Do

1. Tell your child you are going to draw a picture of your street. Explain that this picture is called a map.
2. Use a flattened, cut-open paper bag or newspaper, and draw your street. Add four or five houses or buildings on each side. Have your child show you on the map the location of your home and write your street number on it.
3. Attach more bags or newspapers to your original map and draw more streets and buildings.
4. Have your child name and draw several places (such as her school, a store, a gas station, etc.). Label these places or have your child do so.

Age of Child

6, 7, 8

Did It Work?

Can your child locate one or two places on the "map"?

Easier and Harder Ideas

1. Have a younger child help you "map" the rooms in your home.
2. If you live near a river, railroad tracks, or a big street, have an older child map the area around it. What buildings are near this area that are different from those in your neighborhood? Look at the same places on a commercial map that you can get from a local gas station.

◇ ◇

Making an Alphabet Line

Reason

To help your child learn to put things in alphabetical order

What You Need

Newspapers or shelf paper to lay out on the floor, a marker or pen

Time Needed

10 to 15 minutes

What to Do

1. On a piece of newspaper, write the first five letters of the alphabet in a row (use large letters).
2. Ask your child to find small objects that start with those letters, then have him put these objects by the appropriate letter on the "Alphabet Line." He can use toys (*b*all, *c*ar), groceries (*c*an, *e*ggs, *f*ruit), or any other objects that are easy to carry.
3. Add more letters.
4. Take turns letting each other find objects to place on the Alphabet Line.

Age of Child

6, 7, 8

Did It Work?

Can your child place two or three things in correct alphabetical order?

Easier and Harder Ideas

1. Write the names of family members on slips of paper and place them on the Alphabet Line.
2. Cut out 10 words from the newspaper and ask an older child to alphabetize them. Let him cut out 10 words for you to alphabetize.

◇ ◇

Timing Your Day

Reason

To help your child learn to plan activities

What You Need

Paper, pencil, pen

Time Needed

10 to 15 minutes

What to Do

1. Help your child make a chart for 5, 6, or 7 days that shows the days of the week.
2. In pencil, write down the times she eats breakfast, goes to school, participates in other activities, and goes to bed.
3. Ask your child to notice what times these activities actually occur; then, with a pen, write down those times.
4. On Saturday morning, use a pencil to write down any plans for the day. In the evening, use a pen to write any changes that occurred.

Age of Child

6, 7, 8

Did It Work?

Does your child enjoy discussing with you the times she will do things? Does she enjoy comparing how close the estimated times came to the real times?

Easier and Harder Ideas

1. For a younger child who does not yet understand the concept of minutes, plan one day by the hour.
2. An older child can help plan an automobile trip. Write down the days you will be traveling, the estimated times that you will be arriving at specific places, and the distances between places. Later, compare the actual travel schedule with the planned schedule.

443

◇ ◇ ◇ ◇ ◇ ◇ ◇ ◇ ◇ ◇ ◇ ◇ ◇ ◇ ◇ ◇ ◇ ◇ ◇ ◇

Measuring My House and Myself

Reason

To help your child practice measuring and numbering skills

What You Need

Yardstick, ruler, or tape measure; paper; pencil

Time Needed

10 to 15 minutes

What to Do

1. Talk with your child about measuring things. Measure a table, a chair, and your child's arm, then write down the numbers.
2. Ask your child to measure more things, such as the length of his shoe, the width of a doorway, the width of a window, the width of the TV, or the length of his little finger.
3. Ask him to guess the measurements of some things and have him write down these guesses (or estimates). Then have him measure these items and write down the actual measurements. Compare the estimates with the actual measurements.
4. Take turns measuring different objects.

Age of Child

6, 7, 8

Did It Work?

Does your child enjoy measuring things? Does he or she enjoy guessing or estimating a measurement and then checking it?

Easier and Harder Ideas

1. Have your child measure the pans in your kitchen.
2. With your child, find things you can measure outside: the width of the sidewalk, the height of a mailbox, or how far he can jump.

◇ ◇

Newspaper Headline Puzzles

Reason

To help your child understand word sequence

What You Need

Scissors, tape, paper, envelopes

Time Needed

10 to 15 minutes

What to Do

1. Ask your child to cut out some newspaper headlines.
2. Cut apart the words of one headline. Ask your child to assemble the headline again.
3. After she succeeds, put that "headline puzzle" in an envelope. Cut up another headline to assemble.
4. Use the headline words to make sentences. Tape these sentences to a page and have your child illustrate the sentences to make a booklet.

Age of Child

6, 7, 8

Did It Work?

Did your child enjoy arranging the puzzles? Did she ask to do this activity again?

Easier and Harder Ideas

1. For a younger child, write on a piece of paper a simple sentence that she knows. Cut it up to make a puzzle.
2. For an older child, use harder and longer sentences. Trade places and let her make a puzzle for you. Use magazine headlines and sentences, too.

◇ ◇

Do I Have Enough?

Reason

To help your child use household objects to practice adding and subtracting

What You Need

Silverware, food items, rocks

Time Needed

10 minutes

What to Do

1. Ask your child to set the table. Give him one or two fewer spoons than he needs. Ask him how many more spoons he needs to be able to complete the task.
2. Do this activity with fruit or any food you are serving. How many more servings do you need?
3. Outside, tell your child you want 10 rocks. Give him 7 and ask if he has enough.
4. Count out pennies to buy something. Have him tell you how many more pennies he needs to buy the item.

Age of Child

6, 7, 8

Did It Work?

Does he figure out the correct answer at least some of the time?

Easier and Harder Ideas

1. Take turns. Have your second grader or a younger child ask you if you have enough of something.
2. Practice subtracting. Give your child 10 spoons. Ask him how many he should give back to have enough left for the family.

PARENT LETTER/FEEDBACK SHEET

(This form is to be sent home with each activity)

_____
(Date)

Dear Parent:

Did you know that you are your child's most important teacher? Would you take 5 minutes this week and do the following activity with your child? Please fill in the sheet below with your ideas and comments, then tear it off and send it back to me. Thank you.

_____
(Teacher's Name)

(Tear Off)

- -

For:_____
(Child's Name, Grade)

1. Did you or someone else do the activity with the child? Me _____Other _____

2. How many times did you do the activity? Once _____More than once _____

3. How much time did the activity take?   _____ 15 minutes or less
                                             _____ 30 minutes or less
                                             _____ More than 30 minutes

4. Did you enjoy this activity with your child?   Yes _____ No _____

5. Do you feel your child understood it?   Yes _____ No _____

6. Do you feel your child needs more help in this area? Yes _____ No _____

7. Please share any adaptation you may have of this activity, or describe a new activity. (Write on the back, if necessary.) Thanks for cooperating!

_____   _____
        Signature   Teacher's Name

_____
(Activity name, grade, and number)

Parent Papers

These Parent Papers may be given as handouts at parent meetings, added as an extra page to newsletters sent home with the children, or given as a single page for children to take home. Parents are important partners in children's learning. The goal of these Parent Papers is to help your center include parents in the learning process in a way that saves time and effort for you, while providing professional resources for parenting. By providing these resources to parents, the children at your center will be helped as well, since one of the most effective and inexpensive ways to reach children is to reach their parents. By providing a variety of formal and informal ways to keep in touch with parents, your center will build trust and two-way communication. Many parents find the guidance and support of knowledgeable adults to be invaluable. By learning some of the ways professional personnel interact with children, parents can feel more confident with their children at home. You may want to share this point of view with your staff at a staff meeting.

WHAT TO EXPECT FROM A CHILD-CARE/PRESCHOOL PROGRAM (#1)

Teacher's Name

◇ ◇

Goals of the Early Childhood Program Experience

Goals for Children

- Be themselves
- Express themselves by using art and play materials freely and constructively
- Learn to be tolerant, creative, cooperative, and imaginative
- Learn independence
- Learn limits of behavior
- Increase ability to handle emotions constructively

Goals for Parents

- Become more aware of your child's world and understand his or her behavior
- Achieve a more positive approach to child-adult relationships by taking advantage of professional guidance and sharing experiences with other parents
- Sympathize with and understand your child's feelings about his or her first experience away from home
- Participate in a worthwhile situation, outside of the home and job, by contributing your abilities and talents
- Learn constructive techniques of working with children

What We Teach . . .

- Is not always evident to the casual observer.
- Sets the stage by guiding unobtrusively.
- Maintains an atmosphere of freedom and friendliness within limits.
- Allows the children to develop their own ideas. Adults stay in the background ready to help if needed.

Objectives of the Early Childhood Program

I. Physical Development

A.   Objective: To provide experiences, equipment, and activities that contribute to physical fitness and coordination. We plan:

1.   To provide each child with a balance of active and quiet activities.
2.   To provide the child with activities for small and large muscle development.
3.   To provide the child with balanced and nutritious meals or snacks.
4.   To help the child to achieve awareness and mastery of his or her physical self.

II. Intellectual Development

A.   Objective: To provide experiences that increase the child's ability to solve problems by interacting with his or her surrounding environment. This will include learning to observe, describe, discover, think, organize, and use the information he or she receives through the five senses. We plan:

1.   To develop language ability and vocabulary through all activities and experiences.
2.   To provide problem-solving and decision-making situations to enhance the child's thinking ability.
3.   To expose the child to as much of the world as possible through field trips and actual experience.
4.   To allow the child to express himself or herself creatively, and to manipulate and explore materials.
5.   To provide the child with a variety of learning experiences including cooking, art, water play, and dramatic play.

III. Emotional Development

A.   Objective: To encourage children to develop and grow in positive feelings about themselves and their abilities; who they are; and what they can do. We plan, with your help:

1.   To develop self-confidence and feelings of achievement.
2.   To provide experiences that teach children to deal constructively with their frustrations.
3.   To encourage children to respect themselves, other children, adults, materials, and equipment.
4.   To encourage children to take pride in their ethnic group, family, and community.

IV. Social Development

A. Objective: To help each child develop an awareness and appreciation of others, moving from preoccupation with self towards involvement with others. We plan:

1. To provide the child with opportunities to enjoy knowing and being with other children and adults.

2. To provide sharing experiences for the child and to provide for give-and-take relationships.

3. To help the child learn to trust adults outside the family and to be able to ask for help when it is needed.

V. Strengthening Families

A. Objective: To build a close and positive relationship with families of children in the program.

Teacher's Name

◇ ◇

What Your Child Will Be Learning

We hope the activities in the program will offer your child a variety of ways to have fun. Play can include spontaneous and productive experiences that help children learn about their world and their relationship to it.

The *dramatic play corner* offers an opportunity for dramatic play through which children can assume the roles of a mother, a father, a baby, and many others. They can act out some of their feelings about people and events. Children can express their fantasies, their fears, their impulses, and their needs. They can have their turn with power.

Art activities such as easel painting, finger painting, and fruit and vegetable painting, allow for the discovery of colors, designs, and shapes. While exploring the creative possibilities of paint, clay, paste, and paper, children can find ways to express their feelings and experiences.

Sand and water play involve the sense of touch and the use of small muscles. In this relaxed play situation, children can use pitchers, funnels, measuring spoons, and sponges for pouring, measuring, and squeezing. This activity also helps future math learning.

Food experiences such as making juice and slicing bananas allow the different characteristics of food to be seen, tested, smelled, and touched. This is one way to help children become more aware of and sensitive to learning through their five senses.

Reading stories and making books available for children to use stimulate many interests. Books become recognized as sources of information. Through discussion of pictures, children observe details. Discussion also promotes language development and self-expression. Books can foster the sharing of experiences such as trips and visits from favorite friends and relatives.

Building with blocks stimulates and promotes creative play. Complex and imaginative structures arise. Selecting the blocks involves making comparisons and classifying sizes and shapes.

Outdoor equipment stimulates climbing, jumping, sliding, and balancing, and helps large muscle development and coordination.

We hope that through these activities, children will have the opportunities to gain confidence in themselves and their abilities. According to recent research, self-direction, interest, curiosity, and genuine pleasure in activities of all kinds promote the best possible intellectual development in children.

Teacher's Name

◇ ◇

What to Expect

Ask yourself:

1. What do I expect from an early childhood experience?

For my child:

- the companionship and challenge of friends
- the guidance and support of knowledgeable adults
- the time and space and opportunity to explore many creative materials
- the excitement and enticement of planned activities that provide foundation concepts and learning
- the strengthened feeling that he or she is a capable, active learner
- the pleasure of a world of his or her own, apart from the family, where he or she is a valued individual
- a head start on specific learning and attitudes that will be expected in later school years

For myself:

- the assurance that my child is safe
- the prospect that he or she will grow and gain knowledge, self-confidence, and social skills
- the hope that he or she will be helped in his or her later school experiences
- the chance to discuss my child and his or her needs with a caring teacher
- the chance to observe other children and stages of development
- the chance to extend my knowledge of effective alternatives in child-rearing practices
- the chance to meet other families with similar-aged children who are facing the same or very different problems
- the opportunity to be reliable in picking up my child and paying fees

Note: Please remember—not everyone expects the same things from a program, so not all of these items will be important to everyone, nor will they all carry the same weight.

2. How can parents know how a program is operating, what it is achieving, and what is happening during the hours of operation?

By asking:

- Do the children in the program seem relaxed and sure of themselves, or do they seem tense and anxious?
- Do the children seem to like each other and get along (some of the time)?
- Are they interested in some activity most of the time?
- Do they seem comfortable chatting and explaining and questioning, or are they silent most of the time?
- Are they using all their senses to discover and handle their play materials?

By observing the teacher:

- Does the teacher welcome each child and seem to be aware of what each child is doing?
- Does the teacher speak naturally and directly to a child, stooping to his or her eye level most of the time?
- Does the teacher step in to stop fights or change activities before behavior becomes disruptive?
- Does the teacher seem upset or blame a child when accidents occur?
- Does he or she show respect and genuine interest in a child's work?

By observing the program:

- Is the schedule a rigid timetable or a natural sequence?
- Are there activities for individuals and small groups as well as the whole class?
- Do some activities offer quiet experiences and opportunities for creating and exploring?
- Are the children's interests and comments taken into consideration in the planning of activities, or are all of the activities planned by the teachers?
- Are children permitted and encouraged to do things for themselves, such as hang up their clothes, pour their own juice, and manage art materials?

By observing the space and equipment:

- Is equipment sturdy and non-frustrating?
- Does the equipment upkeep show concern for the health and safety of the children, or are splinters and wobbles allowed to develop?
- Is there imaginative use of color and shape?
- Are there enough materials to really carry out an idea, or are there just a few blocks or dishes, for example?
- Are bathrooms clean, fresh-smelling, and equipped with sturdy step stools?
- Are examples of children's art work displayed around the classroom to be admired and shared?
- Are materials stored so that children may take them out and put them away independently?

By observing the outdoor area:

- Is there an enclosed space for outdoor play?
- Is the outdoor equipment sturdy and secure?
- Does the outdoor play equipment allow children the chance to run, stretch, pull, climb, yell, and, in general, use up stored energy?

By asking about teacher and director credentials:

- Are certificates and diplomas that staff members received for training prominently displayed?

I can help this program and its activities in the following way:

DEVELOPING YOUR CHILD'S SELF-IMAGE (#1)

Teacher's Name

◇ ◇ ◇ ◇ ◇ ◇ ◇ ◇ ◇ ◇ ◇ ◇ ◇ ◇ ◇ ◇ ◇ ◇ ◇ ◇

Building Self-Esteem

Self-esteem or self-confidence affects how a person manages his or her needs, deals with others, produces in life, solves conflicts, and searches for meaning in life; these qualities also affect whether or not a person is able to develop close relationships and take responsibility for meeting others' needs. Self-esteem and a positive self-image go hand in hand.

The feelings of belonging and significance that a child gains in the family can help him or her to be successful in every area of life. Self-confidence and a sense of achievement can be developed in children in much the same way it is developed in adults, but in smaller steps. Children need to feel worth-while and to have a sense of self-respect just as adults do. Aggression in children often is a symptom of a poor self-image.

Steps that build self-esteem include opportunities for decision-making. Children need a chance to make decisions. When providing such opportunities, limit choices to two or three, since too many choices are frustrating and confusing to young children. Some appropriate decision-making opportunities for a young child include:

1. Choosing which vegetable or fruit or dessert the family will eat for supper. Talk about color, smell, size, and taste. Alternatively or in addition, allow your child to choose the appropriate-sized dish to serve the food in—not too big and not too small.

2. Selecting the clothes he or she will wear. Again, allow your child to make selections from a limited number of options.

3. Sharing a grocery shopping trip with you. Make a "shopping list" for your child by pasting onto a piece of cardboard various labels from empty cans or boxes of food that you plan to purchase during the shopping trip. Ask your child to find these items and put them in the cart. Your child will feel good because he or she is big enough to help, which boosts his or her self-image. You benefit, too, because the responsibility of helping keeps your child busy in a productive way.

4. Offering your child the opportunity to choose between two items to buy in the hardware or clothing store, when you have no preference for one or the other. How nice it is to have one's opinion valued and respected!

5. Offering a choice of alternatives to your child when he or she is absorbed in a behavior of which you disapprove. This opportunity can turn an

unhappy situation into a learning experience. It also will help avoid a power struggle and will give your child the responsibility of making an appropriate decision. For example, you can explain to your child, "Crayons are for paper or coloring books, not for magazines (or walls). Which would you like to have, a coloring book or some paper?" This calm approach teaches the child something important: Some things are for coloring on, others are not. It may take several reminders before your child remembers and obeys the rule, but he or she has not been "put down" by a frustrated, angry adult. Your child has learned something, and he or she knows what materials to ask for next time.

More Ideas

Respect for children, respect for materials and equipment, and respect for adults could well be a "theme for the year" for many homes and centers. After two weeks, can you see your child's progress? Is he or she handling some objects more carefully?

Teacher's Name

◇ ◇

You and Children—Your Child is "Somebody Special"

1. *Treat your child as "somebody special."* Call your child by his or her name. Help your child to feel that you like him or her. Try to learn what skills your child's age-group is capable of, then let your child know you think he or she is able to do those things. Be as polite to your child as you would be to an adult; for example, say "please" and "thank you" to your child.

2. *Try to see your child's point of view.* The things children do make sense to them. Try to think like a child to discover why he or she is acting in a particular way. Find out why something makes sense to your child. It can be an enjoyable experience.

3. *Touch your child to get his or her attention.* Put your hand on your child's shoulder, take his or her hand or bend down and put your arm around your child to get his or her attention. Speak in a quiet voice and speak slowly so he or she understands what you are saying. This method of gaining your child's attention takes more time, but it works better than does calling loudly across the room.

4. *Talk to your child.* Talking to children builds their language ability. Give sincere approval when your child successfully masters a difficult situation: "Good job" or "Good idea." Try not to talk *for* your child, or *about* your child, in his or her presence.

5. *Listen to your child.* Pay attention to children when they talk to you. This may take some time, but it lets children feel that someone thinks they are important enough to listen to. It also helps them develop their language abilities. This is a fine way to let children know they are worthwhile.

6. *Accept your child's feelings.* Being sad, glad, lonely, or mad is part of being human. Try to let a child know you understand his or her feelings by saying, "You're angry that your brother took your doll," or "You're frightened by that loud noise that you heard," instead of telling a child to stop crying.

7. *Give your child choices.* Whenever possible, give children a chance to choose. A young child, even a two-year-old, can choose between two things. Ask, "Do you want to wear the red shirt or the blue shirt?" A three- or four-year-old can manage three, four, or five choices. The

offered choices should be as equal as possible; then be willing to accept what your child chooses!

8. *Give directions carefully.* If you want your child to do something:

- *Get* his or her attention.
- *Explain* carefully what you want your child to do.
- *Tell* your child why he or she should do it.
- *Show* him or her how to do it.
- *Give* your child appreciation. For example, you might say, "You picked up all your blocks." Then give your child a hug or do something else that shows you are proud of his or her accomplishment.

9. *Avoid comparing.* Avoid making comparisons between your children. When you compare, one child may think that he or she is not as good as a sibling, or that he or she is better. For example, don't say, "Why can't you finish the food on your plate like Tommy does?"

10. *Let your child know you respect his or her decisions, wishes, and needs.* Giving your child this respect will give him or her a brighter opinion of himself or herself. Your child will also be better able to demonstrate respect for others.

11. *Build your child's positive self-image with encouragement and praise.* A child who THINKS he or she can succeed has a better chance of succeeding than does a child who expects to fail.

12. *Say to your child, "You're O.K.!"* Tell him or her: "I will support your efforts, encourage your skills, respect your decisions, value your opinions, help you through rough spots, and watch you succeed!"

Additional Notes

Teacher's Name

◇ ◇ ◇ ◇ ◇ ◇ ◇ ◇ ◇ ◇ ◇ ◇ ◇ ◇ ◇ ◇ ◇ ◇ ◇ ◇

Building Success and Confidence in Children

"Nothing succeeds like success." Children who learn this concept early—that they CAN succeed in small efforts—will have confidence in their own abilities to tackle greater tasks later. What children think about themselves and their abilities will greatly influence their potential for success as they grow older. It will also affect their enthusiasm for meeting new challenges and will shape their outlook on life.

We can help children build a positive self-image by providing opportunities for them to prove to themselves that they are capable, worthwhile people who are worthy of our respect.

Cooperating and Carrying Out Tasks

1. Know your child's limits and abilities and provide only those tasks that he or she can complete successfully. At this age, your child's attention span is short, and muscle coordination is not fully developed. It takes a long time to accomplish things, and rushing won't help.

2. Your child will be confused and frustrated if you give too many directions at one time. It's best to keep jobs simple or give them one step at a time. For example, "Let's put some of the toys to bed in the toy box" is a less overwhelming instruction than, "Clean up this mess!" Giving your child genuine praise after each successfully completed step encourages good behavior and helps your child to continue one step at a time. Too big a chore can result in failure and disapproval, and a negative self-image could follow.

Help a Child Help Himself or Herself

1. Let your child spread his or her own butter, jelly, or peanut butter.

2. Let your child serve himself or herself from bowls or plates of food at mealtimes.

3. Let children help set and clear the table. Build confidence and self-esteem by making this job a learning game. Talk about sizes, colors, numbers, and new concepts, such as the words *on, in, under, beside,* and *on top of.*

4. Even a young child can feel important when propped up on a stool and allowed to help his or her mother "wash" some dishes (unbreakable

461

ones). Try this activity before mealtimes when young children may be underfoot and impatient to eat. Give your child an apron, a stool, some sudsy water, and the cooking spoons and pans you've finished using.

5. Encourage a child to dress himself or herself. This is a big accomplishment and one that a child can be proud of. Praise the effort and ignore the fact that the pants are on backwards. To redo it tells children that they are not good enough to do it by themselves. As a result, your child may not want to try again. Try to buy clothing that is easy for your child to put on.

6. Remember, praising your child after he or she completes a job and does it well can help to build a good self-image.

Additional Notes

Teacher's Name

◇ ◇ ◇ ◇ ◇ ◇ ◇ ◇ ◇ ◇ ◇ ◇ ◇ ◇ ◇ ◇ ◇ ◇ ◇ ◇

Talking to Young Children

Between the ages of two years and four years, a child will have rapid language development—from a few words to an average of 2,000. Adults can help enormously with this development by reading and talking to young children. By helping their children gain new words, parents smooth many of the frustrations felt by young children when they can't explain what they mean. A child who is able to communicate frustration is ultimately a happier child.

What can a parent do to help a child see and describe:

- himself or herself?
- his or her actions?
- his or her world?

1. Play a game about the clothing you are wearing. Tell your child about something you are wearing and then ask him to tell you something about what he is wearing. For example:

   Parent: "I'm wearing blue pants."

   Child: "I'm wearing a red shirt." (Or, "I'm wearing a shirt with green stripes.")

   Work up to more and more comments until your child can tell you all about what he is wearing. Suggest that your child go in sequence from head to toes so he won't forget anything. An older child can tell you the materials that his clothes are made of, such as cotton or wool.

2. Tell your child about herself as a baby and as a younger child. Often this becomes a favorite story. Point out all the things your child can do NOW that she couldn't do then. For example:

   Parent: "When you were a little baby, you couldn't tell me when you were hungry. You just cried and screamed. How do you tell me now?"

   Child: "I say, 'May I have something to eat?'"

   Build an older child's observation skills by having her describe a younger child in the family.

3. Ask your child to close his eyes and tell you everything that is in the room you're in. Write down what your child says. Then ask him to look around and find what was left out.

463

4. Play "Simon Says." In the role of Simon, ask your child to touch a part of the body that you name. Think of body parts that children don't always know, such as forehead, eyelids, knuckles, hips, elbows, and thighs. Then let your child be Simon. Talk together about parts of the body that come in pairs.

5. Play a game called "Giving Directions." For example, tell your child: "Go get the blue pencil on the table." Work up to two-part directions, such as, "Go get the blue pencil in the middle drawer of the desk upstairs." Add more directions until your child can remember three or four at one time. Add fun directions such as "Hop to the chair," "Jump two times," "Smile at the cat."

6. In the car (or anywhere), play the "Guess What I'm Thinking Of" game. For instance, say, "I'm thinking of something in this car that has two hands wearing mittens (or whatever)." Your child can answer, "That's me!" Let your child ask you to guess what she is thinking of.

7. Talk about the different emotions people feel. Look at pictures of people in magazines or in a photo album. Do they look happy or sad? Rushed or relaxed? Ask your child to tell you what makes him happy, angry, or worried. Share some of your feelings with your child. Talk about how the way we move around sometimes tells how we feel. Ask your child to show you how he would move if he were feeling happy, scared, or angry.

8. Sing any songs you know to your child. From babyhood on, a child's favorite voices are those of his or her mother and father. Your child doesn't care if you can't sing or think you can't. Sing lullabies, folk songs, holiday songs, patriotic songs, popular songs, or songs with motions that your child can participate in. Make up your own words. Any song that includes your child's name will be a big hit.

Books for Young Children (Part I)

Ahlberg, Janet, & Allan Ahlberg. *Each Peach Pear Plum*. Viking, 1978. An "I Spy" story.

Anno, Mitsumasa. *Anno's Counting Book*. Crowell, 1975. Watercolor scenes take the reader through the year, with mathematical concepts suggested on each page.

Arkin, Alan. *Tony's Hard Work Day*. Harper, 1972. Tony wants to work too, and he proves that he can.

Asbjornsen, Peter C., & J. E. Moe. *Three Billy Goats Gruff*. Illustrated by Marcia Brown. Harcourt, 1957. "Who's that tripping over my bridge?" roared the troll.

Barton, Byron. *I Want to Be an Astronaut*. Crowell/HarperCollins, 1988. Sharing a space shuttle with young dreamers.

Bemelmans, Ludwig. *Madeline*. Viking, 1960. Twelve little French school girls in two straight lines, the youngest one is Madeline.

Birnbaum, Abe. *Green Eyes*. Golden, 1953. A white kitten experiences the four seasons of his first year.

Brenner, Barbara. *Bodies*. Dutton, 1973. We are all alike, yet we each have "a body and a mind, one of a kind." Also see *Faces* by the same author.

Brett, Jan. *The Mitten*. Putnam, 1989. A Ukrainian folktale.

Brooke, L. Leslie. *Golden Goose Book*. Warne, 1906. Four stories: "Golden Goose," "Three Bears," "The Three Little Pigs," and "Tom Thumb," brought to life by the irresistible Brooke illustrations.

Brown, Margaret Wise. *Goodnight Moon*. Harper, 1947. A warm and cozy book for quiet night talk.

Burningham, John. *John Burningham's ABC*. Bobbs, 1964.

Burningham, John. *Mr. Gumpy's Outing*. Hold, 1970. The riders tip the boat, but all ends well with a grand tea party.

Burton, Virginia Lee. *Mike Mulligan and His Steam Shovel*. Houghton, 1939. Mike and Mary Ann accomplish great things.

Carle, Eric. *The Very Hungry Caterpillar*. World, 1970. An imaginative look at the life cycle of a butterfly.

Crews, Donald. *Freight Train*. Morrow, 1978. A colorful train experience—one of the best to come down the tracks.

de Brunhoff, Jean. *Story of Babar, the Little Elephant*. Random, 1933. Babar, born in a great forest, learns to enjoy the amenities of civilization. Also see more books about Babar by the same author and his son, Laurent de Brunhoff.

de Regniers, Beatrice Schenk. *May I Bring a Friend*? Illustrated by Beni Montresor. Atheneum, 1964. "Any friend of our friend is welcome here!" say the hospitable king and queen.

de Regniers, Beatrice Schenk. *It Does Not Say Meow*. Illustrated by Paul Galdone. Seabury, 1972. Animal riddle rhymes for guessing games.

Ets, Marie Hall. *Play with Me*. Viking, 1955. Small animals and a little girl meet quietly in a sunny window.

Flack, Marjorie, & Kurt Wiese. *The Story About Ping*. Viking, 1933. A duckling has a narrow escape before he reaches his houseboat home on the Yangtze River.

Fox Went Out on a Chilly Night. Doubleday, 1961. An old song illustrated by Peter Spier.

Teacher's Name

◇ ◇

Reading to Young Children

One of the best ways young children learn new words is from parents reading out loud to them. A young two-year-old may be happy with a question-and-answer conversation about one or two of the pictures in a storybook. Reading two or three pages of a book and then discussing the story may be just right for a child who is almost three years old. The story line is not important at this age—identifying objects, enjoying time with Mom or Dad, and cuddling close are what is important. An older child may want to hear the whole story.

Take your child to the library. Let your child pick out his or her own books. He or she may be ready for non-fiction books from the children's section of the library. Books about rockets, Native Americans, the Coast Guard, railroads, or almost any subject are great and can be used for the pictures alone. Discussing the captions of the pictures will help your child learn more about his or her world. Ask the children's librarian for book suggestions.

Repeat a Lot!

When young children (two- and three-year-olds) enjoy a story, they want to hear it over and over again. Help your children enjoy language by substituting new words for old ones and see if they catch you. Or, skip a section of the story and see if they notice. Make up a new ending to the story and then encourage them to do the same.

How Do You Read a Book to Young Children?

When reading to young children, use a lot of sound effects! Read enthusiastically and with drama. Encourage your children to observe details, ask questions, guess what happens next, and discuss what's going on. Point out that the page numbers change as you turn the page.

How to Tell If a Book Is Good

Do you and your child enjoy the experience?

- Are there brightly colored, realistic pictures? Can you tell what they are?
- Is the story simple and easy to identify with? Since two-, three-, and four-year-olds are the center of their own worlds, they like stories in

which they can see themselves. They particularly enjoy and identify with talking animals or machines, such as in *Goldilocks and the Three Bears* or *The Little Engine That Could*.

- Is there a lot of repetition? A young child likes to know what to expect. This gives him a chance to join in the fun.
- Does it have clear language?
- Do the books show men and women, and people of all races, doing a variety of things?

More Benefits of Reading to Young Children

- It lets them know you think reading is important in your home.
- According to research, it helps your children do better in school.
- Reading together is a time for closeness and warmth; it helps children associate this intellectual and stimulating experience with a loving and friendly time.

Books for Young Children (Part II)

Freeman, Don. *Corduroy*. Viking, 1968. A department store bear finds a friend named Lisa.

Gag, Wanda. *Millions of Cats*. Coward, 1928. The rhythm and repetition of the text entice listener participation.

Galdone, Paul. *The Gingerbread Boy*. Seabury, 1975. He eludes everyone but the wily fox.

Galdone, Paul. *The Little Red Hen*. Seabury, 1973. The brave little hen prevails over her lazy housemates.

Ginsburg, Mirra. *Mushroom in the Rain*. Pictures by Jose Aruego and Ariane Dewey. Macmillan, 1974. A mushroom growing in the rain always shelters one more.

Gretz, Susanna. *The Bears Who Stayed Indoors*. Follett, 1971. Five furry bears and their spotted dog find fun on a rainy day.

Grimm, Brothers. *The Wolf and the Seven Little Kids*. Translated by Katya Sheppard with pictures by Felix Hoffmann. Harcourt, 1959. One of Hoffmann's most felicitous renditions of Grimm.

Harper, Wilhelmina. *The Gunniwolf*. Dutton, 1967. Little Girl goes "pit-pat, pit-pat" and the almost scary Gunniwolf goes "hunker-cha, hunker-cha."

Hissey, Jane. *Little Bear's Trousers*. Philomel, 1987. Little bear loses his trousers.

Hoban, Tana. *Count and See*. Macmillan, 1972. Clear photographs illustrate and expand number concepts.

Hoban, Tana. *Exactly the Opposite*. Greenwillow, 1990. Engaging photographs that teach the concept of opposites.

Hutchins, Pat. *Titch*. Macmillan, 1971. The littlest one wins. Also try Hutchins' *Good Night Owl*.

Keats, Ezra. *The Snowy Day*. Viking, 1963. All the wonder of snow seen through a little boy's eyes. See also *Whistle for Willie*.

Langstaff, John. *Oh, a-Hunting We Will Go*. Pictures by Nancy Winslow Parker. Atheneum, 1974. "We'll catch a fox and put him in a _____ ?" With piano and guitar accompaniment.

Lionni, Leo. *Swimmy*. Pantheon, 1963. Swimmy teaches other little fishes the advantage of working together.

Maestro, Betsy. *Dollars and Cents for Harriet*. Crown, 1988. Harriet is a roller-skating elephant.

McCloskey, Robert. *Blueberries for Sal*. Viking, 1948. Sal and her mother meet a mother bear and her cub on Blueberry Hill.

McCloskey, Robert. *Make Way for Ducklings*. Viking, 1941. Mrs. Mallard and her eight ducklings travel to the Boston Public Gardens with the help of the police.

McPhail, David. *Emma's Vacation*. Dutton, 1987. A family of three bears on vacation.

Mother Goose: Ring o'Roses. Warne, 1922. A nursery rhyme picture book by L. Leslie Brooke. Incomparable pigs, and *the* Humpty Dumpty. See also *The Real Mother Goose* by B. Wright. Rand, 1916.

Petersham, Maud & Miska. *Circus Baby*. Macmillan, 1950. Mother Elephant tries to teach her baby table manners with hilarious results.

Potter, Beatrix. *The Tale of Peter Rabbit*. Warne, 1903. Naughty Peter explores Mr. McGregor's garden.

Rey, H. A. *Curious George*. Houghton, 1941. George's adventures on land and sea, in jail, and free.

Rice, Eve. *Sam Who Never Forgets*. Greenwillow, 1977. Dependable Sam feeds the zoo animals every day.

Sandburg, Carl. *Wedding Procession of the Rag Doll*. Harcourt, 1967. An unlikely but lively procession described by a poet.

Teacher's Name

◇ ◇ ◇ ◇ ◇ ◇ ◇ ◇ ◇ ◇ ◇ ◇ ◇ ◇ ◇ ◇ ◇ ◇ ◇

Thinking, Talking, and Reading to Young Children

Thinking Activities for Young Children

Observing, noticing, and describing

Encourage your children to use all their senses when noticing. Making popcorn and walking in the rain are two activities that involve a lot of the senses. As you participate in different activities, ask your child:

How does it look?

How does it feel?

How does it taste?

How does it sound?

How does it smell?

Comparing

Have your child compare characters in a story or song.

Categorizing

Have your child make categories for things or feelings. For instance, ask your child to stack up all the red books, the books she likes, or all the books she dislikes. Have your child stack up all the little books. Another day, have her stack up all the big books.

Collecting and organizing

Help your child think in terms of groups and categories. For example, ask him:

What do you need for a backyard picnic?

What do you need for a family picture album?

What do you need for a birthday party?

Summarizing

Ask your child to give a new title to a story, a song, or a TV show.

Predicting and proving

Ask your child a question in which she must predict the correct answer. For example, ask: "Which box is heavier, the large one or the small one?" Then ask, "How do you know? How can you tell if your answer is true?"

Guessing

In science, guessing is called hypothesizing, but this activity is often discouraged in school. In the preschool years, encourage your child to guess what will happen next and to tell you why.

Talking Activities with Young Children

Ask children the following questions (ask only three or four questions at any one time):

> What is happening?
>
> What has happened?
>
> What do you think will happen now?
>
> How did this happen?
>
> What caused this to happen?
>
> What took place before this happened?
>
> Where have you seen something like this happen?
>
> How could we make something like this happen?
>
> How does this compare with what we saw or did?
>
> How can we do this more easily?
>
> How can you do this more quickly?

Or ask:

> What kind of a thing is it?
>
> What is it called?
>
> Where is it found?
>
> What does it look like?

Have you seen anything else like it? Where? When?

How is it like other things?

How is it different from other things?

How can you recognize or identify it?

How did it get its name?

What other names does it have?

What can you do with it?

What is it made of?

How was it made?

What is its purpose?

How does it work or operate?

Best Kinds of Books for Children

Simple stories, animal stories

ABC books that are clever and different

Counting books for beginners

Mother Goose rhymes

Learning books

Lullabies and bedtime/sleepy stories

Books about themselves and other people

Any book you think your child would enjoy

Books for Young Children (Part III)

Seuss, Dr. *Horton Hatches the Egg*. Random, 1940. Dedicated Horton is 100 percent faithful.

Slobodkina, Esphyr. *Caps for Sale*. Young Scott, 1947. A tale of a peddler, some monkeys, and their monkey business.

Steig, William. *Sylvester and the Magic Pebble*. Windmill, 1969. A careless wish turns Sylvester into a rock, but the tragedy is resolved with humor and tenderness.

Yolen, Jane. *Owl Moon*. Philomel, 1987. Caldecott medal winner, 1988.

Zemach, Harve, & Margot Zemach. *Mommy Buy Me a China Doll*. Follett, 1966. From an Ozark song. Liza Lou has outlandish plans.

Zion, Gene. *Harry the Dirty Dog*. Pictures by Margaret Bloy Graham. Harper, 1956. Harry has such fun getting dirty, but then Harry's family can't recognize him.

More Books to Read Aloud

Five-, six-, and seven-year-olds will enjoy these books, too.

Ackerman, K., & D. Ray. *The Banshee*. Philomel, 1990.

Alexander, M. *Move Over, Twerp*. Dial Books, 1981.

Alexander, S. *Dear Phoebe*. Little, Brown, 1984.

Aliki. *We Are Best Friends*. Greenwillow, 1982.

Allard, H., & J. Marshall. *Miss Nelson is Missing*. Houghton Mifflin, 1977.

Allender, D. *Shake My Sillies Out*. Crown Publishers, 1987.

Anno, M. *All in a Day*. Philomel, 1986.

Base, G. *My Grandma Lived in Gooligulch*. Harry A. Abrahams, 1983.

Belloc, H. *Matilda. . . .* Knopf, 1991.

Carle, E. *The Grouchy Ladybug*. Crowell, 1977.

Chorao, D. *Grumley the Grouch*. Holiday House, 1980.

Cohen, M., & L. Hoban. *Jim Meets the Thing*. Greenwillow, 1981.

Cole, J. *It's Too Noisy*. Crowell, 1989.

Coleridge, A., and R. Harvey. *The Friends of Emily Culpepper*. Putnam, 1987.

Conrad, P. *The Tub People*. Harper & Row, 1989.

Couzyn, J. *Bad Day*. Dutton, 1988.

Cuyler, M. *That's Good! That's Bad!* Holt, 1991.

Ehlert, L. *Fish Eyes*. Harcourt Brace Jovanovich, 1990.

Farber, N. *I Found Them in the Yellow Pages*. Little, Brown, 1973.

Gackenbach, D. *Harry and the Terrible Whatzit*. Houghton Mifflin, 1977.

Geissert, A. *Pigs from A to Z*. Houghton Mifflin, 1986.

Goode, D. *I Hear a Noise*. Dutton, 1988.

Holder, H. *Crows*. Farrar, Straus and Giroux, 1987.

Kellog, S. *Aster Aardvark's Alphabet Adventure*. Morrow, 1987.

Mahy, M. *The Great White Man-Eating Shark*. Dial, 1989.

Mayer, M. *There's Something in My Attic*. Dial, 1988.

Meddaugh, S. *Too Many Monsters*. Houghton Mifflin, 1982.

Merrian, E. *Fighting Words*. Morrow, 1992.

Nordqvist, S. *Willie in the Big World*. Morrow, 1985.

Parkinson, K. *The Enormous Turnip*. Whitman, 1986.

Pelavin, C. *Ruby's Revenge*. Punam, 1972.

Rice, E. *What Sadie Sang*. Greenwillow, 1976.

Sendak, M. *One Was Johnny*. Harper & Row, 1962.

Sendak, M. *Pierre, A Cautionary Tale. . . .* Harper & Row, 1962.

Sendak, M. *Where the Wild Things Are*. Harper & Row, 1963.

Seuss, Dr. *The Sneetches*. Random House, 1950.

Seuss, Dr. *Thidwick the Big-Hearted Moose*. Random House, 1948.

Seuss, Dr. *Yertle the Turtle*. Random House, 1950.

Sheeter, B. *The Discontented Mother.* Harcourt, Brace, Jovanovich, 1980.

Slobodkin, L. *Excuse Me Certainly.* Vanguard Press, 1959.

Smith, L. *Glasses—Who Needs 'Em?* Viking, 1991.

Steig, W. *Amos and Boris.* Farrar, Straus and Giroux, 1971.

Steig, W. *Rotten Island.* Goldine, 1984.

Steptoe, J. *Mufaro's Beautiful Daughters.* Lothrop, Lee & Shepard, 1987.

Stevensen, J. *"Could Be Worse!"* Greenwillow, 1977.

Stevensen, J. *No Friends.* Greenwillow, 1986.

Stevensen, J. *That Dreadful Day.* Greenwillow, 1985.

Stevensen, J. *The Worst Person in the World at Crab Beach.* Greenwillow, 1988.

Stevensen, J. *Yuch!* Greenwillow, 1984.

Udry, J. *A Tree is Nice.* Harper & Row, 1956.

Ungerer, T. *No Kiss for Mother.* Harper & Row, 1973.

Ungerer, T. *The Three Robbers.* Antheneum, 1962.

Vincent, G. *Smile, Ernest and Celeste.* Greenwillow, 1982.

Viorst, J. *Alexander and the Terrible, Horrible, No Good, Very Bad Day.* Antheneum, 1972.

Vogel, M. *1 Is No Fun But 20 Is Plenty.* Antheneum, 1965.

Williams, L. *The Little Old Lady Who Was Not Afraid of Anything.* Crowell, 1986.

Zemach, M. *It Could Always Be Worse.* Farrar, Straus and Giroux, 1976.

Zion, G. *The Meanest Squirrel I Ever Met.* Scribner, 1962.

For these and other children's favorites, please see your children's librarian.

UNDERSTANDING 2-, 3-, AND 4-YEAR-OLDS (#1)

Teacher's Name

◇ ◇

Understanding Two-Year-Olds

Every child is different, as every parent knows. Still, it is helpful to know what other children might be doing developmentally at a particular age. If your child doesn't fit this particular age group, read the Parent Paper that discusses older children or read other materials about younger children. By exploring and keeping in mind the general stages of child development, you may be able to better understand your child's everyday behavior as well as his or her occasional behavior.

Did you know that you (the parent) are your child's most important teacher? Research has shown this over and over. Research also shows that the most important factor in a child's success and development is an adult who thinks he or she is wonderful.

General Characteristics of the Two-Year-Old

- Demonstrates unevenly developed motor skills. Large muscle coordination is good (the child can walk and climb), but small muscle and eye-hand coordination are still not well-developed.
- Goes through rapid language development. Vocabulary increases from a few words or short sentences to up to 2,000 words by age four.
- Gradually acquires skills in dressing and feeding self.
- Goes through changes in sleep patterns. He or she is gradually giving up daytime naps, but still needs a nap or rest period and about 12 hours of sleep at night.
- Has almost a complete set of baby teeth.
- Often has begun to establish toilet habits and usually will be able to handle his or her own needs by age four.

Characteristic Behavior

- Plays alone, or plays beside, but not with, others.
- Does not share or take turns too well.
- Often says "no," but gradually becomes able to accept adult limits. Wants adult approval and likes to be close to mother and father.

- Helps around the house and is beginning to understand his or her surroundings and the demands of daily life. Likes to feel familiar with things and have a sense of security.
- Imitates language, manners, and habits.
- Is constantly active and shows tiredness by becoming irritable or restless. Seems to have an urgent need to explore.
- Gradually learns what is acceptable and what is not. Much repetition is important.
- Demonstrates great curiosity and asks countless questions.

Special Needs

- A need for love and affection from parents. Two-year-olds also need guidance and a pattern of behavior to follow.
- A need for time, patience, understanding, and genuine interest from adults.
- A need for simple, clear routines and limited choices.
- A need for opportunities to learn sharing and taking turns, to learn to play cooperatively with other children.

Teacher's Name

◊ ◊ ◊ ◊ ◊ ◊ ◊ ◊ ◊ ◊ ◊ ◊ ◊ ◊ ◊ ◊ ◊ ◊ ◊ ◊

Understanding Three-Year-Olds

Every child is different, as every parent knows. Still, it is helpful to know what other children might be doing developmentally at a particular age. If your child doesn't fit this particular age group, read the selection on older or younger children in these Parent Papers. By discovering more about general stages of child development, you may be able to better understand your child's everyday behavior as well as his or her occasional behavior.

Did you know that you (the parent) are your child's most important teacher? Research has shown this over and over again. Research also shows that the most important factor in a child's success and development is an adult who thinks he or she is wonderful.

General Characteristics of the Three-Year-Old

- Demonstrates motor skills that are still unevenly developed. Large muscle coordination is still much better than small muscle and eye-hand coordination.
- Has a full set of baby teeth.
- Shows an awareness of the sequence of steps and the probable outcomes of his or her activities. The three-year-old begins to plan ahead.
- Continues to develop language ability at full speed. The most important and amazing verbal development occurs this year.
- Acquires more skills in feeding and dressing self.
- Goes through changes in sleep patterns, but still needs a daytime nap or rest period and nearly 12 hours of sleep at night. A three-year-old may get tired easily.
- Toilet habits are improving.

Characteristic Behaviors

- Shows more interest in playing with other children. He or she still needs to play alone some, and is not ready to share or take turns too often.
- Wants adult approval and likes to cuddle. The three-year-old may reject adults, but still needs them.
- Becomes even more interested in helping around the house.

476

- Likes to imitate language, manners, and habits.
- Experiments and explores within adult limits.
- Gradually learns what is acceptable behavior and what is not.
- Enjoys looking at picture and story books, and has a better understanding of words. A three-year-old shows great curiosity and still asks many questions.

Special Needs

- A need for the security of love and affection from parents, adult direction, and a consistent pattern of behavior to follow.
- A need for time, patience, understanding, and genuine interest from adults.
- A need for simple, clear daily schedules and limited choices.
- A need for opportunities to learn give-and-take, and to play with other children.
- A need for a wider scope of activity.

Teacher's Name

◇ ◇

Understanding Four-Year-Olds

Every child is different, as every parent knows. Still, it is helpful to know what other children might be doing developmentally at a particular age. If your child doesn't fit his or her particular age group, read the material about younger children in these Parent Papers or look for material about older children. By finding out more about the general stages of child development, you may be better able to understand your child's everyday behavior as well as his or her occasional behavior.

Did you know that you (the parent) are your child's most important teacher? Research has shown this over and over; research also shows that the most important factor in a child's success and achievement is an adult who thinks he or she is wonderful.

General Characteristics of the Four-Year-Old

- The desire to run, not walk, and the desire to yell, not talk. However, a four-year-old still wants adult approval.
- Motor development is still better in terms of large muscles than small muscles or hand-eye coordination.
- Rapid language development continues up to and past 2,000 words.
- Becomes quite skillful in feeding and dressing himself or herself, but may need occasional help.
- Develops sleep patterns that still incorporate up to 12 hours of sleep each night.
- Toilet habits are established. The four-year-old child usually takes care of his or her own needs by this age period.

Characteristic Behaviors

- Shows more independence and reliability.
- Has more interests in many things, including an interest in people and the way they act.
- Plays with real purpose, and engages in much more imaginative play. He or she begins to pretend to be other people or animals.

- Better understands surrounding environment and enjoys trips. He or she asks searching questions about people and their relationships to others.
- Is able to accept necessary limits and restraints from adults.
- Likes to be close to mother and father.
- Is constantly active. Likes to help around the house, and imitates language and habits.
- Becomes capable of longer stretches of quiet activity as he or she approaches five.
- Learns many new words and asks many questions.

Special Needs

- A need for love and affection from parents. Four-year-olds also need guidance and a pattern of behavior they can imitate. They need to feel valued.
- A need for time, patience, understanding, and genuine interest from adults.
- A need for a wider scope of activity and limited freedom to move about, and to move away from the home surroundings.
- A need for opportunities to do things for himself or herself.

Teacher's Name

◇ ◇

Discipline: A Learning Process

A *disciple* is someone who learns. *Discipline*, then, should be a learning process, not a process of scaring a child into NOT doing something. By explaining and helping a child to understand, you help her learn how to behave. You also help her to communicate better and to develop self-control. A child who is scared into not doing something or saying something in front of one adult, may well say or do that very thing at school or in the center.

1. *Show children what to do instead of saying "Don't," "Stop," and "Quit."* Children learn how to act when you show them what to do. Just stopping their negative behavior doesn't teach them what to do next time. For example, telling a child, "Wait until the floor is dry" is better than saying, "Don't walk on the wet floor." Saying, "Hold it this way" is better than saying, "Don't drop it."

2. *Use substitutes.* If you have to take something away from a child, give him something different to play with. Provide active or noisy activities that are acceptable ways to let off aggression. Digging, shouting at the trees outside, and mopping are all good. (Saw about 2 feet off the handle of a mop for a very useful new toy.)

3. *Encourage children to think of something else when they are unhappy.* Children forget quickly. Call a child's attention to something else. This distraction will take her mind off the cause of the unhappiness. This works *very* well with children under two years of age.

4. *Show a child how to help you when he bothers you.* If a child is bothering you as you work, find something else for him to do. Show the child how to help. Giving him your attention may be more necessary right then than the job you are doing.

5. *Establish trust; build a positive relationship.* Build trust with your child by giving praise when she comes closer and closer to doing something the way you want her to do it. This is called "shaping behavior," and lets your child know you are cheering her efforts.

6. *Aim for consistency.* A child learns best if the rules don't change too much. It's better to have just a few rules and then really stick to those few. If you have too many rules, you forget them and so does your child. Wait to add new rules until some old situations have been resolved.

7. *Consider your body language.* Reminding a child with a frown or a smile becomes more effective in shaping behavior as a child grows older. Explain your facial expressions to a young child. For example, say, "I'm smiling because . . ." or "I am frowning because. . . ."

8. *Know your child.* Some children respond to different rewards or different instructions in various ways. This can be true even in the same family. Study your child and determine what methods help him to understand. Learn what a child this age is capable of handling. By doing some research, you won't ask more of your child than he can deliver.

9. *Understand your own personal style.* Your child can get used to your style, but it helps if you both come to understand it. Try to respond to situations as a thinking adult rather than as a "super parent" or an infuriated child. (This is hard to do, but worth it.) You can tell your child what your style is. "I may not seem upset now, but if you do that three times, I'm really going to be upset." Some parents have a "quick to anger, quick to hug" style, while other parents are calmer.

10. *Consider your child's verbal development.* How well a child understands your directions and can express to you what he or she needs or wants can be the single most important factor in the smoothness of your relationship. The more you help your child learn new words by reading and talking with her, the faster frustrations can be resolved.

11. *Encourage decision-making.* Saying such things as, "Well, Michael, you make the decision—either this or this," helps your child build self-control. To your child, a decision *he* makes is more interesting to him than one you make for him. This skill will also help your child in later life.

12. *Do some scheduling.* Children do best when quiet and active play are alternated. Think over the most difficult times of the day. Reflect on what a small (or large) scheduling change might accomplish. If both parents work, some singing in the morning might get the day off to a happier start, for instance.

13. *Set up rooms to make them "child-friendly."* Placing furniture and belongings so your child can do things for herself greatly helps to remove frustrations and build her competence. The child who is helped to believe "I can do it" feels good about herself, and develops self-control.

Summary

Think of something in the course of your childhood that helped to build *your* self-esteem and thus your self-control. It is important for a child to learn that his efforts toward a goal are as important as the goal itself. With this view, failure is less of a defeat because learning occurs along the way. "We'll try again and we'll learn from this" are wonderful words everyone likes to hear.

Parents' attitudes and moods convey either healthy respect to children or discouragement. If parents reinforce good behavior, children will grow to do what parents expect.

HELPING A YOUNG CHILD DEVELOP SELF-CONTROL (#2)

Teacher's Name _____

◇ ◇

Self-Control

1. What is the most difficult task for *you* in the area of self-control in connection with your child?

2. What is the most difficult task for *your child* in the area of self-control?

3. What is the most difficult task for *you* in teaching and guiding your child to control his or her emotions and actions?

4. If you have visited our classroom, what are some of the ways the adults involved here tried to behave in a socially acceptable manner? (Adult behavior that a child *sees* is much more impressive than what an adult *says*.)

5. Watch your child playing with some of his or her friends. At home, observe several children who are involved in frustrating situations. On another sheet of paper, describe the reactions of the children. Try to observe children older and younger than your own child, as well as children of both sexes.

Discussion

1. *Children may need different kinds of self-control for different situations.* A big concept for a young child to learn is to use such words as, "Please give me that. That's mine!" or "Stop it! I don't like that!" instead of using actions such as pushing, shoving, grabbing, or hitting to express themselves. Supply your child with the words he could use to replace unacceptable actions. For example, supply the words, "Please open the door!" Then say: "Do not kick the door when you want it opened." A child needs to be told what to do as well as what not to do. If your first attempts of the "use words and not actions" approach are not 100 percent successful, that's alright; your child is learning new words and will soon be able to use them at the appropriate time. Repeated trials will teach the idea. Try to use words and not actions yourself so your child will see you using acceptable behavior.

2. *Sometimes a young child needs to be completely removed from a situation.* If your child is playing with friends or with older children and is getting tired, removing him to a quiet activity may prevent a quarrel. A chair or place for a "time out" period can be quite successful. In this approach, the child sits with a book or a toy in the "time out" chair or place, until he feels like being with people again.

3. *Anticipate that when the parent is preoccupied, the child's self-control will deteriorate.* If a parent is visiting with guests, on the telephone, or occupied in some other way and a young child starts to fuss and whine, it is better for the parent to interrupt an activity briefly than to accept the formation of a bad habit. The parent can take the child to a quiet place, give her a book or toy, then say quite firmly, "You may not fuss while I am on the phone." Even if the child comes out again, the idea has been planted. If the parent does this every time there is a problem, the desired learning soon occurs. On the other hand, if the parent hands the child a cookie to quiet her, this will teach the child that if she fusses and whines while Mom or Dad is busy, a reward will be coming.

After one or two weeks, answer the questions at the beginning of this Parent Paper again. See if any answers have changed. If you have extra time, list good and bad examples of adults guiding children. Refer to this list of good examples when you need to. Some parents keep this list handy for a crisis moment.

Additional Notes

HELPING A YOUNG CHILD DEVELOP SELF-CONTROL (#3)

Teacher's Name

◇ ◇

Children Need Adults for Guidance

As children grow, their need to be independent often leads them into trouble. Sometimes they put themselves in danger and often they put the people around them into uncomfortable situations. Young children frequently handle things too roughly, using small, eager, but awkward, fingers. This Parent Paper points out some planning ideas and techniques that can be used in your child's classroom or at home to redirect children's actions into acceptable behavior.

1. Look around your child's classroom. Consider the reasons why materials are placed where they are, and why specific amounts of each material are made available. What are some ways children are guided to use materials in a beneficial way?

2. What happens when there is a quarrel over materials or toys? What language does the adult who is dealing with the children use in this situation?

3. Children learn very quickly by imitation. Adult behavior that children see is much more impressive to them than what adults may say. How does the teacher show good relations between people? How does he or she show respect for others? How does the teacher demonstrate care for materials and equipment?

In guiding children, adults can:

- *Strengthen their self-control.* Often boosting the child's interest in what he or she is doing, or providing the child with extra materials, will accomplish this.

- *Reduce frustrations.* When a child can't reach his or her goals, the adult can:

   Remove temptations

   Restructure the situation; provide for a quiet activity; lend a helping hand

   See that the child's possessions are easy to take out and put away (i.e., check the child's room layout)

Remove the child until he regains self-control (allow the child to ride a truck outside, go to his room with a book, or use the time-out chair, for example)

- *Appeal to understanding.* Explain how and why you want something done (or not done). You might say, for example, "Can you pick up two toys and I'll pick up two toys? How many toys do we have now?"
- *Use imagination.* Set up some role playing situations: "You be the Baby Bear and I'll be Mama Bear and then we can. . . ." Using special voices during role play is a big help in capturing the child's attention. Have children take turns giving you instructions.

Remember:

- A positive approach brings positive results.
- The ripple effect works both negatively and positively. A highly emotional approach to a situation distracts the family. If adults yell, children will too.
- Focus on what is being done rather than on feelings or on the child. Say, "Please paint on the paper and not on your chair."

More ideas:

- Give gifts that help with future quiet times, such as crayons, drawing paper, spiral notebooks, or photo albums.
- Have children make memory books of vacations. These books might include pictures, photographs, even pressed weeds from summer or from a walk with grandmother.
- Keep paper, old magazines, paste, blunt scissors, and other interesting materials in a special box for quiet times.

Evaluation

Have you tried two of these ideas in the last two weeks? Give yourself a blue ribbon or a pat on the back as a "Good Parent Award."

Additional Notes

Teacher's Name

◇ ◇

Toys That Teach: What to Choose

When choosing toys, consider the major areas in which a child develops. Toys that teach and enhance development will be the result of careful selection. The major areas of a child's development are physical, mental, social, and emotional. The following list gives some ideas of appropriate toys for preschoolers that focus on developing skills in these four areas. Write your own ideas in the margins and keep this Parent Paper handy for birthdays, Christmas, calls from grandparents, or other special occasions.

Toys for Two- and Three-year-olds

Children this age especially need toys that build physical coordination, develop independence, and satisfy curiosity.

Physical Development ("Fitness")

Steps for climbing to reach sink and toilet

Large balls

Doll carriages

Large trucks to ride

Large, light, hollow blocks (See the Parent Paper "How to Make Toys for Your Child")

Swing set, climbing gym, tricycles, outdoor equipment

Outdoor sandbox

Mental Development ("Brainwork")

Simple inlay puzzles (just a few pieces to start)

Put-it-together train, boat

Colored beads to string

Legos, table toys that interlock (store and use these in gift-type flat boxes with lids)

Blocks

Rubber animals and people to use with blocks

Picture books, song records

Shiny metal or unbreakable mirror

Water toys for bath tub or sink

Social Development ("Teamwork")

Housekeeping equipment

Dress-up hats and clothes for boys and girls (make-believe helps learning)

Large unbreakable washable doll

Ride-a-stick horse

Clothespins, clothesline for hanging artwork, doll clothes

Paper bags, grocery boxes, and cans to play "store"

Tea set, plastic dishes, eggbeater, pots and pans

Small cars and trucks

Emotional Development ("Tension Releasers")

Rocking chair/rocking horse

Pounding toys

Large brushes, poster paints, crayons

Clay and/or play dough

Finger paint (use in bathtub for easy cleanup)

Sand and cups, pails, spoons, strainer, shovels, orange juice cans—for pouring, digging, modeling

Musical instruments—bells, xylophone, triangle, drums, pans

Straws to blow bubbles

Toys for Four- and Five-year-olds

Children this age have a special need for plenty of activity. They want to learn about their world by seeing and doing things. Their teamwork is getting better and toys that help with all these needs are sure to teach. All the toys listed for two- and three-year-olds are still good, along with the following:

Physical Development ("Fitness")

Old tires on the ground for jumping

Bean bags and baskets or boxes to throw them in

Large wooden or cardboard boxes to play train

Wagons

Mental Development ("Brainwork")

Blackboard and white chalk (materials that will be used in grade school)

Small-sized desk or table and chair

Bulletin board to pin up artwork

Books and records with more detail than for age three

Puzzles with more pieces

Crayons, markers, paper of several sizes, including newspapers

More put-together toys

Lotto games

Scissors with rounded points

Glue or paste

Social Development ("Teamwork")

Small cars and trucks (play "gas station")

Finger and hand puppets

More blocks to add to original set

Doctor kit, hospital kit

Flannel board and flannel cut-outs

More props for make-believe, such as costume jewelry and hats from different adult occupations

Emotional Development ("Tension Releasers")

More toys or cans for sand and water play

Eggbeater for water play

Hammer and nails for supervised woodworking

Painting of all kinds (plain water and a roller can be used outside in the summer)

Musical instruments and record or tape player

Teacher's Name

◇ ◇

What Toys Can Teach

Math

Math learning begins when a child learns that two parts of a whole can be taken apart and put back together again. This realization can occur while cutting a cupcake or an apple in half, or while playing with blocks—one long block and two short blocks that combine in length to equal the long one. Learning the vocabulary for math is very important in early years. Using terms such as *how much, too much, half full, all gone, a quarter full,* and other measurement phrases can be incorporated into sand and water play.

Estimating is a process used throughout life and can be learned during block and water play. For example, watch a child estimate where to put two blocks to make the bottom of his or her bridge. This skill improves as three-year-olds become four-year-olds. During water play, ask a child to guess how many more spoonfuls (or cupfuls) of water are needed to fill up a pot. Fractions will not be so strange in elementary school if a child has been talking about them for years. Look for activities that require the child to make comparisons: More or less? Light or heavy? Thick or thin? Long or short?

Toys that help math learning include:

Blocks

Sand or pouring materials that are contained within a large pan, such as rice, macaroni, bird seed, or cornmeal

Water, cups, and utensils

Ruler

Tape measure

Puzzles

Straws

Language/Prereading

A child must learn to talk and think before she can learn to read. Any activity that "gives" a child new words is valuable in the early years. Looking at and talking about a book or some pictures a few minutes every day will do a great deal to help your child in first grade. Records and songs also help children develop vocabulary.

Any toys that help a child to see sameness or difference in objects, pictures, shapes, colors, or symbols help build reading skills. Stringing beads, working with "fit-together" table toys, looking at details in pictures, and talking about what people are doing can all help to develop reading readiness and language skills.

Toys that encourage language/prereading skills include:

Books

Records

Lotto games (make your own from two matching catalogs)

Puppets

Games, especially board games

Old magazines that contain lots of pictures

Props that can be used to act out stories read in books

"Fit-together" toys

Dice or dominoes to match and do groupings

Sensory Learning

The more senses involved in a child's learning experience, the stronger the learning will be. An example of this is how the smells and tastes of holiday foods can take us back to certain times and events in our own childhoods.

In addition to *seeing* and learning to observe carefully, *hearing* samenesses and differences in sounds and recognizing common sounds are important for learning. *Touching* concrete objects, actually handling materials, is essential for young children and doubles or triples the impact of learning for adults, too. Learning to identify substances by their *smell* is fun for young children and can be a springboard to new conversations and thus to new words.

Children need to use their sense of *taste* to learn such words as *crunchy, sweet, sour, mushy,* and *sticky.* Most two-year-olds, who can barely talk, can tell you the name of their favorite cereal. Talking about food while you are eating with a child is a wonderful time to build vocabulary that identifies foods and their textures. For example: "This cracker tastes very crunchy and salty."

Toys and activities that help children learn through the senses include:

Musical toys or instruments

Objects placed inside small boxes for a listen-and-describe activity: rice, pebbles, pennies, beans. Fasten the boxes securely. For a younger child, make matching pairs of "listening boxes." Ask the child to find a box that sounds the same as yours.

Records, song books

Making popcorn

Kitchen items placed inside jars for a smell-and-describe activity: tea bag, mustard, peanut butter, chocolate

Objects placed inside a sock such as a stone, a stick, a pine cone, a spoon, or a cotton ball, to provide a feel-and-describe activity. Have the child describe how the object feels.

Activities in the kitchen, such as tearing lettuce for salad, making instant pudding, and pouring ingredients into a bowl are good for young helpers.

Teacher's Name

◇ ◇

How to Make Toys for Your Child

Toys or activities that are made at home are especially interesting to young children. They carry an extra ingredient of love and the child feels important, like "somebody special." The low price of homemade toys is especially attractive, and often the play value of these toys is long-lasting.

1. *Blocks.* Rinse out and stuff half-gallon milk cartons with crumpled newspaper. Tape the cartons securely closed to form a square end. You might also want to jam one carton inside a second to form a stronger block. These blocks can be covered with colored contact paper, but this is not necessary. (Tip: This can be done two or three at a time while watching television.)

2. *Puzzles.* Glue a colorful magazine picture onto a piece of cardboard. Cut the cardboard into three or four shapes for a two- or three-year-old; five to ten shapes for a four- or five-year-old. Store each puzzle in a separate envelope.

3. *Ride-in Train.* Line up three or four cardboard boxes to make a train that children can sit in. Add slips of paper for "tickets" and appoint a "ticket taker." This is a good activity for rainy weather.

4. *Play House.* Obtain a very large carton, such as a box from a washing machine or from a moving company. Use a marker to draw a door and windows onto the box. Cut out the doors and at least one window. This house will last about two weeks or more and is greatly appreciated.

5. *Tent.* Place a blanket over a card table. This makeshift tent allows children to invent games about camping, army, or whatever the child's imagination chooses. With a pillow inside and some books, the tent can be left up in a child's room as a reading corner.

6. *Puppets.* Stuff brown paper lunch bags with newspaper. Secure them with a wire twist-tie or rubber band. Draw faces and hair with markers. Show your child how to use a table as a stage by holding the puppets up from behind the table. Discarded white or light-colored socks also make good puppets. Draw faces on them with markers.

7. *Indoor Sandbox.* Fill a large roasting pan or basin with macaroni, birdseed, cornmeal, or beans. Any substance that will pour is good. Provide cans, measuring cups, and a funnel. When your child is finished playing,

store the "sand" in a plastic bag or cover the container with aluminum foil. (This activity is good for early math learning.)

8. *Beads for Stringing*. Provide your child with empty spools and a shoelace. The spools can be painted if desired. Using a needle and thread to string round-shaped cereal (such as Cheerios™™) for the birds is an activity young children enjoy. Rigatoni can be strung on a shoelace to make a "necklace" or a "bracelet." It also can be painted.

9. *Easel for Painting*. Tape paper to the bottom of the refrigerator door. Place newspaper on the floor beneath and let your child sit on the floor and create artwork with crayons or paint.

10. *Homemade Paint*. Add food coloring to liquid starch to create some paints. For finger paints, use instant vanilla pudding that has food coloring added.

11. *Food Coloring*. During water play, put a few drops of red food coloring into the water. Later, add a few drops of yellow and ask the child what happens. Do this with blue and yellow and with red and blue. Freeze ice cubes of different colors. Put a red and yellow ice cube into a bowl and ask your child to tell you what happens. Add a squirt of liquid soap to the water to make bubbles.

12. *Play Dough*. Mix or let your child mix 2 cups flour with 1 cup salt, ¼ to ½ cup water, ¼ cup oil, and a few drops of food coloring of your choice. Keep the dough in a plastic bag.

Additional Notes

Leadership Enablers

The following leadership enablers represent just a few ideas for making changes in causal variables as described in chapter 2. These changes should help to build loyalty, gratitude, or a feeling of self-worth in persons, and these attitudes may lead to a climate conducive to higher quality child care. Many other types of causal variables might be considered when deciding to make changes, such as encouraging workers to take courses and workshops, improving personnel policies, creating more flexible hours or schedules, and any others discussed in chapter 2 of the text. In these leadership enablers, the causal variables that are addressed are described in the "How to Do It" sections. Output variables and intervening variables are described in the "Did It Work?" sections.

◇ ◇

A Certificate of Recognition

Benefits

Building the self-esteem of staff members and encouraging them to foster positive attitudes towards the program; showing that the staff's efforts are noticed and appreciated

Time Needed

30 to 45 minutes per month

How to Do It

1. Make certificates or "Happy Grams" based on notes in each teacher's file. See the following example:

> _____ Day Care Center
> Date _____
>
> A Personal Note
> To: Susie Williams
>
> Thank you so much for previewing the new six month goals for Child Development at our total staff meeting. You did a great job!
>
> _____
> Director

2. Present the certificate at a staff meeting or share the information and appreciation at a staff meeting.

Did It Work?

Was the certificate appreciated? Was the work attitude of this staff member changed? Did it make a difference? (Intervening variables)

Other Possibilities

Give similar certificates to children or parents.

◇ ◇

(Your Center Name) Child Care Center Seal of Approval

Benefits

Developing a staff file of art and seasonal activities to be used in the center program

Time Needed

1 hour

What You Need

Children's activities and art books borrowed from the library

How to Do It

1. Everyone takes a book and looks for *good* activities; when an activity is found, its place is marked with a bookmark.
2. The staff votes on the selected choices (i.e., gives them the "Seal of Approval").
3. The chosen activities can be filed under appropriate titles, such as pasting, printing, cutting, etc.
4. Activities can also be filed according to the ages they serve: 6- to 12-year-olds for the after-school program; 2- to 4-year-olds, or 4- to 6-year-olds for your child-care program.

Did It Work?

At staff meetings, the director or head teacher can ask for feedback on activities tried and for any success reports (output variables). Did teachers appreciate having new activities at their fingertips? (Intervening variable)

Other Possibilities

Find books about games, music, woodworking, or any other topic on which the staff wants to build a file.

◇ ◇

Teacher of the Month

Benefits

Building self-esteem and feelings of self-worth for teachers

Time Needed

30 minutes once a month

How to Do It

1. During a staff meeting, make a chart of teacher goals, jobs, and activities that are important to the group.
2. Casually observe class areas or classrooms at 3-day intervals.
3. Keep a record in the form of a checklist of teachers who are meeting the goals or implementing the activities discussed at the staff meeting.
4. Choose a "Teacher of the Month" based on goals met. Make a bulletin board that features a different teacher each month.
5. Give a special small gift to the teacher chosen, or buy him or her lunch.

Did It Work?

After a few months, take note of whether teachers are working towards the goal of "Teacher of the Month" (output variable).

Other Possibilities

1. Choose a "Teacher of the Year" based on the same criteria used for choosing a "Teacher of the Month."
2. Feature a "Child of the Month" for perfect attendance or for meeting other criteria.
3. Choose a "Parent of the Year" or "Parent of the Month." Brainstorm criteria and activities at a parents' meeting.
4. Recognize six months of perfect attendance for teachers.
5. Do a bulletin board on yourself if you accomplish a difficult task or meet important goals.

◇ ◇

Staff Recognition at Board Meetings

Benefits

Building self-esteem of staff members and reinforcing staff strengths; keeping the Board informed and giving the Board knowledge of "good" child-care activities; improving staff and parent and/or staff and Board relations

Time Needed

5 minutes every 2 months

How to Do It

1. Mention in a parent newsletter that the director would welcome notes from parents praising teachers' strengths.
2. Keep a file and present the notes at Board meetings.

Did It Work?

Does the Board seem to have more concrete or positive feelings about the program or the teachers? Do they seem to be learning through this experience? Is the director's choice of staff reaffirmed? Does the staff enjoy receiving additional recognition from someone other than the director? (Intervening variables)

Other Possibilities

Encourage parents to verbally praise teachers for their efforts. Parents might put together a "Staff Scrapbook" to present to the staff on a special day. This scrapbook can be shared with the Board as well and can include children's artwork. This makes a wonderful end-of-the-year (or five- or ten-year) "award" presentation when done for an individual.

◇ ◇ ◇ ◇ ◇ ◇ ◇ ◇ ◇ ◇ ◇ ◇ ◇ ◇ ◇ ◇ ◇ ◇ ◇ ◇

Secret Santa or Holiday Fun

Benefits

Building concern and understanding about each other; building staff interaction

Time Needed

5 minutes a day of school/center time for 5 days, and 15 minutes a day of home or work time

How to Do It

1. Each staff member hangs a stocking in a central place.
2. The staff draws names for a person for whom each will be "Secret Santa."
3. Each day, each Secret Santa sneaks a "gift" into the stocking of the person whose name he or she drew.
4. Inexpensive, homemade, funny, and creative gifts are to be used. For example, if the teacher likes burned popcorn, Santa fills the stocking with burned popcorn one day. Obviously, Secret Santa has to learn a lot about his or her "person."

Did It Work?

Do teachers want to do similar things throughout the year? Do teachers ask to draw names in October so they have plenty of time to think of gifts? (Intervening variables)

Other Possibilities

Have a "Secret Ghost" at Halloween or a "Secret Bunny" at Easter. Instead of stockings, have staff members hunt for gifts each day in a scavenger hunt.

◇ ◇

Meet the Staff

Benefits

Informing parents and other staff members about a particular staff person so they can get to know him or her better; motivating staff, building self-esteem, and giving recognition

Time Needed

15 to 30 minutes once a month

How to Do It

1. Write an article for the parent newsletter that features a different staff person each month. Include information such as his or her background, skills, hobbies, family, etc.
2. Interview the staff person or let him or her help write the article, if you wish.

Did It Work?

Is the chosen staff person proud to see the article and to be recognized or "chosen?" Is he or she happier and more motivated? Do other staff members look forward to their turns? (Intervening variables)

Other Possibilities

Try selecting a "Child of the Month" or "Child of the Week."

LEADERSHIP ENABLERS

◊ ◊

Swap Day

Benefits

Encouraging teaching diversity and sharing ideas

Time Needed

15 minutes 2 days per week

How to Do It

1. On the first day, ask teachers to spend 15 minutes writing an informal classroom activity. List how the activity is done and what materials are needed.
2. On the second day, use the 15 minutes to discuss the activities with another teacher. Swap places with him or her and implement the activity.
3. Directors can do this too, but must be very tactful, as the goal is creativity, not evaluation.

Did It Work?

Did this activity generate enthusiasm and teacher interaction? Did it encourage creativity? (Intervening variables)

Other Possibilities

Swap classrooms for longer parts of the day or for a full day, but not if a child in the classroom is too new to the center.

◊ ◊

Staff Recognition Day

Benefits

Recognizing special achievements and highlighting the worth of the staff's work

Time Needed

About 2 hours sometime during the year; the director will have to spend some time planning and setting this up

How to Do It

1. Call in substitute teachers or parents to stay with the children and invite all the staff to a tea (or whatever event you decide).
2. Have special refreshments.
3. Talk about how worthwhile the work of providing quality care for young children is, and how well it is being done.
4. Give each staff person a small gift, such as a small pin that is a symbol of their dedication and hard work.
5. Give something special to staff members who have accomplished something unusual during the year, such as having received a degree, having good attendance, or having been with the center a long time.
6. Invite other interested persons in addition to the staff.

Did It Work?

Does the staff ask if it will be done every year? Is the staff morale improved? (Intervening variables)

Other Possibilities

Write about special achievements in a staff newsletter.

Motivator Activities

The following Motivator Activities represent a few ideas for making changes in the motivator variables in your center as described in chapter 7. These changes should help to build recognition, self-esteem, growth, a sense of achievement, and a sense of the worth of the work for staff members, parents, and children. Four motivator activities are described for each group, in no particular sequence. Many other possible "motivators" are discussed in chapter 7. The hygiene variables are easier to address and many personnel books contain ideas for improving rules and regulations, hours, pay, and interpersonal relations. Of course, these motivator ideas also help to improve interpersonal relations.

MOTIVATOR ACTIVITIES

◇ ◇ ◇ ◇ ◇ ◇ ◇ ◇ ◇ ◇ ◇ ◇ ◇ ◇ ◇ ◇ ◇ ◇ ◇ ◇

Alumni Day

Motivators

Sense of achievement, self-esteem, and worth of the work

Time Needed

2 hours a year

Materials Needed

Invitations, refreshments

How to Do It

1. Formally invite alumni and parents to the child-care center.
2. Encourage former enrollees to tell about their present successes and experiences.
3. Encourage parents to express their gratitude to teachers.
4. Offer refreshments.

Did It Work?

Does the staff want to do this again? Encourage feedback from the staff.

Other Possibilities

1. Invite local media, child-care administrators, and politicians to this event.
2. Give teachers a flower or a big decorative name tag to wear for the day.

◇ ◇

"We're Proud" Open House

Motivators

Growth, self-esteem (other benefits include sharing ideas with other child-care center staff)

Time Needed

2 hours twice a year

Materials

Refreshments, which can be prepared by the children and can highlight nutrition, if desired

How to Do It

1. Formally invite staff from a nearby child-care center.
2. Encourage the hosting staff to allow visitors to view their rooms and activity ideas.
3. Encourage informal conversations about your program and teaching techniques. Encourage visitors to share their ideas.
4. Offer refreshments.

Did It Work?

Do employees want to do this again? Ask for feedback about how to improve this activity the next time. Ask staff what they gained from this experience.

Other Possibilities

1. Visit the center of the other staff.
2. Invite parents and grandparents to the same open house.
3. Have a "drop in" afternoon once a month to encourage staff from other centers and parents to visit. Coffee or simple refreshments may be set up in a central location.
4. Provide recognition in general for the center by printing the center's logo on helium balloons.
5. Invite a local newspaper photographer to take pictures of a center event relating to the community, such as a story hour in the library or attendance at an Arbor Day event.

MOTIVATOR ACTIVITIES

◇ ◇ ◇ ◇ ◇ ◇ ◇ ◇ ◇ ◇ ◇ ◇ ◇ ◇ ◇ ◇ ◇ ◇ ◇ ◇

Mountain Climbing

Motivators

Esteem, achievement

Time Needed

5 minutes

Materials

A badge with a picture on it of a mountain climber who has reached the top (this can be drawn as a stick figure or can be clipped from a magazine); book about a curriculum topic of interest to the receiver

How to Do It

1. Honor teachers or other staff who have completed a course or degree.
2. Have a ceremony and deliver the badge during morning opening time.
3. Decorate the teacher's lunch table and have his or her food delivered to the table as special music is played or sung.
4. Present the gift-wrapped book.
5. Allow for the book's expense in the training section of the budget. Encourage the use of this book for planning.

Did It Work?

Was the teacher surprised and pleased? Do you give more books each year?

Other Possibilities

1. Give a "You're Number One!" badge.
2. Honor the teacher who has been with the school the most number of years.
3. Honor teachers for other large or small reasons, for example, give a prize for the brightest smile on the second floor.

508

◇ ◇

The Political Game of Life

Motivators

Responsibility, growth, autonomy (as well as enhancing awareness of the political establishment, improving child-care services for all persons)

Time Needed

1 hour during a staff meeting

Materials

Writing paper (personal stationery is fine); envelopes; stamps; addresses of local, state, or federal legislators

How to Do It

1. As a group, select one child-care law or bill that is under consideration.
2. Encourage each staff member to write his or her feelings about the bill and send it to a political official.
3. Invite the official to visit your center at any time or for an upcoming event with parents. Enclose a copy of your newsletter or other information about your center. (Some legislators do not know what good child-care programs look like.)

Did It Work?

Does the staff want to do this again? What did they gain from this project? Was the bill or law passed or defeated? Repeat the activity several times.

Other Possibilities

1. Encourage other centers to participate in this project.
2. If a legislator visits your center, pin a badge on him or her saying, "Friend of Children."
3. Have a newspaper or other media representative present to photograph and report the visit.
4. Take a snapshot of the official wearing the "Friend of Children" badge and enclose a copy of the photo the next time you write that legislator about supporting child-care services. Note: Non-profit organizations may not spend more than 10% of their budget on this type of activity—a far more generous amount than is needed here.

◇ ◇

Ice Breaker Nutrition Game

Motivator

Responsibility, growth

Time Needed

30 to 45 minutes

Materials

Empty food boxes, cans, and grocery bags; large (4' x 4') white sheet, cloth, paper, or oil cloth divided into 4 blocks representing the 4 food groups (a bed sheet is fine). Cut out and paste pictures that represent a particular food group into the corresponding box.

meat fish poultry	dairy
breads cereals	fruits vegetables

Hint: Have parents send in empty food containers for 3 or 4 weeks beforehand; in addition to being available for this activity, children can later use these containers to play store or to play in the housekeeping corner.

How to Do It

1. Have the mat or sheet lying on the floor where all can see it.
2. Give each parent a prefilled bag of groceries as he or she comes in.
3. Start the game by explaining the food groups.
4. Ask each parent to place each article of food on the mat in the proper food group block. Parents might also do this as they gather for a meeting as a "warm-up" game.
5. All "junk" food should be placed off the mat.
6. When everyone has finished, see how many items have been placed in the proper food blocks. Read the ingredients lists on items that have been misplaced.

Did It Work?

Do parents agree that it is important to look at ingredients on food boxes?

Other Possibilities

1. Display refreshments on a table after organizing them by food groups and labeling them.
2. Have handouts available that give several recipes for parents to take home.

◇ ◇

Center Decorations

Motivators

Growth, sense of achievement (other benefits include gaining new decorations for the center, promoting positive parent/child interaction, boosting parent creativity and encouraging home decoration, increasing parents' skills in saving money, helping staff and parents realize that scrap materials can be creatively recycled)

Time Needed

1 to 2 hours at the end of the center day

Materials Needed

Decorative pieces of scrap paper, egg cartons, pieces of wood, scrap pieces of plastic, tempera paint, glitter, shoe polish, egg shells, ribbon, scissors, glue, string, plastic bottles, milk containers, foam pieces, empty spools, wall paper scraps (Hint: Request that parents send in these items for 3 to 4 weeks before the event.)

How to Do It

1. Have children make bologna, peanut butter or other easy-to-make sandwiches and cut up some fruit to eat as a snack with parents when they arrive.
2. Lay out supplies on tables. Talk about some possibilities, then break into small groups to brainstorm. Assign different bulletin boards or planning locations to different groups.
3. Start and have fun. Give a lot of praise.

Did It Work?

Do children and parents display their work? Is staff and parent interaction benefited? Does the group want to decorate again for other seasons? Do other centers copy the idea?

Other Possibilities

1. Have parent and staff workshops to help parents make Christmas or holiday presents for their children. Ideas for presents might be puppets, simple toys, games, bean bags, or stuffed animals. Provide a babysitter and let parents share the cost.

2. List ideas in an "Idea Book" that parents can take home, or devote a page in the newsletter to ideas contributed by parents and staff. Use ideas from the "How to Make Toys" Parent Paper in Appendix B.

3. Make Christmas or holiday cards or ornaments.

◇ ◇ ◇ ◇ ◇ ◇ ◇ ◇ ◇ ◇ ◇ ◇ ◇ ◇ ◇ ◇ ◇ ◇ ◇ ◇

"My News for Mom" Calendar

Motivator

Autonomy, responsibility (other benefits include promoting communication between parent and child, providing opportunities for language development, and recalling activities for child)

Time Needed

5 to 10 minutes for parents, and 5 to 10 minutes for teachers to prepare

Materials Needed

Copies of calendar forms, enough to send home one with each child

How to Do It

Teachers prepare each child's calendar on Thursday to send home with him or her on Friday.

Monday	Tuesday	Wednesday	Thursday
Susie brought turtle to school. Learned finger play "there was a little turtle who lived in a box."	Policeman came to school. Ask me how to cross the street safely.	Painted with Q tips. I'll tell you the colors I used.	Made play doh. Here's the recipe: 2 cups flour, 1 cup salt, ½ cup water, ¼ cup oil, food coloring. Let's make it at home!

Did It Work?

Do the parents feel more involved with the child's school life? Does the child communicate more readily about school activities?

Other Possibilities

1. Include one or more home learning activity suggestions with the calendar.
2. Make a calendar with activity suggestions for each day in December to use at home. Some example activities might include feeding the birds, singing holiday music together, or making Christmas or holiday cards.

◇ ◇ ◇ ◇ ◇ ◇ ◇ ◇ ◇ ◇ ◇ ◇ ◇ ◇ ◇ ◇ ◇ ◇ ◇ ◇

Father-Grandfather Hour

Motivator

Recognition, growth (other benefits include introducing fathers and grand-fathers to the program the center or school offers; giving the children a time with important males in their lives)

Time Needed

1 hour or more at the end of the center day or on a Saturday morning

Materials

Magic markers, paint, cardboard, collage materials, and a snack, if desired

How to Do It

1. Invite fathers, grandfathers or an uncle or other male important to the child to the "Hour."
2. Have the staff plan the schedule so that everyone starts together in a large room with a music person. Sing easy songs that adults can join in on, then end with an action dance such as "Hokey Pokey."
3. Using materials in the child's classroom, have the men and the children make a game to take home. Serve a snack if this is planned. Close the session with a good-bye song.

Did It Work?

Was there positive feedback from all? Did the staff have a good feeling about the event? Were the children pleased about it?

Other Possibilities

1. Have a Mother/Grandmother Hour.
2. Do this activity with Executive Board members or other adults who need orientation to good child care.
3. Have a special day (perhaps a Saturday) to involve spouses who are usually prevented from involvement by work. Plan a special center project that these adults can participate in.

MOTIVATOR ACTIVITIES

◇ ◇

Car Chatter

Motivator

Growth (other benefits include making the ride to and from the child-care center a "quality time," and promoting language development and initial sounds concepts)

Time Needed

A few minutes

Materials

None

How to Do It

1. Play an "I see" game that focuses on beginning sounds. For example, say, "I see something in the front seat that starts with 'buh'." The child might guess blue jeans, book, bottle, etc.
2. Try other starting sounds.
3. Trade roles with the child or children.
4. Try a variation of this game: "I'm thinking of a (toy, person, or animal) whose name begins with the sound 'duh'." The child might guess Dad, dog, doll, etc.

Did It Work?

Does the child ask to play the game again? Will he or she play both roles? Are some sounds easier for the child than others? Is the ride pleasant?

Other Possibilities

1. Use the same game format with colors, shapes, or descriptions.
2. Talk about what you are thinking, feeling, seeing, or hearing. Then ask the child to tell you what he or she is thinking, feeling, seeing, or hearing.

◇ ◇

I Did It!

Motivator

Recognition, achievement, and self-esteem (other benefits include a reward for learning the rules)

Time Needed

1 minute

Materials

Construction paper, magic marker, safety pin

How to Do It

1. Make a badge for whatever goal you are working on with a particular child.
2. Write the goal on the badge.
3. Reward the child with the badge when he or she remembers to do what was requested.

Did It Work?

Does the child ask for the badge when he or she has reached a particular goal?

Other Possibilities

1. Suggest that parents use the badge idea at home.
2. Make a badge for eating vegetables, helping a friend, learning to fasten buttons, or putting away toys.
3. Take a picture of the child wearing the badge and send the picture to a special relative.

MOTIVATOR ACTIVITIES

◇ ◇

Use Your Great Big Voice

Motivator

Recognition (other benefits include getting a child to talk in a voice louder than a whisper)

Time Needed

A few minutes weekly, over a 3-month period

How to Do It

1. Have the children as a group discuss talking loud enough for friends to hear you.
2. When a particular child speaks too softly, have the children tell this child that they can't hear what he or she is saying.
3. Allow the child to use the tape recorder to record and play back his or her voice. Encourage him or her to take deep breaths while talking. (This relaxes the vocal cords.)
4. Ask the staff to give verbal and physical praise (pats on the back) when the child talks in a louder voice.
5. Ask other children to give the child verbal and physical praise when the child talks in a louder voice.
6. Encourage the parent to give a reward to the child when the teacher communicates that the child is talking louder at school.

Did It Work?

Does the child speak with normal loudness 80 percent of the time?

Other Possibilities

1. Refer the child to a speech pathologist.
2. Encourage the parent to take turns at storytelling at home with the child. Allow the child to use the tape recorder and play it back at home.

MOTIVATOR ACTIVITIES

◇ ◇

Spring Garden Project

Motivator

Worth of the work, achievement (other benefits include involving parents, teachers, and children in a cooperative venture; learning about nature and the growth patterns of plants)

Time Needed

2 to 3 months

Materials

Garden plot, garden tools, seeds

How to Do It

1. Have a Saturday or Sunday "Sowing Social." Invite parents, children, and teachers to get the garden soil ready. Have parents purchase the seeds and allow the children to plant them in a corner of the outdoor play area.
2. Caring for the garden and additional planting can be done by children and teachers during outdoor activity times.
3. Discuss ways of growing food and the principles of good nutrition with the children.
4. Have a harvest picnic and/or dinner when the garden is ready for harvest. For example, lettuce, radishes, and carrots could all go in a salad. Children could make the salad the afternoon before the planned event.

Did It Work?

How successful was the harvest? Did children learn about nutrition and growing "crops?" Did parents, children, and teachers cooperate together?

Other Possibilities

1. Keep growth charts for different vegetables.
2. Have each family grow something at home in a flower pot, garden, yard, or orange crate lined with a trash bag.

14 Volunteer Program Papers (VPPs)— Classroom Volunteers

Parent Involvement Helps Teachers and Children: Possibilities for Volunteers and Paid Aides in Child Care Centers and Public Schools (School-Wide Concept or Individual Teacher)

A children's classroom is busy at work time. The paint spills at the easel, the tape or record at the listening station needs changing, Suzy needs her smock buttoned, and the guinea pig is suddenly loose. The extra pair of hands that a teacher so often needs can be available through a Volunteer Helper program.

Since extra pairs of hands are especially needed during September, recruiting of Volunteer Helpers is best done during the spring. If a center or school doesn't start that early, the fall is also a good time to recruit. (Remind prospective volunteers that they must have a TB test, if it is required in your state).

A volunteer coordinator (which could be a parent) sets up the schedules and plans monthly in-service training meetings at a nearby home or at the school from 3 to 4 P.M. or after the center day. An assistant coordinator duplicates the materials given out in training and plans with the coordinator and the teachers for the content of the meetings. (Mathematics readiness? Language readiness? Are the paint cans too full?)

Orientation meetings for new volunteers are held before the program starts with teachers attending and the coordinator giving instructions, such as: Be on time; If you can't come, exchange your day with another volunteer; Never discuss the children outside of class; Call the teacher for any disciplinary action.

The teachers go over the goals of the program for the children, the helpers, and the teachers, and together the group reviews the "Rules of the Road" and "Tips for Conversations" (included in this section) to set the tone and provide the facts needed by the helpers.

Later meetings (to which small children of the volunteers are invited in order to prevent babysitting problems) can deal with areas of curriculum learning, so that volunteers may become even more useful, by, for example, suggesting a domino game and knowing that this is appropriate to mathematics readiness.

The format of these meetings is generally: (1) Science-Math-Reading (or other) readiness in kindergarten (or appropriate topics for the program being discussed); (2) How the aides can help at school (direct children to the nature table, help the children use the computer or the magnifying glass, etc.); (3) What parents can do at home in this field (discuss the egg's form changing when scrambling eggs, talk about seeds and leaves when raking leaves together). There is a mutual discussion of these projects with interesting questions and comments. Parent education is achieved at the same time volunteers are becoming better trained for their jobs. As one parent put it: "Now when my child wants to help me in the kitchen, I think of it as science readiness rather than as a nuisance." These principles can also be applied by individual teachers in their own classrooms or by groups of two or three teachers.

Ways Teachers Can Contribute to the Program

1. Fill out the questionnaire of your needs carefully. Think about the ways you would feel comfortable having a volunteer help you. Would you like help with bulletin board work? Perhaps you want him or her to come twice a week during afternoon time? Could he or she give nominal supervision to the class while you work with a small group or individual needing help?

2. Attend at least one session of the volunteer aide training program, if one is already in place, so that you are familiar with the training being given. You will probably want to add to what's been said, but do make sure you know something about the philosophy of the entire program.

3. Accept invitations—or offers—to discuss your volunteer needs at an orientation meeting. (Incidentally, a panel is an interesting way to present different needs).

4. Meet with your volunteer aide to discuss scheduling and duties, even if these details have been partly prearranged.

5. Let the volunteer aide know in advance if you won't need him or her during a certain week.

6. Make an effort to chat with the coordinator periodically. He or she would like to hear your point of view, and is interested in your suggestions for making the program better.

What Kinds of Help Are Needed?

(An example of the job descriptions that a steering committee can provide)
Note: Most volunteers prefer to give one morning or one afternoon per week.
Hence, most jobs are described to coincide with this preference.

Story aides—To write down stories dictated by the children. One person; two to three hours per week; responsible to the classroom teacher.

Art Aides—To oversee the children using art materials and to keep materials in order; to help change bulletin boards and displays throughout the school. One person; three to four hours per week; responsible to a teacher or a team coordinator.

Carpentry aides—To make scenery and play props, storage boxes, etc. May work at home as needed; responsible to the aide coordinator.

Book makers—To bind children's writings into book form. Three to four hours per week; responsible to the librarian in a school setting.

Music aides—To play piano or guitar and lead the children in singing. Three hours per week; responsible to team coordinator.

Computer tutors—To work with children using the different types of software available.

Keyboarding—To type/keyboard in for teachers or children (for the center or school newspapers, plays), etc. Three hours per week; responsible to aide or teacher coordinator.

Instructional materials aides—To get assignments from the instructional materials coordinator (who has received requests from teachers) to mount magazine pictures, make puppets, costumes, flash cards, games, charts. May work at home; three hours per week.

Reading tutors—To work under supervision of the reading or classroom teacher with individual children or with small groups. Three hours per week.

Resource people—To serve as experts in a particular subject or interest area; to talk with a class or teachers as requested, or on a continuing basis (visiting classrooms regularly to help children grow plants, for example) or to conduct classes in cooking, sewing, or other areas of interest as the resource person's schedule will allow. Three hours per week or on a one-time-only basis.

As always, the teacher has the responsibility for planning and providing the instructional program and designing the activities which the volunteer carries through.

Parents in the Room . . . What Happens to the Child?

In setting up Volunteer Helper programs, some teachers prefer not to have a parent working in his or her own child's room. The coordinator, of course, respects this preference. However, it has been found that some parents can work in their child's room without undue disruption, "clinging," or other undesirable behaviors.

Often the parent himself/herself will sense which child of his/hers they can work successfully alongside of and which child would respond uncomfortably to his/her presence. In today's creative schools, many children might take note of their parent's presence the first one or two times scheduled, but continue busily with their own work. If this type of scheduling does not seem to be working out after three or four helper scheduling periods, then the coordinator reserves the right, as in all cases, to assign the helper to another room or task.

What happens to the child? Often he or she benefits—or is proud of his/her work and class. The parent helper benefits from the weekly hour in a different perspective gaining insight into child guidance techniques. With proper structure, training, and guidelines, many successful programs have been built on direct parent involvement.

Steering Committee Helps Volunteer Programs Grow

"A classroom volunteer program must start small and grow gradually" believes Peg Rich, coordinator of one successful volunteer program. The steering committee that works with Peg wholeheartedly agrees. Established to provide regular communication between the professionals and the volunteer staff, the steering committee includes teachers and directors. However, the school's teachers, volunteers, curricula and neighborhood are all changing and as its volunteer program grows, the committee membership will change also.

The members of the steering committee provided the following services:

1. Using a questionnaire, they found out which teachers wanted volunteer aides, and the types of duties they wanted the volunteers to perform in the classrooms. Then, they developed job descriptions based upon this information—spending quite a lot of time to do this carefully.

2. They distributed a questionnaire to parents to find out who would be interested in helping in specific ways. Included in this questionnaire was the opportunity to learn to use a personal computer as part of the training. (Keeping the program relevant to volunteer interests was very important.) This questionnaire was handed out at a volunteers orientation meeting in the fall. A booklet describing the philosophy of the school or center and details of the volunteer program was given out at the meeting. (Some volunteers decided *not* to sign up after reading the booklet. However, the committee felt that this, too, was good.)

3. The steering committee screened the questionnaires carefully and assigned volunteers to the teachers.

4. The members set up an interview between the teacher and the volunteer.

5. If problems arose, the coordinator counseled both parties and helped them to work together. Her extra effort was an important factor in the success of the program. "Of course," says Peg Rich, "sometimes I counseled a volunteer right out of the program if she or he wasn't working out well." Peg also stresses the importance of coordinators and volunteers maintaining a professional attitude about their jobs, and not discussing personalities at all outside of the program. Peg says, "sometimes I feel a part of neither world. There's so much you can't tell parents, and so many things you can't tell teachers."

Checklist for Coordinators

1. Set up a steering committee. This must include teachers (we recommend at least three) as well as the director and/or assistant director, the coordinator, and the various program chairpersons (instructional materials, classroom aides, art center, etc.). This group will prepare job descriptions, with teachers' input, and screen volunteers for various positions. The steering committee may also:

   - Provide regular reports on each program, with attention to any problems. (Each teacher and chairperson can give a brief report at each meeting.)
   - Design forms to be used in the instructional materials and keyboarding programs, making sure the instructions are clear to both teachers and aides.
   - Report feedback from staff meetings, and plan presentations for future staff meetings.
   - Provide opportunities for parents and teachers to come together—allowing the aide coordinator to plan monthly in-service training meetings with the teacher, for example.
   - Design new questionnaires or announcements for various aide groups, the newsletter, or the staff.
   - Design and plan a workshop about the total volunteer program for teachers and parents.

2. Send questionnaires to teachers asking about their volunteer needs. Chat with them personally if necessary.

3. Meet with the director and steering committee to plan an orientation meeting (see Hints for Volunteers, a part of an Orientation Meeting Agenda, elsewhere in this section.)

4. Prepare the materials to be given out at the fall orientation meeting. These could include (1) A brochure of job descriptions. (2) An orientation booklet including the philosophy of the school and listing pointers for parents. (3) A questionnaire on the volunteer's interests, time available, ability to babysit, previous experience with children.

5. Plan with the director (and steering committee) to provide some orientation for teachers about the volunteer program. This could include:

   - the opportunity for teachers to discuss where, what, when, and why they might want volunteers.
   - distribution of the orientation materials that volunteer aides receive.

- an explanation for teachers of why parents volunteer and how to use them to best advantage. It is important for teachers to understand that parents and teachers have a mutual interest in the school or program community as well as in the children.

6. Keep a supply of little jobs on hand, so that volunteers can do something useful even if a plan with a teacher doesn't materialize some particular morning. This technique gets odd jobs done and insures the volunteer's continuing interest. Instructional materials lend themselves beautifully to this category.

Helpful Hints for Training Parents and Volunteer Helpers

(These may be distributed and/or used as part of the orientation meeting agenda).

- The aim of the program is to aid the teachers. Volunteers receive no pay, but, hopefully, do merit appreciation. The volunteer motto is "A job worth doing is a job worth doing well." When a volunteer is happy it benefits the whole center or school.

- Everyone in the program is responsible to another person, as in any professional organization.

- Volunteers are responsible for rescheduling their service times or arranging a switch with another aide, depending on the program they're in, if they have to miss a scheduled time. Let the teacher know of the change.

- Aides may help remind children to behave appropriately, but must assume no responsibility for disciplinary measures. They should call a teacher if such action is necessary.

- The coordinator is the person to contact for help. Teachers or volunteers should contact the coordinator when they have a question, a serious problem, a suggestion, or a complaint. Volunteers must maintain a professional attitude. There is no place for gossip in the program.

- Since volunteers and professional staff are working together to benefit the children, both groups of adults must be flexible enough to work together for their common goal. When there is a personality clash, the coordinator is the person who should be contacted to solve it. Teachers and volunteers should call her immediately for a change of station or personnel.

- The coordinator tries to honor volunteers' preferences for jobs. However if one art aide is needed and six people want the job, obviously they can't all have it. Coordinators may have to rotate people from time to time as needed, within their time choices.

- Volunteers must be careful not to discuss any child. Criticism, even if constructive, should remain in the school or center.

- Volunteers should chat with the coordinator periodically. He or she welcomes their suggestions for making the program better.

- Volunteers must have a chest x-ray, if it is required.

Rules of the Road for the Novice Volunteer

Sample rules of the road from one Volunteer Helper Program might be adapted for use in your program with appropriate changes made by your teachers and okayed by your Director.

Sand table and work bench activities:

To be used only during work time. Work bench activities must be supervised by an adult and only four children may be there at one time. The children may paint their woodworking project. The child can paint the project on newspaper that has been put down on the floor. He can take only one can of paint (from the easel) at a time, returning it before choosing another color. When painting, the child must wear his smock. Growth in responsibility comes with the child's getting the newspaper, paint and smock himself and returning them to the proper place when finished with that activity.

Easel painting:

Paints will be placed on the easel for use at work time every day unless the whole group is participating in a painting activity. Children wear the provided smocks. Paints are left in the juice cans and stored in the sink cupboard at the end of the day. In the morning, check the amount (half full) and the consistency of the paint and place on the easel, adding to it if needed.

Blocks, toys, and games:

During free work time, each child chooses his activity. However, he may not move on to another activity until he has put away the equipment he is using. Blocks should be grouped by size and shape. Because of limited space, only two children may play in each of the two block areas, two children with the railroad set, four in the dramatic play corner, two with the guinea pigs, two with tinker toys, flannel board, and magnetic numbers and shapes.

Children may use the bathroom as needed, but they are discouraged from going during rest time. Only one child uses the bathroom at a time, except in an emergency. Check on the child if he or she stays in the bathroom for an unusual length of time. Insist that the child wash his or her hands after using the toilet. Children may also wash hands at the sink but encourage them to wash quickly so those waiting may have a turn.

The role of the volunteer helper will be that of one who stays unobtrusively in the background. Resist an urge to step into a situation too quickly, thus depriving the child of an educational experience. Instead of buttoning or zipping the child's jacket, show the child how he or she can start it, or try talking the child through it as he/she attempts it. Cheerful encouragement and praise will produce amazing results, not the least being the child's satisfaction derived from doing it himself or herself!

A few general suggestions: Write the child's name and date on art work. Don't suggest what to draw or make. Do not ask the child what he/she is drawing or making, he/she may be simply trying out the medium. Listen to the child if he wishes to talk about his/her work. If a child loses interest or forgets about self-control, direct him/her to another activity or another play area.

Tips for Conversations

1. Adults should keep voices low. Bend down or use a low chair when talking to the children. Listen to the children. Learn from them. Talking *at* the children bores them.

2. Do not disturb a child unnecessarily. When he or she is looking for approval, use generalities, not comparisons. Say: "What a fine building" or "What nice colors."

3. Establish possessions and turns by saying, "he is using it now, you may use it later."

4. Give sincere approval when a child meets a difficult situation: "good idea."

5. Admit "that really did hurt," if a child falls or hurts himself.

6. Try to anticipate the deterioration of group play. The right suggestion at the right time will help.

7. Be careful not to discuss any child (in his or her presence or any other time).

8. State suggestions in a positive manner. For example, "Let's wash hands" or "We paint on paper." With this approach, you are less likely to arouse resistance.

9. Use a positive tone of voice where no choice is given. "Rest time now." Where there is a choice, phrase it so: "Would you like to pass the crayons?"

10. Use a negative approach only for important or dangerous situations: "You may not throw blocks." To a child who is tempted to throw a rock: "Balls are for throwing, rocks are not."

Goals of the Early Childhood Program Experience

For Children

- Be themselves
- Express themselves by using art and play materials freely and constructively
- Learn to be tolerant, creative, cooperative, and imaginative
- Learn independence
- Learn limits of behavior
- Increase ability to handle emotions constructively

For Volunteer Helpers

- Become more aware of a child's world and understand his or her behavior
- Achieve a more positive approach to our child-adult relationships through professional guidance and shared experiences with other parents
- Be sympathetic, understanding that this may be a child's first experience away from home
- Provide worthwhile outlets for energies and abilities of parents outside of the home
- Learn constructive techniques of working with children

What We Teach

- Is not evident to the casual observer
- Setting the stage means guiding unobtrusively
- Maintaining an atmosphere of freedom and friendliness within limits
- Allowing the children to develop their own ideas but with the adults in the background ready to help if needed

Instructional Materials—One Way to Get Started

A teacher can't work without materials. Surrounded by puppets lined up in plastic bags, window shades that pull down to show number charts, and parents busily laminating puzzles and pictures, we began to see that the term "materials" covers a pretty wide range.

Volunteer parents have produced instructional materials related to visual perception, cognitive skills (association, classification, memory, interpretation), language and math development, creative play, as well as materials and equipment (i.e., listening stations, puppets, flannel board stories, picture files, puzzles, tables for sitting or writing, puppet stages, number boards, cookie-cutter shaped crayons, etc.)

Program parents and administrators cooperatively nominate two volunteer parents who serve as co-chairpersons of the program where the instructional materials are made. One of the main characteristics of a good co-chairperson is "public relations" talents (salesmanship). The co-chairperson helps to tell the community about the program via letters, telephone, or personal contacts with parents, and also recruits and schedules sufficient volunteers to produce the instructional materials.

Professional staff members create models of the instructional material to be made. Members of the instructional advisory committee (teachers and administrators) decide which instructional materials should be made, taking into account the cost of production, how the item will be used for the instructional program in the school or center, how often it will be used and how many people will use it. As they are produced, the materials are housed in the resource media center for loaning out under the same procedure as library books.

The Educational Director is responsible for coordinating and supervising the work of the volunteer parents—including instructing the parents, laying out the work and materials to be used, purchasing raw materials such as window shades or linoleum, and even making a model for the parents from teachers' rough drafts, etc.

All program teachers check out materials from the resource center with library cards (in pockets glued right to the plastic bags) for an indeterminate length of time. Children may also check out these materials.

The philosophy behind the "check out" procedure is that the parents can find the job more satisfying if they can see numerous teachers and children using the instructional materials which they have made. Central storage also insures more efficient use of these instructional resources.

A good and orderly check-out system, including an overall catalog of the total number of each item, and perhaps a code for types of items, is a must. A smaller and newer instructional materials program at another program purchased a file cabinet to store "made" materials. Shelves are useful as well.

At some schools, a parent "instructional materials coordinator" assumes the job of Educational Director described above. The parent coordinator meets regularly with the volunteer aide committee, which includes the director and at least three teachers.

Tips on Getting Organized

In the beginning of most instructional materials programs, a certain amount of "selling" is needed. One program started with puppets, flannel board characters and a picture file. As the teachers begin to see the excellent products that parents are willing to turn out and see colleagues using these items and requesting new items, the requests and ideas will grow. Note: The professional person should always be the one to determine all the details of a given product.

A flyer sent to parents followed by an orientation coffee is a good way to recruit volunteers and parents willing to work as instructional materials aides. Sign-up sheets should include room for a variety of interests—sewing, printing, pasting, etc.—or even babysitting for others. Some groups meet at the school or center, if there is room to work. Some meet in a home weekly and some work individually.

One school that was starting an instructional materials program, with no school secretary to help or room to work in, used the following procedures:

1. The coordinator met with the director to determine how costs were to be met. The director underwrote the program to the extent of $100 and requested that the coordinator make up a list of needs to help determine future underwriting, at a later date, when he/she had more of a "feel" for the requirements. They decided which supply items would be purchased through the center and which supply items the parent coordinator should buy.

2. The coordinator decided to keep the supply of materials in her home, to be delivered or picked up by the volunteers working on certain projects. (There was no room at this center. It is generally agreed that a room at the center is preferred, if such a room is available.)

3. A teacher needing something (three charts, for example) would fill out a form listing his/her name and class, a brief description of the charts desired, date needed, and indicating he/she would either call the volunteer at home about the project, or giving his/her phone number so the volunteer could call him/her. This form was placed in the coordinator's box in the office.

4. The coordinator received the request and assigned a volunteer. She first checked with the volunteer about the acceptability of the assignment (time, interests, etc.) and explained the project, then returned the form with the name and phone number of the volunteer to the teacher.

5. The teacher and volunteer picked a date and time for the volunteer to come in and look at sample charts and receive information about the details of the new charts. (This school discovered that a self-explana-

tory item, like ten bean bags, needs no personal interview if good instructions about size and material were indicated on the form.)

6. Frequently, a teacher and a volunteer developed a special rapport and continued to work on other projects together. (However, it was found that it was best if the teacher submitted another form requesting that volunteer in order to prevent the volunteer from being led into a larger commitment than she had originally planned.)

The Volunteer-Crafted Instructional Material Product: What If It Isn't Good Enough?

What do you do if a product comes in that isn't good enough? Perhaps the workmanship isn't good, or perhaps a chart is written in script. Or perhaps there is some other problem related to misunderstood directions.

One school graciously accepts everything the parent does, and then assigns this worker to an easier task or job. It is generally agreed that you must never criticize the volunteer or ask her to re-do the project. Ask another volunteer to re-do it, if necessary. But also take the time to review your instruction-giving channels.

Perhaps the coordinators need additional details from certain teachers who haven't time to write down specific instructions. Perhaps certain people work better in a group with patterns cut out and materials already assembled. (These might include felt, liquid embroidery, sequins, etc. for flannel board characters. Note: Many programs make two of every flannel board set and use double felt for extra durability.)

An evaluation sheet used regularly with each project, for parents and for teachers, gives valuable clues about what constitutes a successful instructional materials program. Use of these sheets, such as the one printed elsewhere in this section, is recommended. Also, have a group evaluation of the entire program once or twice a year, so that new ideas may be included and old problems solved.

Sample Evaluation Sheet

(Note: Add questions to these samples based on your own school or program needs)

For the Teacher

1. Did this project meet your need? If not, why not?
2. Did you write or call in instructions? Did you discuss the project personally with the coordinator or volunteer? Which do you prefer?
3. Was the request sheet clear and did it provide sufficient information?
4. Did you get the project on time?

For the Volunteer

1. Were the instructions clear?

Oral   _____
Written   _____
In person   _____

2. Did the project take more time or less time than expected?
3. Is this the type of thing you enjoy doing?
4. What else would you prefer?

Early Childhood Websites

Early childhood professionals can find many and varied resources on the Internet. Included here is a sampling of interesting and useful sites, many with more links to additional early childhood sites.

List servs

ECEOL-L@MAINE.MAINE.EDU is a major early childhood listserv with more than 600 teachers, directors, professors and students on it, and is still growing.

PROJECTS-L@POSTOFFICE.CSO.UIUC.EDU is the Project Approach Listserv and includes input from well-known authors in this area, such as Sylvia Chard.

REGGIO-L@POSTOFFICE.CSO.UIUC.EDU is the Reggio Emilia Preschool Discussion Group.

Director and Teacher Resources

http://nccic.org is the National Childcare Information Center

http://www.lib.uconn.edu/CANR/ces/child is the National Network for Child Care Connections Newsletters which targets child care providers, home providers, child care center management and staff, and before-and-after-school program providers.

http://www.worldbank.org/children is the Inter-American Development Bank group on Early Childhood Development website.

http://members.aol.com/aactchrday is a fairly new message board for Preschool Directors and Administrators on which they can share and exchange ideas.

http://www.nauticom.net/www/cokids/ is a popular site with many links.

http://www.naeyc.org is the NAEYC website. The Public Policy and News section of the website is updated regularly.

http://www.insidetheweb.com/messageboard/mbs.cgi/mb38135 is a new message board for Preschool Education.

http://www.cwla.org is the Child Welfare League of America with many useful sub-pages and statistics.

http://www.kidscampaign.org is an advocacy site featuring the state of child care in America.

http://www.cdc.gov/ncidod/hip/abc/contents.htm is the Center for Disease Control's (CDC) site for The ABCs of Safe and Healthy Childcare.

http://www.daycare.miningco.com/ is a good resource list for special days throughout the year with seasonal activities, art activities, and many great links to other resources.

http://www.homelearning.net/ is a website with many resources for parent send-home activity sheets for children of all ages—infant-toddler, preschool, primary, and even later elementary grade (appropriate for after-school programs). www.homelearning.org/ is similar, but with fewer graphics. www.home-learning.org/ features parenting classes and a bibliography.

http://www.ume.maine.edu/~cofed/eceol/welcome/shtml is a collection of sites of interest to early childhood educators on the ECEOL website. There is also a large collection of websites for children within it, that are described briefly and rated.

http://ericir.syr.edu is AskERIC.

http://www.aap.org is the American Academy of Pediatrics.

http://www.careguide.net is the CareGuide child care resource.

http://ericps.crc.uiuc.edu/ccdece/ccdece.html is the Center for Career Development in Early Care and Education.

http://www.ccw.org/ is the Center for the Child Care Workforce.

http://www.childrensdefense.org/ is the Children's Defense Fund.

http://www.cyfc.umn.edu/ is the Children, Youth and Family Consortium.

http://www.paaap.org/ is the Early Childhood Educaton Linkage System.

http://www.ehsnrc.org/ is the Early Headstart National Resource Center.

http://ericeece.org/ is the ERIC Clearinghouse on Elementary and Early Childhood Education (ERIC/EECE).

http://www.families and workinst.org/ is the Families and Work Institute.

http://www.naccp.org/ is the National Association of Child Care Professionals.

http://www.naccrra.net/ is the National Association of Child Care Resource and Referral Agencies.

http://www.nccanet.org/ is the National Child Care Association.

http://www.calib.com/nccanch/ is the National Clearinghouse on Child Abuse and Neglect.

http://www.nectas.unc.edu http://www/ is the National Early Childhood Technical Assistance System.

http://www.nhsa.org/ is the National Headstart Association.

http://npin.org/ is the National Parent Information Network.

http://www.nsaca.org/ is the National School Age Care Alliance.

http://www.zerotothree.org/ is the Zero to Three: National Center for Infants, Toddlers and Families.

http://www.acf.dhhs.gov/ is the Administration for Children and Families.

http://www.acf.dhhs.gov/programs/ccb/index.html/ is the Child Care Bureau.

http://dticaw.dtic.mil/childcare/ is the Department of Defense Child Development System.

http://www.acf.dhhs.gov/programs/hsb/ is the Head Start Bureau.

Resources for Children and Educators

www.childrenssoftware.com/ is the website for Children's Software Revue (CSR), also available by telephone at 1-800-993-9499. CSR is written by experienced educators with input from families and children. Very useful for those interested in using computers with children.

http://www.kidsatrandom.com is Random House Children's Publishing site for young readers.

www.funschool.com has free online games for preschool, kindergarten and first grade.

http://www.brigadoon.com/~owlmouse/megamaps.htm is a site from which one can download a free U.S. map. It can be printed out to be over 6 feet across (8 sheets across and 8 sheets of paper long.)

www.familyeducation.com/ is sponsored by the National P.T.A.

www.capecod.net/schrockguide/index.htm

www.tenet.edu/academia/earlychild.html

www.earlychildhood.com

www.worldvillage.com/ideabox

INDEX